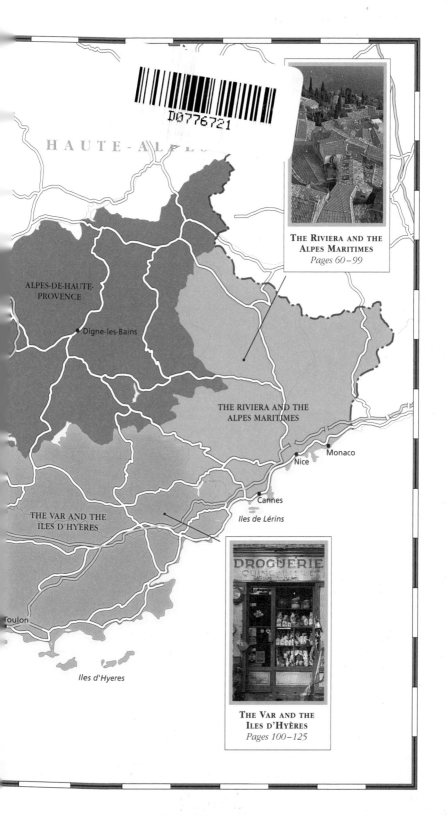

HAUTE-ALPES

THE RIVIERA AND THE ALPES MARITIMES
Pages 60–99

ALPES-DE-HAUTE-
PROVENCE

Digne-les-Bains

THE RIVIERA AND THE
ALPES MARITIMES

Monaco

Nice

THE VAR AND THE
ILES D'HYERES

Cannes

Iles de Lérins

Toulon

Iles d'Hyeres

**THE VAR AND THE
ILES D'HYÈRES**
Pages 100–125

DK TRAVEL GUIDES

PROVENCE
& THE CÔTE D'AZUR

DORLING KINDERSLEY *TRAVEL GUIDES*

PROVENCE
& THE CÔTE D'AZUR

Main Contributor: ROGER WILLIAMS

DORLING KINDERSLEY, INC.
LONDON • NEW YORK • SYDNEY • MOSCOW • DELHI
www.dk.com

DORLING KINDERSLEY, INC.

www.dk.com

PROJECT EDITOR Jane Simmonds
ART EDITOR Jane Ewart
SENIOR EDITOR Fay Franklin
EDITORS Tom Fraser, Elaine Harries, Fiona Morgan
DESIGNERS Claire Edwards, Pippa Hurst, Malcolm Parchment

CONTRIBUTORS
John Flower, Jim Keeble, Martin Walters

PHOTOGRAPHERS
Max Alexander, John Heseltine, Kim Sayer, Alan Williams

ILLUSTRATORS
Stephen Conlin, Richard Draper, Steve Gyapay,
Chris D Orr Illustration, John Woodcock

Film outputting bureau Cooling Brown, England
Reproduced by Colourscan, Singapore
Printed and bound by L. Rex Printing Company Limited, China

First American Edition 1995
6 8 10 9 7 5

Published in the United States by Dorling Kindersley, Inc.,
95 Madison Avenue, New York. NY 10016

Reprinted with revisions 1995, 1997 (twice), 2000

Copyright 1995, 2000 © Dorling Kindersley Limited, London

Library of Congress Cataloging-in-Publication Data
Provence and the Côte d'Azur. – – 1st American ed.
p.   cm. – – (Dorling Kindersley travel guides)
Includes index.
ISBN 1–56458–860–2
1. Provence–Côte d'Azur (France) – – Guidebooks.
I. Series
DC611.P958P735 1995   94-44323
914.4'904839 – – dc20   CIP

THROUGHOUT THIS BOOK, FLOORS ARE REFERRED TO IN ACCORDANCE WITH EUROPEAN
USAGE, I.E., THE "FIRST FLOOR" IS ONE FLIGHT UP.

CONTENTS

HOW TO USE THIS GUIDE 6

Poppy field outside Sisteron

INTRODUCING PROVENCE

PUTTING PROVENCE ON THE MAP 10

**Busy Pampelonne beach to the
south of fashionable St-Tropez**

Marseille fisherman and his catch

A PORTRAIT OF
PROVENCE *12*

PROVENCE THROUGH
THE YEAR *30*

THE HISTORY
OF PROVENCE *36*

**PROVENCE
AREA BY AREA**

PROVENCE
AT A GLANCE *58*

Tarascon's château by the Rhône

THE RIVIERA AND THE
ALPES MARITIMES *60*

THE VAR AND THE
ILES D'HYÈRES *100*

BOUCHES-DU-RHÔNE
AND NÎMES *126*

VAUCLUSE *154*

ALPES-DE-HAUTE-
PROVENCE *174*

Goat cheese in chestnut leaves

**TRAVELLERS'
NEEDS**

WHERE TO STAY *190*

One of the perfumes of Provence

RESTAURANTS, CAFÉS
AND BARS *202*

SHOPS AND
MARKETS *218*

ENTERTAINMENT *222*

SURVIVAL GUIDE

PRACTICAL
INFORMATION *228*

TRAVEL
INFORMATION *238*

GENERAL INDEX *246*

PHRASE BOOK *262*

**Typical Provençal countryside
between Grasse and Castellane**

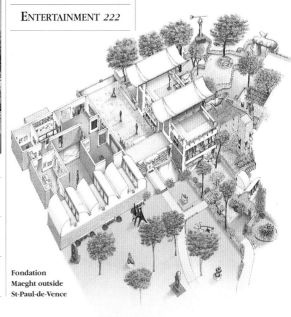

**Fondation
Maeght outside
St-Paul-de-Vence**

HOW TO USE THIS GUIDE

THIS GUIDE will help you get the most from your stay in Provence. It provides both expert recommendations and detailed practical information. *Introducing Provence* maps the region and sets it in its historical and cultural context. *Provence Area by Area* describes the important sights, with maps, photographs and detailed illustrations. Suggestions for food, drink, accommodation, shopping and entertainment are in *Travellers' Needs*, and the *Survival Guide* has tips on everything from the French telephone system to getting to Provence and travelling around the region.

PROVENCE AREA BY AREA

In this guide, Provence has been divided into five separate regions, each of which has its own chapter. A map of these regions can be found inside the front cover of the book. The most interesting places to visit in each region have been numbered and plotted on a *Pictorial Map*.

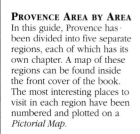

Each area of Provence can be quickly identified by its colour coding.

1 Introduction
The landscape, history and character of each region is described here, showing how the area has developed over the centuries and what it has to offer the visitor today.

A locator map shows the region in relation to the whole of Provence.

2 Pictorial Map
This gives an illustrated overview of the whole region. All the sights are numbered and there are also useful tips on getting around by car and public transport.

Features and story boxes highlight special or unique aspects of a particular sight.

3 Detailed information on each sight
All the important towns and other places to visit are described individually. They are listed in order, following the numbering on the Pictorial Map. *Within each town or city, there is detailed information on important buildings and other major sights.*

4 Major Towns
An introduction covers the history, character and geography of the town. The main sights are described individually and plotted on a Town Map.

A Visitors' Checklist gives contact points for tourist and transport information, plus details of market days and local festival dates.

The town map shows all main through roads as well as minor streets of interest to visitors. All the sights are plotted, along with the bus and train stations, parking, tourist offices and churches.

5 Street-by-Street Map
Towns or districts of special interest to visitors are shown in detailed 3D, with photographs of the most important sights. This gives a bird's-eye view of towns or districts of special interest.

A suggested route for a walk covers the most interesting streets in the area.

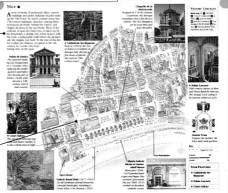

For all the top sights, a Visitors' Checklist provides the practical information you will need to plan your visit.

6 The top sights
These are given two or more pages. Important buildings are dissected to reveal their interiors; museums have colour-coded floorplans to help you locate the most interesting exhibits.

The gallery guide explains the layout of the museum and gives details on the arrangement and display of the collection.

Stars indicate the works of art or sights that no visitor should miss.

INTRODUCING
PROVENCE

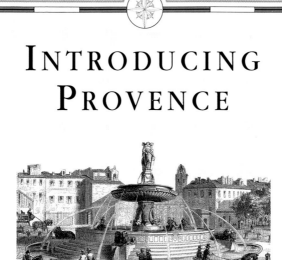

PUTTING PROVENCE ON THE MAP 10-11
A PORTRAIT OF PROVENCE 12-29
PROVENCE THROUGH THE YEAR 30-35
THE HISTORY OF PROVENCE 36-55

Putting Provence on the Map

Provence is situated in the sun-blessed south-east corner of France, edged to the south by the Mediterranean. Its most illustrious stretch of coastline, roughly from Menton to Bandol, is also known as the Côte d'Azur although, the nearer to Italy it gets, the more likely it is to be referred to as the Riviera. To the east are Italy and the Alps, to the west, the Rhône river. The region covers an area of over 30,000 sq km (18,650 sq miles) with a population of about 4.25 million.

KEY

☐	Area covered by this guide
⬓	Ferry service
✈	Airport
═	Motorway
▬	Major road
—	Railway line

0 kilometres   100

0 miles   100

View of the impressive Palais des Papes in Avignon next to the Rhône

A PORTRAIT OF PROVENCE

I N A COMPARATIVELY *short time, Provence has changed its face. A generation or two ago it was, to the French, a place of indolent southern bumpkins. To foreigners, it was an idyllic spot, but one reserved, it seemed to many, for the rich or artistic. Now, Provence, more than any other region, is where the French would choose to live and work, and its holiday routes buzz with traffic all year round.*

The high-tech industry based here can attract top-flight staff, not just from France but from all over the world.

Still, Provence remains an essentially rural region. At its edges, it has a lively Latin beat: almost Spanish among the *gardians* of the Camargue in the west, Italian in Nice to the east. The rest of the region is mostly traditional and conservative. Only in games of *boules* or discussions about European bureaucracy does the talk become animated. But, once engaged in conversation, Provençals are the most generous and warmest of hosts. There is an all-pervading Frenchness, of course, which means that people are polite and punctual.

Monaco Grand Prix poster

Shopkeepers always greet you as you enter, but will close at the stroke of noon. Other institutions open and close on the dot, too. Lunch, in Provence, is sacrosanct.

Traditions are important to the people of Provence. Local crafts are not quaint revivals, but respected, time-honoured occupations. Artists who came here for the light and the scenery found other inspirations, too. Picasso himself learned the potter's art at the wheel of a Provençal craftsman. Homes will have hand-turned local chestnut or oak furniture, *terre rouge* clay pots, Moustiers *faïence*, Biot glassware and furnishings using the traditional *indiennes* patterns of Arles and Nîmes.

A leisurely game of *boules* at Châteauneuf-du-Pape

◁ **One of the many narrow, Italianate streets in the Old Town of Nice**

Vendor of delicious cakes and pastries in Sisteron

The home is run as it has been for generations. Provençal kitchens, at the heart of family life, are famous. Combining simplicity with bounty, they mix the aroma of herbs with the generosity of wine. In the envious and admiring eyes of visitors, they are the epitome of taste.

Good taste is inbred. In this rural community, the familiarity of the weather, the seasons and the harvests are sources of constant discussion. Gardens, full of fruit trees, vegetables and flowers, are a matter of pride. Even city-dwellers know how the best produce should be grown, and may well have access to a country relation's plot. Market stalls are beautifully laid out and carefully scrutinized and, no matter how abundant the fruit, the vegetables or the wine, they are all grist for debate.

The most heated discussions today are fuelled by the European Union, whose legislation, the farmers say, has set aside acres of productive Provençal land. They see ancient vineyards being grubbed up, no new ones to be planted. They cite towns such as Cavaillon, once among the richest in the country because of its fruit and vegetables, now no longer in the same league, with its landowners' wealth in similar decline.

The harvest cycle is close to the gods, whose benificence can affect the crops as surely as any EU bureaucrat. As Catholic as the rest of France, the people of Provence are also touched with a mystic sense that has been influenced by Mithraism and Islam, as well as by pagan gods. Religious beliefs are so well mixed that it is often difficult to separate them. Carnival and Corpus Christi extend Easter, which has more importance here than in many other parts of Europe. Christmas, too, is an elaborate affair. The rituals begin as early as 4 December, St Barb's day, with the planting of grains of wheat, a pagan symbol of renewal and rebirth.

Superstitions linger in the countryside. An egg, salt, bread and matches, humble representations of elemental concepts, may be given to a newborn baby, while carline thistles may be seen nailed to front doors for good luck.

Fish, straight from the sea to the market

Provence has a typically Mediterranean landscape: the mountains drop down to the sea; communities perch on crags or cling to remote hillsides. It is little wonder that traditions live on here. For centuries, too, it was a place for outlaws from France, who could assume new identities here and carry on with their lives.

Harvesting linden blossoms to make *tilleul* infusion

The dramatic, isolated crags of Les Penitents des Mées, in Alpes-de-Haute-Provence

Strangers were not to be trusted, and remained outsiders for ever. A seemingly trivial slight might spark a feud which could last for generations. There are still villages where one family does not speak to another, even though each has long forgotten why. This attitude, and its tragic implications, was finely portrayed by Yves Montand, with Gérard Depardieu as the shunned outsider, in Claud Berri's films of Marcel Pagnol's *Jean de Florette* and *Manon des Sources*. The more cosmopolitan coast is the territory of *film noir*. Here, the tradition of silence and strong family ties has not always been to the common good. Jean-Paul Belmondo and Alain Delon romanticized it in *Borsalino* but Gene Hackman revealed its dark underside in *The French Connection*.

In 1982, the Antibes-based novelist Graham Greene published an exposé of corruption in nearby Nice. In 1994, Yann Piat, anti-drugs campaigner and member of parliament for the Var, was assassinated in Hyères.

The fact that Piat was a woman made no difference to her enemies, ironic in a region where women are not always treated as equals. Alphonse Daudet noted the Provençal male's "incurable contempt" for women. Still, the annual Festival Queen of Arles is elected for her virtues as an upholder of the traditional Provençal values, and it was this region that nurtured the 20th century's ultimate icon of French womanhood, Brigitte Bardot.

There are great rewards for the visitor who appreciates the many facets of Provence – its ingrained traditions as well as its beauty and glamour. But, the more often you return, the more you will realize, as have some of the world's greatest artists and writers, that part of the allure of Provence lies in the secrets it refuses to surrender.

Pavement café on cours Mirabeau, Aix

The Natural History of Provence

AFASCINATING ARRAY of insects, birds, animals and flowers flourish in the varied habitats available in Provence, from the Mediterranean to coastal wetlands, rocky gorges and the remote peaks of the Alpes Maritimes. The area has the mildest climate in France: hot, mainly dry summers, and warm, mild winters near the coast. In early spring the myriad flowers are at their best, while numbers of unusual birds are at their highest in late spring. Many of the wilder areas have been made into reserves, often with routes marked out for exploration.

A two-tailed pasha butterfly

The Luberon (see pp170–72) *is a huge limestone range, rich in orchids, such as this military orchid. It is also good hunting ground for birds of prey.*

Mont Ventoux's lower slopes are flower-covered in the spring *(see p160).*

Les Alpilles' *limestone ridge* (see p141) *attracts birds of prey, including Bonelli's eagles, Egyptian vultures and eagle owls, as well as this more mild-mannered bee-eater.*

• Orange

Carpentras •

• Avignon

VAUCLUSE

• Arles

BOUCHES-DU-RHONE AND NIMES

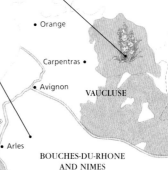

The Camargue, *at the delta of the river Rhône, is one of Europe's most important wetlands* (see pp136–9). *Water birds that thrive here include purple herons and the magnificent greater flamingo. Lizards, such as this ocellated lizard, can also be seen here.*

• Marseille

The Côte Bleue is rich in marine life, such as octopuses, in the deeper waters.

Les Calanques *(see p153)* are narrow inlets bounded by cliffs. Pine and oak trees grow on the rocky slopes, home to woodland birds such as owls.

The Plaine de la Crau *is 50,000 ha (193 sq miles) of stony plains and steppe-like grasslands southeast of Arles, home to birds like this hoopoe, and the rare pin-tailed sandgrouse.*

The Parc National du Mercantour is one of the finest Alpine reserves (see p97), containing wildlife such as this marmot, and chamois, ibex and mouflon (wild sheep). It is also good walking country.

The Haute Provence Geological Reserve near Digne (see p180) has a spectacular collection of giant ammonites embedded in rock.

The Cime de la Bonette (see p179) is a lofty pass where chamois roam.

Barcelonnette ●

ALPES-DE-HAUTE-PROVENCE

Digne-les-Bains

The Gorges du Verdon area, between the Alps and the Mediterranean, is a beautiful nature reserve with a dramatic canyon at its centre (see pp184–5). A footpath along the canyon floor allows detailed examination of the rock formations, rare plants and birds.

The Gorges de la Vésubie (see p95) has viewpoints from which to spot migrating birds such as swallows.

THE RIVIERA AND THE ALPES MARITIMES

Nice ●

THE VAR AND THE ILES D'HYERES

● Fréjus

The Massif de l'Esterel's (see p124) high rocky coves and scrubland are home to various species of snakes.

In the Massif des Maures (see pp116–17), dense maquis and cork oak woods contain bee-eaters, woodchat shrikes and hoopoes. They also provide sanctuary for the rare Hermann's tortoise.

The Massif de la Ste-Baume is clothed with many broadleaved trees that are vividly coloured in autumn.

● Toulon

KEY

☐	National park
☐	Regional natural park
☐	Protected site
☐	Reserve

0 kilometres   25

0 miles   25

The Iles d'Hyères (see pp114–15), scattered a ferry-ride away from the most southerly point of Provence, are best known for their abundant sea life, including fish such as this wrasse. Geckos and rare birds like the great spotted cuckoo can be seen.

Perched Villages

SOME OF THE MOST ATTRACTIVE architectural features of Provence are the *villages perchés* or perched villages. They rise like jagged summits on the hill-tops where they were built for safety in the political turmoil of the Middle Ages. From their lofty heights they kept vigil over the hinterland as well as the coast. They were built around castle keeps and wrapped in thick ramparts, a huddle of cobbled streets, steps, alleys and archways. Few were able to sustain their peasant communities beyond the 19th-century agrarian reforms, and a century of poverty and depopulation followed. Today many of the villages have been restored by a new generation of artists, craftworkers and holiday-makers.

The mountainous site *of Peillon (see p95) is typical of the way perched villages blend organically with the landscape.*

ST-PAUL-DE-VENCE
St-Paul is a typical *village perché*, with many of the key features preserved. The medieval ramparts were com-pletely reinforced by Francis I in the 16th century. Today it is again besieged – as one of the most popular tourist sights in France *(see p75)*.

RUE DE LA POURTOUNE
GRANDE PLACE
RUE C
RUE DES DORIERS
RUE DE LA CASTRE
RUE DES BAUQUES
RUE GRANDE
COURTINE ST PAUL
BASTION ST REMY
REMPAR

Complicated entrances confused invaders and provided extra security against attack.

The chapel was always the focal point of the village.

Side entrances *were never obtrusive or elaborate, but were usually small and, as in Eze (see p88), opened onto narrow, winding lanes. Some-times there were more gates or abrupt turns within the walls to confuse attacking soldiers, making the town easier to defend.*

Castles and keeps *(donjons), and sometimes fortified churches, were always sited with the best viewpoint in the village, and provided sanctuary in times of crisis. Many, like the castle at Eze (see p88), were often attacked and are now in ruins.*

The chapel sustained the religious life of the community. As in Les Baux (see p142), it was usually built near the keep of the castle, part of a central core of communal buildings, and was often fortified. The bell would be rung to warn of impending attack.

Fountains were essential to the village, often being the sole source of water. Many, like this one in Vence (see p74), were elaborately embellished.

The arcades lent support to the buildings in the narrow, winding streets, as here in Roquebrune (see p98). They also gave shelter from sun and rain.

Fountain

Arched and stepped streets

RUE DU HAUT FOUR

LE PONTIS

RUE GRANDE

RUE GRANDE

PLACE DE L'HOSPICE

REMPARTS OUEST

OUEST

A narrow gateway was easily secured.

Ramparts and bastions provided solid defences.

Main gates were always narrow so they could be closed off and defended in times of attack. Some gates had the additional protection of portcullises. This example is one of four 12th-century gates built into the ramparts of the ancient village of Bargemon (see p106) in the Var.

The ramparts surrounded the entire village with thick stone walls, often with houses built into them. The defences, like those of St-Paul (see p75), were strengthened in the 16th century under Francis I and by Vauban, Louis XIV's military architect. Today they offer excellent panoramas.

Rural Architecture in Provence

Shutters to keep out the sun and wind

Traditional architectural features are reminders of how influential the weather is on living conditions in rural Provence. Great efforts are made to ease the biting gusts of the Mistral and the relentless heat of the summer sun. Thick stone walls, small windows and reinforced doors are all recognizable characteristics. Traditional farmhouses were built entirely from wood, clay, stone and soil, all locally found materials. Rows of hardy cypress trees were planted to act as a windbreak on the north side; plane and lotus trees provided shade to the south.

Bories (see p169) *are drystone huts built using techniques dating back to 3,500 BC.*

THE PROVENÇAL MAS

Found across rural Provence, the *mas* is a low, squat stone farmhouse. Protection and strength are vital to its construction – walls are made of compact stone blocks and the wooden doors and shutters are thick and reinforced. Outbuildings often included a cellar, stables, a bread oven and dovecote.

Canal roof tiling, *or* tuiles romaines, *is typical of the south.*

Dovecot

Chimneys are stone-built, low and squat, and lie close to the roof.

Roughly cut stone bricks are used to make the walls.

The most exposed part of the roof is unthatched.

The roof is gently sloping and thatched with marsh reeds.

The north wall is rounded for protection against the Mistral.

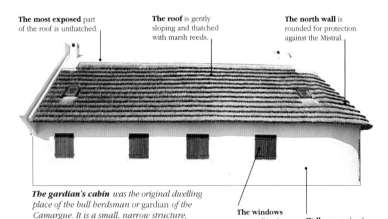

The gardian's cabin *was the original dwelling place of the bull herdsman or gardian of the Camargue. It is a small, narrow structure, consisting of a dining room and bedroom, divided by a reed screen and furnished simply.*

The windows are small and reinforced.

Walls are made of compressed clay and straw, known as cob.

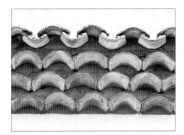

The tiled roofs are gently sloping and are influenced by Roman design, with a decorative frieze (génoise) under the eaves. The tiles are made of thick, red terracotta and curved in shape – a double or triple layer of tiles are set in mortar and protrude beyond the wall.

Windows are built on three sides of the mas but none on the north to avoid the Mistral's full blast. They are kept small to prevent the winter winds coming in, but large enough to let light in.

Interlocking clay tiles form canals, allowing rainwater to run down and drain off the roof.

The Mistral winds blow so fiercely that the mas was often built facing the southeast to minimize the wind's impact. Roofs are built low to the ground, covering the living quarters and annexes. The gentle slope prevents the tiles blowing and sliding off.

The walls are rendered smooth with plaster.

Stone ice houses were built near the mas and used for storage during the winter months. Blocks of ice were cut and put in the huts, insulated with hay.

IRONWORK BELL TOWERS

Wrought-iron bell towers have been a speciality in Provence since the 16th century. Their light, open framework allows strong winds to blow through and the sound of the bells to carry for miles. The design and complexity depends on the size and purpose of the building. These examples illustrate the skills of local craftsmen across the region.

Highly ornate bell tower in Aix

The bell tower of St-Jérôme in Digne

The Hôtel de Ville bell tower in Orange

Notre Dame's bell tower in Sisteron

Architectural Styles in Provence

FROM THE IMPERIAL GRANDEUR of Roman constructions to the modern domestic designs of Le Corbusier, Provence has a magnificent array of architectural styles. The Middle Ages saw a flourishing of great Romanesque abbeys and churches and from the 16th to the 18th centuries, as prosperity increased, châteaux and town houses were built. With the expansion of towns in the 19th century came an increase in apartment blocks and public buildings to accommodate the fast-growing population. Today, successful restoration has taken place, but often in haste. The demands of tourism have taken their toll, particularly on the coast, resulting in ugly developments.

An 18th-century fountain in Pernes-les-Fontaines

ROMAN ARCHITECTURE (20 BC–AD 400)

The quality of Roman architecture is illustrated by the many extant amphitheatres, triumphal arches and thermal baths found across the region, all built with large blocks of local limestone.

Ornate high-relief

The triumphal arch of Glanum (pp140–41) *is the original entrance to the oldest Roman city in Provence. Carvings on the outer arch show Caesar's victory over the Gauls and Greeks.*

Doric columns on second storey

Both storeys have 60 arcades

Nîmes Arènes, built in the 1st century AD *(p132)*

Nîmes' well-preserved Maison Carrée *(p132)*

ROMANESQUE ARCHITECTURE (11–12TH CENTURIES)

The high point of Provençal architecture came after the Dark Ages. It was a combination of Classical order and perfection, inspired by Roman design and new styles from northern and southern Europe. This style is characterized especially in religious buildings by elegant symmetry and simplicity.

Multiple arches

Elaborate religious carvings

This church entrance in Seyne (see p178) *is an example of 13th-century Romanesque architecture. The slight point of the multiple arches hints at a move away from strict Romanesque purity.*

Clustered pillar

Decorated capital with interlaced leaves

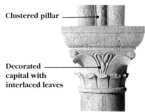

Capital from the Abbaye du Thoronet *(p108)*

The Abbaye de Sénanque, founded in 1148 *(pp164–5)*

Late Middle Ages (13th–16th centuries)

Feuding and religious wars led to people withdrawing to towns, protected by fortified walls and gates. Communication between houses was often by underground passages. Streets were roughly paved and water and sewage were carried away by a central gutter.

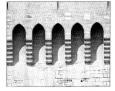

Tour de la Campana in the Palais des Papes (pp44–5)

Street in St-Martin-Vésubie (p95) showing central gutter

Crenellation or battlements

Portcullis used against invaders

Aigues-Mortes (see pp134–5) was built by Louis IX in the 13th century, according to a strict grid pattern. This strategically placed fort overlooks both sea and land.

Classical Architecture (17th–18th centuries)

The severity and order of the Classical style was relieved by elaborate carvings on doorways and windows. Gardens became more formal and symmetrical.

The 17th-century Barbentane château, fronted by formal gardens (p130)

Tablet with symbol of authority

Carved Regency doorway

The Musée des Tapisseries in Aix (see p148) has elaborately carved wooden entrance doors.

Refined stone

Neo-Classical pillar

Pavillon de Vendôme detail, Aix-en-Provence (p149)

Modern Architecture (1890–present day)

The magnificent hotels and villas of the Belle Epoque have given way to more utilitarian housing and public buildings. But the numerous modern art galleries represent the highest standards of 20th-century architecture.

Le Corbusier's Cité Radieuse (p152)

Rounded pavilion

Cupola above a round corner tower

The palatial Négresco hotel in Nice (p84)

The Musée d'Art Contemporain in Nice (see p85) was built in 1990. It is made up of square towers, linked by glass passageways.

Artists of Provence

PROVENCE INSPIRED MANY of the most original 19th- and 20th-century painters. They were attracted by the luminescent quality of the light here, and the consequent brilliance of the colours. Cézanne, who was a native, and Van Gogh, a convert, were both fired by the vibrant shades of the landscape. The Impressionists Monet and Renoir came early, and followers included Bonnard, Signac and Dufy. The two giants of 20th-century painting, Matisse and Picasso, both settled here. The artistic tradition is kept alive by small galleries in almost every town, as well as major museums throughout the region.

Jean Cocteau *(1889–1963) spent many years on the coast and created his museum in Menton (see p99). Noce imaginaire (1957) is one of his murals from the Salle des Mariages.*

Victor Vasarely *(1908–97) has his Kinetic and Op Art on display at Gordes, in the château (see p169).*

Hans Van Meegeren *(1889–1947), the Dutch master-forger of Vermeer, was living in Roquebrune (see p98) when found out.*

REGIONS OF PROVENCE

Roquebrune

Menton

Gordes

Arles

Aix-en-Provence

Martigues

St-Tropez

Vincent Van Gogh *(1853–90) painted* Van Gogh's Chair *(1888) in Arles (see pp144–6). His two years here and in St-Rémy (see pp140–41) were his most prolific.*

Paul Cézanne *(1839–1906), in his desire to scour the "depth of reality", often painted his native Aix (see pp148–9).*

Vallauris

Paul Signac *(1863–1935) came to St-Tropez in 1892, painting it in his palette of rainbow dots (see pp118–22).*

Félix Ziem *(1821–1911) was born in Burgundy but was a great traveller. He adored Venice, and found the same romantic inspiration by the canals of Martigues (see p147), where he painted* Camargue, Côté Soleil.

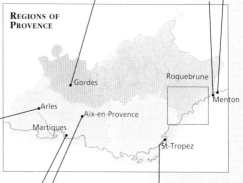

Pablo Picasso *(1881–1973) created this goat-like jug,* Cabri *(1947), while in Vallauris, where he learned the potter's craft. It is now in the Musée Picasso, Antibes (see p73).*

0 kilometres   3

0 miles   3

Marc Chagall *(1887–1985), Russian painter of light-hearted and biblically inspired works, lived in St-Paul-de-Vence from 1949 (see p75).*

Raoul Dufy *(1877–1953) appreciated the pleasures of the coast. A twilight stroll beneath the palm trees is fondly evoked in* La Jetée Promenade à Nice *(1928).*

• Vence

• Nice

• Cagnes-sur-Mer

Henri Matisse
(1869–1954) captured the Riviera's light and colour even in homely settings such as Intérieur au Phonographe *(1924) (see pp82–3).*

• Biot

Pierre Auguste Renoir
(1841–1919) sought relief from his rheumatism at Cagnes in 1906 and found new inspiration (see p78).

Fernand Léger *(1881–1955) is celebrated for his vivid Cubist and industrial works in oils and ceramics, on show in Biot (see p74).*

Antibes

ARTISTS IN PROVENÇAL HISTORY

Provence was home to great artists long before the advent of modern art. In the Middle Ages, the Schools of Avignon and Nice flourished. The latter was dominated by the Bréa family, whose works can be seen in churches throughout the region. Sculptor Pierre Puget (1620–94) is called the "Michelangelo of Provence". His birthplace, Marseille, has several of his works *(see p150-2)*. But Jean-Honoré Fragonard (1732–1806) is most Provençal of them all – his Romantic paintings are filled with Grasse flowers *(see p66)*.

Crucifixion (1512) by Louis Bréa, monastery of Notre-Dame, Cimiez (see p84)

Nicolas de Staël *(1914–55) was born in Russia. When successful, he bought a house in the Luberon for his wife, but chose to live with his mistress in Antibes (see p72). His* Paysage Méditerranéen *was painted in 1953.*

Writers in Provence

Victor Hugo

T HE NOBEL LAUREATE Frédéric Mistral (1830–1914) was the champion of the Provençal language, but better known are the local writers who have captured the Provençal character: Alphonse Daudet, Jean Giono, Emile Zola and Marcel Pagnol. French writers such as Dumas and Hugo used Provençal backdrops for their fiction, and writers from many other countries found inspiration in the region.

1892 The last part of *Thus Spake Zarathustra* by German Friedrich Nietzsche is published. He devised it after traversing the path in Eze *(see p88)* which was later named after him.

1895 Jean Giono is born in Manosque *(see p182)*. Work like *The Man who Planted Trees* evokes the region.

An early edition of The Count of Monte Cristo

Frédéric Mistral

Alphonse Daudet

1869 Alphonse Daudet publishes *Collected Letters from my Windmill*, set in a windmill at Fontvieille *(see p143)*.

1844 Alexander Dumas publishes *The Count of Monte Cristo*, set in the Château d'If, Marseille *(see p152)*.

1870 Death in Cannes of Prosper Mérimée, author of *Carmen*, Bizet's opera.

1904 Frédéric Mistral wins the Nobel Prize with his poem, *Mirèio*.

1840	1855	1870	1885	1900	1915
1840	1855	1870	1885	1900	1915

1862 *Les Misérables* by Victor Hugo is published. The early chapters are set in Digne-les-Bains *(see p180)*.

1868 Edmond Rostand, author of *Cyrano de Bergerac* (1897) is born in Marseille *(see pp150–51)*.

1907 Provençal poet, René Char, is born in L'Isle sur-la-Sorgue.

EARLY WRITERS

For centuries, troubadour ballads and religious poems, or *Noels*, formed the core of literature in Provence. While certain unique individuals stand out, it was not until 1854, with Mistral's help, that Provençal writers found their own "voice".
1327 Petrarch *(see p45)* falls in unrequited love with Laura de Noves in Avignon, inspiring his *Canzonière* poems.
1555 Nostradamus, from St-Rémy, publishes *The Centuries*, prophecies outlawed by the Vatican.
1764 Tobias Smollett "discovers" Nice. (He published his book, *Travels through France and Italy,* in 1766).
1791 Marquis de Sade, the original sadist, publishes *Justine*, written while imprisoned in the Bastille.

Petrarch's Laura de Noves

Edith Wharton

1915 Edith Wharton, American author of *The Age of Innocence*, visits Hyères *(see p115)* with French writer, André Gide. A street is named after her.

1887 Journalist Stéphen Liégeard introduces the term, *Cote d'Azur*.

1885 *Germinal* published by Emile Zola, boyhood friend of Cézanne, as part of his 20-novel cycle, *The Fortunes of the Rouge* (1871–93), set partly round Aix.

Emile Zola

Poster for film version of Colette's story, Gigi

Marcel Pagnol

1981 British actor Dirk Bogarde moves to Provence and publishes his first novel, *A Gentle Occupation*.

1925 Colette, author of *Gigi* (1944), buys a house, *La Treille Muscat*, in St-Tropez *(see pp118-22)* which features in some of her short stories.

1974 Death of film director and writer Marcel Pagnol, whose *Marseille Trilogy* explored his Provençal childhood.

Lawrence Durrell

1932 Briton Aldous Huxley writes *Brave New World* in Sanary-sur-Mer *(see p112)*, the setting for *Eyeless in Gaza* (1936).

1985 The last volume of Briton Lawrence Durrell's *Avignon Quintet* is published.

1933 Thomas Mann, who wrote *Death in Venice* (1913) and brother Heinrich, flee Germany for Sanary *(see p112)*.

St-Exupéry's poignant fable, Le Petit Prince

1989 Briton Peter Mayle's book *A Year in Provence* generates interest in the Luberon.

1944 Antoine de St-Exupéry, aviator and author of *Vol de Nuit* (1931) and *Le Petit Prince* (1943), goes missing. His last flight passed his sister's house at Agay.

1930	1945	1960	1975	1990
1930	1945	1960	1975	1990

1954 Françoise Sagan, aged 18, writes *Bonjour Tristesse* (1954) about the Esterel coast.

1982 Britain's Graham Greene writes *J'Accuse – The Dark Side of Nice.*

Albert Camus

Graham Greene

1957 Albert Camus buys a house in Lourmarin *(see p171)*, where he writes his autobiography, not published until 1994.

The Fitzgeralds

1993 Briton Anthony Burgess, the author of *A Clockwork Orange* (1962), writes his final work, *Dead Man in Deptford*, in Monaco.

1934 American author F Scott Fitzgerald's South of France-based *Tender is the Night* is published. Scott and his wife Zelda stay in a villa at Juan-Les-Pins in 1926.

1926 American author Ernest Hemingway sets *The Garden of Eden* in La Napoule. Britain's W Somerset Maugham buys the Villa Mauresque, Cap Ferrat, and writes *Cakes and Ale* (1930).

1920 Consumptive New Zealand short story writer Katherine Mansfield recuperates in Menton *(see p99)* and writes *Miss Bull* and *Passion* among other pieces.

Somerset Maugham

Malcolm McDowell plays Alex, the antihero, in the controversial film, A Clockwork Orange (1966).

The Beaches of Provence

FROM THE UNTAMED EXPANSES of the Rhône delta to the hot spots of the Riviera, via the cliffs and coves of the Var, the coastline of Provence is extremely varied. Resort beaches around the towns of the Riviera, such as Menton, Nice and Monte-Carlo, are crowded and noisy in the height of summer. They often charge a fee, but are usually well-kept and offer good watersports facilities. It is, however, possible to seek out quieter corners away from the crowds if you know where to look.

The Côte d'Azur beaches offer warmth and sunshine all year long, as advertised in this 1930s poster by Roger Broders.

The Camargue beaches (see pp136–8) *at the mouth of the Rhône delta, are often deserted. The long, flat sands are ideal for horse riding, but there is a shortage of amenities.*

The Côte Bleue is dotted with fishing ports and elegant summer residences. Pine trees line the beaches.

Stes-Maries-de-la-Mer   ①

Plage de Piémanson

Carry-le-Rouet

C O T E B L E U E

Marseille

C A M A R G U E

② Bandol

C A L A N Q U E S

Sanary ③

Les Calanques (see p153) *are beautiful and dramatic fjord-like inlets situated east of Marseille. The sheer white cliffs, some 400 m (1,312 ft) high, drop vertically into the tempting, blue water.*

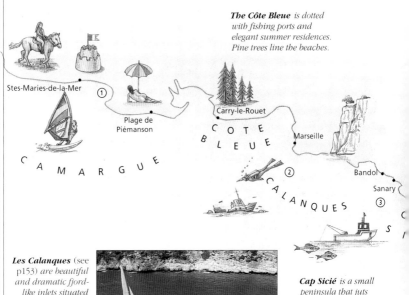

Cap Sicié is a small peninsula that juts out from the Var mainland. It is famed for its strong winds and waves, ideal for experienced windsurfers.

PROVENCE'S TEN BEST BEACHES

Best sandy beach ①
Plage de Piémanson, east of the Camargue, is remote enough for nudist bathing.

Best deep-sea diving ②
The deep Calanques waters are ideal for exploring.

Best sea fishing ③
Bandol and Sanary are charming resorts, where the tuna boats make their daily catch.

Best small resort beach ④
Le Lavandou offers all amenities on a small scale.

Best trendy beach ⑤
Tahiti-Plage in St-Tropez is the coast's showcase for fun, sun, fashion and glamour.

Best family beaches ⑥
Fréjus-Plage and the beach of St-Raphaël are clean, safe and have excellent facilities.

Best star-spotter's beach ⑦
Cannes' beautiful setting, with its scenic harbour, casino and stylish beaches, attracts the rich and famous.

Best teen and twenties beach ⑧
The all-night bars, cafés and nightclubs of Juan-les-Pins make this a lively resort.

Best activity beach ⑨
Watersports fanatics gather at the Ruhl-Plage in Nice for the jet-skiing and parasailing.

Best winter beach ⑩
Menton is the warmest resort on the Riviera and the sun shines all year round, ideal for relaxing winter holidays.

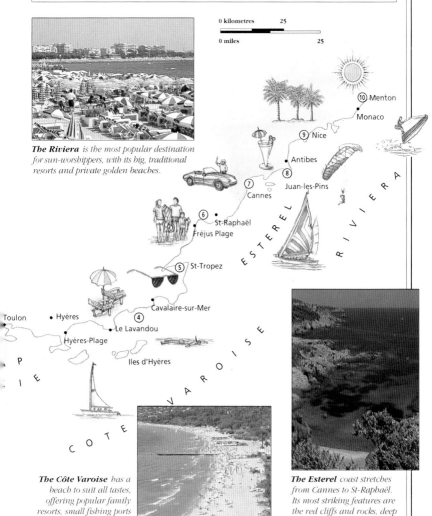

0 kilometres 25

0 miles 25

The Riviera is the most popular destination for sun-worshippers, with its big, traditional resorts and private golden beaches.

⑩ Menton

Monaco

⑨ Nice

Antibes

⑧

Juan-les-Pins

⑦ Cannes

⑥ St-Raphaël

Fréjus Plage

⑤ St-Tropez

Cavalaire-sur-Mer

Toulon • Hyères

④ Le Lavandou

Hyères-Plage

Iles d'Hyères

ESTEREL

RIVIERA

CÔTE VAROISE

P I E

The Côte Varoise has a beach to suit all tastes, offering popular family resorts, small fishing ports and excellent snorkelling.

The Esterel coast stretches from Cannes to St-Raphaël. Its most striking features are the red cliffs and rocks, deep ravines and secluded coves.

PROVENCE THROUGH THE YEAR

P ROVENCE IS at its prettiest in spring, when flowers bring livelihoods to perfume-makers and please to passers-by. It can also be surprisingly cold as this is when the Mistral blows its strongest.

Summer fruit and vegetables are both abundant and beautiful, filling the local markets. The midsummer heat is added to by the fires of St Jean and the Valensole plains are striped with lavender, the indelible colour of the region.

Medieval-style grape harvest or *vendange*

To entertain the thousands of holiday-makers, July and August are filled with music festivals. Come autumn, vineyards turn to copper and the grapes are harvested. Snows blanket the mountains from December and skiers take to the slopes. Throughout the year, every town and village celebrates with a *fête*, often with traditional costume and lively activities. For information, contact the local tourist office (*see p229*).

The first strawberries of the year

SPRING

B Y THE TIME March begins, lemons have already been harvested and the almond blossom faded. The landscape is brightened with pear, plum and apricot blossom and the first vegetables of spring are ready for the markets: beans, asparagus and green artichokes known as *mourre de gats*. By May, fruit markets are coloured with the first ripe cherries and strawberries of the year.

Southern mountain slopes warm to the sunshine and come alive with alpine flowers but the northern slopes remain wintery. Broom turns hillsides deep yellow and bees start to make honey from the sweet-smelling rosemary flowers. Flocks of sheep begin the journey of transhumance up to the summer pastures, and on the vast plains maize, wheat and rape push their way up through the softening earth.

MARCH

Exposition International de la Fleur (*end-March–April*), Cagnes-sur-Mer (*p78*). One of the region's many flower festivals to celebrate spring.
Festin es Courgourdons (*last Sun*), Nice (*pp84–5*). Folklore and sculpted gourd *fête*.
Festival International de Musique Classique (*biennial, mid-month*), Cannes (*pp68–9*). Features top orchestras.

APRIL

Procession aux Limaces (*Good Friday*), Roquebrune-Cap-Martin (*p98*). The streets are lit with shell lamps and a parade of locals dressed as disciples and legionnaires recreate the entombment of Christ.
Féria Pascale (*Easter*), Arles (*pp144–6*). Arletans turn out in their traditional costume for a *féria*. The *farandole* is danced to the accompaniment of the *tambourin* drum and *galoubet* flute to mark the beginning of the famous bullfighting season.

Fête des Gardians (*last Sunday in April*), Arles (*pp144–6*). The town is taken over by the *gardians* or cowboys who look after the Camargue cattle herds.
Fête des Vignerons (*24–25 April*), Châteauneuf-du-Pape (*p164*). The blessing of the vintage in the region's best-known wine-producing community.

MAY

Pèlerinage des Gitans avec Procession à la Mer de Sainte Sarah (*24–25 May*), Stes-Maries-de-la-Mer (*pp34–5*).
Festival International du Film (*two weeks in May*), Cannes (*pp68–9*). The most prestigious annual film festival.
La Bravade (*16–18 May*), St-Tropez (*see p34*).
Grand Prix Automobile de Formula 1 (weekend after Ascension), Monaco (*p94*). The only Grand Prix raced on public roads laps up an impressive 3,145 km (1,954 miles).
Feria (*Pentecost*), Nîmes (*see pp132–3*). The first major bullfighting event of the year.

Rodeo-style horse games at the Fête des Gardians in Arles

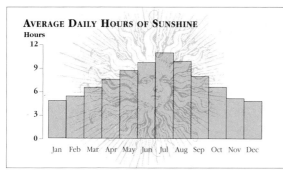

AVERAGE DAILY HOURS OF SUNSHINE

Hours
12
9
6
3
0

Jan Feb Mar Apr May Jun Jul Aug Sep Oct Nov Dec

Sunshine Chart
The summer months are guaranteed to be hot, with the intensity climaxing in July. Even in the winter, coastal towns can have up to 150 hours of sunshine a month, but be warned: it is often the icy Mistral that blows the clouds away in early spring.

SUMMER

The CÔTE D'AZUR is essentially a playground in summer, particularly in August when the French take their holidays. Rafters take to the rivers and scuba divers explore the varied sea-life. For laid-on entertainment, there are music festivals throughout the region.

Three national celebrations are also manifest: fireworks and bonfires brighten the skies on the **Fête de St-Jean** (June 24). **Bastille Day** (July 14) is celebrated with fireworks while **Assumption Day** (August 15) is a time for great feasting.

Celebrating the Fête de St-Jean with fireworks over Marseille harbour

JUNE

Fête de la Tarasque *(last Sun)*, Tarascon *(p140)*. According to local legend, the Tarasque monster once terrorized the region. An effigy of the monster is paraded through the town.
Festival International d'Aix *(all month)*, Aix-en-Provence *(pp148–9)*. Extensive programme of classical music concerts and opera is staged in the courtyard theatre of the Archbishop's Palace.

The legendary Tarasque

JULY

Festival d'Avignon *(last three weeks)*, Avignon *(see p35)*.
Son-et-Lumière *(Jul – Aug)*, Fontaine-de-Vaucluse *(p165)*. A sound and light show is staged by the town's famous mystical fountain, the source of the river Sorgue.
Chorégies d'Orange *(last two*

weeks), Orange. This long-established opera season is held in the accoustically perfect Roman theatre *(pp162–3)*.
Jazz à Juan *(second week)*, Juan-les-Pins *(p72)*. One of the top jazz festivals in Provence.
Festival du Jazz *(mid-month)*, Toulon *(p112–13)*. A week of free concerts in different squares every day throughout the town.
Recontres Internationales de la Photographie *(first two weeks)*, Arles *(p144–6)*. The National School of Photography was set up in 1982 as a result of this festival and each year the town is transformed into a photographic arena.

AUGUST

Corso de la Lavande *(first weekend)*, Digne-les-Bains *(see p35)*.
Les Journées Médiévales *(biennial, weekend before Assumption)*, Entrevaux

(p187). The quiet streets come to life with a 16th- and 17th-century music *fête*.
Fête du Jasmin *(first weekend)*, Grasse *(pp66–7)*. Floats, music and dancing in the town.
Procession de la Passion *(5 Aug)*, Roquebrune-Cap-Martin *(p98)*. Over 500 locals take part in staging Christ's passion, enacted since the Virgin saved the town from plague in 1467.
Le Festival de Musique *(all month)*, Menton *(pp98–9)*. Chamber music in the square.

Holiday-makers on the crowded beaches of the Côte d'Azur

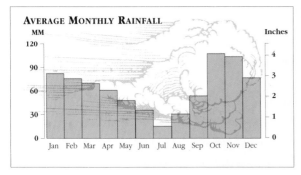

Rainfall Chart

Spring and autumn are the wettest times, with the amount of rainfall increasing as you head inland. November rain is the most violent, often with storms and flooding. Summer is virtually rain-free, causing drought in some forest areas.

AUTUMN

WHEN THE summer holidays are over it is time for the *vendange*, the grape harvest, when everyone lends a hand. In the Camargue, rice is ready to be brought in. Walnuts are picked and, in the Maures, sweet chestnuts are collected. The woods also yield rewards for mushroom hunters, while in Vaucluse and the Var truffles are harvested from oak woods and sold on the market stalls.

The hunting season begins in November. Small birds, such as thrushes, and ducks fall from flight into the pot and wild boar are bagged, their feet kept as talismans. Sheep are brought down to their winter pastures.

A grape picker at work during the autumn harvest

On the hunt for truffles in the woods of Haute Provence

SEPTEMBER

Fête des Prémices du Riz *(early Sep)*, Arles *(pp144–6)*. This festival of the rice harvest coincides with the last Spanish-style bullfights of the year.

Féria des Vendanges *(second week)*, Nîmes *(pp132–3)*. An enjoyable combination of wine, dancing and bullfights.

Festival de la Navigation de Plaisance *(mid-Sep)*, Cannes *(pp68–9)*. Yachts from around the world meet in the harbour.

Fête de Vent *(mid-Sep)*, Marseille *(pp150–2)*. Kites from all over the world decorate the sky for two days down on the Plages du Prado.

OCTOBER

Fête de Sainte Marie Salome *(Sunday nearest 22 Oct)*, Stes-Maries-de-la-Mer. A similar festival to the Gypsy Pilgrimage held in May *(see p34–5)* with a procession through the town's streets to the beach and the ritual blessing of the sea.

Foire Internationale de Marseille *(end of Sep–early Oct)*, Marseille *(pp150–52)*. Thousands of visitors pour into the city to enjoy the annual fair. Various activities and sports are organized with crafts, music and folklore entertainment from over 40 different countries.

NOVEMBER

Jour de Nationale *(19 Nov)*, Monaco *(pp90–94)*. The second smallest independent state in Europe celebrates its national day with a firework display over the harbour.

Festival International de la Danse *(biennial, late-Nov or early Dec)*, Cannes *(pp68–9)*. A festival of contemporary dance and ballet with an impressive programme of international performances.

Performers at the Festival International de la Danse in Cannes

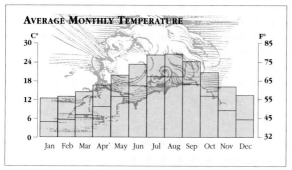

AVERAGE MONTHLY TEMPERATURE

Temperature Chart
The Mistral has a substantial effect on the temperature. During the winter and early spring, it can drop 10˚C (50˚F) in only a few hours. The summer heat can be uncomfortable, but the evenings cool down and are perfect for sitting outside.

WINTER

THERE IS AN old saying in Provence used to describe winter: *"l'hiver a ges d'ouro,"* "winter has no hours". It is a time to open the jams of the summer, to make the geese and duck *confits* and to turn the olive harvest into oil.

Snow soon cuts off mountain passes and, at weekends, locals and visitors take to the many ski resorts, warmed by juniper or wild strawberry liqueurs.

Christmas is heralded by the sale of *santons*, the figurines used to decorate Provence's distinctive cribs. Epiphany is another important festival, when the Three Kings are fêted with crown-shaped pastries.

DECEMBER

Foire aux Santons *(all month)*, Marseille *(pp150–52)*. The largest fair honouring the symbolic clay figures that are an integral part of Christmas.
Fête du Vin *(early December)*, Bandol *(p112)*. Every wine-grower in the town has their own stand and there is free wine-tasting. A different theme is chosen every year with activities and much merriment.
Fête des Bergers and mid-night mass *(24 Dec)*, Les Baux-de-Provence *(pp142–3)*. A traditional festive feast of the shepherds before mass.

JANUARY

Rallye de Monte-Carlo *(late Jan, pp92–3)*. A major event in the motor sporting calendar.
Festival du Cirque *(end of month)*, Monaco *(p94)*. Circus shows from around the globe.

Relaxing in the winter sun in the Alpes-de-Haute-Provence

FEBRUARY

Fête du Citron, *(late Feb–early Mar)*, Menton *(pp98–9)*. Floats and music fill the town during the lemon festival.
Fête de Mimosa *(third Sunday)*, Bormes-les-Mimosas

(pp116–17). The annual festival in celebration of the perched village's favourite flower.
Carnaval de Nice, *(all month)*, Nice *(see p34)*.

PUBLIC HOLIDAYS

New Year's Day (1 Jan)
Easter Sunday and Monday
Ascension (sixth Thursday after Easter)
Whit Monday (second Monday after Ascension)
Labour Day (1 May)
VE Day (8 May)
Bastille Day (14 Jul)
Assumption Day (15 Aug)
All Saints' Day (1 Nov)
Remembrance Day (11 Nov)
Christmas Day and Boxing Day (25–26 Dec)

The Taj Mahal re-created at the Fête du Citron in Menton

Festivals in Provence

FESTIVALS IN PROVENCE are very much part of the way of life. They are not staged purely for the benefit of visitors and tourism, but more to continue the seasonal celebrations that are deeply rooted in tradition. Many *fêtes* are based on pagan rites while others are celebrations of historic occasions – only a few have been hijacked by fun-loving holiday-makers on the coast. Here is a selection of the best festivals from each of the *départements*.

One of the spectacular floats in the procession at the Nice Carnival

THE RIVIERA AND THE ALPES MARITIMES

THE BRILLIANT explosion of fireworks at the Carnaval de Nice above the Baie des Anges is one of the most popular images of Nice *(see pp84–5)*. It is the largest pre-Lent carnival in France, and crescendos on Shrove Tuesday with fireworks and the immolation of King Carnival, *Sa Majesté Carnaval.*

Carnival festivities, held in all Catholic countries, are based on the pagan celebrations of the death of winter and the birth of spring and life. It is a time of feasting (*mardi gras* means "fat Tuesday") before the fasting of Lent (*carne vale* is Latin for "farewell to meat").

Festivities begin three weeks before Mardi Gras, when the king is wheeled out into the streets. During the two weekends between then and his departure, the colourful, flower-decked floats of the procession parade along the 2-km (1-mile) route round Jardin Albert I, amid confetti battles, bands and mounted escorts.

Carnival characters in the streets of Nice

By the 19th century, the Nice Carnival had developed into little more than a chalk and flour battle. The floats did not appear until 1873, inspired by the local artist, Alexis Mossa, who also resurrected the figure of King Carnival. Since then, great effort and time has been put into making the costumes.

Meanwhile, the whole town is *en fête*, and parties and balls are held in hotels and public venues all night long. Visitors should book well in advance to secure accommodation.

THE VAR AND THE ILES D'HYÈRES

A NUMBER OF FESTIVALS in the region feature the firing of muskets, reminiscent of ancient witch-scaring rites. Spectacular volleys are set off into the air in St-Tropez *(see pp118–19)* for the biannual *bravade*, commemorating two significant events.

The first one takes place on May 16 and 17 and is a religious procession devoted to the town's patron, Saint Torpès, He was a Roman soldier in the

service of the emperor, Nero. In AD 68, Torpès converted to Christianity and was martyred by decapitation. His body was placed in a boat along with a hungry dog and a cockerel. Miraculously, the saint's body was untouched. The vessel was washed up onto the shores of southern France, on the spot where St-Tropez stands today.

The May *bravade* honours his arrival. Celebrations begin with the blessing of a lance by the town's priest in the Eglise de St-Tropez. From here, the saint's gilded wooden bust is taken and carried around the flag-decked town in a terrific flurry of musket volleys. The procession winds down to the beach, and the sea is blessed for safely conveying the saint.

The second *bravade* takes place on 15 June and is honoured with earth-shattering fusillades and military parades. It marks the anniversary of the day in 1637, when the local militia saw off a Spanish fleet, about 22 vessels strong, after an attempt to capture four ships of the Royal French fleet.

La bravade procession in St-Tropez, honouring the town's patron saint

BOUCHES-DU-RHÔNE AND NÎMES

EUROPE'S LARGEST Romany festival, the Pèlerinage des Gitans in Saintes-Maries-de-la-Mer *(see p138)*, is a simple yet very moving occasion. At the end of May, usually 24–26, Romanies from all over the continent gather to pay their

Procession of the saints down to the sea in Saintes-Maries-de-la-Mer

Papal Palace and his Théâtre National Populair still performs every year. Other venues include the theatres and cinemas, where films are shown all day, the opera house and churches.

Since the 1960s, the fringe-style Avignon Public Off, brings some 520 events to over 100 venues including many specially set-up theatres. Amateur performers can be seen for free in the main square outside the opera, the place de l'Horloge.

ALPES-DE-HAUTE-PROVENCE

Provence's most particular flower has its festival, the Corso de la Lavande, in the mountain spa town of Digne-les-Baines *(see p180)*.

The colourful event, which lasts for four days, takes place in August and celebrates the harvesting of the crop. There are jars and pots of honey and all kinds of lavender produce for sale in the town, and events centre on the main street, boulevard Gassendi. The climax of the festival comes on the last day when the flower-decked floats, representing a variety of themes, parade through the streets, accompanied by music, dancing and cheering. Preceding the floats is a municipal truck spraying the roads with litres of lavender water leaving the whole town heady with the distinctive, sweet perfume.

respects to the patron saint of gypsies, Saint Sarah, known as the Black Madonna. This takes place in the picturesque town of Saintes-Maries-de-la-Mer.

The pilgrimage is a colourful occasion, brightened by traditional Arlesian costumes and *gardian* cowboys. The object of their veneration is Saint Sarah, the Ethiopian servant. As legend has it, she arrived on the shores of the Camargue by boat. Also on board was Mary Magdalene, and the saints Mary Jacobea (sister of the Virgin Mary) and the elderly Mary Salome (mother of the apostles Saint James and Saint John). Sarah and the Marys decided to stay in the town and they built an oratory on which the fortified church of Notre-Dame-de-la-Mer was built. The saints started to preach the gospel and the town became known as the "Mecca of Provence".

Saint Sarah stands serene and excessively robed in the crypt. On the two nights and days of celebration in May, she is remembered with a Mass and all-night vigil. The next day, the statues of the saints are borne down to the sea where the Camargue cowboys take their horses, neck-deep, into the water and the Bishop of Arles blesses the sea.

After the statues have been returned to the church, the great folk festival begins, with rodeos, bull-running, horse racing, Arletan dancing and all manner of entertainment. The *gardians* return for a smaller celebration of Mary Salome in October, when there is a procession around the church.

VAUCLUSE

The papal city of Avignon *(see pp166–8)* is a splendid setting for the foremost arts festival in Provence, the Festival d'Avignon. Theatre, music, dance and film are all covered in the month-long programme which runs from mid-July to early August. More than a quarter of a million visitors travel to Avignon every year to attend the largest arts festival in France. It is advisable to reserve hotels and tickets in advance to avoid disappointment *(see pp224–5 for reservations)*.

The festival was established in 1947 by the late Jean Vilar whose aim was to bring theatre to the masses. He devised a number of productions to be staged in the courtyard of the

Lavender from the festival in Digne

Lively street performers at the summer Festival d'Avignon

THE HISTORY
OF PROVENCE

FEW REGIONS of France have experienced such a varied and turbulent history as Provence. There is evidence, in the form of carvings, tools and weapons, of nomadic tribes and human settlements from 300,000 BC. The introduction of the vine, so important today, can be credited to the Phoenicians and Greeks who traded along the coast. Perhaps more crucially, Provence was the Romans' "Province" and few regions of their vast empire have retained such dramatic buildings; the theatre at Orange, the arenas of Arles and Nîmes, the Pont du Gard and the imposing trophy of La Turbie are all testimony to past Roman power.

Virgin and Child, Aix-en-Provence

The Middle Ages proved a stormy period of feuding warlords and invasions; the many well-fortified hilltop villages that characterize the region were a desperate attempt at defence. The presence of the papacy dominated the 14th century, and the magnificent palace that the popes built in Avignon remains today. The arts flourished too, especially under King René in his elegant capital of Aix. Following his death in 1480, Provence lost its independence and its history became enmeshed with that of France. Religious war took its toll and the Great Plague killed tens of thousands in 1720.

A beguiling climate and improved transport in the 19th century began to attract artists and foreign nobility. Tiny fishing villages grew into glamorous Riviera resorts. The allure remains for millions of tourists while economic investment means it is also a boom area for the technology industry.

16th-century map of Marseille and its harbour

◁ **Detail of an illuminated 13th-century manuscript showing a troubadour playing to a royal audience**

Ancient Provence

ROCK CARVINGS, FRAGMENTS OF PAINTINGS and remains from primitive settlements suggest that Provence was first inhabited a million years ago. Carvings in the Grotte de l'Observatoire in Monaco and the decorated Grotte Cosquer near Marseille are among the oldest of their kind in the world. Nomadic tribes roamed the land for centuries, notably the Celts from the north and the Ligurians from the east. Not until the arrival of the Phoenicians and the Greeks did trade flourish in a more structured way and Provençal society become more stable.

Stone fertility figurine (1,000,000 BC)

"Double Head" Carving
This stone figure (3rd century BC) probably decorated a Celtic sanctuary.

The bories at Gordes date back to 3,500 BC.

Celtic Doorway
(3rd century BC) The niches in the pillars held the embalmed heads of Celtic heroes.

The Grotte des Fées at Mont de Cordes contain prehistoric carvings often associated with modern astrological symbols.

THE FOUNDATION OF MARSEILLE

When Greek traders arrived in 600 BC, their captain, Protis, attended a feast in honour of the local chief's daughter, Gyptis. She chose Protis as her husband. The chief's dowry to Protis and Gyptis was the strip of land on which Marseille grew.

St-Blaise, once a heavily fortified Greek trading centre, has only minimal remains.

The Grotte Cosquer, with paintings dating to 30,000 BC, is accessible only from the sea.

Wine jars, bound for Greece from 1,000 BC onwards, were found in Les Calanques near Marseille.

TIMELINE

1,000,000 BC Earliest human presence in Provence at Grotte de l'Observatoire in Monaco; use of bone as a tool

400,000 BC Fire first used in Nice

60,000 BC Neanderthal hunters on the Riviera

1,000,000 BC	5,000		4,000	3,500

30,000 BC Appearance of *Homo sapiens* (modern man); cave painting at Grotte Cosquer

Cave painting from Grotte Cosquer

3,500 BC First borie villages

Vallée des Merveilles
About 100,000 carvings date from 2,500– 2,000 BC. Among them are strange, witch-like figures known as orants.

The Vallée des Merveilles carvings suggest that nearby Mont Bégo was a focus for worship.

WHERE TO SEE ANCIENT PROVENCE

Many museums, such as the Musée Archéologique, Nîmes *(see p132)*, have excellent collections of ancient artifacts. The well-preserved bories in the Luberon *(p169)* illustrate early village communities; the Grotte de l'Observatoire in Monaco *(p94)* is an example of an even more primitive settlement.

Borie Village at Gordes
These dry-stone dwellings (p169) *have for centuries been used by nomadic shepherds.*

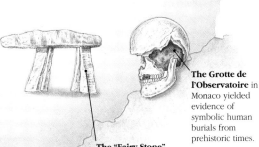

The Grotte de l'Observatoire in Monaco yielded evidence of symbolic human burials from prehistoric times.

The "Fairy Stone", *Peïro de la fado* in Provençal, is the only true prehistoric dolmen in Provence.

Grotte de l'Observatoire
Skeletons uncovered here have characteristics linking them with southern African tribes.

ANCIENT SITES OF PROVENCE

Most sites lie along the coast, but there are some pockets of settlement inland near Tende, in the Luberon, and in the inaccessible Vallée des Merveilles, which stands at about 2,500 m (8,200 ft).

Standing Stone
Prehistoric stelae, like this carved stone from the Luberon, are scattered throughout Provence.

Hannibal crossing the Alps

2,500–2,000 BC
Carvings at Vallée des Merveilles

218 BC Hannibal passes through region to reach Italy

3,000	2,500	2,000	1,500	1,000	500 BC

2,000 BC Tombs carved at Cordes

600 BC Greek traders settle at St-Blaise. Founding of Marseille

380 BC Celtic invasions of Provence

Gallo-Roman Provence

Mosaic from Vaison-la-Romaine (40 BC)

THE ROMANS EXTENDED THEIR EMPIRE into Provence towards the end of the 2nd century BC. They enjoyed good relations with the local people and within 100 years created a wealthy province. Nîmes and Arles became two of the most significant Roman towns outside Italy; colonies at Glanum and Vaison-la-Romaine flourished. Many fine monuments remain and museums, for instance at Vaison-la-Romaine, display smaller Roman treasures.

Christ's followers are reputed to have brought Christianity to the region when they landed at Les-Saintes-Maries-de-la-Mer in AD 40.

Pont Julien (*3 BC*)
This magnificently preserved triple-arched bridge stands 8 km (5 miles) west of Apt.

Twin temples, dedicated to the emperor Augustus's adopted sons, Caius and Lucius, date from 30 BC.

Marble Sarcophagus (*4th century*)
The Alyscamps in Arles (see p146), once a vast Roman necropolis, contains many carved marble and stone coffins.

Triumphal Arch at Orange
Built in about 20 BC this is, in spite of much restoration, one of the best preserved Roman triumphal arches. Carvings depict the conquest of Gaul and sea battle scenes.

The fortified gate was built by the original Greek community that occupied Glanum from the 4th century BC.

ROMAN GLANUM
The impressive ruined site at Glanum reveals much earlier Roman and Greek settlements. This reconstruction shows it after it was rebuilt in AD 49.

TIMELINE

118 BC Provincia founded – first Gallo-Roman Province

125 BC Roman legions defend Marseille against Celto-Ligurian invaders

Consul Marius

49 BC Emperor Julius Caesar lays siege to Marseille for supporting his rival, Pompey. Romans rebuild Glanum

40 BC Vaison-la-Romaine ranks among Roman Gaul's wealthiest towns

100 BC	AD 1	100

123 BC Romans make Entremont first Provençal settlement

121 BC Foundation of Aquae Sextiae, later to become Aix-en-Provence

102 BC Consul Marius defeats invading German tribes; over 200,000 killed

14 BC Emperor Augustus defeats Ligurians in Alpes Maritimes. Trophy at La Turbie erected (*see p89*)

3 BC Pont Julien built

AD 40 "Boat of Bethany" lands at Les-Saintes-Maries-de-la-Mer

2nd-century BC Venus d'Arles

Les-Stes-Maries-de-la-Mer
*Mary Magdalene, Mary
Salome and Mary Jacobea
reputedly sailed to
Provence in AD 40. The
town where they
landed is named in
their honour and still
attracts pilgrims* (see p138).

(see p138)

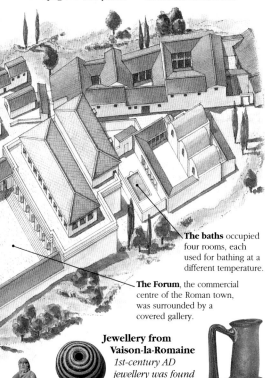

The baths occupied
four rooms, each
used for bathing at a
different temperature.

The Forum, the commercial
centre of the Roman town,
was surrounded by a
covered gallery.

**Jewellery from
Vaison-la-Romaine**
*1st-century AD
jewellery was found
in excavations of the
Roman necropolis.*

Roman Flask
*Well-preserved ancient
Roman glassware and
everyday items have
been found in many
areas of Provence.*

WHERE TO SEE GALLO-ROMAN PROVENCE

Arles *(see pp144–6)* and
Nîmes *(pp132–3)*, with their
amphitheatres and religious
and secular buildings, offer
the most complete examples
of Roman civilization. Orange
(p161) and Vaison-la-Romaine
(p158) contain important
monuments, and the Pont du
Gard *(p131)* and Le Trophée
des Alpes *(p89)* are unique.

Théâtre Antique d'Orange
*Built into a hill, this Roman
theatre would have held over
10,000 spectators* (pp162–3).

Cryptoporticus
*The foundations of Arles' forum,
these horseshoe-shaped underground galleries were probably
used as grain stores* (p146).

200	300	400	500

413 Visigoths
seize Languedoc

476 Western Roman
Empire collapses

300 Arles reaches
height of its prestige
as a Roman town

*Basilique St-Victor,
founded 416,
in Marseille*

Medieval Provence

13th-century manuscript illustration

WITH THE FALL of the Roman Empire, stability and relative prosperity began to disappear. Although Provence became part of the Holy Roman Empire, the local counts retained considerable autonomy and the towns became fiercely independent. People withdrew to hilltops to protect themselves from attack by a series of invaders, and *villages perchés (see p18–19)* began to develop. Provence became a major base for Christian Crusaders, intent on conquering Muslim territories in Africa and Asia.

The Great Walls, finally completed in 1300, 30 years after Louis IX's death, were over 1.6 km (1 mile) long and formed an almost perfect rectangle.

St-Trophime Carving
The monumental 12th-century portal at St-Trophime in Arles (see p144) is adorned with intricate carvings of saints and scenes from the Last Judgment.

Louis IX's army
consisted of 35,000 men plus horses and military equipment.

Louis IX

St Martha and the Tarasque
The 9th-century legend of St Martha and the Tarasque, a ferocious dragon, proved the strength of Christianity. The beast fled at the sight of her crucifix.
(See p140.)

THE SEVENTH CRUSADE

Hoping to drive the Muslims out of the Holy Land, Louis IX (St Louis) of France set sail from his new port, Aigues-Mortes *(see p134–5)*, in 1248. It was a spectacular occasion, with banners waving and his army singing hymns.

TIMELINE

536 Provence ceded to the Franks	**737–9** Anti-Frankish rebellions in Avignon, Marseille and Arles brutally suppressed by Charles Martel	**855** Kingdom of Provence created for Charles the Bald, grandson of Charlemagne	**949** Provence divided into four counties
600	**700**	**800**	**900**
Saracen warrior and Provençal maiden		**800** First wave of Saracen invasions	**924** Hungarians sack Nîmes

Charles the Bald

Troubadour Ivory (c.1300)
The poetry of Provençal troubadours tells how knights wooed virtuous women through patience, courtesy and skill.

Notre-Dame-de-Beauvoir Chapel
At the top of a path from Moustiers (see p186), the chapel has a fine Romanesque porch and nave.

1500 ships set sail for the Holy Land on 28 August 1248.

WHERE TO SEE MEDIEVAL PROVENCE

The highlights are undoubtedly the Romanesque abbeys and churches, especially the "three sisters": Silvacane (p147), Le Thoronet (p108) and Sénanque (p164). Fortified *villages perchés*, such as Gordes (p169) and the spectacular 11th-century citadel at Les Baux-de-Provence (p142), testify to the unrest and horrific violence that scarred this period of Provence's history.

Les Penitents des Mées
These are said to be 6th-century monks turned to stone for gazing at Saracen women (p181).

St Christopher Fresco
The Tour Ferrande in Pernes-les-Fontaines (see p164) contains religious frescoes from 1285. They are among the oldest in France.

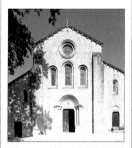

Silvacane Abbey (1175–1230)
This beautiful, austere Cistercian abbey was Provence's last great Romanesque abbey.

974 Saracens defeated at La Garde-Freinet

Seal of Simon de Montfort

1213 Battle of Muret: de Montfort defeats count of Toulouse and King of Aragon

1209 French military leader Simon de Montfort marches on Provence

1246 Charles of Anjou marries Béatrice, heiress of Provence, to become Count of Provence

1248 Louis IX embarks on Seventh Crusade from Aigues-Mortes

1000	1100	1200	1300

1032 Provence becomes part of Holy Roman Empire

1096–1099 First Crusade

1112 Raymond-Bérenger III, Count of Barcelona, marries the Duchess of Provence

1186 Counts of Provence declare Aix their capital

1125 Provence shared between Barcelona and Toulouse

1187 Remains of St Martha discovered at Tarascon

1274 Papacy acquires Comtat Venaissin

1295 Death of Guiraut Riquier, the "Last Troubadour"

1280 Relics of Mary Magdalene found at St-Maximin-la-Ste-Baume

Papal Avignon

14th-century carving, Palais des Papes

WHEN THE PAPACY TEMPORARILY abandoned war-torn Italy, Avignon became the centre of the Roman Catholic world. From 1309 until 1377 seven French popes ruled unchallenged. When a new Italian pope, Urban VI, was elected, the French cardinals rebelled. In 1378 they chose a rival pope, Clement VII, thus causing a major schism that lasted until 1403. During the 14th century the papal court in Avignon became a wealthy centre for both learning and the arts, extending its influence across the region.

The Palais Vieux (1334–42), built by Benedict XII in typically austere Cistercian style, is more of a fortress than a church.

Benedict XII's cloister

Grand Tinel

Consistory Hall

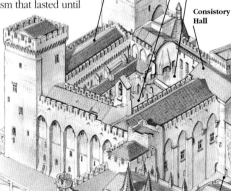

Bargème, Northern Var
Instability across Provence led to villages like Bargème building strong fortifications.

Papal Throne
The Pope's Room in the Palais des Papes contains copies of the original 14th-century furniture, like this carved wooden throne.

Great Courtyard

Prophets Fresco (1344–5)
Matteo Giovanetti from Viterbo was the principal fresco-master of Clement VI. His realism contrasts with earlier medieval artists.

TIMELINE

1316–34 Reign of John XXII

1327 Petrarch first catches sight of Laura of Avignon, his muse

1342–52 Reign of Clement VI

Coin of Pope Innocent VI

1352–62 Reign of Innocent VI

1310	1320	1330	1340	1350

1309 Papacy moves to Avignon

1334–42 Reign of Benedict XII

1348 Clement VI acquires Avignon

1349 Jews take refuge in the Comtat Venaissin, part of the Papal lands

Pope John XXII

Death of Clement VI
Clement VI came to Avignon to "forget he was pope". In 1348 he bought the town for 80,000 florins and built the splendid Palais Neuf.

Stag Room Frescoes
The hunting scenes are a reminder that monastic life was not only about learning and prayer.

Stag Room

The Great Chapel, covering 780 sq m (8,400 sq ft), contains the restored papal altar.

The Palais Neuf was built by Clement VI in 1342–52.

Great Audience Hall

PALAIS DES PAPES

The maze of corridors and rooms in the Palais des Papes *(see p168)*, built over 18 years (1334–52), were richly decorated by skilled artists and craftsmen introduced from Italy. The building's scale is overwhelming.

WHERE TO SEE PAPAL PROVENCE

Avignon is surrounded by evidence of religious and aristocratic splendour. With the presence of the wealthy papacy – a kind of miniature Vatican – abbeys, churches and chapels flourished. The Musée du Petit Palais *(see p168)* in Avignon contains examples of work by the artists who were encouraged to work at the papal court.

Villeneuve Charterhouse
Innocent VI established this, the oldest charterhouse in France, in the 1350s (p130).

Châteauneuf-du-Pape
John XXII's early 14th-century castle became the popes' second residence. The keep and walls are still standing today (p164).

Petrarch *(1304–74)*
The great Renaissance poet Petrarch considered papal Avignon to be a "sewer" and a place of corruption.

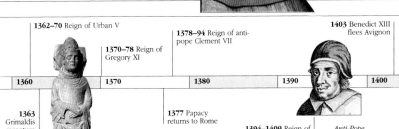

1362–70 Reign of Urban V

1370–78 Reign of Gregory XI

1378–94 Reign of anti-pope Clement VII

1403 Benedict XIII flees Avignon

| 1360 | 1370 | 1380 | 1390 | 1400 |

1363 Grimaldis recapture Monaco

Effigy of Urban V

1377 Papacy returns to Rome

1394–1409 Reign of anti-pope Benedict XIII

Anti-Pope Benedict XIII

René and the Wars of Religion

Pietà, Notre-Dame-de-l'Assomption

THE END of the 15th century saw the golden age of Aix *(see pp148–9)*, then Provence's capital. Under the patronage of King René, art and culture flourished and the Flemish-influenced Avignon School was formed. After René's death, Provence was annexed by the French king, Louis XI. Loss of independence and subsequent involvement with French politics led to brutal invasions by Charles V. The 16th-century Wars of Religion between "heretic" Protestants and Catholics resulted in a wave of massacres, and the wholesale destruction of churches and their contents.

Detail of the Triptych
René's favourite château of Tarascon (p140) on the Rhône is realistically painted.

King René, himself a poet, painter and musician, was a great influence on Provençal culture.

Nostradamus
Born in St-Rémy (pp140–41), the physician and astrologer is best known for his predictions, Les Centuries *(1555).*

Massacres of Protestants and Catholics
The religious wars were brutal. Thousands of Protestants were massacred in 1545, and 200 Catholics died in Nîmes in 1567.

BURNING BUSH TRIPTYCH
Nicolas Froment's painting (1476) was commissioned by King René. The star of the Cathédrale de St-Sauveur, Aix, it depicts a vision of the Virgin and Child surrounded by the eternal Burning Bush of Moses.

TIMELINE

King René

1434–80 Reign of Good King René

Retable from Avignon

1486 Union of Provence with France

1501 Parliament de Provence created

1425	1450	1475	1500

1481 Charles du Maine, Count of Provence and René's nephew, gives Provence to King of France

1496 Military port built at Toulon

The Annunciation
The Master of Aix, one of René's artistic circle, painted this Annunciation. Dark symbolism, including the owl's wings of the angel Gabriel, undercuts this usually joyful subject.

The Bush, burning but unconsumed, was a pagan and Christian symbol of eternal life.

Holy Roman Emperor, Charles V, by Titian
Between 1524 and 1536, Charles V (Charles I of Spain) attacked Provence frequently as part of his war against France.

The saints John the Evangelist, Catherine of Alexandria and Nicolas of Myra are behind Queen Jeanne.

Moses is seen receiving the word of God from an angel.

Queen Jeanne, René's second wife, is shown kneeling in adoration.

WHERE TO SEE 15TH- AND 16TH-CENTURY PROVENCE

Architecture from this period can be seen today in the fine town houses and elegant streets of Aix (pp148–9) and Avignon (pp166–8). The Musée Granet, also in Aix, contains several interesting examples of religious paintings. A collection of period furniture is exhibited in the Musée Grobet-Labadié in Marseille (p151).

Château at Tarascon
This 13th-century château (p140) was partly rebuilt by Louis II and then completed by King René, his son.

Rhinoceros Woodcut by Albrecht Dürer
In 1515, Marseille's Château d'If (p152) was briefly home to the first rhinoceros to set foot in Europe. It was in transit as a gift for the Pope, but died later in the journey.

1524 Invasion of Charles V			**1598** Edict of Nantes signals end of Wars of Religion	
	1545 Massacre of Protestants in Luberon villages	**1577** First soap factory in Marseille		
1525	**1550**	**1575**	**1600**
		1562 Wars of Religion commence		
1525 Jews in Comtat Venaissin forced to wear yellow hats		*Protestant martyrdom*		

Classical Provence

PROVENCE IN THE 17th and 18th centuries saw a decrease in regional allegiance and growth of national awareness. Towns grew and majestic monuments, town houses (*hôtels*) and châteaux proliferated. But despite economic development in the textile industry and the growth of the ports of Toulon and Marseille, the period was bleak for many, culminating in the devastating plague of 1720. The storming of the Bastille in Paris in 1789 sparked popular uprisings and revolutionary marches on Paris.

Pavillon de Vendôme
Jean-Claude Rambot made the Atlantes for this building (1667) in Aix (see pp148–9).

The death toll
was over 100,000 in the last plague in Europe.

Boat-Building in Toulon
Toulon, a strategic port, was famous for its boat-building. Galley slaves, chained to their oars, were a great tourist attraction in the 17th century.

Corpses were hauled in carts to mass graves.

THE GREAT PLAGUE
Vue du Cours pendant la Peste by Michel Serre depicts the 1720 plague in Marseille, brought by a cargo boat from Syria. Over half of Marseille's population died. All contact with the city was banned and huge walls were built to halt the epidemic, but it still spread as far as Aix, Arles and Toulon.

Santon Crib Scene
The santon ("little saints" in Provençal) cribs were first made after the Revolution, when the churches were shut. They soon became a very popular local craft.

TIMELINE

1622 Louis XIII visits Arles, Aix and Marseille

1660 Louis XIV, the "Sun King", enters Marseille

Sun King emblem

1707 English siege of Toulon fails

1696 France returns Nice to Savoy

1625	1650	1675	1700

1646 Jews confined to ghettos, notably in Carpentras

1666 Work begins on the Canal du Midi

1679 Vauban starts work on new port at Toulon

1691 Nice occupied by the French

1707 Provence invaded by Eugène of Savoy

Louis XIII

Napoleon Seizes Toulon
Junior officer Napoleon Bonaparte first made his name when he took Toulon from occupying English troops in 1793.

Cours Belsunce, built in 1670 in the Italian style, was lined with trees and Baroque palaces.

Monks, led by the devout Jean Belsunce, the Bishop of Marseille, gave succour to the dying.

Marshal Sébastien Vauban
Louis XIV's brilliant military architect, Vauban, fortified towns and ports including Toulon and Antibes.

Moustiers Faïence
Brought to France from Italy in the 17th century, traditional faïence *features pastoral scenes in delicate colours.*

WHERE TO SEE CLASSICAL PROVENCE

Avignon *(see pp166–8)* and Aix *(pp148–9)* have period town houses with fine door-ways and staircases. Jewish synagogues and remains of Jewish enclaves can be found in Cavaillon *(p170)*, Forcal-quier *(p182)* and Carpentras *(p164)*. The 18th-century Jardin de la Fontaine in Nîmes *(pp132–3)* can still be visited.

Pharmacy at Carpentras
The 18th-century Hôtel-Dieu (hospital) houses a chapel and a pharmacy containing faïence *apothecary jars.*

Fontaine du Cormoran
The best known of the 36 foun-tains in Pernes-les-Fontaines (p164) is the 18th-century carved Cormorant fountain.

1713 Treaty of Utrecht cedes Orange to France

1718 Nice becomes part of new Kingdom of Sardinia

1791 Avignon and Comtat Venaissin annexed to France

1779 Roman mausoleum at Aix demolished

1793 Breaking of siege of Toulon catapults Napoleon Bonaparte to fame

1725	1750	1775	1800

1720 Great Plague strikes Marseille and spreads throughout Provence

1771 Aix parliament suppressed

1787 Provençal silk harvest fails

1789 Storming of the Bastille, Paris; Provençal peasants pillage local châteaux and monasteries

1792 Republicans adopt Rouget de Lisle's army song: *La Marseillaise*

The Great Plague, Marseille

The Belle Epoque

Marseille soap advert, 1880

FROM THE START of the 19th century the beguiling climate, particularly the mild winters, of coastal Provence attracted foreign visitors, from invalids and artists to distinguished royalty and courtesans. Railways, grand hotels, exotic gardens, opulent villas and the chic promenade des Anglais in Nice were built to meet their needs. Queen Victoria, the Aga Khan, King Leopold of Belgium and Empress Eugénie – Napoleon III's wife and doyenne of Riviera royalty – all held court. Artists and writers came in droves to revel in the light and freedom.

Homage à Mistral
Frédéric Mistral created the Félibrige group in 1854 to preserve Provençal culture.

Printing in Marseille
Cheap labour, ample paper supplies and good communications fostered the development of printing.

Casino tables were sometimes draped in black mourning when a gambler succeeded in breaking the bank with a major win.

Grasse Perfume
More modern methods of cultivation and distillation played an important role in the expanding 19th-century perfume-making industry.

MONTE-CARLO CASINO INTERIOR

From being the poorest state in Europe in 1850, Monaco boomed with the opening of the first Monte-Carlo casino in 1865, as seen in Christian Bokelman's painting. The fashionable flocked to enjoy the luxury and glamour, while fortunes were won and lost *(see pp92–4).*

TIMELINE

1814
Napoleon lands at Golfe-Juan

1830 Beginnings of tourism around Nice

1861 Monaco sells Roquebrune and Menton to France

1860 Nice votes for union with France

1820   1840   1860

Paul Cézanne

1839 Marseille-Sète railroad begun. Birth of Cézanne

1854 Founding of Félibrige, the Provençal cultural school

1859 Mistral publishes his epic poem, *Mirèio*

Vineyard blight
Ravaged by phylloxera, vines in Provence and across France were replaced by resistant American root stocks.

Tourism
By the late 19th century, sun and sea air were considered beneficial to health.

Belle Epoque decor had interiors lavish with ornate chandeliers, gilt and coloured marble.

High society included famous courtesans as well as their rich and royal lovers.

WHERE TO SEE BELLE EPOQUE PROVENCE

Although many have been destroyed, villas and hotels built in the extravagant Belle Epoque style still survive on the Côte d'Azur. The Négresco in Nice *(see pp84–5)* is especially fine. Other period pieces include the Cathédrale Orthodoxe Russe, also in Nice, and, on glamorous Cap Ferrat, the Musée Ephrussi de Rothschild *(pp86–7)*. In Beaulieu the Villa Kerylos, Rotunda and lush exotic gardens are all typical of the era *(p88)*.

The Carlton Hotel, Cannes
Built in 1911, this ostentatious Riviera landmark is still an exclusive hotel overlooking the beach (pp68–9).

Monte-Carlo Opéra
Charles Garnier designed this opera house (pp92–3), as well as the Casino.

Van Gogh's Provence
Van Gogh produced turbulent works in the Clinique St-Paul in St-Rémy (see pp140–41).

1879 Monte-Carlo Opéra opens

Casino at Monte-Carlo

1909 Earthquake centred on Rognes in the Bouches-du-Rhône causes widespread damage

1880	1900	1920

1869 Opening of Suez Canal brings trade to Marseille; railway extended to Nice

1888–90 Van Gogh works in Provence

1904 Mistral wins Nobel prize for Literature for *Mirèio*

Provence at War

AFTER THE ECONOMIC DRAIN caused by World War I, Provence enjoyed increasing prosperity as the tourist industry boomed. While much of the interior remained remote and rural, the vogue for sea-bathing drew crowds to resorts such as Cannes and Nice from the 1920s onwards. Provence continued to build on its image as a playground for the rich and famous, attracting visitors from Noël Coward to Wallis Simpson. The 1942–44 German occupation brought an end to the glamorous social life for many, and some towns, including St-Tropez and Marseille, were badly damaged by Germans and Allies.

Tourism
As swimming in the sea and sunbathing became fashionable pursuits, resorts along the Riviera attracted many new visitors. In the 1930s a nudist colony opened on the Ile du Levant.

Monaco Grand Prix
This race around the principality's streets was started on the initiative of Prince Louis II in 1929. It is still one of the most colourful and dangerous Formula 1 races.

Precious ammunition and arms were dropped from Allied planes or captured from the Nazis.

Antoine de Saint-Exupéry
France's legendary writer-pilot disappeared on 31 July 1944 while on a reconnaissance flight (see p27).

LA RÉSISTANCE
After 1942 the Résistance (or *maquis* after the scrubland that made a good hiding place) was active in Provence. The fighters were successful in Marseille and in preparing the coastal areas for the 1944 Allied invasion.

TIMELINE

Coco Chanel

1930 Novelist DH Lawrence dies in Vence

1925 Coco Chanel arrives on the Riviera

1920	1925	1930

1924 Scott and Zelda Fitzgerald spend a year on the Riviera

1928 Camargue National Park created

1930 Pagnol begins filming *Marius, Fanny* and *César* trilogy in Marseille

F Scott Fitzgerald

Marcel Pagnol (1905–74)
Pagnol immortalized Provence and its inhabitants in his plays, novels and films, depicting a simple, rural life (see p27).

Many who joined the Résistance had scarcely left school. Training was often only by experience.

Allied Landings
On 14 August 1944, Allied troops bombarded the coast between Toulon and Marseille and soon gained ground.

Marseille Exhibition
The 1922 exhibition was an invitation to enjoy the cosmopolitan delights of Marseille.

WHERE TO SEE 1920s TO 1940s PROVENCE

The now slightly seedy suburbs of Hyères *(see p115)* retain evidence of graceful living after World War I. Toulon harbour's bristling warships *(pp112–13)* are a reminder of the French navy's former power. The activities of the Résistance are well documented in the Musée de la Résistance in Fontaine-de-Vaucluse *(p165)*.

Les Deux Garçons, Aix
This still chic café was frequented by Churchill and Cocteau among others (pp148–9).

Citadelle, Sisteron
Rebuilt after the Allied bombing in 1944, the citadel has displays on its turbulent history (p178).

1940 Italians occupy Menton

1942 Nazis invade southern France; French fleet scuttled in Toulon harbour

1943 *Maquis* resistance cells formed

1935	1940	1945

1939 Cannes Film Festival inaugurated, but first festival delayed by war

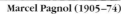

Liberation of Marseille

1944 American and French troops land near St-Tropez; liberation of Marseille

Post-War Provence

PAID VACATIONS, post-war optimism, and the St-Tropez sun cult all made the Riviera the magnet it has remained for holiday-makers. The region still offers a rich variety of produce – olive oil, wine, fruit, flowers and perfume – though industry, especially in the high-tech sector, grows apace. The environment has suffered from overdevelopment, pollution and forest fires. The 1960s saw massive North African immigration, and today unemployment creates racial and political tension.

Scooter rider in St-Tropez

Port-Grimaud
The successful "Provençal Venice", a car-free leisure port, was built by François Spoerry in 1966 in regional village style (see p123).

Bus Stop by Philippe Starck
The modern architecture of Nîmes typifies many bold projects in the region.

Beach at Nice
Though many are pebbly, the Riviera beaches still attract dedicated sun-worshippers.

Fires
The devastating forest fires which ravage the region are fought with planes scooping up sea water.

TIMELINE

1946 Picasso starts painting in the Grimaldi Castle, Antibes

1952 Le Corbusier's Cité Radieuse built

Grace Kelly

1956 Grace Kelly marries Monaco's Prince Rainier III

1961 Art festival of new Ecole de Nice

1962 Algerian Independence – French North Africans *(pieds-noirs)* settle in Provence

1950

1960

1954 Matisse dies

1956 Roger Vadim films *And God Created Woman*, starring Brigitte Bardot, in St-Tropez

1959 Floods in Fréjus

1962 Lower Durance engineered to develop hydro-electric power

Ben's Il y a trop d'art (1985) in Nice

Winter Sports
Skiing has become increasingly popular (see p96). Isola 2000, near Nice, a purpose-built, futuristic resort, was built in 1972.

Colombe d'Or, St-Paul
Once an artists' café, this is now one of many chic venues for the rich and famous (see p75).

WHERE TO SEE MODERN PROVENCE
Some of the most striking modern architecture includes Le Corbusier's Cité Radieuse in Marseille *(see p152)*, the Musée d'Art Contemporain in Nice *(p85)* and the Norman Foster-designed Carré d'Art in Nîmes *(p132)*. Large-scale rebuilding programmes in towns such as St-Tropez *(pp118–22)* and Ste-Maxime *(p123)* have concentrated on new buildings that blend well with the existing ones.

St-Tropez
Successful post-war restoration means it is often difficult to tell new buildings from old.

Fondation Maeght
The building reflects the modern use of traditional Provençal style and materials (pp76–7).

CANNES FILM FESTIVAL
Brigitte Bardot   **Kim Novak**

First held in 1946, the festival *(see p68)* has become the world's annual film event, a glamorous jamboree of directors, stars and aspiring starlets. *And God Created Woman,* starring Brigitte Bardot, became a *succès de scandale* in 1956.

Picasso

1970 Autoroute du Soleil completed

1973 Picasso dies at Mougins

1977 First section of Marseille underground railway opened

1981 TGV link with Paris completed

1982 *J'Accuse* by Graham Greene exposes corruption in Nice

Jacques Médecin

1998 Jacques Médecin dies in Uruguay, self-exiled after a year in jail in France

1970	1980	1990

1971 The "French Connection" drug ring is exposed

TGV train

1970 Sophia-Antipolis technology park opens near Antibes

1982 Princess Grace is killed in car accident

1990 Jacques Médecin, Mayor of Nice, flees to Uruguay to avoid trial for corruption and tax arrears

1992 Floods in Vaison-la-Romaine

PROVENCE
AREA BY AREA

PROVENCE AT A GLANCE 58-59

THE RIVIERA AND
THE ALPES MARITIMES 60-99

THE VAR AND
THE ILES D'HYÈRES 100-125

BOUCHES-DU-RHÔNE
AND NÎMES 126-153

VAUCLUSE 154-173

ALPES-DE-HAUTE-PROVENCE 174-187

Provence at a Glance

FROM NATURAL WONDERS and historic architecture to
the cream of modern art, Provence is a region with
something for everyone. Even the most ardent sun-
worshipper will be tempted into the cool shade of its
treasure-filled museums and churches. Visitors who
come in the footsteps of the world's greatest artists will
be equally dazzled by the wild beauty of the Gorges
du Verdon and the Camargue. In a region packed with
delights, those shown here are among the very best.

**Papal Avignon's medieval archi-
tectural splendour** *(see pp166–7)*

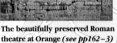

• Avignon

VAUCLUSE

**The beautifully preserved Roman
theatre at Orange** *(see pp162–3)*

**BOUCHES-DU-RHONE
AND NIMES**

• La Camargue

Marseille •

**Wildlife in its natural habitat in
the Camargue** *(see pp136–7)*

0 kilometres　　20

0 miles　　　　20

**The massive basilica of St-Maximin-la-Ste-Baume,
housing relics of St Mary Magdalene** *(see pp110–11)*

**Unspoiled and tranquil, the
Iles d'Hyères** *(see pp114–5)*

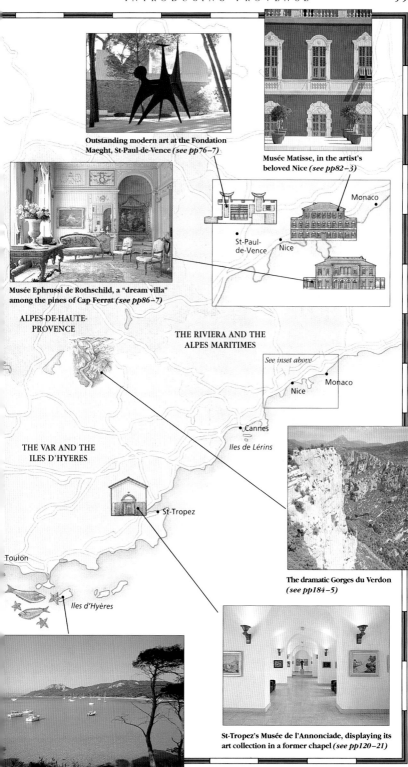

Outstanding modern art at the Fondation
Maeght, St-Paul-de-Vence *(see pp76–7)*

Musée Matisse, in the artist's
beloved Nice *(see pp82–3)*

Musée Ephrussi de Rothschild, a "dream villa"
among the pines of Cap Ferrat *(see pp86–7)*

ALPES-DE-HAUTE-
PROVENCE

THE RIVIERA AND THE
ALPES MARITIMES

See inset above

Monaco

St-Paul-
de-Vence

Nice

Monaco

Nice

THE VAR AND THE
ILES D'HYERES

Cannes
Iles de Lérins

St-Tropez

Toulon

Iles d'Hyères

The dramatic Gorges du Verdon
(see pp184–5)

St-Tropez's Musée de l'Annonciade, displaying its
art collection in a former chapel *(see pp120–21)*

THE RIVIERA AND THE ALPES MARITIMES

THE FRENCH RIVIERA *is, without doubt, the most celebrated seaside in Europe. Just about everybody who has been anybody for the past 100 years has succumbed to its glittering allure. This is the holiday playground of kings and courtesans, movie stars and millionaires, where the seriously rich never stand out in the crowd.*

There is a continual complaint that the Riviera is not what it used to be, that the Cannes Film Festival is mere hype, that grand old Monte-Carlo has lost all sense of taste and that Nice isn't worth the trouble of finding a parking space. But look at the boats in Antibes harbour, glimpse a villa or two on Cap Martin, or observe the baubles on the guests at the Hôtel de Paris in Monte-Carlo. Money and class still rule.

The Riviera is not just a millionaire's watering hole: a diversity of talent has visited, seeking patrons and taking advantage of the luminous Mediterranean light. This coast is irrevocably linked with the life and works of Matisse and Picasso, Chagall, Cocteau and Renoir. It lent them the scenery of its shores and the rich environment of hill villages like St-Paul-de-Vence. St-Paul has echoed to the voices of such luminaries as Bonnard and Modigliani, F Scott Fitzgerald and Greta Garbo. Today, its galleries still spill canvases on to its medieval lanes.

The Alpes Maritimes, which incorporates the principality of Monaco, is renowned for its temperate winter climate. The abundance of flowers here attracted the perfume industry and the English – who created some of the finest gardens on the coast. Inland, the mountainous areas of Provence offer a range of skiing activities in superb mountain scenery, and a chance to try traditional Alpine food.

Relaxing on the promenade des Anglais, Nice

◁ **View of Roquebrune village from the castle**

Exploring the Riviera and the Alpes Maritimes

THE ROCKY HEIGHTS of the pre-Alps lie in tiers, running east to west and tumbling down to the Riviera's dramatic, Corniche-hemmed coast. On bluffs and pinnacles, towns and villages keep a watchful eye on the distant blue sea. Towards the Italian border, the Alpine ridges run from north to south, cut by torrents and gorges which provide snowy winter slopes for skiers. Much of the higher ground is occupied by the Parc National du Mercantour *(see p97)*, home of the ibex and the chamoix. Its jewel is the prehistoric Vallée des Merveilles, less than two hours from the contrasting bustle of the Riviera.

GETTING AROUND

The A8 from Italy runs inland, parallel to the coast. Between this highway and the sea, from Nice to Menton, are three corniches. The Grande Corniche follows the Roman road, Julia Augusta, via La Turbie. The Moyenne Corniche passes through Eze, and the Corniche Inférieure visits all coastal resorts. The inland roads are narrow and winding, so allow more time for your journey. Grasse and Cannes are linked by the regular Metazur train service, and bikes can be hired at some railway stations. Bus links are also good. The largest airport in the region and second busiest in France, is at Nice, west of the city.

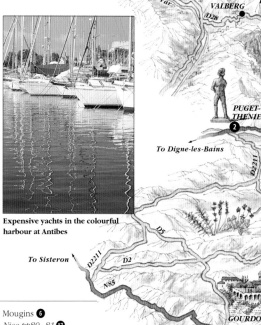

Expensive yachts in the colourful harbour at Antibes

SIGHTS AT A GLANCE

Antibes ⑩
Beaulieu ⑳
Biot ⑫
Cagnes-sur-Mer ⑯
Cannes pp68–9 ⑦
Cap Ferrat ⑱
Eze ㉑
Forêt de Turini ㉘
Gorbio ㉝
Gorges du Cians ①
Gourdon ④
Grasse ⑤
Iles de Lérins pp70–71 ⑧
Juan-les-Pins ⑨
La Turbie ㉒
Lucéram ㉖
Menton ㉟
Monaco pp90–94 ㉓

Mougins ⑥
Nice pp80–81 ⑰
Parc National du
　Mercantour ㉙
Peille ㉕
Peillon ㉔
Puget-Théniers ②
Roquebrune-Cap-Martin ㉞
St-Cézaire-sur-Siagne ③
St-Paul-de-Vence ⑮
Saorge ㉛
Sospel ㉜
Tende ㉚
Vallauris ⑪
Vallée de la Vésubie ㉗
Vence ⑭
Villefranche ⑲
Villeneuve-Loubet ⑬

AURON ●

P A R C　N

VALBERG　BEU

●

PUGET-THENIERS
②

To Digne-les-Bains

To Sisteron

GOURDON ④

GRASSE
⑤

③
ST-CÉZAIRE-SUR-SIAGNE

To Draguignan

0 kilometres　　10

0 miles　　　　10

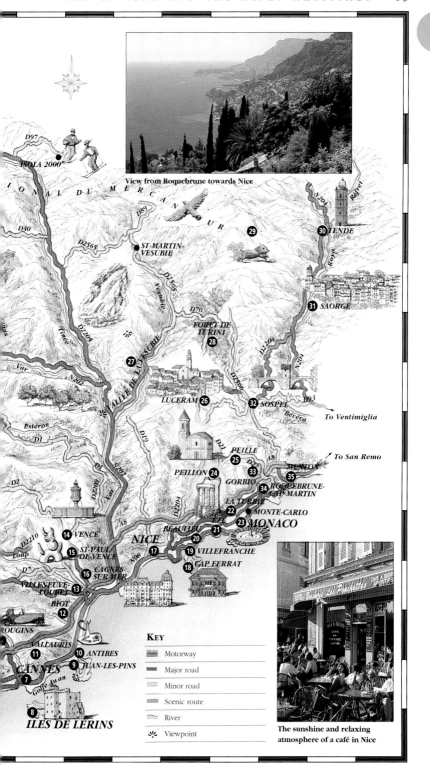

View from Roquebrune towards Nice

KEY

Motorway

Major road

Minor road

Scenic route

River

Viewpoint

The sunshine and relaxing
atmosphere of a café in Nice

To Ventimiglia

To San Remo

Upstream view of the upper Gorges du Cians

Gorges du Cians ●

✈ Nice. ▣ Touët-sur-Var. ▣ Nice,
Touët-sur-Var, Valberg. ℹ Valberg
(04 93 23 24 25).

AMONG THE FINEST natural
sights in the region, these
gorges are a startling combination of deep red slate and
vivid mountain greenery. They
follow the course of the river
Cians, which drops 1,600 m
(5,250 ft) in 25 km (15 miles)
from Beuil to Touët-sur-Var.
At Touët, through a grille in
the floor of the church nave,
you can see the torrent below.

Approaching from the lower
gorges, olives give way to
scrubland. It is not until Pra
d'Astier that the gorges become steep and narrow: at
their narrowest, the rock walls
entirely obliterate the sky.
Higher still up the gorge, you
may spot saffron lilies in June.

At the upper end of the
gorges, overlooking the Vallée
du Cians, is the 1,430-m
(4,770-ft) eyrie of Beuil. A winter sports centre and summer
retreat, it was first fortified by
the counts of Beuil, members
of the aristocratic Grimaldi
family (see p91). They lived
here until 1621, despite staff
revolt: one count had his throat
cut by his barber and another
was stabbed by his valet. The
last, Hannibal Grimaldi, was
tied to a chair and strangled
by two Muslim slaves. Stones
from their château were used
to build the Renaissance chapel
of the White Penitents in the
1687 Eglise St-Jean-Baptiste.

Puget-Théniers ●

Road map E3. 👥 1,700. ▣ ▣ ℹ
202 route nationale (04 93 05 05 05).

THIS ATTRACTIVE village lies at
the foot of a rocky peak,
nestling at the confluence of
the Roudole and the Var
beneath the ruins of a château
that belonged to the Grimaldi
family (see p91). The old
town has some fine manorial
homes with overhanging roofs,
but the chief attraction is the
13th-century parish church
Notre-Dame de l'Assomption
built by the Templars. The
delightful altarpiece, Notre-
Dame de Secours (1525), is
by Antoine Ronzen. In-
side the entrance, the
reredos of the Passion
(1515–1520) is by
Flemish craftsmen,
possibly working with
the architect and sculp-
tor Matthieu d'Anvers.

Beside the main road,
the striking statue of a
woman with her hands
tied is called L'Action
Enchaînée, by Aristide
Maillol (1861–1944).
It commemorates
the local revolution-
ary and master of
insurrection, Louis-
Auguste Blanqui. He was born
in the town hall in 1805 and
became one of the socialist

L'Action Enchaînée, in
Puget-Théniers square

heroes of the Paris Commune
in 1871. A year later he was
imprisoned for life and served
seven years, having already
spent 30 years in jail.

St-Cézaire-sur-Siagne ●

Road map E3. 👥 2,500. ▣
ℹ Hôtel de Ville (04 93 60 84 30).
▣ Tue & Sat.

DOMINATING the steep-sided
Siagne valley, St-Cézaire
has been occupied since pre-
Roman times. The walls and
towers of the village are
reminders of its feudal
past. At its heart is the
13th-century **Chapelle du
Cimetière**, which houses
a Gallo-Roman tomb dis-
covered nearby – a fine
example of Provençal
Romanesque design. A
path from the church
leads to a viewpoint.

To the northeast of the
village are the **Grottes
de St-Cézaire-sur-
Siagne** – iron-rich
caves filled with
beautiful rock
crystallization.
Dramatic stalactites
and stalagmites have
formed on the cave ceilings
and floor. If touched, the
stalactites become remarkably

Antoine Ronzen's altarpiece *Notre-Dame de Secours* (1525), Puget-Théniers

resonant, but leave this to the guide. Both the stalactites and stalagmites have created some enchanting shapes, reminiscent of flowers, animals and toadstools. Red oxide in the limestone gives a rich colour to the caves' chambers, which are named the Hall of Draperies, Organ Chamber, Fairies' Alcove and Great Hall. The chambers are connected by narrow underground passages. One of these ends suddenly, 40 m (130 ft) below ground level, at the edge of an abyss.

Grottes de St-Cézaire-sur-Siagne

St-Cézaire-sur-Siagne. 04 93 60 22 35. Jun–Sep: daily; Feb–late-May, Oct: daily pm only.

Inside the remarkable Grottes de St-Cézaire-sur-Siagne

The village of Gourdon, on the edge of a rocky cliff

Gourdon ④

Road map E3. 395. pl de l'Eglise (04 93 09 68 25).

FOR CENTURIES, villages were built on hilltops, surrounded by ramparts. Gourdon is a typical *village perché (see pp18–19)*, its shops filled with regional produce, perfume and local art. From the square at its precipitous edge, there is a spectacular view of the Loup valley and the sea with Antibes and Cap Roux in the distance.

There are good views, too, from the terrace of the Château de Gourdon, which was built around 1610 under Louis de Lombard, overlord of Gourdon, on the foundations of what was once a Saracen fortress. Its vaulted rooms are remnants of Saracen occupation. The terrace gardens, now mostly alpine, were laid out by André Le Nôtre when the château was restored in the 17th century. Although it is still privately owned, it has two museums. The **Musée Historique** has an Aubusson tapestry, a writing desk which once belonged to Marie-Antoinette, and a self-portrait by Rembrandt. There is also an adjoining **Musée d'Art Naïf** which features naïve painting from 1925 to 1970. Included are a portrait by Douanier Rousseau and works by his European imitators.

Musée Historique et Musée d'Art Naïf

Château de Gourdon. 04 93 09 68 02. Jun–Sep: daily; Oct–May: Wed–Mon pm only.

JOURNEY IN THE GORGES DU LOUP

The village of Gourdon is on the edge of the Gorges du Loup, the most accessible of many dramatic gorges running down to the coast. The route up to the Gorges du Loup begins at Pré-du-Loup, just east of Grasse, and leads to Gourdon. From Gourdon, the D3 goes up into the gorge and offers the best views, turning back down the D6 after 6.5 km (4 miles).

Descending on the left bank, the road passes the great pothole of Saut du Loup and the Cascades des Demoiselles, where the river's lime carbonate content has partly solidified the vegetation. Just beyond is the 40-m (130-ft) Cascade de Courmes, which has a treacherously slippery stairway under it.

The N210 continues to Vence, passing via Tourrettes-sur-Loup, an art and craft centre on a high plateau. The 15th-century church has a triptych by the Bréa school and a 1st-century altar dedicated to the Roman god Mercury.

The 40-m (130-ft) Cascade de Courmes

Grasse ⑤

Road map E3. 🚶 *43,000.* 🚌
ℹ *cours Honoré Cresp (04 93 36 03 56).* 🛒 *Tue–Sun.*

ONCE KNOWN FOR its leather tanning industry, Grasse became a perfume centre in the 16th century. The tanneries have vanished, but three major perfume houses are still in business. Today, perfume is mainly made from imported flowers, but each year, this attractive, fragrance-filled town holds a Jasmine festival *(see p31).* The best place to find out more is the **Musée International de la Parfumerie**.

Grasse became fashionable after 1807–8 when Princess Pauline Bonaparte recuperated here. Queen Victoria often wintered at the Grand Hotel.

Artist Jean-Honoré Fragonard (1732– 1806) was born here and the walls of the **Villa-Musée Fragonard** are covered with his son's murals. The artist's one known religious work, *Washing of the Feet*, hangs in the 12th-century **Ancienne Cathédral Notre-Dame-du-Puy**, in the old town. The cathedral also houses three works by Rubens. Grasse's marine links are revealed in the **Musée de la Marine**. The 18th-century **Musée d'Art et d'Histoire de Provence** displays *bergamots*, decorated, scented *papier-mâché* boxes lined with peel from the fruit. Provençal costumes and jewellery from the 18th and 19th centuries can be seen at the Parfumerie Fragonard's own museum.

🏛 **Musée International de la Parfumerie**
8 place du Cours. 📞 *04 93 36 80 20.*
🕐 *Jun–Oct: daily; Oct & 9 Dec–May: Wed–Sun.* ⬤ *public hols.* 🖼 ♿
🏛 **Musée de la Marine**
2 bd Jeu-de-Ballon. 📞 *04 93 09 10 71.*
🕐 *Jun–Sep, Oct & Dec–May: Mon–Fri.* ⬤ *public hols.* 🖼
🏛 **Villa-Musée Fragonard**
23 bd Fragonard. 📞 *04 93 36 01 61.*
🕐 *Jun–Oct: daily; Oct & 9 Dec–May: Wed–Sun.* ⬤ *public hols.* 🖼
🏛 **Musée d'Art et d'Histoire de Provence**
2 rue Mirabeau. 📞 *04 93 36 01 61.*
🕐 *Jun–Sep daily; Oct–May: Wed–Sun.* ⬤ *public hols.* 🖼

Exterior of the Musée International de la Parfumerie in Grasse

Mougins ⑥

Road map E3. 🚶 *15,000.* 🚌
ℹ *av Charles Mallet (04 93 75 87 67).*

THIS OLD HILLTOP town *(see pp18–19)*, huddled inside the remains of 15th-century ramparts and fortified Saracen Gate, is one of the finest in the region. Mougins is a smart address: it has been used by royalty and film stars as well as Yves St Laurent and Picasso, who spent his last years in a house opposite the Chapelle de Notre-Dame-de-Vie.

Mougins is also one of the smartest places in France to eat. Among its many high-class restaurants, is Roger Vergé's **Moulin de Mougins** *(see pp210–11)*, set in an old mill just outside the village. Diners can also browse through his quality kitchen equipment shop, open until midnight.

The **Musée de la Photographie** has a fine permanent collection of work by Brassaï, Doisneau and Lartigue, who lived at nearby Opio. The radiator-shaped **Musée de l'Automobiliste**, some 5 km (3 miles) south of Mougins, has a classic car collection, notably Bugattis, on show.

🏛 **Musée de la Photographie**
Porte Sarrasine. 📞 *04 93 75 85 67.*
🕐 *Jul–Aug: daily pm; Sep–Oct & Dec–Jun: Wed–Sun pm.* ⬤ *1 Jan.* 🖼
🏛 **Musée de l'Automobiliste**
Aire de Breguieres, autoroute A8.
📞 *04 93 69 27 80.* 🕐 *mid-Dec–mid-Nov: daily.* 🖼 ♿

Jacques-Henri and Florette Lartigue, Musée de la Photographie, Mougins

The Perfumes of Provence

FOR THE PAST 400 years, the town of Grasse has been the centre of the perfume industry. Before that it was a tannery town, but in the 16th century, Italian immigrant glove-makers began to use the scents of local flowers to perfume soft leather gloves, a fashion made popular by the Queen, Catherine de' Médici. Enormous acres of lavender, roses, jonquils, jasmine and aromatic herbs were cultivated. Today, cheaper imports of flowers and high land prices mean that Grasse focuses on the creation of scent. The power of perfume is evoked in Patrick Süskind's disturbing novel, *Perfume*, set partly in Grasse, in which the murderous perfumer exploits his knowledge of perfume extraction to grisly effect.

Catherine de'Médici, 1581

Picking early morning jasmine

Jasmine waiting to be processed

CREATING A PERFUME
Essences are extracted by various methods, including distillation by steam or volatile solvents, which separate the essential oils. *Enfleurage* is a costly and lengthy method for delicate flowers such as jasmine and violet. The blossoms are layered with lard which becomes impregnated with scent.

Steam distillation is one of the oldest extraction processes originally developed by the Arabs. It is now used mainly for flowers such as orange blossom. Flowers and water are boiled together in a still and the essential oils are extracted by steam in an essencier, or oil decanter.

Vast quantities of blossoms are required to create the essence or "absolut" perfume concentrate. For example, almost a ton of jasmine flowers are needed to obtain just one litre of jasmine essence.

The best perfumes are created by a perfumer known as a "nose" who possesses an exceptional sense of smell. The nose harmonizes fragrances rather like a musician, blending as many as 300 essences for a perfume. Today, scents can be synthesized by using "head-space analysis" which analyzes the components of the air above a flower.

Cannes ❼

LORD BROUGHAM, BRITISH LORD CHANCELLOR, put Cannes on the map in 1834 when he stopped on his way to Nice. He was so entranced by the climate of what was then a tiny fishing village that he built a villa and started a trend for upper-class English visitors. Today, Cannes may not attract blue blood but it has become a town of festivals, the resort of the rich and famous. It is busy all year round, its image reinforced by the Film Festival *(see p30)*. With its casinos, fairs, beach, boat and street life, there is plenty to do, even though Cannes lacks the great museums and monuments of less glamorous resorts.

Cannes beach and Carlton Hotel

Exploring Cannes
The heart of the city is built round the Bay of Cannes and the palm-fringed seafront boulevard de la Croisette. Here there are luxury boutiques and hotels and fine views of La Napoule Bay and the Esterel heights. The eastern end of the bay curves out to Pointe de la Croisette and the summertime Palm Beach Casino, built on the ruins of the medieval Fort de la Croix, which has a night-club, restaurant and swimming pool. The town's other gaming house is **Casino Croisette**, which is open all year.

Brougham persuaded King Louis-Philippe to donate two million francs to build the Cannes harbour wall. Between La Pantiero and rue Felix Faure are the allées de la Liberté. Shaded by plane trees and surveyed by a statue of Lord Brougham, this open space is ideal both for *boules* and the colourful morning flower market. It provides a fine view of the harbour, which is filled with pleasure craft and fishing boats. Behind the allées is the rue Meynadier, where you can buy delicious pasta, bread and cheese. This leads you to the sumptuous **Marché Forville**. Succulent regional produce turns up here fresh every day. The small streets and lanes meander up from the *marché* to the old Roman town of Canoïs Castrum. This area was named after the reeds that grew by the seashore, and is now known as Le Suquet (which is also the Provençal name for a kind of fish soup). The church in the centre of the old town, **Notre-Dame de l'Espérance**, was completed in 1648.

The Cannes Film Festival has been held here every May since 1946. The main venue is the **Palais des Festivals**, but there are cinemas all over town, and some film screenings start as early as 8:30am. The beach has been a focus for paparazzi since 1953, when Brigitte Bardot pouted so beautifully that the world's press were moved to put her on its front pages.

The main hotels in Cannes have their own beaches with bars and restaurants, where prices match their standing. Celebrities are most likely to be seen at the Carlton, Majestic and Martinez. There is a small charge to enter most beaches in Cannes, where imported sand covers the natural pebbles, and sun-loungers cost extra. Just next to the festival building is a free public beach.

🎬 Palais des Festivals et des Congrès
1 la Croisette. **☎** *04 93 39 01 01.* **ℹ** *04 93 39 24 53.* ⭕ *daily.*

Built in 1982, this unmistakable modern slab, known as The Bunker, stands beside the Vieux Port at the west end of the promenade. It is the chief venue for the *Palmes d'Or* and *Grands Prix*, both sufficiently prestigious for the film business to take them seriously, and much business goes on, so that the festival is not all hype and publicity. Some 30,000 official tickets are distributed and only 10 per cent are taken up by locals. Apart from its use for the great Film Festival, the Palais des Festivals has a casino and a night-club, and is a regular conference venue. In the nearby allée des Stars, handprints of such famous celebrities as the film director Roman Polanski are immortalized in pavement cement.

Famous handprint

Model Carla Bruni and friends at the 47th Cannes Film Festival

Cannes Old Town, known locally as Le Suquet, overlooking the harbour

VISITORS' CHECKLIST

Road map E4. 🗺 *69,000.*
🚉 *rue Jean-Jaurès.* 🚌 *pl de l'Hôtel de Ville.* ℹ️ *palais des Festivals (04 93 39 24 53).* 🚢 *daily.* 🎬 *Film Festival: May.*

🏛 Musée de la Castre

Château de la Castre, Le Suquet.
📞 *04 93 38 55 26.* ⏰ *Feb–Dec: Wed–Mon.* ● *public hols.*

The old Cannes castle, erected by the Lérins monks in the 11th and 12th centuries, houses this museum. Set up in 1877, it contains some fine archaeological and ethnographical collections from all over the world, ranging from South Sea Island costumes to Asian art and African masks. Also housed in the Cistercian St-Anne chapel is a collection of musical instruments whose sounds can be heard at the touch of a button. The 11th-century **Tour de la Castre** is worth climbing for the view.

🏨 Carlton Hotel

58 la Croisette. 📞 *04 93 06 40 06.*
See **Where to Stay** p196.

This ultimate symbol of comfort and grace contains 355 rooms and apartments. It was designed and built in 1911 by the architect, Henri Ruhl. The huge Rococo-style dining room, where the colonnades rise to an ornately decorated ceiling with finely wrought cornices, is unchanged. The hotel's wedding-cake exterior is studded with tiny balconies, and the window frames, cornices and attic pediments are decorated with stucco. The hotel's twin black cupolas are said to be modelled on the breasts of the notorious Belle Otéro, a half-gypsy courtesan who captivated Ruhl. The Carlton was so revered that in World War II, a *New York Times* journalist asked a commanding officer to protect what he considered the world's finest hotel.

The height of luxury

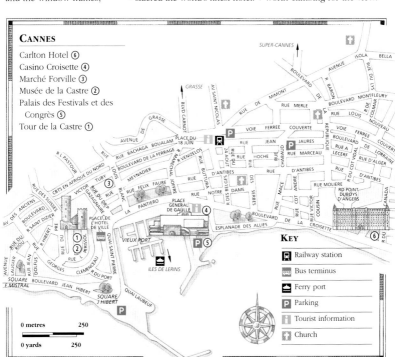

CANNES

Carlton Hotel ⑥
Casino Croisette ④
Marché Forville ③
Musée de la Castre ②
Palais des Festivals et des
   Congrès ⑤
Tour de la Castre ①

KEY

🚉 Railway station

🚌 Bus terminus

🚢 Ferry port

🅿 Parking

ℹ️ Tourist information

🕀 Church

0 metres 250

0 yards 250

Iles de Lérins ●

ALTHOUGH ONLY a 15-minute boat ride from the glitter of Cannes, the Iles de Lérins reflect a contrasting lifestyle, with their forests of eucalyptus and Aleppo pine and their tiny chapels. The two islands, separated only by a narrow strait, were once the most powerful religious centres in the south of France. St-Honorat is named after the Gallo-Roman, Honoratus, who visited the smaller island at the end of the 4th century and founded a monastery. Ste-Marguerite was named after his sister, who set up a nunnery there. Its fort is well known as the prison of the mysterious 17th-century Man in the Iron Mask, who spent 11 years here.

Lerina liqueur

★ **Fort Ste-Marguerite**
Built under Richelieu and strengthened by Vauban in 1712, its ground floor has a maritime museum.

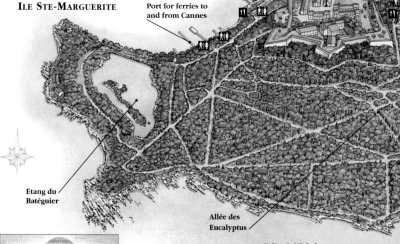

ILE STE-MARGUERITE

Port for ferries to and from Cannes

Etang du Batéguier

Allée des Eucalyptus

Eglise St-Michel

ILE ST-HONORAT

Chapelle St-Saveur

St-Honorat et les Saints de Lérins
This icon of St-Honorat can be found in the Abbaye de Lérins.

Chapelle St-Caprais
St-Caprais was the disciple of St-Honorat during his first visit to Provence.

0 metres   1000

0 yards   1000

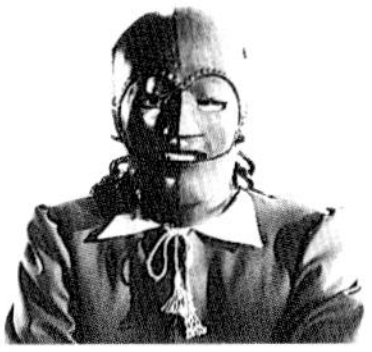

The Man in the Iron Mask
The mystery man was imprisoned in Fort Royal from 1687 to 1698, then moved to the Bastille, where he died in 1703.

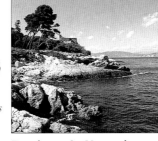

Remains on Ste-Marguerite
Excavations on the coast near the fort have revealed houses, mosaics, wall paintings and ceramics which date back to around the 3rd century BC.

Visitors' Checklist

Road map D5. Gare Maritime, Cannes. *04 93 39 11 82.* ***Ferries*** *7:30am–4:15pm summer, last return 7pm (5pm winter).* **Fort Ste-Marguerite** *04 93 43 18 17. 10:30am–noon, 2–6:30pm Wed–Mon (4:30pm winter). Tue, Jan, public hols.* **Monastère Fortifié** *04 92 99 54 00. 9:30am–4:30pm daily.*

Allée de la Convention
Both the islands have many paths leading through the densely wooded interior as well as round

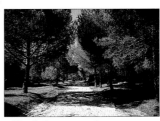

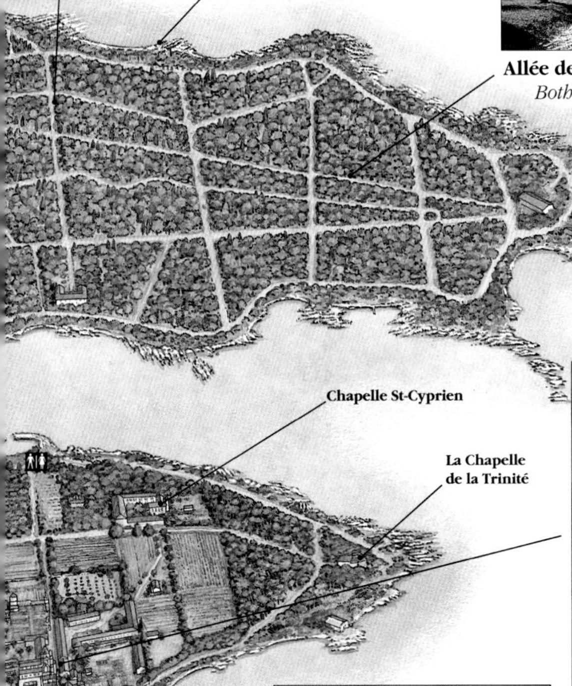

Allée du Grand Jardin
Chapelle St-Cyprien
La Chapelle de la Trinité

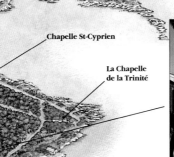

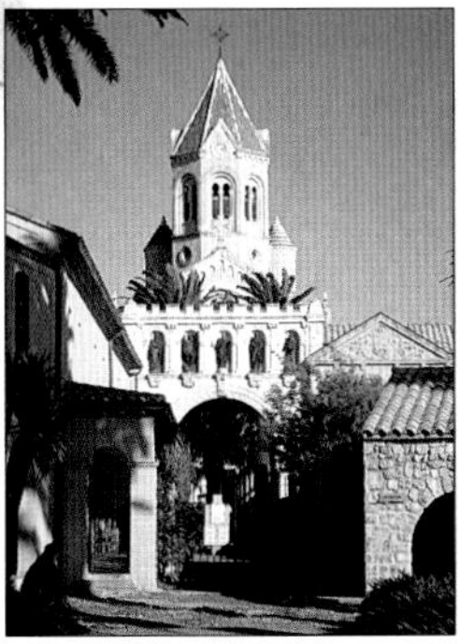

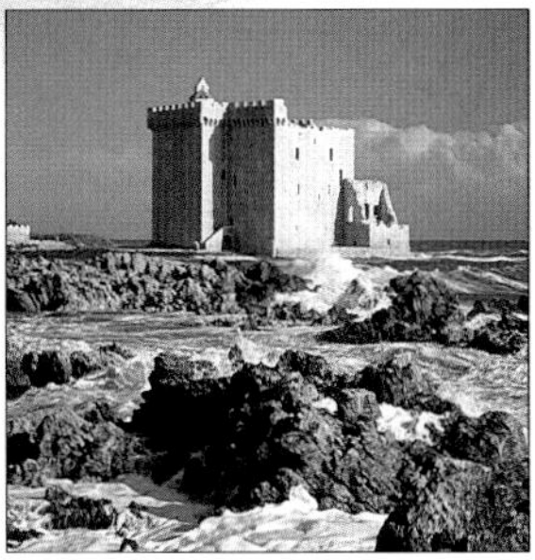

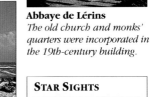

Abbaye de Lérins
The old church and monks' quarters were incorporated in the 19th-century building.

★ Monastère Fortifié
Built in 1073 by Abbot Aldebert, to protect the monks from Saracen pirates, this "keep" gives views as far as Esterel.

Star Sights

★ **Fort Ste-Marguerite**

★ **Monastère Fortifié**

Juan-les-Pins **⑨**

Road map E3. 🏛 *80,000 (Commune of Antibes)*. 🚉 🚌 🛈 *51 bd Guillaumont (04 92 90 53 05).*

To THE EAST of Cannes is the hammerhead peninsula of Cap d'Antibes, a promontory of pines and coves where millionaires' mansions grow. Its finest beach is tucked in the west side of the cape in Golfe-Juan, where Napoleon came ashore from Elba in 1815. This is a 20th-century resort, promoted by American railroad heir Frank Jay Gould, who attracted high society in the 1920s and 1930s when writers F Scott Fitzgerald and Ernest Hemingway stayed.

Today, in the high season, it is filled with a young crowd. The area at the junctions of boulevards Baudoin and Wilson is filled with colourful bars which make it seem like an open-air *mardi gras*. Action centres round the 1908 casino, the Palais des Congrès, and Penedès pine grove, which reaches down to the shore and gives shelter to the World Jazz Festival *(see p31)* in July.

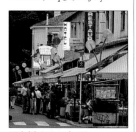
Nightlife in Juan-les-Pins

Antibes **⑩**

Road map E3. 🏛 *80,000*. 🚉 🚌 🚢 🛈 *11 place du Gen de Gaulle (04 92 90 53 00).* 🕐 *Tue–Sun.*

ORIGINALLY THE ancient Greek trading post of Antipolis, Antibes became heavily fortified over the centuries, notably by Vauban in the 17th century, who built the main port and Fort Carré, where Napoleon lived and was temporarily imprisoned.

There are some pleasant lanes splashed with flowers in the old town, and a market place in cours Masséna. The

Spectacular pleasure yachts in Antibes harbour

town's high points include the 12th-century towers of the church and Grimaldi castle on the site of Antipolis. The **Eglise de l'Immaculée Conception**, which took over the town's watchtower as a belfry, has a wooden crucifix from 1447, a 16th-century Christ and a fine Louis Bréa altarpiece depicting the Virgin Mary, dating from the same period.

The Château Grimaldi nearby houses the **Musée Picasso**, over 50 drawings, paintings, prints and ceramics which the artist exe-
cuted when he used the museum as a studio during 1946. Also on show is Antoine Aundi's *La Vierge de Douleur* (1539), with one of the earliest views of Antibes. The archaeological collection has a 2nd-century BC inscription to the spirit of Septentrion, a boy who danced for crowds at the Antipolis theatre for two days.

The modern art collection includes works by Ernst, Léger, Miró and Nicolas de Staël in the last two years of his life. Further south, the **Musée d'Histoire et d'Archéologie** at the fortified Bastion St-André houses Greek and Etruscan finds from the Mediterranean.

🏛 **Musée Picasso**
Château Grimaldi. [*04 92 90 54 20.* 🕐 *Tue–Sun.* 🌑 *public hols.* 📷
🏛 **Musée d'Histoire et d'Archéologie**
Bastion St-André. [*04 92 90 54 35.* 🕐 *Tue–Sun.* 🌑 *public hols.* 📷 🛗

Local pottery from Vallauris

Vallauris **⑪**

Road map E3. 🏛 *24,000.* 🚉 🛈 *square 8 mai 1945 (04 93 63 82 58).* 🚢 *Tue–Sun.*

IN SUMMER, the wares of over 100 potters spill on to the central avenue of this coastal pottery capital. Pablo Picasso revitalized this dying industry, and the **Musée Magnelli** traces its history from Roman times. In the square is *L'Homme au Mouton* (1943), and his *La Guerre et la Paix* (1951) is the chief exhibit on show in the **Musée Picasso**. The pottery museum has a wax model of Picasso at his wheel.

🏛 **Musée Magnelli**
Pl de la Libération. [*04 93 64 16 05.* 🕐 *Wed–Mon.* 🌑 *public hols.* 📷
🏛 **Musée Picasso**
Pl de la Libération. [*04 93 64 98 05.* 🕐 *Wed–Mon.* 🌑 *public hols.* 📷

78-year-old Pablo Picasso with a man-sized dalmatian companion

Pablo Picasso (1881–1973)

Picasso, the giant of 20th-century art, spent most of his later life in Provence, inspired by its luminous light and brilliant colours. He came first to Juan-les-Pins in 1920, and returned to Antibes in 1946 with Françoise Gilot. He was given a studio in the seafront Grimaldi palace, where, after wartime Paris, his work became infused with Mediterranean light and joyful images. No other artist has succeeded with so many art forms, and the Antibes collection is a taste of his versatility. He died at Mougins, aged 92.

Violin and Sheet of Music *(1912), now in Paris, is a Cubist collage from the period when Picasso experimented with different forms.*

Les Demoiselles d'Avignon *(1907), now in New York, was the first Cubist painting. Its bold style shocked the art world of the day.*

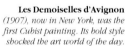

La Joie de Vivre *(1946), is one of Picasso's main works from the Antibes period, using favourite mythological themes. He is the bearded centaur playing the flute, and Françoise Gilot is the Maenad who dances while two fauns leap about and a satyr plays a panpipe.*

The Goat *(1946), also in Antibes, is one of his best-known images. In 1950 he made his famous goat sculpture using a wicker basket as the ribcage.*

L'Homme au Mouton *(1943) was sculpted in an afternoon. It stands in the main square of Vallauris, also home of La Guerre et la Paix (1951).*

Biot ⑫

Road map E3. 🏔 8,000. 🚉 🚌 ⓘ
rue Saint Sébastien (04 93 65 05 85).

THE PICTURESQUE VILLAGE of Biot was the main pottery town in the region until Pablo Picasso revived the industry in Vallauris after World War II. Today, Biot is renowned for its bubble-flecked glassware, with seven glass works. Visitors to **La Verrerie de Biot** can marvel at master craftsmen at work.

Biot was once the domain of the Knights Templar (see p123), and some fortifications remain, such as the 1566 Porte des Migraniers (grenadiers).

The church has two fine 16th-century works: *L'Ecce Homo*, attributed to Canavesio, and *La Vièrge au Rosaire*, attributed to Louis Bréa.

The dramatically modern **Musée Fernand Léger** was built on the land the artist bought to use as studio just before he died in 1955. Léger's mosaic celebrating sport decorates the external wall. Inside are more than 400 works in a bold style that developed from Cubism.

🏛 **Musée Fernand Léger**
Chemin du Val-de-Pôme. 【 04 92 91 50 30. ◯ Wed–Mon. ● 1 Jan, 1 May, 25 Dec. 🎫 &.
🏛 **La Verrerie de Biot**
Chemin des Combes. 【 04 93 65 03 00. ◯ daily. ● 25 Dec. &.

Detail of Léger mosaic from the eastern façade of the museum, Biot

Villeneuve-Loubet ⑬

Road map E3. 🏔 15,000. 🚉
ⓘ 16 av de la Mer (04 93 20 20 09).
🛒 Wed & Sat.

THIS OLD VILLAGE IS dominated by a restored medieval castle belonging to the Villeneuve family. It is also where France's most celebrated chef, Auguste Escoffier, (1847–1935) was born. The man who invented the *bombe Néro* and *pêche Melba* was *chef de cuisine* at the Grand Hotel, Monte-Carlo before Mr Ritz persuaded him to become head chef at the Savoy in London. The **Fondation Escoffier**, in the house of his birth, contains many showpieces in almond paste and icing sugar, and 5,000 menus,

Chef Auguste Escoffier, born in Villeneuve-Loubet

some dating back to 1820. The **Marineland** leisure park includes a children's farm, a butterfly park, a marine zoo and a shark-filled aquarium.

🏛 **Fondation Escoffier**
1 rue Escoffier. 【 04 93 20 80 51.
◯ Dec–Oct: Tue–Sun pm only.
● public hols. 🎫
🐟 **Marineland**
306 av Mozart. 【 04 93 33 49 49.
◯ daily. 🎫 &.

Vence ⑭

Road map E3. 🏔 15,000. 🚉
ⓘ place du Grand-Jardin (04 93 58 06 38). 🛒 Tue & Fri.

A DELIGHTFUL OLD cathedral town on a rocky ridge, Vence has long attracted artists. English writer DH Lawrence died here in 1930.

The old town is entered by the Porte de Peyra (1441), beside the place du Frêne, named after its giant ash tree planted to commemorate the visits of King François I and Pope Paul III. The adjoining 16th-century castle of the lords of Villeneuve, seigneurs of Vence, houses the museum and the **Fondation Emile Hughes**, named after a former mayor, which holds many temporary exhibitions. Inside the gate, the place du Peyra has an urn-shaped fountain built in 1822.

The town's cathedral, one of the smallest in France, stands by the site of the forum of the Roman city of Vintium. Vence was a bishopric from the 4th to the 19th centuries. Its notable prelates included Saint Véran (d AD 492), and

THE CREATION OF BIOT GLASSWARE

Biot is the capital of glassblowing on the coast. Local soils provide sand for glassmaking, and typical Biot glass is sturdy, with tiny air bubbles (known as *verre à boules*). The opening of Léger's museum led to an increased interest in all local crafts, and to the arrival of the Verrerie de Biot workshop in 1956. This revived old methods of making oil lamps, carafes and narrow-spouted *ponons*, from which a jet of liquid can be poured straight into the mouth.

the former wit and ladies' confidant, Bishop Godeau (1605–72). The 51 oak and pear choir stalls are carved with satirical figures. Marc Chagall designed the mosaic of *Moses in the Bulrushes* in the chapel (1979).

Henri Matisse *(see pp82–3)* decorated the **Chapelle du Rosaire** between 1947 and 1951 to thank the Dominican nuns who nursed him through an illness. The stations of the cross are reduced to black lines tinted with stained glass.

⛫ Fondation Emile Hughes
Château de Villeneuve. **▐** *04 93 24 24 23.* ○ *Tue–Sun.* ● *1 May.* 🖼
⛫ Chapelle du Rosaire
Av Henri Matisse. **▐** *04 93 58 03 26.* ○ *Tue–Fri (Wed, Fri & Sat by appt only, 48 hrs notice); school hols: Tue–Sat pm only.* ● *Nov.* 🖼 ♿

St-Paul-de-Vence ⓯

Road map E3. 🏠 *2,900.* 🚌 *Vence.* ℹ *Maison de la Tour, 2 rue Grande (04 93 32 86 95).*

Simone Signoret and Yves Montand in St-Paul-de-Vence

THIS CLASSIC MEDIEVAL *village perché (see pp18–19)* was built behind the coast to avoid Saracen attack. In 1537 it was re-ramparted, under François I, to stand up to Savoy, Austria and Piedmont. A celebrity village, it was first "discovered" by Bonnard, Modigliani and other artists of the 1920s. Since that time, many of the rich and famous literati and glitterati have flocked to St-Paul. A photographic display in the local museum includes Simone de Beauvoir, Jean-Paul Sartre, F Scott Fitzgerald, Catherine Deneuve, Sophia Loren and the elusive Greta Garbo.

Most famously, these personalities slept, dined, and, in the case of Yves Montand and Simone Signoret, even had their wedding reception at the **Colombe d'Or** *auberge (see p211).* Today it has one of the finest 20th-century private art collections, built up over the years in lieu of payment of bills. The priceless dining-room décor includes paintings by such world-famous artists as Miró, Picasso and Braque.

In the 12th-century Gothic church, there is a painting, *Catherine of Alexandria,* attributed to Tintoretto. There are also gold reliquaries and a fine local 13th-century enamel Virgin. The **Musée d'Histoire de St-Paul** nearby features costumed tableaux of scenes from the town's rich past, and the old castle keep opposite is now the town hall.

The main street runs from the 13th-century entrance gate of Porte Royale and past the Grande Fontaine to Porte Sud. This gives on to the cemetery, a resting place for Chagall, the Maeghts, Escoffier and many locals. It also offers wonderful views and true serenity.

Just outside St-Paul, on La Gardette Hill, is Josep Lluis Sert's striking concrete and rose **Fondation Maeght** *(see pp76–7),* one of Europe's finest modern art museums.

⛫ Musée d'Histoire de St-Paul
Place de la Castre. **▐** *04 93 32 41 13.* ○ *daily.* ● *1 Jan, 1 May, 25 Dec.* 🖼

Entrance to Chapelle du Rosaire in Vence, decorated by Henri Matisse

Fondation Maeght

Nestling amid the umbrella pines in the hills above St-Paul-de-Vence, this small modern art museum is one of the world's finest. Aimé and Marguerite Maeght were Cannes art dealers who numbered the likes of Chagall, Matisse and Miró among their clients and friends. Their private collection formed the basis for the museum, which opened in 1964. Like St-Paul itself, the Maeght has been a magnet for celebrities: Duke Ellington, Samuel Beckett, André Malraux, Merce Cunningham and, of course, a galaxy of the artists themselves have mingled at fundraising events. The museum now receives over 250,000 visitors each year.

★ Cour Giacometti
Slender bronze figures by Alberto Giacometti, such as l'Homme Qui Marche I *(1960), inhabit their own shady courtyard or appear about the grounds as if they have a life of their own.*

La Vie *(1964)*
Marc Chagall's painting is full of humanity: here is love, parenthood, religion, society, nature; all part of a swirling, circus-like tableau of dancers and musicians, acrobats and clowns.

Les Poissons
is a mosaic pool designed by Georges Braque in 1962.

Les Renforts *(1965)*
One of many works of art that greet arriving visitors, Alexander Calder's creation is a "stabile" – a counterpart to his more familiar mobiles.

L'Eté *(1909)*
Pierre Bonnard settled in Provence for the last 22 years of his life, becoming a close friend of Aimé Maeght. Matisse called Bonnard "the greatest of us all".

Cowled roofs
allow indirect light to filter into the galleries. The building was designed by Spanish architect Josep Lluis Sert.

La Partie de Campagne *(1954) Fernand Léger lends his unique vision to the classic artistic scene of a country outing.*

VISITORS' CHECKLIST

Route de Pass-Prest, St-Paul-de-Vence. **[** 04 93 32 81 63. **[]** Jul–Sep: 10am–7pm; Oct–Jun: 10am–12:30pm, 2:30–6pm. **[]**
[] *Bookshop.*

★ Labyrinthe de Miró
Joan Miró's l'Oiseau Lunaire *(1968) is one of the many statues in this multi-levelled maze of trees, water and gargoyles.*

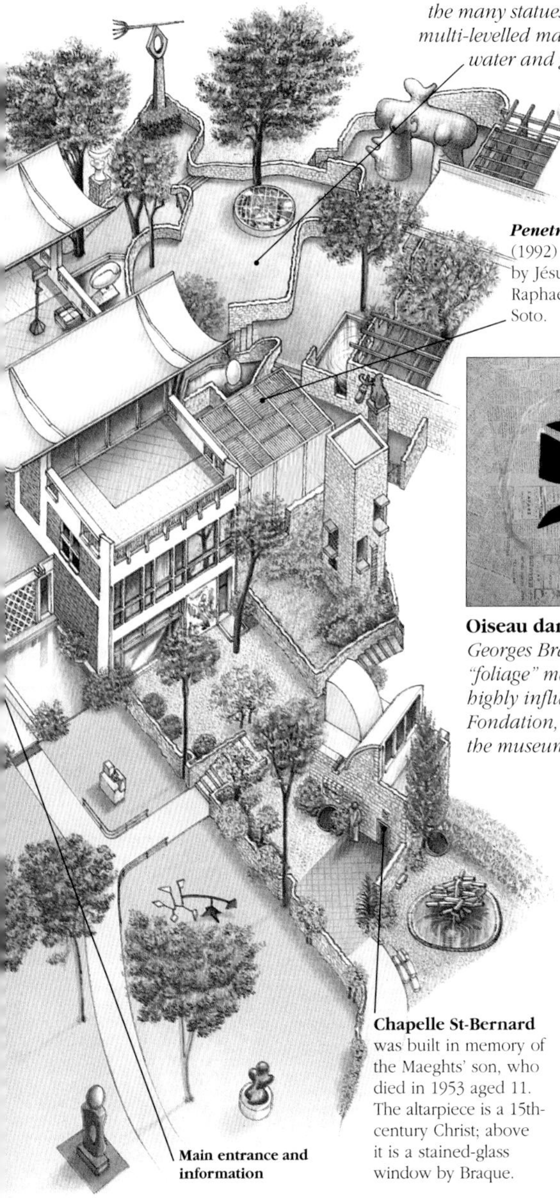

Penetrable (1992) is by Jésus Raphael Soto.

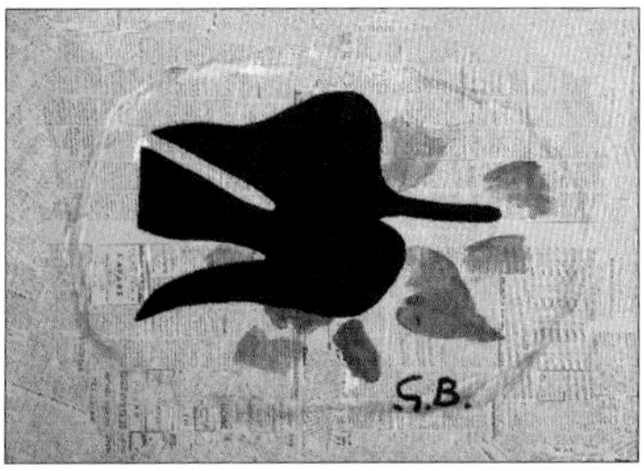

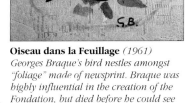

Oiseau dans la Feuillage *(1961) Georges Braque's bird nestles amongst "foliage" made of newsprint. Braque was highly influential in the creation of the Fondation, but died before he could see the museum finally opened to the public.*

GALLERY GUIDE

The permanent collection is comprised entirely of 20th-century art. The only items on permanent view are the large sculptures in the grounds. The indoor galleries display works from the collection in rotation but, in summer, only temporary exhibitions are held.

Chapelle St-Bernard was built in memory of the Maeghts' son, who died in 1953 aged 11. The altarpiece is a 15th-century Christ; above it is a stained-glass window by Braque.

Main entrance and information

STAR SIGHTS

★ **Cour Giacometti**

★ **Labyrinthe de Miró**

Renoir's studio at Les Collettes

Cagnes-sur-Mer ⑯

Road map E3. 🏛 43,000. 🚗 🚉
ℹ 6 bd Maréchal Juin (04 93 20 61
64). 🛒 Tue–Sun.

T HERE ARE THREE parts to
Cagnes-sur-Mer: Cros-de-
Cagnes, the fishing village
and beach; Cagnes-Ville, the
commercial centre; and Haut-
de-Cagnes, the upper town.

Haut-de-Cagnes is the place
to head for. This ancient hilltop town is riven with lanes,
steps and vaulted passages. It
is dominated by the **Château
Grimaldi** but also has some
fine Renaissance houses and
the church of St-Pierre, with a
Gothic nave in which the
Grimaldis are entombed.

East of Cagnes-Ville is Les
Collettes, built among ancient
olive trees by Pierre-Auguste
Renoir (1841–1919). He came
here in the 1890s, hoping that
the climate would relieve his
rheumatism. He bought the
house in 1908 and stayed for
the rest of his life. A picture of
Renoir in his last year shows
him still at work, a brush tied
to his crippled hand.

Now the **Musée Renoir** at
Les Collettes is almost exactly
as it was when the artist died.
In the house are ten of Renoir's
paintings, as well as works by
his friends Bonnard and Dufy.
Visitors can also explore his
beloved olive groves, the
setting for the fine bronze
Venus Victrix (1914).

🏛 **Musée Renoir**
19 chemin des Collettes. 📞 04 93
20 61 07. ⏰ Dec–Oct: Wed–Mon.
⬛ 1 Jan, Nov, 25 Dec. 🎫

Château Grimaldi

I N THE MIDDLE AGES the Grimaldi family held sway over
many of the Mediterranean coastal towns. The castle
that towers over Haut-de-Cagnes was built by Rainier in
1309 as a fortress-prison; in 1620 his descendant, Jean-
Henri, transformed it into the handsome palace which
shelters behind its dramatic battlements. Mercifully, the
château survived the worst ravages of the Revolution and
later occupation by Piedmontese troops in 1815. It now
houses an eclectic mixture of
museums, from olives to
modern art.

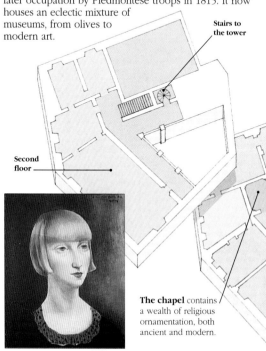

**Stairs to
the tower**

**Second
floor**

The chapel contains
a wealth of religious
ornamentation, both
ancient and modern.

★ **Donation Suzy Solidor**
*This 1930s chanteuse was
painted by 244 artists during
her lifetime. The 40 works
on display include portraits
by Jean Cocteau (above)
and Kisling (top).*

GALLERY GUIDE
*The olive tree museum is on
the ground floor, along with
exhibits about life in the medieval castle. The Suzy Solidor
collection is displayed in a
former boudoir on the first
floor. Selections from the permanent collection of modern
Mediterranean art, as well as
temporary exhibitions, are on
the first and second floors.*

KEY TO FLOORPLAN
☐ Donation Suzy Solidor
☐ Musée d'Art Modern Méditérranéen
☐ Musée de l'Olivier
☐ Permanent collection
☐ Temporary exhibition space
☐ Non-exhibition space

Renaissance Courtyard
This central space rises past two levels of marble-columned galleries to the open sky. Among its lush greenery is a 200-year-old pepper tree.

VISITORS' CHECKLIST

Cagnes-sur-Mer. **[** 04 93 20 87 29. **○** May–Sep: 10am–noon, 2–6pm Wed–Mon; Oct, Dec–Apr: 10am–noon, 2–5pm Wed–Mon. **●** 1 May, Nov, 25 Dec. 🖉

★ La Chute de Phaëton by Giovanni Carlone
The Piedmontese soldiers occupying the château in the 19th century had little respect for this spectacular 1620s illusionistic ceiling – and used it for target practice.

Musée de l'Olivier
A massive wooden oil mill, vast terracotta jars and other arti-facts illustrate the time-honoured Provençal tra dition of olive cultivation.

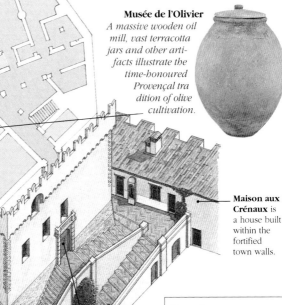

First floor

Ground floor

Maison aux Crénaux is a house built within the fortified town walls.

To place du Château

Main entrance and ticket office

STAR SIGHTS

★ La Chute de Phaëton by Giovanni Carlone

★ Donation Suzy Solidor

Street-by-Street: Nice ⓱

A DENSE NETWORK of pedestrian alleys, narrow buildings and pastel, Italianate façades make up the Old Town. Its streets contain many fine 17th-century Italianate churches, among them St-François-de-Paule, behind the Opéra, and l'Eglise du Jésus in the rue Droite. Most of the seafront, at quai des Etats-Unis, is taken up by the Ponchettes, a double row of low houses with flat roofs, a fashionable walk before the promenade des Anglais was built. To the east of this lies the Colline du Château, occupied in the 4th century by Greeks who kept fishing nets on the quay.

★ Cathédrale Ste-Réparate
Built in 1650 by the Nice architect J-A Guiberto in Baroque style, this has a fine dome of glazed tiles and an 18th-century tower.

Palais de Justice
This awesome building was inaugurated on 17 October 1892, replacing the smaller quarters used before Nice became part of France. On the same site was a 13th-century church and convent.

★ Cours Saleya
The site of an enticing vegetable and flower market, it is also a lively area at night.

RUE DE LA BOUCHERIE
RUE F GALLO
RUE COLONA D' ISTRIA
RUE DE L
RUE DU MARCHE
PLACE DU PALAIS
PLACE PIERRE GAUTIE
RUE DE LA TERRASSE
RUE ALEXANDRE MARI
RUE L GASSIN
COUR
RUE ST-F DE PAULE

Opera House
Built in 1855, the ornate and sumptuous Opéra de Nice has its entrance just off the quai des Etats-Unis.

Chapelle de la Miséricorde

Designed in 1740 by Guarino Guarinone, this Baroque masterpiece has a fine Rococo interior. The Nice altarpieces are by Louis Bréa and Jean Mirailhet.

VISITORS' CHECKLIST

Road map F3. 🏠 342,000. ✈ 7 km (4.5 miles) SW. 🚌 av Thiers. 🚉 12 av Félix Faure. 🚢 quai du Commerce. 🛈 5 prom des Anglais (04 92 14 48 00). 🅰 Mon, Tue & Sun. 🎭 Carnival (before Lent), Festival du Jazz et Folk (July).

★ **Palais Lascaris**
18th-century statues of Mars and Venus flank the staircase. The trompe l'oeil *ceiling is by Genoese artists.*

Tourist Tram
It passes the market, old town and castle gardens.

KEY

- - - Suggested route

0 metres 100

0 yards 100

Les Ponchettes

Musée Mossa
Alexis Mossa is remembered here both as the man who dreamt up Nice's carnival procession, and, together with his son Gustav-Adolf, as a gifted landscape painter.

STAR FEATURES

★ **Cathédrale Ste-Réparate**

★ **Palais Lascaris**

★ **Cours Saleya**

Musée Matisse

Henri Matisse (1869–1954) first came to Nice in 1916, and lived at several addresses in the city before settling in Cimiez for the rest of his life. His devotion to the city and its "clear, crystalline, precise, limpid" light culminated, just before his death in 1954, with a bequest of works. Nine years later they formed the museum's core collection, sharing space with archaeological relics in the Villa des Arènes, next to the Cimiez cemetery, which holds the artist's simple memorial. Since 1993 the entire villa, complete with its new extension, has been devoted to celebrating his life, work and influence.

★ Nu Bleu IV *(1952)*
The celebrated "cut-outs" were made in later life when Matisse was bedridden.

Matisse in his Studio *(1948)*
The museum's photographic collection offers a unique insight into the man and his work. Robert Capa's picture shows him drafting the murals for the Chapelle du Rosaire at Vence (see pp74–5).

First floor

To stairs up to villa

Ground floor

★ Fauteuil Rocaille
A gilded Rococo armchair, painted by Matisse in 1946, is among many of his personal belongings that are on display in the museum.

STAR EXHIBITS

- ★ **Nature Morte aux Grenades**
- ★ **Fauteuil Rocaille**
- ★ **Nu Bleu IV**

GALLERY GUIDE

The ground and first floors of the villa are used to display works from the museum's ever-expanding permanent collection. The new subterranean wing is used for changing thematic exhibitions devoted to Matisse and his contemporaries.

KEY TO FLOORPLAN

- ☐ Permanent collection
- ☐ Temporary exhibition space
- ☐ Non-exhibition space

Lectrice à la Table Jaune *(1944)*
The tranquillity of this work belies the troubles that beset Matisse in World War II, including a major operation and the arrest of his wife for Resistance work.

VISITORS' CHECKLIST

164 av des Arènes de Cimiez, Nice. **[** *04 93 81 08 08.*
◯ *10am–6pm Wed–Mon (5pm Nov–Mar).* **●** *1 Jan, 1 May, 25 Dec.*

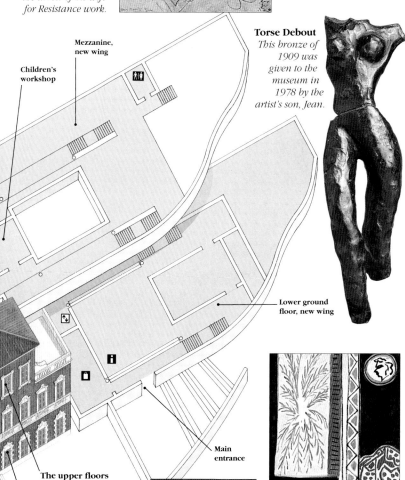

Torse Debout
This bronze of 1909 was given to the museum in 1978 by the artist's son, Jean.

Mezzanine, new wing

Children's workshop

Lower ground floor, new wing

Main entrance

The upper floors of the villa hold a library and resource centre for students and researchers.

Trompe l'Oeil Façade
The decorative stonework that adorns the 17th-century Villa des Arènes is, in fact, a masterful disguise of plain walls, only visible close to.

★ Nature Morte aux Grenades *(1947)*
Ripe pomegranates feature in a favourite setting: an interior with a window to "skies ... as brilliantly blue as Matisse's eyes", as the poet Aragon put it.

Exploring Nice

Nice is France's largest tourist resort and fifth biggest city. It has the second busiest airport in France and more banks, galleries and museums than anywhere else outside the capital. Each year, Nice hosts a lavish pre-Lent carnival, ending with a fireworks display and the Battle of the Flowers (see p34). The city has its own dialect and its own cuisine of *socca*, chickpea pancakes, but the ubiquitous pizza ovens lend a rich Italian flavour.

Beach and promenade des Anglais

A glimpse of the city

Nice lies at the foot of a hill known as the Château, after the castle which once stood there. The daily flower and vegetable market in the cours Saleya is a shoppers' paradise. The fashionable quarter is the Cimiez district, up on the hills overlooking the town, where the old monastery of **Notre-Dame** is worth a visit. Lower down, next to the handsome **Musée Matisse** (see p82–3), are the remains of a Roman amphitheatre and baths. Artifacts are on show at the nearby archaeological museum.

The city's most remarkable feature is the 19th-century promenade des Anglais which runs right along the seafront. It was built in the 1820s, using funds raised by the English colony. Today it is an eight-lane 5-km (3-mile) highway. Until World War II, Nice was popular with aristocrats. Queen Victoria stayed here in 1895, and in 1912, Tsar Nicholas II built the onion-domed **Cathédrale Orthodoxe Russe** in St-Philippe. The old town is now gentrified, although it once had a bad reputation. In 1982 English author Graham Greene criticized Jacques Médecin, the city's right-wing mayor, who was eventually imprisoned for corruption and died in exile.

🏨 Hotel Négresco

37 promenade des Anglais. **(** *04 93 16 64 00. See* **Where to Stay** *p197.* This palatial hotel was built in 1912 for Henri Négresco, once a gypsy-violin serenader, who went bankrupt eight years later.

The fountain in place Masséna

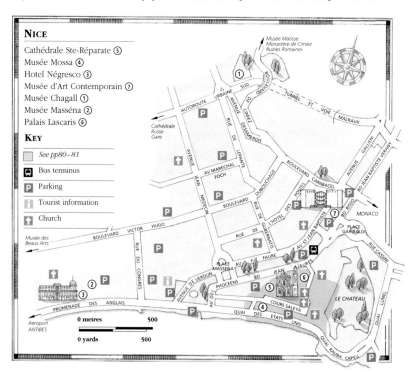

NICE

Cathédrale Ste-Réparate ⑤
Musée Mossa ④
Hotel Négresco ③
Musée d'Art Contemporain ⑦
Musée Chagall ①
Musée Masséna ②
Palais Lascaris ⑥

KEY

▨	See pp80–81
🚌	Bus terminus
P	Parking
ℹ	Tourist information
✝	Church

0 metres   500

0 yards   500

In the *salon royale* hangs a Baccarat chandelier made from 16,000 stones. The infamous American dancer Isadora Duncan spent her last months here in 1927. She died tragically outside the hotel when her trailing scarf caught in the wheel of her Bugatti and broke her neck.

🏛 Musée Masséna
67 rue de France. **☎** 04 93 88 11 34. **○** Tue–Sun. **●** until late 2000, public hols. 🖼
This 19th-century Italianate villa belonged to the great-grandson of Napoleon's Nice-born Marshal. Its Empire-style main hall has a bust of the Marshal by Canova. Among its exhibits are religious works, paintings by Niçois primitives, white-glazed faïence pottery *(see p186)* and Josephine's gold cloak.

🏛 Musée Chagall
16 av Dr Ménard. **☎** 04 93 53 87 20. **○** Wed–Mon. **●** 1 Jan, 1 May, 25 Dec. 🖼 🅰
Built in 1972, this museum houses the largest collection of Marc Chagall's work. The 17 canvases from his Biblical Message series include *Noah's Ark*, *The Creation of Man* and five versions of *The Song of Songs*. Three stained-glass windows depict the *Creation of the World* and a large mosaic reflected in the pool represents the prophet Elijah.

Russian Orthodox cathedral

✝ Cathédrale Ste-Réparate
Place Rossetti. **○** daily. .
This 17th-century Baroque building has a handsome tiled dome. The interior is lavishly decored with plasterwork, marble and original panelling.

⚓ Palais Lascaris
15 rue Droite. **☎** 04 93 62 05 54. **○** Dec–Oct: Tue–Sun. **●** 1 Jan, Easter, 1 May, 2 weeks in Nov, 25 Dec.
This salon of this stuccoed 17th-century palace has a *trompe l'oeil* ceiling, said to be by Carlone. An 18th-century pharmacy has been re-created on the ground floor.

🏛 Musée des Arts Asiatiques
405 prom des Anglais. **☎** 04 92 29 37 00. **○** Wed–Sun. **●** 1 Jan, 1 May, 25 Dec. 🅰
This museum has outstanding examples of ancient and contemporary art from across Asia in Kenzo Tange's uncluttered white marble setting.

🏛 Musée des Beaux-Arts
33 av des Baumettes. **☎** 04 92 15 28 28. **○** Tue–Sun. **●** 1 Jan, Easter, 1 May, 25 Dec. 🖼
Once home to a Ukranian princess, this 1876 villa houses a collection begun with a donation by Napoleon III. Three centuries of art cover work by Jules Chéret, Carle Van Loo, Van Dongen, and Impressionists and Post-impressionists such as Bonnard, Dufy and Vuillard.

🏛 Musée d'Art Contemporain
Promenade des Arts. **☎** 04 93 62 61 62. **○** Wed–Mon. **●** 1 Jan, Easter, 1 May, 25 Dec. 🖼 🅰
Based in a strikingly original building with marble-faced towers and glass passageways, the collection reflects the history of the *avant-garde*, including Pop Art by Andy Warhol and work by Ecole de Nice artists such as Yves Klein.

Hillside view over Cap Ferrat

Cap Ferrat ⑱

Road map F3. ✈ Nice. 🚉 Villefranche. 🚌 St-Jean-Cap-Ferrat. **ℹ** St-Jean-Cap-Ferrat (04 93 76 08 90).

THE CAP FERRAT peninsula is a playground for the rich, with exclusive villas, luxury gardens and fabulous yachts in the St-Jean marina.

King Léopold II of Belgium started the trend in the 19th century when he built Les Cèdres on the west side of the cape overlooking Villefranche. Today, the 14-ha (35-acre) park is open to the public and a 3-ha (7-acre) lake on Leopold's estate has been turned into the **Parc Zoologique**, complete with chimps' tea parties. In 1906 he built the Villa Mauresque for his personal priest; it was bought by Somerset Maugham 20 years later. The Duke and Duchess of Windsor added *cachet* when they rented a villa here in 1938, and postwar residents have included David Niven and Edith Piaf. High hedges and gates protect these exotic villas, but one of the finest, **Musée Ephrussi de Rothschild** *(see pp86–7)*, is open to the public.

There is a superb view from the little garden around the 1837 lighthouse at the end of the cape. A pretty shoreside walk leads around the Pointe St-Hospice, east of the port at **St-Jean-Cap-Ferrat**, a former fishing village with old houses overlooking the harbour.

🐾 Parc Zoologique
Cap Ferrat. **☎** 04 93 76 04 98. **○** daily. 🖼 🅰

Yves Klein's *Anthropométrie* (1960) in the Musée d'Art Contemporain

Musée Ephrussi de Rothschild

BÉATRICE EPHRUSSI DE ROTHSCHILD (1864–1934) could have led a life of indolent luxury, but her passions for travel and fine art, combined with an iron will, led to the creation of the most perfect "dream villa" of the Riviera, Villa Ile-de-France. She competed with King Léopold II of Belgium for the land, and later supervised every aspect of the villa's creation. It was completed in 1912 but Béatrice had only four years in which to enjoy its beauty. After the death in 1916 of her beloved husband, whom she called "Frousse", she never lived there again. The villa remains a monument to a woman of spirit and vision.

★ Fragonard Room
The unrivalled collection of working drawings by Jean-Honoré Fragonard (1732–1806) includes this sketch, wryly named If he were as faithful to me.

Béatrice, Aged 19
Her meek appearance belies a woman who, a contemporary once observed, "commands flowers to grow during the Mistral".

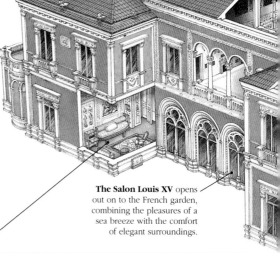

The Salon Louis XV opens out on to the French garden, combining the pleasures of a sea breeze with the comfort of elegant surroundings.

Béatrice's Boudoir
Valuable miniature antique sofas and footstools made cosy day beds for Béatrice's dogs. Her writing desk dates from the 18th century and belonged to Marie-Antoinette.

STAR SIGHTS

★ Fragonard Room

★ Salon Louis XVI

★ Gardens

Villa Ile-de-France
Béatrice christened her villa in memory of an ocean voyage on the luxury liner of the same name. Its stucco walls are coloured in her favourite shade of rose pink.

Covered Patio

Combining Moorish and Italian elements, this airy space rises the full height of the villa. The marble columns, mosaic flooring and diffused light complement the Renaissance religious works and 16th–17th-century tapestries on the walls.

First-floor apartments

Entrance to villa and assembly point for guided tours

To ticket office and car park

Cabinet des Singes

Béatrice's love of porcelain animals is epitomized by this tiny room. Its screens are painted with monkeys dancing to the music of the diminutive 1740s Meissen monkey orchestra.

★ Gardens

The French garden is designed to resemble the prow of a ship. At parties, staff wore sailors' uniforms to enhance the illusion. Other garden themes include Florence and Japan, complete with a miniature Pagoda.

★ Salon Louis XVI

Like every room in the villa, the decor here is lavish, with wood ornamentation from the Crillon in Paris, Savonnerie carpets, and chairs upholstered in 18th-century Beauvais tapestries.

Villefranche ⑲

Road map F3. 🏠 8,125. 🚉 🚌
ℹ️ Jardin François Binon (04 93 01
73 68).

THIS UNSPOILT TOWN over-
looks a beautiful natural
harbour, deep enough to be a
naval port, with a lively waterfront lined by bars and cafés.
   The medieval **Chapelle St-
Pierre** on the quay, once used
for storing fishing nets, was
renovated in 1957, when Jean
Cocteau added lavish frescoes.
Steep lanes climb up from the
harbour, turning into tunnels
beneath the tightly packed
buildings. The vaulted rue
Obscure has provided shelter
from bombardment as recently
as World War II.
   In one narrow street, the tiny
Baroque **Eglise St-Michel**
contains a 16th-century carving
of St Rock and his dog.
   Within the sturdy grey walls
of the 16th-century Citadelle de
St-Elme are the chapel, open-
air theatre and several galleries.

Fishing in the natural harbour at Villefranche

🏠 **Chapelle St-Pierre**
Quai Amiral Courbet.
📞 04 93 76 90 70. ⏰ Tue–Sun.
● mid-Nov–mid-Dec, 25 Dec. 🅿️

Beaulieu ⑳

Road map F3. 🏠 4,000. 🚉 🚌
ℹ️ pl Clemenceau (04 93 01 02 21).
🚌 Mon–Sat.

HEMMED IN and protected
by a rock face, this is one
of the Riviera's warmest
resorts in winter. Its palm-lined
promenade overlooking the
Baïe des Fourmis is known as
"Petite Afrique". The casino,
formal gardens and the Belle
Epoque Rotunda, now a
conference centre, add to
Beaulieu's old-fashioned air.
Among its hotels is La
Réserve, founded by Gordon
Bennett, the owner of the *New
York Herald*. As a stunt, in
1871, he sent journalist HM
Stanley to rescue the Scottish
missionary and explorer Dr
Livingstone, who was looking
for the source of the Nile.
   Beaulieu is the site of the
Villa Kerylos. Built by arche-
ologist Théodore Reinach, it
resembles an ancient Greek
villa. Authentic techniques
and precious materials were
used to create lavish mosaics,
frescoes and inlaid furniture.
There are also numerous
original Greek ornaments.

🏛️ **Villa Kerylos**
Impasse Eiffel. 📞 04 93 01 01 44.
⏰ mid-Dec–mid-Nov daily.
● 1 Jan, 25 Dec. 🅿️

Eze ㉑

Road map F3. 🏠 2,450. 🚉 🚌
ℹ️ pl Général de Gaulle
(04 93 41 26 00).

EZE IS A DRAMATIC *village
perché (see pp18–19)*, a
cluster of ancient buildings
some 427 m (1,400 ft) above
the sea. At its summit are the
bat-filled ruins of a 14th-
century castle. Around it, is the
Jardin Exotique, offering
views as far as Corsica.
   The flower-decked, car-free
streets lead to an 18th-century
church. Its bust of Christ is
made from olive wood that
survived the terrible fires that
raged close by in 1986.

🌷 **Jardin Exotique**
Rue du Château. 📞 04 93 41 10 30.
⏰ daily. 🅿️

Steps of the elegant Belle Epoque Rotunda (1886), Beaulieu

La Turbie ❷

Road map F3. 🏘 *2,600.* 🚌
ℹ️ *La Mairie (04 93 41 10 10).*

HIGH ABOVE MONTE-CARLO is one of the finest views on the Riviera, reached by a stretch of the Grande Corniche which crosses ravines and tunnels through mountains. The charming old village of La Turbie, scented with jasmine and bougainvillea, still retains two medieval gateways. Its oldest houses, which date from the 11th–13th centuries, are on the Roman via Julia.

View of Le Trophée des Alpes from the village of La Turbie

🏛 Musée du Trophée des Alpes

Av Albert 1er. 📞 *04 93 41 20 84.* ⬜ *Apr–Sep: daily; Oct–Mar: Tue–Sun.* ⬛ *1 Jan, 1 May, 1 & 11 Nov, 25 Dec.* 📷

The most spectacular feature of La Turbie is the Trophée des Alpes, a huge Roman monument, built out of white local stone, which marked the division between Italy and Gaul. Its construction was ordered in 6 BC by the Roman Senate to honour Augustus's victory in 13 BC over 44 fractious Ligurian tribes. The original trophy was 50 m (164 ft) tall and had niches with statues of each of the campaign's victors. There were stairs leading to all parts of the structure.

When the Romans left, the trophy was gradually dismantled. In the 4th century, St Honorat chipped away at the monument because it had become the object of pagan worship. Later it served both as a fort and as a stone quarry. It was partly destroyed on the orders of Louis XIV, who feared it would fall into enemy hands during the invasion of Provence by Savoy in 1707. Restoration did not begin until 1920, when a philanthropic American, called Edward Tuck, stepped in. Today, the triumphal inscription of Roman victory has been restored to its original position.

A small museum on the site documents the history of the trophy, with fragments of the monument, pieces of sculpture, inscriptions, drawings and a small-scale model.

The spectacular panorama from the terraces of the trophy takes in Cap Ferrat and Eze. Monaco, at 480 m (1,575 ft) below, seems breathtakingly close, like an urban stage set seen from a seat in the gods.

Among visitors impressed with La Turbie and its trophy, was the poet Dante (1265–1321), and his comments are inscribed on a plaque in rue Comte-de-Cessole. From the end of this street there is a fine view of the monument.

Monument detail

LE TROPHÉE DES ALPES

This triumphal monument had a square podium, a circular colonnade and a stepped cone which was surmounted by the statue of Augustus.

6-m (20-ft) statue of Emperor Augustus

The original colonnade included niches for the statues of Augustus's campaign generals.

The inscription records the names of the 44 tribes subjugated by Augustus, with a dedication to the emperor.

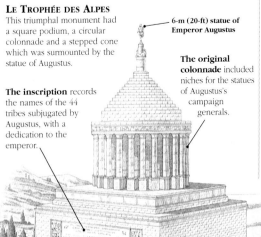

🔒 Eglise St-Michel-Archange

⬜ *daily.* ♿

The 18th-century Nice Baroque church was built with stones plundered from the trophy. Inside there is an altar of multi-coloured marble and a 17th-century onyx and agate table, which was used for communion. Its religious paintings include two works by the Niçois artist Jean-Baptiste Van Loo, a portrait of St Mark attributed to Veronese, and a Piéta from the Bréa School.

Monaco ㉓

Grimaldi family crest

IF YOU COME to Monaco by car, you may well travel in on the Moyenne Corniche, one of the world's most beautiful coastal highways. Arriving amid the skyscrapers of present-day Monaco, it is hard to imagine its turbulent history, much of it centred on Monaco-Ville. The palace, cathedral and museums are all in this old part of town, set on the Rock, a sheer-sided, flat-topped finger of land extending 792 m (2,600 ft) into the sea. First a Greek and later a Roman colony, it was bought from the Genoese in 1309 by François Grimaldi. In spite of family feuds and at least one political assassination, the Grimaldis, whose crest shows two sword-waving monks, remain the world's oldest ruling monarchy.

Modern Monaco
Lack of space has led to vertical building, and a striking skyline of skyscrapers and apartment blocks.

Musée des Souvenirs Napoléoniens

Palais du Prince
The Grimaldis have ruled from here since the 14th century. The palace dates from the 16th–17th centuries but its towers are Genoese of 1215. The constitution insists it is guarded by French carabiniers. (See p94).

Cathédrale
This Neo-Romanesque construction in cream-coloured stone sits on a rocky spur. Among its treasures are two early 16th-century screens by Bréa, La Pietà *and* St-Nicolas. *(See p94).*

Musée Océano-graphique

Erected on a sheer cliff, high above the Mediterranean, it has one of the best aquaria in Europe. It is also used as a scientific research institute. (See p94).

VISITORS' CHECKLIST

Road map F3. 🚶 *30,000.*
✈ *7 km (4.5 miles) SW Nice.*
🚉 *pl Saint Dévote (00 377 93 25 54 54).* ℹ *2a boulevard des Moulins (00 377 92 16 61 16).*
🗓 *daily.* 🎪 *Festival du Cirque (Jan); Grand Prix (May); Fête Nationale Monégasque (19 Nov).*

Théâtre du Fort Antoine

This ancient fort has been converted into a theatre which shows a wide range of productions throughout the year.

Monte Carlo Story is a multi-visual history in film and photographs, recorded in different languages.

Typical Old Town Villa
Hidden in a labyrinth of passages are fountains, tiny squares and elegant façades.

THE ROYAL FAMILY

Since 1949, Monaco has been ruled by the businesslike Prince Rainier Louis Henri Maxence Bertrand de Grimaldi. He is the 26th ruling prince, a descendant of the Grimaldi who, disguised as a monk, entered the Monaco fortress in 1297. At that time the territory extended to Antibes and Menton. Prince Rainier's wife, the former film star Grace Kelly, whom he married in 1956, died tragically in 1982. Their son, Albert, is heir to the $200 million throne, and an extemely eligible bachelor, but it is his beautiful, sometimes wayward sisters, Stephanie and Caroline who have taken up most media attention in recent years.

Prince Rainier III and Grace Kelly at their engagement party in 1956

Monte-Carlo

**Art Deco entrance,
Le Café de Paris**

THE DRAMATIC HEIGHTS of Monte-Carlo are the best-known area of Monaco. People flock to the annual car rally in January and many of the world's greatest singers perform here in the opera season. Monte-Carlo is named after Charles III, who opened the first casino in 1865, to save himself from bankruptcy. Such was his success that, five years later he abolished taxation. Although Queen Victoria thought Monte-Carlo a den of iniquity, her view was not shared by other aristocrats, including Edward VII, who were regular visitors. The stunning Casino and Opera House were built by Charles Garnier, architect of the Paris Opéra. Between Monaco-Ville and Monte-Carlo lies La Condamine, a shopping and commercial centre surrounding the luxury yachts.

View of Monte-Carlo
*It is worth pausing at
La Turbie (see p89) to
admire the panorama.*

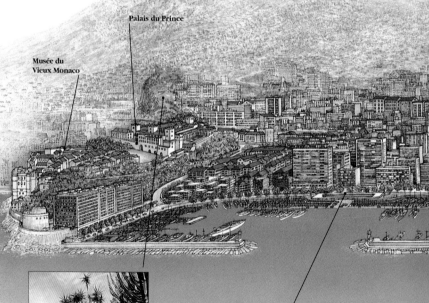

Palais du Prince

Musée du
Vieux Monaco

Jardin Exotique
*Plants normally grown in
balmy climates flourish here,
and its grottoes housed prehistoric animals and humans
200,000 years ago (see p94).*

La Condamine
*The quays are pleasant
yacht-watching promen-
ades laid out by Albert I.
The current prince added
a watersports pool, and
it is also a popular
setting for funfairs.*

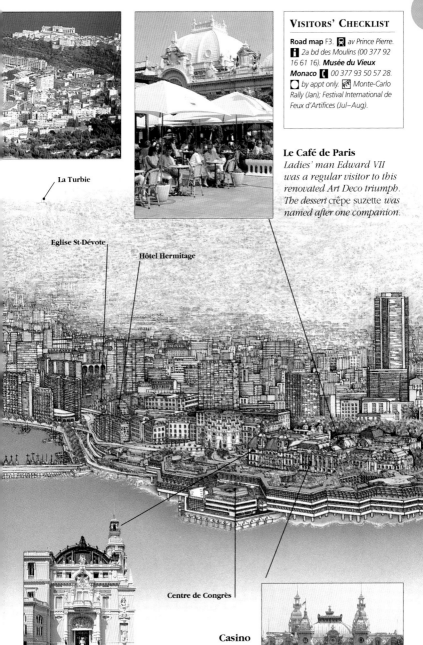

VISITORS' CHECKLIST

Road map F3. 🚌 *av Prince Pierre.*
🛈 *2a bd des Moulins (00 377 92
16 61 16).* **Musée du Vieux
Monaco** 📞 *00 377 93 50 57 28.*
🕐 *by appt only.* 🎉 *Monte-Carlo
Rally (Jan); Festival International de
Feux d'Artifices (Jul–Aug).*

Le Café de Paris
*Ladies' man Edward VII
was a regular visitor to this
renovated Art Deco triumph.
The dessert* crêpe suzette *was
named after one companion.*

La Turbie

Eglise St-Dévote

Hôtel Hermitage

Centre de Congrès

Salle Garnier
*Designed by Charles Garnier
in 1878, this was where ballet
innovators such as Diaghilev
and Nijinksy congregated.*

Casino
*In a 3-day gambling
spree in 1891, Charles
Deville Wells turned
$400 into $40,000
and inspired the tune,*
The Man Who Broke
the Bank at Monte-
Carlo *(see p94).*

Exploring Monaco

AFTER THE VATICAN, Monaco is the world's smallest sovereign state. It covers less than 1.9 sq km (0.74 sq miles), about half the size of New York City's Central Park. Its inhabitants, 20 per cent Monégasque citizens, pay no taxes and enjoy the world's highest per capita income. Monégasque, a dialect of Provençal, is reflected in street names, such as *piaca* for place, *carrigiu* for rue. But the official language is French, its currency can be used here and most of its laws apply here. Monaco's road network is complicated, so drivers should plan routes with care.

Marine explorer Jacques Cousteau

Monaco Grand Prix route

♦ Palais de Monaco
Pl du Palais. **☎** 00 377 93 25 18 31. ⬜ Jun–Oct: daily. 📷
Monaco's seat of government is an attractive castle-palace, protected by cannons donated by Louis XIV, and sentries who change daily at 11:55am. The palace, with its priceless furniture and frescoes, is only open to the public when the prince is away. Summer concerts are held in the Cour d'Honneur.

⏛ Musée des Souvenirs Napoléoniens
Pl du Palais. **☎** 00 377 93 25 18 31. ⬜ Jun–mid-Nov: daily; mid-Dec–May: Tue–Sun. ● 1 Jan, 1 May, Grand Prix, 25 Dec. 📷
The palace museum combines local history with Napoleonic memorabilia. A large family tree traces links between the Bonapartes and the Grimaldis, while the ground floor is devoted to Napoleon, with busts of him and Josephine.

♜ Casino
Pl du Casino. **☎** 00 377 92 16 23 00. ⬜ daily, from noon. ♿
Designed in 1878 by Charles Garnier (*see p51*), architect of the Paris Opéra, the casino sits on a terrace with superb views

of Monaco. Its interior is still decorated in Belle Epoque style. Roulette is played in the opulent Salle Europe, while the Salle de Jeux Americains includes slot machines. Female nudes smoking cigars deck the ceiling of the Salon Rose bar.

⏛ Musée National (Poupées et Automates d'Autrefois)
17 av Princesse Grace. **☎** 00 377 93 30 91 26. ⬜ daily. ● 1 Jan, 1 May, 25 Dec. 📷
Charles Garnier built this pretty villa, set in a rose garden with sculptures including the *Young Faun* by Carpeaux. It has 400 dolls dating from the 18th century. The automata are set in motion daily: some are opened to show their inner workings.

⛪ Cathédrale
4 rue Colonel Bellando del Caste. ⬜ daily. ♿
The 12th-century church of St-Nicolas was replaced by this 19th-century Neo-Romanesque building in La Turbie stone. Its old altarpiece, by Louis Bréa, is by the ambulatory, with its tombs of princes and bishops. The much-mourned Princess Grace is buried here.

⏛ Musée Océanographique
Av St-Martin. **☎** 00 377 93 15 36 00. ⬜ daily. 📷 ♿
Founded by Prince Albert I in 1910, this clifftop museum has an aquarium filled with rare marine plants and animals, a collection of shells, coral and pearls, and a life-sized model of a giant squid. Marine explorer Jacques Cousteau was director here for 30 years until 1988. The roof terrace offers a superb coastal view.

♣ Jardin Exotique
62 bd du Jardin Exotique. **☎** 00 377 93 30 33 65. ⬜ daily. ● 19 Nov, 25 Dec. 📷 ♿ (small part of garden only).
These gardens are among the finest in Europe, with a vast range of tropical and sub-tropical plants. Off the gardens are the **Grotte de l'Observatoire**, where prehistoric animals and humans lived 200,000 years ago. The **Musée d'Anthropologie Préhistorique**, accessible via the garden, has a collection of prehistoric tools, figurines, bones and Roman treasure.

Roulette tables in the Salle Europe of the Casino

Peillon ⓔ

Road map F3. 🏘 *1,100.*
🚌 *La Mairie (04 93 79 91 04).*

A T A LEVEL OF 373 m (1,225 ft),
this pretty *village perché*
is said by locals to mark the
extremity of the inhabited
world. Its streets are stepped
and narrow, with houses that
have scarcely changed since
the Middle Ages. There is an
attractive cobbled square with
fine views, and the 18th-cen-
tury parish church has an
unusual octagonal lantern. But
most impressive of all are
Giovanni Canavesio's frescoes
in the Chapelle des Pénitents
Blancs. Peillon is ideally placed
for woodland walks leading
to both Peille and La Turbie.

Ancient arch across Peillon street

Peille ⓕ

Road map F3. 🏘 *1,800.* 🚌
🚌 *La Mairie (04 93 91 71 71).*

P EILLE IS A CHARMING medieval
village with a view from its
war memorial across the Paillon
Valley and as far as the Baie
des Anges. Behind the village
looms the vast Pic de Baudon,
rising to 1,264 m (4,160 ft).

The town is full of cobbled
alleys and covered passages.
At the end of place A-Laugier,
beyond a Gothic fountain, two
arches beneath a house rest on
a Romanesque pillar.

The Counts of Provence
were lords of the castle, and
the 12th-century church of Ste-
Marie has a picture of Peille in
the Middle Ages. There is also
a fine 16th-century altarpiece

The Gorges de la Vésubie in the pine-forested Vallée de la Vésubie

by Honoré Bertone. The Hôtel
de Ville is in the domed 18th-
century former Chapelle de
St-Sébastien, and there is a
museum in rue de la Turbie.

Lucéram ⓖ

Road map F3. 🏘 *1,000.* 🚌 🚌 *1
rue de la Placette (04 93 79 46 50).*

I N THE MIDST of this pretty,
Italianate village is the tiled
roof of the 15th-century Eglise
Ste-Marguerite, which contains
many art treasures from the
Nice school. Its master, Louis
Bréa, used Lucéram as a centre
for religious painting, and his
contribution is the 10-panelled
altarpiece. Other treasures include a silver reliquary of the
Tarascon dragon *(see p140).*
The church is the setting for
a Christmas service, where
shepherds, accompanied by
flutes and tambourines, bring
lambs and fruit as offerings.

**Italian-style houses in Lucéram, set
between two ravines**

Vallée de la Vésubie ⓗ

🚌 *Nice.* 🚌 *St-Martin-Vésubie.* 🚌
St-Martin-Vésubie (04 93 03 21 28).

S OME OF THE most attractive
landscape around Nice can
be uncovered and enjoyed in
the valley of the river
Vésubie, with its dense pine
forests, alpine pastures, peaks
and cascades. The river rises
high in the snowy Alps near
the Italian border, courses past
Roquebillière to the west of the
Parc National du Mercantour
(see p97) and dives through the
Gorges de la Vésubie before
entering the river Var, 24 km
(15 miles) north of Nice airport.

The Vésubie is created from
the Madone de Fenestre and
the Boréon torrents, which
meet at St-Martin-Vésubie. This
popular summer mountaineer-
ing centre is surrounded by
waterfalls, summits and lakes.
In its fine 17th-century church
is a 12th-century statue of
Notre-Dame-de-Fenestre. Each
year this statue is carried to
the Chapelle de la Madone de
Fenestre, in a craggy alpine
setting, 12 km (8 miles) to the
east, for a three-month stay.

The Gorges de la Vésubie
begins at St-Jean-la-Rivière, and
there is a spectacular panorama
at la Madonne d'Utelle, above
the fortified village of Utelle.
In places, the dramatic gorge,
etched with coloured rock,
runs up to 244 m (800 ft) deep.
Sadly, the road beside it has
few stopping places from
which to admire the view.

Skiing in the Alpes d'Azur

PROVENCE OFFERS a wide range of ski-ing activities in the Alpes d'Azur. Around one hour from the coast, in breathtaking mountain scenery, there are more than 20 resorts, with over 250 ski-runs. The *après-ski* includes ice-skating, riding on a snowmobile and a chance to sample traditional Alpine food such as delicious melted cheese *raclette*. In summer, Auron and Isola 2000, resorts in the Parc National du Mercantour, offer swimming, cycling and horse-riding in dramatically con-trasting surroundings to the Côte d'Azur.

Snowbound Valberg, a winter resort since 1935

AURON

ALTITUDE *1,600 m (5,250 ft) –
2,100 m (6,890 ft).*
LOCATION *97 km (60 miles) from Nice via RN 202 and D 2205.*
SKI RUNS *5 black, 14 red, 13 blue, 4 green.*
SKI LIFTS *23 including 8 chair lifts and 3 cable cars.*

ISOLA 2000

ALTITUDE *1,600 m (5,250 ft) –
2,610m (8,563 ft).*
LOCATION *90 km (56 miles) from Nice via RN 202, D 2205 and D 97.*
SKI RUNS *5 black, 16 red, 18 blue, 7 green.*
SKI LIFTS *23 including a cable car and 10 chairlifts. Funicular railway.*

VALBERG

ALTITUDE *1,430 m (4,690 ft) –
2,100 m (6,890 ft).*
LOCATION *81 km (50 miles) from Nice via RN 202, CD 28, CD 202 or CD 30.*
SKI RUNS *12 black, 22 red, 13 blue, 11 green.*
SKI LIFTS *26 including 6 chair lifts.*

Getting ready for a few hours of snow-shoe trekking

Climbing a frozen waterfall, or frozen fall climbing, in one of the many alpine resorts

ALPINE ACTIVITIES

	Auron	Isola 2000	Valberg	
		•		ATC (three-wheeled motorbikes)
	•			Bungee jumping
	•	•	•	Cross-country skiing
		•		Frozen fall climbing
		•		Horse-driven buggy rides
		•		Ice circuit driving
	•	•		Ice skating
		•	•	Mono-skiing
		•		Night skiing
		•		Para-skiing
		•		Ski jumping
	•	•	•	Ski school
	•	•	•	Ski touring
		•		Snowboarding
		•		Snow buggies
		•		Snow motorbikes
	•	•	•	Snow scooter circuits
		•		Snow-shoe trekking
		•		Speed ski school

Snowboarding in the alpine resort of Isola 2000

Forêt de Turini

🚌 l'Escarène, Sospel. 🚌 Sospel, Moulinet. ℹ️ Sospel (04 93 04 15 80).

BETWEEN THE WARM coast and the chilly Alps, from the Gorges de la Vésubie to the Vallée de la Bévéra, lies this humid, 3,497-sq km (1,350-sq mile) forest. Beech, maple and sweet chestnut thrive here, and pines grow to great heights.

At the forest's northeastern edge is the 1,889-m (6,197-ft) mountain of l'Authion, site of heavy fighting in the German retreat of 1945. Casualties are recorded on a war memorial.

The neighbouring Pointe des Trois-Communes, at 2,082 m (6,830 ft), offers superb views of the pre-Alps of Nice and the peaks of the Mercantour national park.

Le Parc National du Mercantour ㉙

Road map E2 & F2. 🚌 Nice. 🚌 St Etienne de Tinée. ℹ️ St Etienne de Tinée (04 93 02 41 96).

SCOURED BY ICY GLACIERS and bristling with rocky summits, this sparsely populated park covers 70,000 ha (270 sq miles). Among its unusual wildlife are the chamois, the ibex and the *mouflon*, a sheep which originated in Corsica. Sometimes visible in the mornings is the marmot, a rodent which is prey to golden eagles, and the exotic lammergeier, a bearded vulture with orange-red feathers and black wings. There are many brightly coloured butterflies and alpine flowers, including the park symbol, *Saxifraga florulenta*.

Tende ㉚

Road map F2. 🏔️ 2,200. 🚌 🚌 ℹ️ av 16 Sep 1947 (04 93 04 73 71). 🗓️ Wed.

SOMBRE TENDE once guarded the mountain pass connecting Piedmont and Provence, now bypassed by a tunnel. Its tall, balconied, green-grey schist buildings appear piled on top of each other. Only a

A street scene in the old border town of Tende

wall remains of the castle of Lascaris feudal lords, near the terraced cemetery above the town. Tende's unusual towers include that of the 16th-century church of **Notre-Dame-de-l'Assomption**. Lions support the pillars around the Renaissance doorway and there are green schist columns inside.

Due to vandalism, the **Vallée des Merveilles**, the most spectacular part of Mercantour national park, can only be visited provided you are accompanied by a guide. For information, contact the tourist office at Tende or St-Dalmas. The most direct route is from Lac des Mesches. A 10-km (6-mile) walk leads to Lac Long and Les Merveilles Refuge. The Mont Bégo area has 100,000 engravings, dating from 1,800 – 1,500 BC, carved into the rock face. They reveal a Bronze Age culture of Ligurian shepherds and farmers who instilled magic into the area around Mont Bégo.

Southeast of Tende, there are fine paintings in the church at La Brigue. Jean Canavasio's 15th-century frescoes of *La Passion du Christ*, and the lurid *Judas pendu* are in the nearby 14th-century **Chapelle Notre-Dame-des-Fontaines**.

Tower at Tende

🥾 Vallée des Merveilles
🚌 Tende, St Dalmas-de-Tende. 🚌 Tende. ℹ️ Tende (04 93 04 73 71).

Saorge ㉛

Road map F3. 🏔️ 360. 🚌 ℹ️ La Mairie (04 93 04 51 23).

SAORGE IS THE PRETTIEST spot in the Roya Valley. Set in a natural amphitheatre high over the river, its slate-roofed houses are tiered between narrow alleys, in the style of a typical stacked village or *village empilé*.

Olive-wood carvings are traditional, and carved lintels date many houses to the 15th century, when Saorge was a stronghold. It was taken by the French under Masséna in 1794.

Churches range from the dank 16th-century St-Sauveur with an Italian organ to the Baroque church of the Franciscan monastery and the octagonal tower and Renaissance frescoes of **La Madone-del-Poggio** (open afternoons).

View of Saorge from the Franciscan monastery terrace

Sospel ❷

Road map F3. 👥 *2,600.* 🚌 🚉 🅸
Vieux Pont (04 93 04 15 80). 🅐 *Thu.*

THIS CHARMING ALPINE resort on the river Bévéra has an 11th-century toll tower, restored since Sospel was badly damaged by bombs in World War II, when the bravery of the town's citizens earned it the Croix de Guerre. Fort St-Roch, built in 1932 against possible Italian invasion, has a museum with details of the Maginot line. The former cathedral, now church of St-Michel, containing one of François Bréa's best works, has an attractive façade, as do the chapels of the Red and Grey Penitents, and the Romanesque Palais Ricci.

🏛 Musée de la Ligne Maginot des Alpes
Fort St-Roch. 📞 *04 93 04 00 70.* ⭘
Apr–Jun, Oct: Sat, Sun & public hols pm only; Jul–Sep: Tue–Sun pm only. 📷

Trompe l'oeil **houses in Sospel**

Gorbio ❸

Road map F3. 👥 *1,135.* 🚉
🅸 *La Mairie, 30 rue Garibaldi (04 92 10 66 50).*

MORE THAN a thousand species of flowers have been identified in the sunny Gorbio valley, which produces vegetables and fruit, wine and oil. Until the last century the area was entirely supported by its olive production.

Often shrouded in mist in the mornings, Gorbio itself is a *village perché (see pp18–19),* with sea views. The old Malaussène fountain stands by the entrance to the narrow cobbled lanes, and an elm tree in the square was planted in

Early morning Gorbio, surrounded by olive groves

1713. The church has a conical belfry, a typical feature of the region. Each June a procession marks the White Penitents' ritual, when the village lanes twinkle with the lights from oil lamps made from snail shells.

A kilometre's walk (0.5 mile) from Gorbio is Ste-Agnès, at 671 m (2,200 ft) the highest *village perché* on the coast, and more commercial than Gorbio.

Roquebrune-Cap-Martin ❹

Road map F3. 👥 *12,400.* 🚌 🚉
🅸 *20 av Paul Doumer (04 93 35 62 87).*

ROQUEBRUNE IS SAID to have the earliest feudal **château** in France, the sole example of the Carolingian style. It was built in the 10th century by Conrad I, Count of Ventimiglia, to ward off Saracen attack, and was later remodelled by the Grimaldis *(see p91).* Wealthy Englishman Sir William Ingram,

View of Château de Roquebrune, overlooking Cap Martin

one of the first wave of tourist residents, bought the château in 1911 and added a mock medieval *tour anglais.*

At the turn of the century, Cap Martin was the smartest resort on the Côte d'Azur, attracting the era's glitterati. Empératrice Eugénie, wife of Napoléon III, and England's Queen Victoria wintered here. Winston Churchill, Coco Chanel and Irish poet WB Yeats also visited. Architect Le Corbusier, who drowned off the cape in 1965, has a coastal path named after him.

A number of important prehistoric remains have been found around Roquebrune, some in caves such as the nearby **Grottes du Vallenot.** Just outside the village, on the Menton road, is the majestic *olivier millénaire,* one of the oldest olive trees in the world, which is believed to be at least 1,000 years old.

Every August since 1467, in gratitude for being spared from the plague, the inhabitants of Roquebrune have taken part in scenes from the Passion *(see p31).*

⚓ Château de Roquebrune
📞 *04 93 35 07 22.*
⭘ *daily.* 📷

Menton ❺

Road map F3. 👥 *30,000.* 🚌 🚉
🅸 *Palais de l'Europe, av Boyer (04 92 41 76 50).* 🅐 *daily.*

JUST A MILE from the border, Menton is the most Italian of the French resorts. Tucked in by mountains, it is a sedate town with a Baroque square and a promenade stretching towards Cap Martin.

Menton has several fine tropical gardens, and citrus fruits thrive in a climate mild enough for the lemon festival in February *(see p33)*. The **Palais de l'Europe** of the Belle Epoque (1909), once a casino, now a tourism and cultural centre, is beside the **Jardin Biovès**. The **Jardin Botanique Exotique** has tropical plants and is in the grounds of Villa Val Rameh. Above the town is the **Jardin des Colombières** designed by artist and writer Ferdinand Bac (1859–1952). It contains what is reputed to be the oldest carob tree in France.

The jetties offer fine views of the old town, and steps lead to Parvis St-Michel, a fine square paved with the Grimaldi coat of arms, where summer concerts are held.

To the left side are the twin towers of the Baroque **Eglise St-Michel**, its main altarpiece by Manchello (1569). Behind the new marina is the suburb of Garavan. The tubercular New Zealand writer Katherine Mansfield lived here in the villa Isola Bella from 1920–22.

⛬ Musée des Beaux-Arts
Palais Carnolès, 3 av de la Madone. **[** 04 93 35 49 71. ⭘ Wed–Mon. ● public hols. **&** restricted.
The 18th-century palace, now Menton's main art museum, was once summer residence of

JEAN COCTEAU (1889–1963)
Born near Paris in 1889, Cocteau spent much of his very public life around the Côte d'Azur. A man of powerful intellect and great *élan*, he became a member of the Académie Française in 1955. Among other talents, Cocteau was a dramatist (*La Machine Infernale*, 1934); the writer of *Les Enfants Terribles* (1929), and a surrealist film director. *Orpheé* (1950) was partly shot against the barren landscape at Les Baux *(see p142)*. He died before his museum opened in 1967.

Mosaic at the entrance of the Musée Jean Cocteau in Menton

the princes of Monaco. It has paintings by Graham Sutherland (1903–80), an honorary citizen, 13th- to 18th-century Italian and French art, and works by Utrillo and Dufy.

♛ Salle des Mariages
Hôtel de Ville. **[** 04 92 10 50 00. ⭘ Mon–Fri. ● public hols. **&**
Jean Cocteau decorated this room in 1957 with colourful images of a fisherman and his bride, and the less happy story of Orpheus and Eurydice, and Provençal motifs such as using a fish for a fisherman's eye.

⛬ Musée Jean Cocteau
quai Monléon. **[** 04 93 57 72 30. ⭘ Wed–Mon. ● public hols. **&**
Cocteau supervised the conversion of this former 17th-

century fort into his museum. He designed the salamander mosaic on the ground floor, and donated his first tapestry, set designs and drawings.

✝ Cimetière du Vieux-Château
Each terrace of this former castle site accommodates a separate faith. Webb Ellis, inventor of rugby is buried here, as is Rasputin's assassin, Prince Youssoupov.

⛬ Musée de la Préhistoire Régionale
Rue Loredan Larchey. **[** 04 93 35 84 64. ⭘ Wed–Mon. ● public hols.
The museum's fine local history and archaeological pieces include the skull of 30,000-year-old "Grimaldi Man".

View over Menton from Ferdinand Bac's Jardin des Colombières

THE VAR AND THE ILES D'HYÈRES

THE VAR IS A REGION of rolling lands, rocky hills, thick forests and swathes of vineyards. To the north, Provençal villages are thinly scattered by mountain streams, on hilltops and in valleys; to the south, a series of massifs slope down to the coast making this stretch of the Côte d'Azur the most varied and delightful shore in France.

Through the centre of the Var, dividing it roughly into two sections, runs the A8 autoroute. To the south of this artery the influence of the sea is unmistakable. Toulon, the departmental capital, occupies a fine deep-water harbour that is home to the French Mediterranean fleet. Beyond it are the pleasant resorts of Bandol and Sanary, where Jacques Cousteau first put scuba-diving to the test. To the east are the sandy beaches beneath the great slab of the Massif des Maures. The Var's most famous resort, St-Tropez, facing north in the crook of a bay, lies in a glorious landscape of vineyards. Beyond it, just past Fréjus, the first Roman settlement in Gaul, the land turns blood red in the twinkling inlets and coves below the beautiful Corniche de l'Esterel, which heads east towards the Riviera. The more remote areas to the north of the autoroute have always provided a retreat from the bustling activity of the coast. This is where the Cistercians built their austere Abbaye du Thoronet. Today visitors escape inland from the summer traffic around St-Tropez to the sparsely populated Haut Var, where towns seem to grow from tufa rock.

Highlights include wines from the Côtes de Provence, and fresh tuna from quayside restaurants. Music enthusiasts should spare time to hear both the organ at St-Maximin-la-Ste-Baume, Provence's finest Gothic building, and the string quartets at the festival in the hill towns near Fayence. Visitors can also go walking, sailing and sunbathing, and enjoy a rich collection of museums and architecture.

Sunrise over the boats in St-Tropez harbour

◁ **A traditional shop in the centre of Cotignac in the Haut Var**

Exploring the Var and the Iles d'Hyères

THE VAR DEPARTEMENT covers about 6,000 sq km (2,300 sq miles). It combines a stunning coastline sprinkled with red cliffs, delightful bays and the Iles d'Hyères, which spill out from its southernmost point, with dramatic chains of hills behind the coast and further inland. Although the hills have been partly depleted by forest fires, they are still home to a fascinating array of flora and fauna as well as to the many producers of Côtes-de-Provence wines.

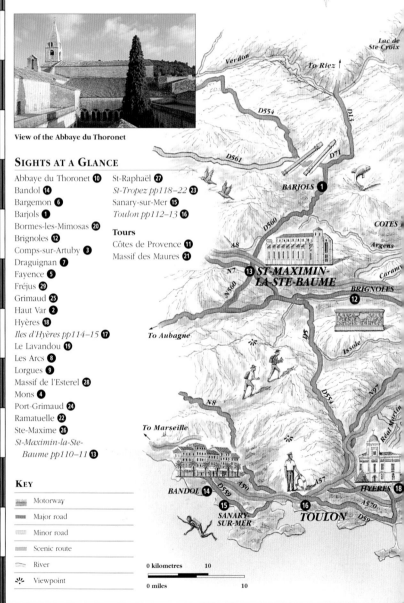

View of the Abbaye du Thoronet

SIGHTS AT A GLANCE

Abbaye du Thoronet ⑩
Bandol ⑭
Bargemon ⑥
Barjols ①
Bormes-les-Mimosas ⑳
Brignoles ⑫
Comps-sur-Artuby ③
Draguignan ⑦
Fayence ⑤
Fréjus ㉙
Grimaud ㉕
Haut Var ②
Hyères ⑱
Iles d'Hyères pp114–15 ⑰
Le Lavandou ⑲
Les Arcs ⑧
Lorgues ⑨
Massif de l'Esterel ㉘
Mons ④
Port-Grimaud ㉔
Ramatuelle ㉒
Ste-Maxime ㉖
St-Maximin-la-Ste-Baume pp110–11 ⑬
St-Raphaël ㉗
St-Tropez pp118–22 ㉓
Sanary-sur-Mer ⑮
Toulon pp112–13 ⑯

Tours

Côtes de Provence ⑪
Massif des Maures ㉑

KEY

Motorway
Major road
Minor road
Scenic route
River
Viewpoint

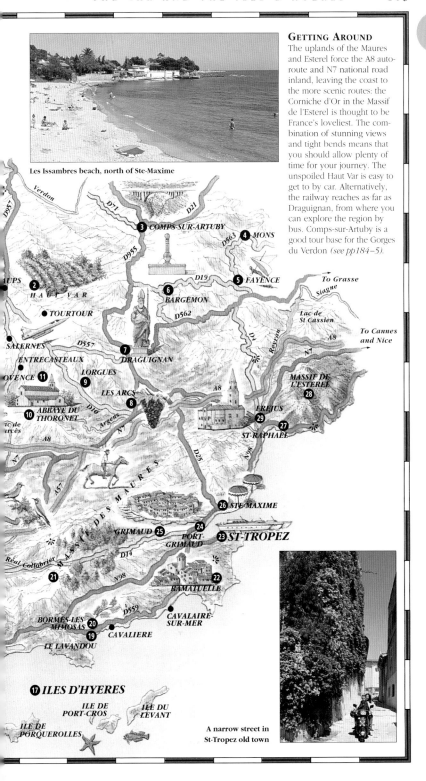

Les Issambres beach, north of Ste-Maxime

GETTING AROUND

The uplands of the Maures and Esterel force the A8 auto-route and N7 national road inland, leaving the coast to the more scenic routes: the Corniche d'Or in the Massif de l'Esterel is thought to be France's loveliest. The combination of stunning views and tight bends means that you should allow plenty of time for your journey. The unspoiled Haut Var is easy to get to by car. Alternatively, the railway reaches as far as Draguignan, from where you can explore the region by bus. Comps-sur-Artuby is a good tour base for the Gorges du Verdon (see pp184–5).

Verdon

D71 D21

3 COMPS-SUR-ARTUBY

D955

D563 4 MONS

UPS

2

HAUT VAR

D19 5 FAYENCE

6

BARGEMON

To Grasse

Siagne

TOURTOUR

D562

Lac de
St Cassien

To Cannes
and Nice

A8

SALERNES

D557

ENTRECASTEAUX

7 DRAGUIGNAN

D4

Reyran

N7

OVENCE 11

LORGUES

9

MASSIF DE
L'ESTEREL

28

LES ARCS

A8

10 ABBAYE DU
THORONET

8

D10

Argens

FRÉJUS

29 27

N7

D25

ST-RAPHAËL

A8

A57

M A S S I F   D E S   M A U R E S

D25

26 STE-MAXIME

Réal Collobrier

21

GRIMAUD 25

24

PORT-
GRIMAUD

23 ST-TROPEZ

D14

N98

22

RAMATUELLE

BORMES-LES-
MIMOSAS 20

D559

CAVALAIRE-
SUR-MER

19 CAVALIERE

LE LAVANDOU

17 ILES D'HYERES

ILE DE
PORT-CROS

ILE DU
LEVANT

ILE DE
PORQUEROLLES

A narrow street in
St-Tropez old town

A traditional flute-maker at work in Barjols

Barjols ❶

Road map D4. 🏛 *2,150.* 🚌
🛈 *bd Grisolle (04 94 77 20 01).*
🚂 *Tue, Thu & Sat.*

ONCE RENOWNED for its seething tanneries, Barjols lies peacefully among woods and fast-flowing streams. In 1983, after almost 400 years, the leather industry finally folded. The many abandoned factories have now become bustling artisans' studios.

Today, it is these local craftsmen who bring manufacturing acclaim to the area. Two traditional Provençal instruments, the three-holed flute *(galoubet)* and the narrow drums *(tambourins)*, are today made only in Barjols.

The *Champignon* fountain in Barjols

These instruments resound each January at the annual festival of St Marcel, the town's patron saint. About every four years the ceremony includes the slaughter and roasting of an ox on the town square. This is followed by a colourful "tripe dance" outside the 16th-century church of Notre-Dame-de-l'Assomption, where Saint Marcel is buried. The ceremony commemorates the survival of the town after a siege in 1350. Roastings are planned for 2000 and 2004.

Of the many stone fountains dotted around the town, the most famous is the mossy *Champignon* in place Capitaine Vincens. It stands under what is reputed to be the largest plane tree in Provence.

Between the church and the old tanneries are the restored buildings of the old quartier du Réal. Exotic porticoes, particularly on the Renaissance Hôtel de Pontevès, add spice to some otherwise drab streets.

Haut Var ❷

🚂 *Toulon-Hyères.* 🚉 *Les Arcs.*
🚌 *Aups.* 🛈 *Aups (04 94 70 00 80).*

THE MOST REMOTE and unspoiled lands of the Var are situated between Barjols and Comps-sur-Artuby, up towards the Gorges du Verdon *(see pp184–5)*. Much of the land near here has been taken over by the military.

Aups, set among undulating hills on the plateau edge, is the region's centre. Epicureans may be drawn by the local honey and the truffle market each Thursday in winter. It is an attractive town with a grand old square and castle ruins. The 15th-century St-Pancrace church has a well-restored Renaissance doorway. Also worth a visit is the **Musée Simon Segal**, which is housed in a former Ursuline convent. The museum contains works by Segal and Paris painters, as well as local scenes.

About 5 km (3 miles) northwest on the D9 is the village of Moissac-Bellevue. Many of its buildings date from the 16th and 17th centuries and its church was mentioned in a papal edict of 1225.

South from Aups is Villecroze. The town is set against a natural backdrop of caves on two levels, which local lords in the 16th century turned into dwellings, known as the **Grottes Troglodytes**. The arcaded streets and the keep of the feudal castle give the town a medieval flavour. A short drive from Villecroze leads up to the hill village of Tourtour, a smaller, prettier and more popular place.

View of Entrecasteaux château near Cotignac, Haut Var

From Tourtour there are fine views of Montagne Ste-Victoire, which was one of Cézanne's favourite painting subjects.

The valley town of Salernes lies in the opposite direction, 5 km (3 miles) west on the D51. Smoke pumps from the kilns of its 15 ceramic factories.

Troglodyte dwellings in Villecroze

The 110 m (361 ft) Artuby bridge spanning the Canyon du Verdon

Salernes is one of the best-known Provençal tile-making centres, noted for *tomettes* – hexagonal terracotta floor-tiles.

Cotignac, west of Salernes, is an echo of Villecroze, with a cave-pocked cliff behind it. Behind the *Mairie*, a river springs from the rocks and beyond is an open-air theatre.

The region's most intriguing château is **Entrecasteaux**, 8 km (5 miles) east of Cotignac on the D50. The 17th-century castle was bought in 1974 by the late Ian McGarvie-Munn, who restored and filled it with his own paintings. The garden, by Le Nôtre, is publicly owned.

🏛 Musée Simon Segal
Rue Albert Premier, Aups. **☎** 04 94 70 01 95. **◯** mid-Jun–mid-Sep: daily. **🞐**
🞖 Grottes Troglodytes
Villecroze. **☎** 04 94 70 63 06. **◯** Feb & Easter hols, mid-May–Jun: daily pm; Jul–mid-Sep: daily; mid-Sep–mid-Oct: Sat–Sun pm. **●** Nov–Easter. **🞐**
🞖 Château d'Entrecasteaux
83570 Entrecasteaux. **☎** 04 94 04 43 95.
◯ Jul–Aug: daily; Sep–Jun: Thu–Tue.
● 25 Dec–2 Jan, Feb. **🞐**

Comps-sur-Artuby ❸

Road map D3. **🏔** 270. **🚌** **🛈** *la Mairie (04 94 76 90 16).*

THE EASTERN APPROACH to the Gorges du Verdon *(see pp184–5)* passes through Comps-sur-Artuby. The village nestles at the foot of a rock topped by the 13th-century chapel of **St-André**, which was restored recently. From the church there are grand views of the Artuby Gorges.

To the east lies Bargème, a village of steep streets and hollyhocks with a population of just 86. At 1,094 m (3,589 ft) it is the highest community in the Var. The village itself is closed to all traffic.

Dominating Bargème is a large, partially ruined but nevertheless remarkably well preserved 14th-century castle. Also worth a visit is the 13th-century Romanesque **Eglise St-Nicolas** which contains a carved, wooden altarpiece depicting Saint Sebastian.

Mons ❹

Road map E3. **🏔** 460. **🚌**
🛈 *pl St Sébastien (04 94 76 39 54).*

DRAMATICALLY SITUATED on a rock-spur, Mons, with its tiny lanes and overhanging arches, has an almost magical appeal. The place St-Sébastien looks out across the entire coast, from Italy to Toulon.

Originally a Celtic-Ligurian settlement, its Château-Vieux quarter dates from the 11th century, but it was mainly built by Genoese who repopulated the village after ravages by the plague in the 14th century. The first families came in 1461 from Figounia near Ventimiglia; their legacy is the local dialect, *figoun*, which still survives thanks to the unusually isolated position of the village. Nearby is the *roche taillée*, a working Roman aqueduct carved from solid rock. There are also many dolmens in the surrounding area.

The Roman-built *roche taillée* aqueduct near Mons

View over Bargemon's terracotta rooftops to the wooded hills beyond

Fayence 5

Road map E3. 🏘 4,000. 🚌
ℹ place Léon Roux (04 94 76 20 08).
🛒 Tue, Thu & Sat.

THE HILLSIDE TOWN of Fayence
is the largest one between
Draguignan and Grasse and is
a centre for both local crafts
and gliding. Dominated by a
wrought-iron clock tower, it
still has a few remains of its
14th-century defences including a Saracen Gate.

The **Eglise St-Jean-Baptiste**
was rebuilt in the 18th century
with a baroque marble altar
(1757) by a local mason, Dominique Fossatti. Its terrace
offers a sweeping view over
the town's glider airfield.

On the hillside opposite, in
the community of Tourettes,

there is a striking château.
Part modelled on the Cadet
school in St Petersburg, it was
constructed in 1824 for General
Alexandre Fabre, who once
worked as a military engineer
for Tsar Alexander I of Russia.
He originally intended to make
the building a public museum,
but failed to finish the task
and so it remains private.

There are a number of attractive villages nearby. Among
the best are Callian and
Montauroux to the east and
Seillans, 5 km (3 miles) to the
west, where the German-born
painter Max Ernst (1891–1976)
chose to spend his last years.
The prestigious Musique en
Pays de Fayence festival in
October brings string quartets
who perform in some of the
charming local churches.

Bargemon 6

Road map E3. 🏘 1,050. 🚌 Les
Arcs. 🚌 ℹ av Pasteur (04 94 47 81
73). 🛒 Thu.

THIS MEDIEVAL TOWN, fortified
in AD 950, has four remaining 12th-century gates. The
town is laid out around a number of squares filled with the
aroma of mimosa and orange
blossom, containing fountains
shaded by plane trees.

The angels' heads on the
high altar of the 15th-century
church, **St-Etienne**, are
attributed to Pierre Puget, as
are those in the **Chapelle
Notre-Dame-de-Montaigu**
which overlooks the town.
The chapel also contains a
"miraculous" olive-wood
carving of the Virgin brought
here from Montaigu in Belgium
by a local monk in 1635.

Draguignan 7

Road map D4. 🏘 33,000. 🚌
ℹ 🚕 bd Georges Clemenceau
(04 94 68 63 30). 🛒 Wed, Sat.

DURING THE DAY, the former
capital of the Var département has the busy air of a
small market town. At night,
however, the only sign of life
is groups of young people in
the place des Herbes. Baron
Haussmann, planner of modern
Paris, laid out Draguignan's
19th-century boulevards.

TRADITIONAL POTTERY AND CRAFTS

Fayence and Tourettes are at the centre of an exciting revitalization of Provençal crafts. A vast
number are practised here – for example
weaving, pottery and stone and wood
carving. A regional speciality is hand-
crafted domestic pottery made using
traditional techniques and designs,
as well as local clays in a wonderful variety of colours. In both
towns, small shops and studios
sell examples of these crafts.
There are good buys to be
had, but do shop around to
avoid being overcharged.

A Fayence potter at work

At the end of his plane-tree-lined allées d'Azémar, there is a Rodin bust of the prime minister Georges Clemenceau (1841–1929) who represented Draguignan for 25 years.

The main interest lies in the pedestrianized old town. Its 24-m (79-ft) clockless clock tower, built in 1663, stands on the site of the original keep and there is a good view from its wrought-iron campanile. The wooden-roofed **Eglise St-Michel**, in the place de la Paroisse, contains a statue of St Hermentaire, first bishop of Antibes. In the 5th century he slew a local dragon, giving the town its name.

Draguignan has two good local museums. The **Musée des Arts et Traditions Populaires de Moyenne Provence** is concerned with the region's social and economic history. It occupies buildings that date back to the 17th century. Regional country life is illustrated using reconstructed kitchens and barns. Exhibits related to leisure include a charming old merry-go-round with hand-painted wooden horses.

The **Musée Municipal** contains works of art from Rembrandt to Renoir as well as eye-catching collections of both ceramics and furniture. Its library houses a lavishly illuminated 14th-century manuscript of the *Roman de la Rose*, considered to be the most important book of courtly love *(see p142)* in France.

Northwest of the town on the D955 is the enormous prehistoric dolmen Pierre de la Fée, or Fairy Stone *(see p39)*.

St Hermentaire slaying the dragon

🏛 **Musée des Arts et Traditions Populaires de Moyenne Provence**
15 rue Joseph-Roumanille. 📞 04 94 47 05 72. ◻ Tue–Sat, Sun pm. ⬤ public hols. 📷
🏛 **Musée Municipal**
9 rue de la République. 📞 04 94 47 28 80. ◻ Mon pm–Sat. ⬤ public hols. ♿

Pierre de la Fée, the giant dolmen outside Draguignan

Les Arcs ⑧

Road map D4. 🏘 *4,750.* 🚌 🚉
ℹ *place du Général de Gaulle (04 94 73 37 30).* 🛒 *Thu.*

WINE CENTRE for the Côtes de Provence *(see p109)*, Les Arcs has a medieval quarter, Le Parage, based around the 13th-century Château de Villeneuve. The **Eglise St-Jean-Baptiste** (1850), in the rue de la République, contains a screen by Louis Bréa (1501) and a mechanical crib.

East of Les Arcs on the D91 is the 11th-century Abbaye de Ste-Roseline, which was named after Roseline de Ville-neuve, daughter of the hard-hearted Arnaud de Villeneuve, Baron of Arcs. Local legend has it that when Roseline was stopped by her father while taking food to the poor, her provisions turned miraculously into roses. She entered the abbey in 1300 and later became its abbess.

The renovated Romanesque **Chapelle Ste-Roseline** contains the well-preserved body of the saint in a glass shrine. There is also an abundance of Renaissance and Baroque detail, and a celebrated Chagall mosaic *(see p25)*.

🔒 **Chapelle Ste-Roseline**
Route Ste-Roseline, between Muy and La Motte. ◻ Tue–Sun pm. ♿

Mosaic by Marc Chagall (1887–1985) in the Chapelle Ste-Roseline

Lorgues **9**

Road map D4. 7,500. pl
d'Entrechaux (04 94 73 92 37). Tue.

Nestling on a slope beneath
oak and pine woodland,
Lorgues is surrounded by vineyards and olive groves. Its old
town was fortified in the 12th
century. Today, two 14th-cen-
tury gates and city wall remains
can be seen. The town centre's
handsome square is shaded by
a large plane tree. Lorgues has
a grand array of 18th-century
municipal buildings and monuments and one of the longest
plane-tree avenues in France.
   In the centre of town is the
stately **Collégiale St-Martin**,
consecrated in 1788. Its organ,
dating from 1857, is the finest
example of the work of the
Augustin Zeiger factory, Lyon.
Also on display is a marble
Virgin and Child (1694) which
came from the Abbaye du
Thoronet and is attributed to
the school of Pierre Puget.

Abbaye du Thoronet **10**

Road map D4. 83340 Le Thoronet.
04 94 60 43 90. daily. 1
Jan, 1 May, 1 & 11 Nov, 25 Dec.

Founded in 1146, Le Thoronet was the first Cistercian
building in Provence. Lost in
deep woodland, it occupies a
typically remote site. Along

**Graceful cloisters on the north
side of the Abbaye du Thoronet**

with the two Romanesque
abbeys of Sénanque (see p164)
and Silvacane (see p147), it is
known as one of the three
"Cistercian sisters" of Provence.
   The cool geometry of the
church, cloister, dormitory
and chapter house reflects the
austerity of Cistercian prin-
ciples. Only the belltower
breaks with the order's strict
building regulations: instead
of wood, it is made of stone,
to enable it to withstand the
strong Provençal winds.
   Dilapidated as early as the
15th century, the abbey was
finally abandoned in 1791. In
common with many medieval
Provençal buildings, its restoration was instigated by Prosper
Mérimée, Romantic novelist
and Napoleon III's Inspector
of Historic Monuments, who
visited in 1834.
   Just beside the abbey is the
modern Monastère de Beth-
léem, home to some 20 silent
Cistercian nuns whose handi-
crafts are on sale in a shop.

Côtes de Provence Tour **11**

The côtes de provence wine-growing
region reaches from the Haut Var to
the coast. Dozens of roadside vineyards offer tastings and a chance to
buy. This rural route suggests a few
accessible and well-regarded producers,
starting at the Maison des Vins in Les
Arcs. Here you can find out about local wines,
plot your own route, buy wine from the producers, and even book to stay at a vineyard.
The tour passes a few interesting towns
en route. For more information on the
region's wines, see pages 206–7.

TIPS FOR DRIVERS

Tour length: 100 km (62 miles).
Stopping-off points: The
Maison des Vins should be your
first stopping point – it is open all
day and has a restaurant. Around
the route motorists should have
no difficulty in spotting places to
stop and sample, though many of
the wine producers close between
noon and 2pm. The Lac de
Carcès makes a good place for a
picnic. (See also pp242–3.)

Carcès 5
As you head north, the Lac de
Carcès is on the left in a steep
valley. The town's castle remains
and gardens are worth seeing.

Entrecasteaux 6
From Entrecasteaux, dominated
by its huge 17th-century
château, follow signs for
Les Saignes to find
Château Mentone.

les Saignes

CHATEAU
MENTONE

D50

D31

⑥

D562

Argens

D562

⑤

D13

DOMAINE
DE L'ABBAYE

D17

D79

④

Le Thoronet 4
The Domaine de l'Abbaye
vineyard is named after Le
Thoronet's beautiful abbey.

D13

KEY

Tour route

Other roads

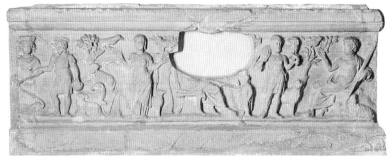

La Gayole sarcophagus, dating from the 2nd or 3rd century, in the Musée du Pays Brignolais

Brignoles ⑫

Road map D4. 🏘 12,500.
🚉 Carrefour de l'Europe (04 94 72
04 21). 🅿 Wed, Sat.

Bauxite mines have stained
the Brignoles countryside
red: vital to the region's econ-
omy, over a million tonnes of
metal are mined here annually.
The medieval town remains
above it all, quiet and empty
for most of the year. An

unexpected delight is the
Musée du Pays Brignolais in
a 12th-century castle that was
built as a summer retreat for
the Counts of Provence. The
eclectic collection includes La
Gayole marble sarcophagus,
which is carved with images
in both the pagan and Christian traditions; a boat made of
cement designed by J Lambot
(1814–87), who gave the
world reinforced concrete; and
a collection of votive offerings.

St Louis, bishop of Toulouse
and patron of Brignoles, was
born in a palace beside the
Eglise St-Sauveur in 1274. The
church has a 12th-century portico and a side entrance in the
rue Grand Escalier where steps
lead to the Carami river.

🏛 **Musée du Pays Brignolais**
Palais des Comtes de Provence. 🄲 04
94 69 45 18. 🕐 Wed–Sun. ● 1
Jan, Easter, 1 May, 1 Nov, 25 Dec. 🈺

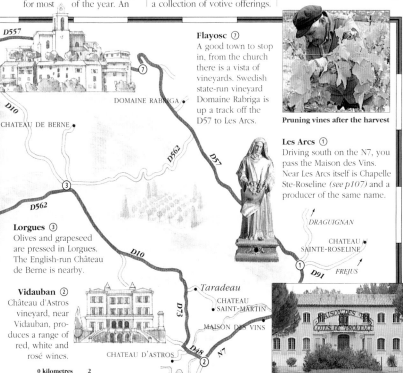

Flayosc ⑦
A good town to stop
in, from the church
there is a vista of
vineyards. Swedish
state-run vineyard
Domaine Rabriga is
up a track off the
D57 to Les Arcs.

DOMAINE RABRIGA

D557

D10

CHATEAU DE BERNE

D562

③

D562

Lorgues ③
Olives and grapeseed
are pressed in Lorgues.
The English-run Château
de Berne is nearby.

D10

Vidauban ②
Château d'Astros
vineyard, near
Vidauban, pro-
duces a range of
red, white and
rosé wines.

CHATEAU D'ASTROS

Taradeau

CHATEAU
SAINT-MARTIN

MAISON DES VINS

D73

D48

N7

②

Pruning vines after the harvest

Les Arcs ①
Driving south on the N7, you
pass the Maison des Vins.
Near Les Arcs itself is Chapelle
Ste-Roseline (see p107) and a
producer of the same name.

DRAGUIGNAN

CHATEAU
SAINTE-ROSELINE

①

D91 FREJUS

Maison des Vins near Les Arcs

0 kilometres   2

0 miles   2

St-Maximin-la-Ste-Baume ⓭

Surrounded by hills and vineyards, St-Maximin-la-Ste-Baume is dominated by the basilica Ste-Marie-Madeleine and its attached monastery. According to legend, the basilica was built on the site of the tombs of St Mary Magdalene and of St Maximin, martyred first bishop of Aix *(see pp148–9)*. The saints' remains, hidden from the Saracens *(see pp42–3)*, were rediscovered in 1279. The building, started 16 years later by Charles II, Count of Provence, is the region's finest example of Gothic architecture.

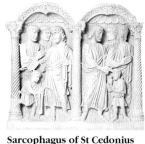

Sarcophagus of St Cedonius
This is one of four 4th-century saints' sarcophagi in the crypt, which was once the burial vault of a Roman villa.

★ Relics of St Mary Magdalene
This bronze gilt reliquary (1860) holds the skull of St Mary Magdalene. Pilgrim popes and princes took away other parts of her body.

Stairs to crypt

The apse
was completed in the early 14th century; a staircase tower has become the belfry.

★ Ronzen's Retable *(1520)*
François Ronzen's wood retable and surrounding panels include the first picture of the Papal Palace in Avignon (pp44–5).

★ Organ
One of the finest in France, with some 3,000 pipes, the organ was made in 1773 by Jean-Esprit Isnard. Napoleon's brother Lucien saved it in the Revolution by having the Marseillaise played on it whenever a visiting official arrived.

Basilica Entrance
The western side of the basilica has two matching wooden doors. They feature studied carving that contrasts sharply with the surrounding façade, which appears to have been crudely chopped off. When work stopped on the building in 1532, this part was left unfinished.

VISITORS' CHECKLIST

Road map D4. Place de l'Hôtel de Ville. 🕿 *04 94 59 84 59.*
Basilica ☐ *9am–6pm daily.*
🕆 *10:30am Sun.*
🖸 ⛔
Monastery ☐ *9am–6pm daily.*
🚫

Hôtel de Ville
The town hall is in the pilgrims' hostelry. It adjoins the refectory and chapel of the Royal Monastery.

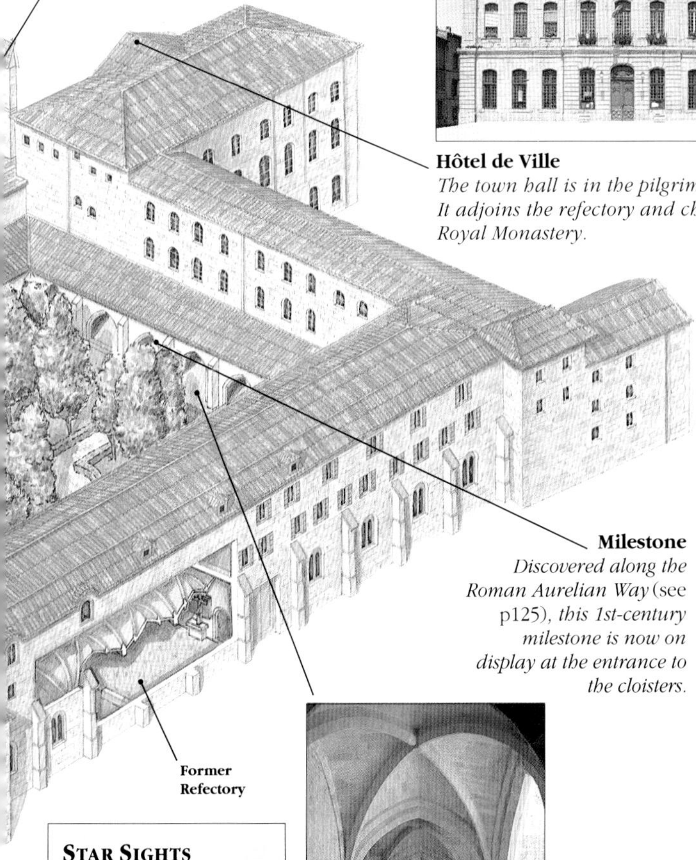

Milestone
Discovered along the Roman Aurelian Way (see p125), this 1st-century milestone is now on display at the entrance to the cloisters.

Former Refectory

STAR SIGHTS

★ **Relics of St Mary Magdalene**

★ **Organ**

★ **Ronzen's Retable**

Cloisters
The cloisters are at the centre of the Royal Monastery, so called because the French kings were its priors. The monks left in 1959 and it is now a cultural centre.

Boats in the colourful, palm-fringed harbour at Sanary-sur-Mer

Bandol ⓮

Road map C4. 🏛 *7,500.* 🚌 🚉
🛈 *Pavillon du Tourisme, allée Vivien
(04 94 29 41 35).* 🛒 *Tue.*

THIS CHEERFUL RESORT has a
tree-lined promenade,
casino, large yachting harbour
and tuna-fishing boats for
hire. Tucked away
in a bay, the shelter
offered by the en-
circling hills makes
for excellent grape-
growing conditions.
Indeed, Bandol has
produced superb
wines since 600 BC.
Outside town, the
**Jardin Exotique
et Zoo de Sanary-
Bandol** contains wildlife and
greenhouses of tropical plants.

Bandol wine label

**⚘ Jardin Exotique et Zoo
de Sanary-Bandol**
Quartier Pont-d'Aran. ☎ *04 94 29 40
38.* ⭘ *Mon–Sat, Sun pm.* 🚫 ♿

Sanary-sur-Mer ⓯

Road map C4. 🏛 *18,000.* 🚌
Ollioules-Sanary. 🚉 🛈 *Maison du
Tourisme, Jardins-de-la-Ville (04 94 74
01 04).* 🛒 *Wed.*

IN THE AGREEABLE, clear blue
waters of Sanary-sur-Mer,
the diver Jacques Cousteau's
experiments to develop the
modern aqualung took place.
Diving and fishing (mainly for
tuna and swordfish) are still
popular pursuits in this delightful resort, where rows of pink
and white houses line the bay.
Its name derives loosely from
St-Nazaire; the lovely local
19th-century church took the
saint's name in its entirety.
   Dating from about
1300, the landmark
medieval tower in
the town still con-
tains the cannon
that saw off an
Anglo-Sardinian
fleet in 1707. It is
now part of a hotel.
   Compact and con-
tained, Sanary-sur-
Mer has enticed
visitors for many years. Once
the home of the British writer
Aldous Huxley (1894–1963), it
was a haven between the wars
for innumerable other authors.
Bertolt Brecht (1898–1956)
and his compatriot Thomas
Mann (1875–1955) both fled
here from Nazi Germany.
   To the east of Sanary, the
coast becomes dramatic and
rocky. By the peninsula's extremity at the Cap Sicié is the
Notre-Dame-du-Mai chapel,
which was built in the 16th
century. A pilgrimage destination full of votive offerings, its
stepped approach offers a
wonderful panorama over the
coast and surrounding hills.

Toulon ⓰

Road map D4. 🏛 *172,000.* ✈ 🚌
🚌 🚢 🛈 *pl Raimu (04 94 18 53 00).*
🛒 *Tue–Sun.*

TUCKED INTO A FINE natural
harbour, Toulon is home to
France's Mediterranean fleet.
In the old town, or along the
quays of the Darse Vieille, the
matelots and the bars reinforce
the maritime connection.
   In Roman times, Toulon was
renowned for its sea snails
(*murex*) which, when boiled,
produced an imperial-quality
purple dye. During the reign
of Louis XIV, Pierre Puget
(1620–94) was in charge of
the port's decoration. Two of
his best-known works now
support the town-hall balcony.

**Ornate Baroque entrance to the
Musée de la Marine**

These are *Strength* and *Tiredness*, his 1657 carved marble figures of Atlantes.

The port was extensively damaged in World War II by the Allies and Nazis. Today it has a large opera house and several interesting museums and much of the town under restoration. A colourful flower and vegetable market takes place in the mornings (except Monday) in cours Lafayette.

🏛 Musée de la Marine

Place Monsenergue. 04 94 02 10 61. Apr–Sep: daily; Oct–Mar: Wed– Mon. 1 Jan, 1 May, Nov, 25 Dec.

The museum's grand entrance is decorated with imposing statues of Mars and Bellona. It was once the gateway to the 17th-century city arsenal. This stretched for more than 240 ha (595 acres) behind it.

Inside, the museum boasts two vast model galleons, *La Sultane* (1765) and *Duquesne* (1790), used for training. There is also a model of Barbarossa's galley, which harried Provence in 1543. Some figureheads and ships' prows are on show, as are two wooden figures that were carved by Pierre Puget.

🏛 Musée d'Art de Toulon

113 bd du Maréchal Leclerc. 04 94 93 15 54. daily pm only. public hols. limited.

A permanent collection of traditional and contemporary Provençal paintings makes up the core of this small museum. Works by international artists are often included in the first-floor temporary exhibitions.

🏛 Musée du Vieux Toulon

69 cours Lafayette. 04 94 92 29 23. Mon–Sat pm only. Sun, public hols.

This quaint museum features the young Napoleon and his

endeavours in the defence of Toulon, as well as old weapons and a number of historical sketches by Puget.

🕌 Cathédrale Ste-Marie-Majeure

Place de la Cathédrale. daily.

Lying directly inland from the town hall in the Darse Vieille is the city's 11th-century cathedral. It was treated to a Classical face-lift and extended during the 17th century.

Inside, there are works by Puget and Jean Baptiste Van Loo (1684–1745) as well as a spectacular Baroque altar.

Place Victor Hugo and the opera house in Toulon

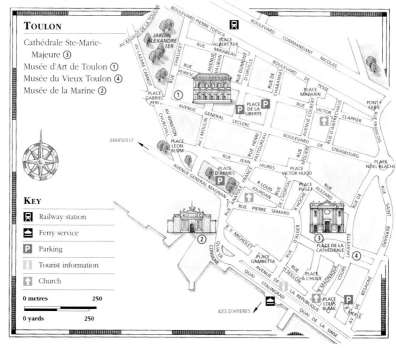

TOULON

Cathédrale Ste-Marie-
   Majeure ③
Musée d'Art de Toulon ①
Musée du Vieux Toulon ④
Musée de la Marine ②

KEY

🚉 Railway station

⛴ Ferry service

🅿 Parking

ℹ Tourist information

✝ Church

0 metres   250
0 yards   250

Iles d'Hyères ⑰

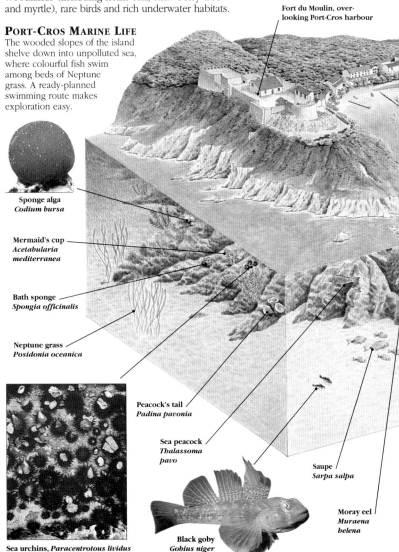

Tʜᴇ ɪʟᴇs ᴅ'ʜʏᴇʀᴇs are three unspoilt islands, found 10 km (6 miles) off the Var coast – Porquerolles, Le Levant and Port-Cros. Their history has been chequered due to their important strategic position: occupiers have included Greeks, Romans and Saracens, as well as ruthless pirates. Today the French Navy uses much of Le Levant. Porquerolles, the largest island, is partly cultivated with vineyards, but also has expanses of pine forest and *maquis*. Port-Cros has been a national park since 1963, protected for its woodlands (including holm oak, strawberry tree and myrtle), rare birds and rich underwater habitats.

Bottle of the rare Côte des Iles wine

LOCATOR MAP

Fort du Moulin, over-looking Port-Cros harbour

PORT-CROS MARINE LIFE

The wooded slopes of the island shelve down into unpolluted sea, where colourful fish swim among beds of Neptune grass. A ready-planned swimming route makes exploration easy.

Sponge alga
Codium bursa

Mermaid's cup
Acetabularia mediterranea

Bath sponge
Spongia officinalis

Neptune grass
Posidonia oceanica

Peacock's tail
Padina pavonia

Sea peacock
Thalassoma pavo

Saupe
Sarpa salpa

Moray eel
Muraena helena

Sea urchins, *Paracentrotous lividus*

Black goby
Gobius niger

Port-Cros Harbour
The tiny, palm-fringed harbour and village of Port-Cros nestle in a sheltered bay to the northwest of the island.

VISITORS' CHECKLIST

Road map D5. ✈ Toulon-Hyères. 🚉 Hyères. 🚌 Hyères. ⛴ from Hyères (Tour Fondu) to Porquerolles daily (every 30 mins in summer); from Hyères and Le Lavandou to Port-Cros and Le Levant daily (Nov–Mar: 3–4 times a week). ℹ Porquerolles (04 94 58 33 76).

Hyères ⑱

Road map D4. 🏘 52,000. ✈ Toulon-Hyères. 🚉 🚌 ⛴ ℹ rotonde Jean Salusse, av de Belgique (04 94 65 18 55). 🛒 Tue, Thu, Sat.

H YÈRES IS ONE of the most agreeable towns on the Côte d'Azur, and the oldest of the south of France winter resorts. The town lies at the centre of well-cultivated land that provides fresh fruit and vegetables all year. It has three leisure ports, 35 km (22 miles) of sandy beach and a peninsula facing the Iles d'Hyères.

The new town, laid out in the 19th century, was called Hyères-les-Palmiers. A palm-growing industry was established here in 1867, soon becoming the largest in Europe. The industry is still important and hundreds of palms line the new town boulevards.

Hyères' main church is **St-Louis** in place de la République just outside the old town. Romanesque and Provençal Gothic, it was completed in 1248. From place Massillon, rue St-Paul leads past the 11th-century **Eglise St-Paul**, full of 17th-century ex-votos. The road continues to the ruined 12th-century Château St-Bernard which has good views. In the gardens is the Cubist-inspired **Villa de Noailles** (1924), built by Robert Mallet-Stevens for the Vicomte de Noailles (tour at 4:30pm Friday). The **Jardins Olbius Riquier** has a zoo and exotic plants.

🌿 Jardins Olbius Riquier
Av Amboise Thomas. ⬤ daily. ♿

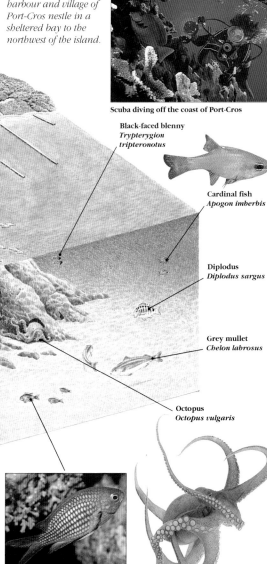

Scuba diving off the coast of Port-Cros

Black-faced blenny
Trypterygion tripteronotus

Cardinal fish
Apogon imberbis

Diplodus
Diplodus sargus

Grey mullet
Chelon labrosus

Octopus
Octopus vulgaris

Damsel fish, *Chromis chromis*

Moorish architecture inspired by the many palms in Hyères

Beach at Le Lavandou overlooked by hotels and exclusive villas

Le Lavandou ⑲

Road map D4. 🏘 5,200. 🚌 🚢
🛈 quai Gabriel Péri (04 94 71 00 61).
🛒 Thu.

AN EMBARKATION PORT for the nearby Iles d'Hyères, Le Lavandou is a fishing village now almost entirely given over to tourism. This is due mostly to its good, sandy stretch of beach, which is backed by a long promenade. It is a centre for water sports and offers moorings for luxury yachts. Full of bars, nightclubs and restaurants, Le Lavandou is a favourite of younger, less well-heeled visitors.

It takes its name not from the lavender fields in the surrounding hills, but from a *lavoir* (wash-house) depicted in a painting of the town by Charles Ginoux dating from 1736. During the last century, when it was no more than a fishing village, Le Lavandou was popular with artists. The most famous, though not so well known outside France, was Ernest Reyer (1823–99), a composer and music critic after whom the main square is named. From this square there is a view over the Iles de Levant and Port-Cros.

Much of nearby Cap Bénat is in the hands of the military and the French president has a summer residence there.

Bormes-les-Mimosas ⑳

Road map D4. 🏘 5,100. 🚌
🛈 1 place Gambetta (04 94 01 38 38).
🛒 Wed.

BORMES IS A MEDIEVAL hill village on the edge of the Dom Forest, bathed in the scent of oleander and eucalyptus and topped with a

Rue Rompi-Cuou, one of the steep, old streets in Bormes-les-Mimosas

Tour of the Massif des Maures ㉑

THE ANCIENT MOUNTAIN RANGE of Maures takes its name from the Provençal *maouro*, meaning dark or gloomy, for the Massif is carpeted in sweet chestnuts, cork trees, oaks and pines with a deeply shaded undergrowth of myrrh and briar, though forest fires have reduced some of it to scrubland. Lying between Hyères and Fréjus, the Massif is nearly 60 km (40 miles) long and 30 km (18 miles) wide. This tour is a simple route that takes you through the wild and often deserted heart of the Massif, through dramatic countryside ranging from flat valley floors covered in cork trees to deep valleys and lofty peaks. A few of the roads are steep and winding.

Gonfaron

Village des Tortues ③
Keep bearing left on the D75 for the "Tortoise Village", which has saved France's only remaining species of wild tortoise.

Notre-Dame-des-Anges ④
Beside this priory and its chapel full of votive offerings, is the highest summit in the Massif at 780 m (2,559 ft).

← TOULON

Collobrières ⑤
This riverside village with its hump-backed bridge is famed for its *marrons glacés*. Nearby forests supply bottle corks.

TIPS FOR DRIVERS

Tour length: 75 km (47 miles).
Stopping-off points: Collobrières is a pleasant lunchtime stop. Allow time to visit Chartreuse de la Verne (04 94 48 08 00 for opening times), which is reached up narrow, steep roads. (See also pp242–3.)

Farm workers at Collobrières

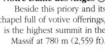

flower-lined walk around its castle. "Les Mimosas" was not added to its name until 1968, a century after the plant was first introduced to the south of France from Mexico. A pretty and popular village, Bormes serves a marina of more than 800 berths. Plummeting streets such as Rompi-Cuou ("bottom-breaker") lead to lively cafés and good coastal views.

A statue of St Francis di Paola stands in front of the attractive 16th-century **Chapelle St-François**, commemorating the saint's timely arrival during a plague outbreak in 1481. The Neo-Romanesque church of **St-Trophyme** has modern (1980) paintings by Alain Nonn. The works of local painter Jean-Charles Cazin (1841–1901) are well represented in the **Musée Arts et Histoire**.

🏛 **Musée Arts et Histoire**
103 rue Carnot. **📞** 04 94 05 34 50. ⭕ Sun–Fri. 🔴 Tue pm, public hols. ♿

Ramatuelle village enclosed by wooded slopes and vineyards

Ramatuelle ㉒

Road map E4. 🏘 1,950. 🚌 ℹ️ pl de l' Ormeau (04 94 79 26 04). 🔷 Thu & Sun.

SURROUNDED BY VINEYARDS, this attractive hilltop village was called "God's Gift" (Rahmatu 'llah) by the Saracens who left two gates, now well-restored, in their fortifications, and a penchant for figs. It is one of three particularly quaint villages on the St-Tropez peninsula (La Croix-Valmer and Gassin are the others). Gérard Philipe (1922–59), the leading young French actor during the 1950s, is buried here. Vibrant theatre and jazz festivals take place in the village annually.

Nearby, Moulins de Paillas, at 248 m (814 ft), offers a panorama. The peninsula ends 5 km (3 miles) east of Ramatuelle at Cap Camarat, where there is a lighthouse and coast views.

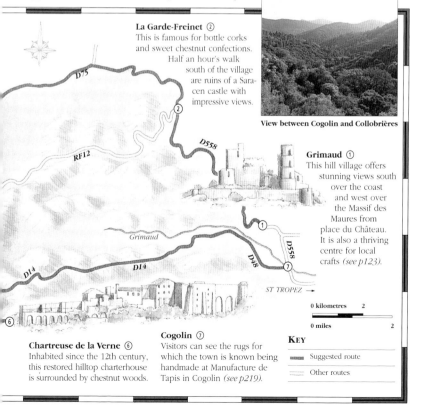

La Garde-Freinet ②
This is famous for bottle corks and sweet chestnut confections. Half an hour's walk south of the village are ruins of a Saracen castle with impressive views.

View between Cogolin and Collobrières

Grimaud ①
This hill village offers stunning views south over the coast and west over the Massif des Maures from place du Château. It is also a thriving centre for local crafts (see p123).

ST TROPEZ →

D75

RF12

D558

Grimaud

D14

D14

D558

D48

Chartreuse de la Verne ⑥
Inhabited since the 12th century, this restored hilltop charterhouse is surrounded by chestnut woods.

Cogolin ⑦
Visitors can see the rugs for which the town is known being handmade at Manufacture de Tapis in Cogolin (see p219).

0 kilometres   2
0 miles   2

KEY

▬▬▬ Suggested route
--- --- Other routes

Street-by-Street: St-Tropez ㉙

St Torpès in his boat

C LUSTERED AROUND the old port and nearby beaches, the centre of St-Tropez, partly rebuilt in its original style after World War II *(see p52)*, is full of fishermen's houses. In the port itself, traditional fishing boats are still to be seen moored side-by-side with sleek luxury cruisers of all shapes and sizes. Behind the port-side cafés of the quai Jean-Jaurès, the narrow, bustling streets are packed with boutiques and restaurants. The town is overlooked by the church's wrought-iron belltower in the centre and the citadel just outside.

La Fontanette beach leads to a coastal walk with views over Ste-Maxime.

The Ponche quarter is a comparatively quiet and unspoiled area of St-Tropez.

Tour Vieille

The Port de Pêche
The Tour Vieille separates this port, still used by fishing boats, from La Glaye next door.

Place de la Ponche

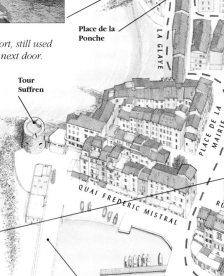

RUE

RUE DE LA PONCHE

LA GLAYE

PLACE DE LA MAIRIE

RUE SIBILLE

RUE DU CEPOUN

Tour Suffren

QUAI FREDERIC MISTRAL

QUAI JEAN

St-Tropez Old Town
Fashionable motorcyclists pose along the narrow streets of central St-Tropez.

Môle Jean Réveille

★ Quai Jean-Jaurès
The attractively painted houses and packed cafés lining the quay have enticed visitors and inspired artists for over a century.

**View from the Ramparts
of the Citadel**
*The hilltop citadel, situated
east of St-Tropez, offers
spectacular views over
the rooftops of the
town and beyond.*

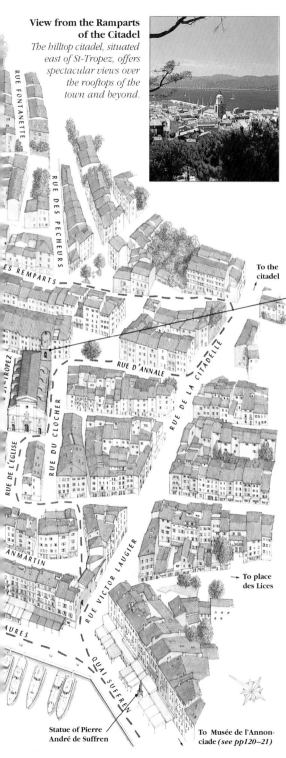

VISITORS' CHECKLIST

Road map E4. 🚗 *5,750.*
🚌 *av 8 mai 1945 (04 94 97 88
51).* ℹ️ *quai Jean-Jaurès (04 94
97 45 21).* 🛒 *Tue & Sat.* 🎉
Bravades: 16–18 May, 15 Jun.

★ Eglise de St-Tropez
*The bust of St Torpès, kept in
the church, is paraded in
the May* bravade *(see p34).*

To the
citadel

RUE FONTANETTE

RUE DES PECHEURS

ES REMPARTS

RUE D'ANNALE

RUE DE LA CITADELLE

RUE DU CLOCHER

RUE DE L'EGLISE

TROPEZ

ANMARTIN

RUE VICTOR LAUGIER

AURES

QUAI SUFFREN

**Open Window on the Har-
bour at St-Tropez** *(1925–6)*
*Charles Camoin's painting
is now in the Annonciade.*

To place
des Lices

KEY

– – – Suggested route

0 metres   50

0 yards   50

**Statue of Pierre
André de Suffren**

To Musée de l'Annon-
ciade *(see pp120–21)*

STAR SIGHTS

★ **Quai Jean-Jaurès**

★ **Eglise de St-Tropez**

Musée de l'Annonciade

THIS INNOVATIVE GALLERY opened in 1955 in the former Chapelle de l'Annonciade by the old port in St-Tropez. Built in 1568, the building was converted into a museum by architect Louis Süe (1875–1968), funded by art collector Georges Grammont. The collection began with the paintings of Paul Signac and the other artists who followed him to St-Tropez, and now contains many stunning Post-Impressionist works from the late 19th and early 20th centuries. In 1961, 65 valuable works were stolen from the museum, but were recovered and restored a year later.

Le Rameur *(1914)*
This bold Cubist work is by Roger de la Fresnaye.

★ **St-Tropez, la Place des Lices et le Café des Arts**
This painting (1925) is one of several that Charles Camoin made of St-Tropez's famous square after he followed Paul Signac and settled in the town.

★ **L'Orage** *(1895)*
Paul Signac's atmospheric work vividly depicts the onset of a storm in St-Tropez harbour.

Temporary exhibition room

GALLERY GUIDE
Exhibition space is too limited for all works to be permanently on view, so the display changes frequently. An exhibition room holds temporary displays linked with the permanent collection.

KEY TO FLOORPLAN

☐	Ground floor
☐	Mezzanine
☐	First floor
☐	Non-exhibition space

★ **Nu Devant la Cheminée** *(1919)*
In this warm, intimate picture, characteristic of the artist, Pierre Bonnard uses delicate tones within a limited colour range to create an effect of light and shade.

Le Temps de l'Harmonie
*In this study (1893–5)
for a larger work, Paul
Signac departs from his
more usual Pointillist
technique, using simple,
fluid lines.*

VISITORS' CHECKLIST

Place Grammont, St-Tropez. 04
94 97 04 01. 10am– noon,
2–6pm (Jun–Sep: 3–7pm) Wed–
Mon . 1 Jan, Ascension, 1 May,
Nov, 25 Dec.

Balcony

La Nymphe *(1930)
This Classically
influenced bronze
sculpture, one of several
excellent works by
Aristide Maillol in
the Annonciade, is a
graceful evocation of
ideal beauty.*

The sculpture garden,
currently undergoing
renovation, contains
several modern works
by François Stahly.

Deauville, le Champ de Courses
*Raoul Dufy's racecourse, painted in
1928, is typical of his interest in
glamorous subjects.*

18th-century
main entrance

STAR PAINTINGS

★ **St-Tropez, la Place
des Lices et le Café
des Arts by Charles
Camoin**

★ **L'Orage by Paul
Signac**

★ **Nu Devant la
Cheminée by Pierre
Bonnard**

Exploring St-Tropez

THIS EXCEPTIONAL RESORT has become a victim of its own charms – the August high season attracts about 80,000 hell-bent hedonists. Following their departure, however, the genuine, peaceful nature of the village still shines through. Surrounded by slopes covered with vineyards, looking out over the millpond bay of Golfe St-Tropez and protected by an imposing citadel, its situation remains inviolate. It does, however, face the northerly Mistral which thunders through the town for much of the winter, ensuring it remains a summer haunt.

Tower of the Eglise de St-Tropez

Paintings by local artists for sale on the quai Jean-Jaurès

A glimpse of the town

Activity is centred north of the Musée de l'Annonciade, beside the little port. Here, local artists sell their wares and people pass the time of day in the Café de Paris, le Gorille or Senequier *(see p217)*.

The pretty, pastel-painted houses lining the quai Jean-Jaurès can be viewed at their best from the harbour breakwater, the Môle Jean Réveille. These buildings were among the town's sights that inspired Paul Signac (1863–1935) to start painting in St-Tropez. Many other artists followed, all well represented in the Annonciade *(see pp120–21)*.

The old town, just behind the waterfront, is flagged by the tower of the Eglise de St-Tropez. To its north lies the Hôtel de Ville and the Tour Suffren, residence of the former local lords. Admiral Pierre André de Suffren (1726–88), "terror of the English", is commemorated by a statue on the quay. Behind the quai Suffren is the place des Lices, a large square crowded with cafés, where locals play *boules*.

Out to the east, beyond the old Ponche quarter and the unspoiled fishing port nearby, lies the 16th-century hexagonal citadel. With fine views from the ramparts, it contains the Musée Naval de St-Tropez. Further east, Brigitte Bardot still lives in La Madrague. *And God Created Woman*, the 1959 film shot in St-Tropez starring Bardot, started the celebrity rush to the town.

🏛 Musée de l'Annonciade
See pp120–21.

🔒 Eglise de St-Tropez
Rue de l'Eglise. ⭕ *daily.*
This 19th-century Baroque church contains several busts of saints, including one of St Torpès after whom St-Tropez is named. Beheaded by the Romans for his Christianity, his body was put in a boat with a dog and a cockerel and the boat landed here in AD 68. Every year, the saint's bust is carried through the town in the 16 May *bravade*.

The hilltop citadel east of St-Tropez

🏛 Musée Naval de St-Tropez
Forteresse. 📞 04 94 97 59 43.
⭕ *Nov, public hols.* ⭕ *Wed–Mon.*
📷 &
Located in the dungeon of the citadel keep, to the east of the town, the collection includes model ships, naval engravings and seascapes. Many of these illustrate the local and naval history and culture of St-Tropez, including the 1944 Allied landing *(see p53)*.

Among the more striking exhibits in the museum are an impressive reconstruction of a Greek galley, a pair of 16th-century Spanish cannons and a full-scale cross-section of a wartime torpedo.

Brigitte Bardot, St-Tropez' most famous resident, in 1973

Port-Grimaud ㉔

Road map E4. 🚗 *150.* 📧 🅱 🖥
*chemin communal (04 94 56 02 01 in
summer) or 1 bd des Aliziers, 83310
Grimaud (04 94 43 26 98).* 🚌 *Thu &
Sun.*

THIS NEWLY CREATED PORT was
dreamed up entirely by
the Alsace architect François
Spoerry (1912–98). In 1962 he
bought up the marshy delta
lands of the River Giscle west
of the Golfe St-Tropez. Four
years later, work began on a
mini-Venice of 2,500 canal-
side houses with moorings
covering 90 ha (222 acres).
There are now three "zones",
a marina and a beach. Its
church, **St-François-d'Assise**,
in the place d'Eglise, contains
some stained glass by Victor
Vasarély (1908–97) and offers
a sweeping view of the port
from the top of its tower.

The whole port is free of
traffic and the *coche d'eau*
offers a water-taxi service. As
one of France's major tourist
attractions, Port-Grimaud
brings in about one million
visitors a year.

Grimaud ㉕

Road map E4. 🚗 *3,300.* 📧 🅱 *1 bd
des Aliziers (04 94 43 26 98).* 🚌 *Thu.*

THE ANCIENT, FORTIFIED, traffic-
free *village perché (see
pp18–19)* of Grimaud is yet
another legacy of the ubiquitous Grimaldi family *(see p91),*
after which the village is
named. Gibelin de Grimaldi, a
doughty Genoese knight, was
rewarded with a fief here after

View of Port-Grimaud from the Eglise de St-François-d'Assise

helping William the Good of
Provence drive the Saracens
out of this part of France in
AD 973, after 83 years of occupation. The castle dates from
the 11th century and was
reduced to ruins under the
direction of Cardinal Richelieu
as punishment for the town's
Protestant leanings.

The view of the coast from
its heights made it an ideal
vantage point from which to
watch for further invasion.
This task was adopted in 1119
by the Knights Templar. These
were a clandestine military
and religious order of knights
founded during the First Crusade to defend Christians.

Their well-preserved **Maison
de Templiers**, closed to the
public, is one of the few surviving Templar buildings in
Provence. It stands in the rue
des Templiers, the town's
oldest street, which is lined
with arcades designed to be
battened down in case of
attack. In the same street is
the pure Romanesque 11th-
century church of St-Michel.

Ste-Maxime ㉖

Road map E4. 🚗 *12,000.* 📧 *St-
Raphaël, St Tropez.* 🅱 *promenade
Simon-Lorière (04 94 96 19 24).* 🚌 *Fri.*

Beach at Ste-Maxime

FACING ST-TROPEZ across the
neck of the Gulf, Ste-
Maxime is protected by hills.
Its year-round clientele
reaches saturation point in
summer. The attractions of
this smart resort are its port,
promenade, good sandy
beaches, watersports, nightlife, fairs and casino.

Ste-Maxime was once pro-
tected by the monks of Lérins,
who named the port after
their patron saint and put up
the defensive Tour Carrée des
Dames which now serves as
the **Musée des Traditions
Locales**. The church opposite
contains a 17th-century green
marble altar that was brought
from the former Carthusian
monastery of La Verne in the
Massif des Maures.

🏛 **Musée des Traditions
Locales**
Place des Aliziers. 📞 *04 94 96 70
30.* ⭕ *Wed–Mon.* ⬤ *1 May,
25 Dec.* 📷

Grimaud, dominated by the castle ruins

St-Raphaël ㉗

Road map E4. 🚶 *30,000.* 🚌 🚉
ℹ️ *rue Waldeck Rousseau (04 94 19 52 52).* 🅿️ *Tue–Sun.*

THIS STAID AND SENSIBLE family resort dates to Roman times when rich families came to stay at a spot near the modern seafront casino. Napoleon put the town on the map when he landed here in 1799 on his return from Egypt, and 15 years later when he left St-Raphaël for exile on Elba.

Popularity came when the Parisian satirical novelist Jean-Baptiste Karr (1808–90) publicized the town's delights. In the old part is the 12th-century church of St-Raphaël and the **Musée Archéologique**, which contains Greek amphorae and other underwater finds.

🏛 Musée Archéologique
Place de la Vieille-Eglise. 📞 *04 94 19 25 75.* ⏰ *Tue–Sat.* ⬤ *public hols.*
♿

Tourist poster of St-Raphaël from the 19th century

Massif de l'Esterel ㉘

Road map E4. 🚉 Nice. 🚌 🚉 *Agay, St-Raphaël.* ℹ️ *rue Waldeck Rousseau, St-Raphaël (04 94 19 52 52).*

THE ESTEREL, a mountainous volcanic mass, is a wilderness compared to the popular coast. Although it rises to no more than 620 m (2,050 ft), and a succession of fires have laid waste its forests, its innate ruggedness and the dramatic colours of its porphyry rocks remain intact. Until the middle of the last century it was a

Château at La Napoule, now the Musée Henry Clews

refuge for highwaymen and escaped prisoners from Toulon. Here, after being fêted on arrival in St Raphaël, Napoleon and his coach were robbed of all their valuables while they were on their way out of town heading towards Paris.

The north side of the massif is bounded by the N7 which runs through the Esterel Gap, following the Roman Aurelian way from Cannes to Fréjus. At the Testannier crossroads 11 km (7 miles) from Fréjus a road leads to Mont Vinaigre; the final 15 minutes of the journey must be made on foot. This is the highest point on the massif and there is a fine panorama from the Alps to the Massif des Maures.

On the seaward side of the massif the N98 from St-Raphaël twists along the top of startlingly red cliffs to Agay. This resort has the best anchorage on the coast. It is famous for its blue porphyry, from which the Romans cut columns for their Provençal monuments.

Round the bay is Pointe de Baumette where there is a memorial to French writer and World War II aviator, Antoine de St-Exupéry *(see p27).* The road continues to Anthéor and the Pointe de l'Observatoire. Just before here, a left turn leads to the circuit of the Cap Roux and Pic de l'Ours. The coast road continues through a series of resorts to La Napoule at the start of the Riviera. In La Napoule is a 14th-century château refurbished by American sculptor Henry Clews (1876–1937) who left work scattered about the estate forming the **Musée Henry Clews**.

The route leading inland to the Col Belle-Barbe from the coast passes on the right a turn to the 452-m (1483-ft) Pic du Cap Roux. An hour's walk to the top is rewarded by a sweeping coast view.

From the car park at Col Belle-Barbe, a path leads to the Mal Infernet, a dramatic ravine that concludes a 40-minute walk away at the Lac de l'Ecureuil. Continuing inland from Col Belle-Barbe over the Col du Mistral up to the Col des Trois Termes, the path then twists south to Col Notre-Dame. A 45-minute or so walk from here leads on to the dramatic Pic de l'Ours, which rises to 496 m (1,627 ft). Between here and the coast is the 323-m (1,060-ft) Pic d'Aurelle which also provides an impressive vista.

🏛 Musée Henry Clews
Château de la Napoule, bd Henry Clews. 📞 *04 93 49 95 05.* ⏰ *Mar–Nov: Wed–Mon pm only.* ♿

Remaining timber on the fire-ravaged Massif de l'Esterel

Fréjus

Road map E4. 🏙 *52,000.* 🚉 *St Raphaël.* 🚌 🛈 *325 rue Jean-Jaurès (04 94 51 83 83).* 🛒 *Wed & Sat.*

VISIBLY, THOUGH not ostentatiously, wealthy in history, Fréjus is one of the highlights of the coast. The oldest Roman city in Gaul, it was founded by Julius Caesar in 49 BC and greatly expanded by Augustus. Lying on the Aurelian way – a huge road built in the reign of Augustus from Rome to Arles – it covered 40 ha (100 acres), had a population of 30–40,000 and, as a port, was second in importance only to Marseille.

Although substantial sections of the Roman city were decimated by the Saracens in the 10th century, a few parts of their walls remain, including a tower of the western Porte des Gaules. The opposite eastern entrance, the Porte de Rome, marks one end of a 40-km (25-mile) aqueduct, the ruins of which amble alongside the N7 towards the Siagnole river

Mosaic in the Musée Archéologique in Fréjus

near Mons. Just to the north of here the remains of the semicircular, 1st-century Théâtre can be viewed. In their midst, performances are still held. The praetorium or Plateforme – military headquarters that formed the eastern citadel – lie to the south. North of the Porte des Gaules, on the road to Brignoles, stands the large 1st–2nd-century **Arènes**, built to hold 10,000 spectators and now used for bullfights.

The spectacular **Cathédrale St-Léonce et Cloître** houses a Musée Archéologique with finds from all around Fréjus. South of the town is the Butte St-Antoine citadel, which at one time overlooked the harbour. The canal connecting the harbour to the sea began silting up in the 10th century; by the 18th century it was entirely filled in, forming Fréjus-Plage. A little over 2 km (1 mile) from the town's centre, this modern resort stretches along a sandy beach towards St-Raphaël. A surprising Fréjus monument is

Well in the centre of the Cathedral cloisters at Fréjus

a Buddhist Pagoda about 2 km (1 mile) north of the Arènes. Built in 1919, it is a sad memorial to those Vietnamese who died while they were serving in the French army during the horrors of World War I.

🏛 **Arènes de Fréjus**
Rue Vadon. 📞 04 94 51 34 31. 🕐 Wed–Mon. 🔴 1 Jan, 1 May, 25 & 31 Dec.

⛪ **Cathédrale St-Léonce et Cloître**
Place Formigé. 📞 04 94 51 26 30. 🕐 Apr–Sep: daily; Oct–Mar: Tue–Sun. 🔴 public hols. 🎫 cloisters. 🅿

CATHÉDRALE ST-LÉONCE ET CLOÎTRE
The fortified cathedral and the marble-columned cloister date from the 12th century, while the 5th-century baptistry is one of the oldest in France.

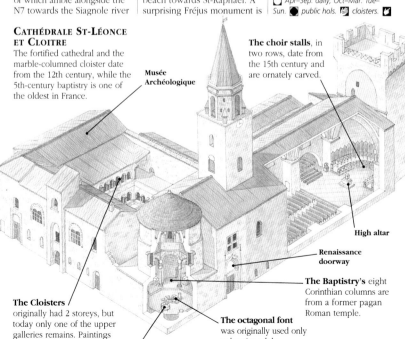

Musée Archéologique

The choir stalls, in two rows, date from the 15th century and are ornately carved.

High altar

Renaissance doorway

The Baptistry's eight Corinthian columns are from a former pagan Roman temple.

The Cloisters originally had 2 storeys, but today only one of the upper galleries remains. Paintings cover the ceilings.

The octagonal font was originally used only to baptize adults.

Earthenware basin

BOUCHES-DU-RHÔNE
AND NÎMES

THIS SOUTHWESTERN CORNER OF PROVENCE *has a feel that's unique in the region. It is the land of Van Gogh, brightly patterned materials and beaches of shifting sands. Its wildest point is the Camargue in the Rhône delta, a place of light and colour, lived in for centuries by gypsies and by cowboys who herd the wild horses and bulls.*

Many inland towns reflect the region's Greek and Roman past. The Greeks first settled in France in circa 600 BC and founded Marseille, now a cosmopolitan cultural centre and the country's second largest city. The Romans, who arrived after them, built the theatre at Arles and the amphitheatre at Nîmes, and left the remains of Classical houses at Glanum. The skeleton of a Roman aqueduct runs beween a spring at Uzès to a water tower at Nîmes, a great feat of engineering best seen at Pont du Gard.

"A race of eagles" is how Frédéric Mistral, the Provençal writer *(see p26)* described the Lords of Baux, bloodthirsty warriors who ruled in the Middle Ages from an extraordinary eyrie in Les Baux-en-Provence. This former fief was paradoxically famous as a Court of Love *(see pp142–3)* during the 13th century. Louis IX (Saint Louis) built the fortified city of Aigues-Mortes for the Crusaders. In the 15th century, Good King René *(see pp46–7)*, held his court in the castle of Tarascon and in Aix-en-Provence, the ancient capital of Provence. Aix's university, founded by René's father in 1409, is still the hub of this lively student town.

The area provides great walks and stunning scenery, particularly in the Alpilles and around Marseille. The films and books of Marcel Pagnol *(see 153)* and the stories of Daudet *(see p143)*, which have influenced perceptions of Provençal people and life, are set in this region. The Camargue maintains a unique collection of flora and fauna, providing, in addition to fine vistas, superb horse riding and birdwatching.

Produce on display in the colourful food market, Aix-en-Provence

◁ Joseph Sec's statue of Saul in Aix-en-Provence, made in 1792 in honour of the French Revolution

Exploring Bouches-du-Rhône and Nîmes

At the mouth of the Rhone lie the flat, wetland marshes and sand dunes of the Camargue wildlife reserve. Further inland, cities such as Aix-en-Provence, Arles and Nîmes are awash with ancient architecture. Northeast of Arles, the herb-covered chain of the Alpilles rises from the surrounding plains to the heady heights of Les Baux, and there are some stunning walks through the mountains. St-Rémy-de-Provence makes a good base for exploring the Alpilles. Popular coastal towns are Marseille and the scenic port of Cassis. A short car or boat trip away lie Les Calanques, deep, narrow inlets set between pine trees and white cliffs.

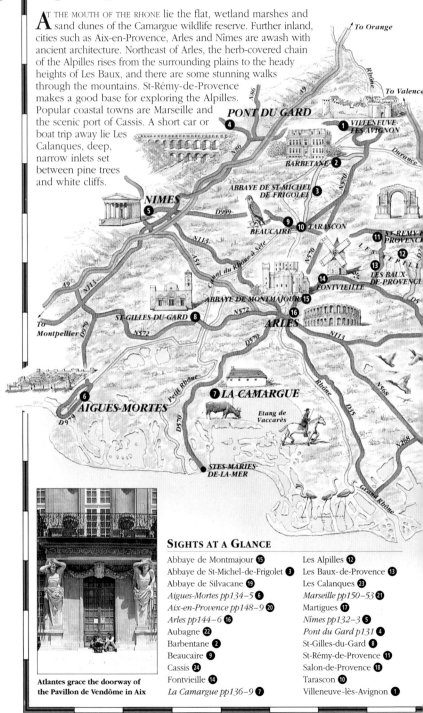

To Orange

To Valence

PONT DU GARD ④

VILLENEUVE-LES-AVIGNON ①

BARBENTANE ②

ABBAYE DE ST-MICHEL DE FRIGOLET ③

NIMES ⑤

BEAUCAIRE ⑨   ⑩ **TARASCON**

ST-RÉMY-PROVENCE ⑪

⑫

LES BAUX-DE-PROVENCE ⑬

FONTVIEILLE ⑭

ABBAYE DE MONTMAJOUR ⑮

ST-GILLES-DU-GARD ⑧

To Montpellier

⑯ **ARLES**

⑦ **LA CAMARGUE**

Etang de Vaccarès

AIGUES-MORTES ⑥

STES-MARIES-DE-LA-MER

Petit Rhône

Grand Rhône

Sights at a Glance

Abbaye de Montmajour ⑮
Abbaye de St-Michel-de-Frigolet ③
Abbaye de Silvacane ⑲
Aigues-Mortes pp134–5 ⑥
Aix-en-Provence pp148–9 ⑳
Arles pp144–6 ⑯
Aubagne ㉒
Barbentane ②
Beaucaire ⑨
Cassis ㉔
Fontvieille ⑭
La Camargue pp136–9 ⑦

Les Alpilles ⑫
Les Baux-de-Provence ⑬
Les Calanques ㉓
Marseille pp150–53 ㉑
Martigues ⑰
Nîmes pp132–3 ⑤
Pont du Gard p131 ④
St-Gilles-du-Gard ⑧
St-Rémy-de-Provence ⑪
Salon-de-Provence ⑱
Tarascon ⑩
Villeneuve-lès-Avignon ①

Atlantes grace the doorway of the Pavillon de Vendôme in Aix

View across the harbour of Fort St-Jean, Marseille

GETTING AROUND

If you have a car, the auto-routes are fast and bypass slow traffic in the towns. The A8 autoroute which leads along the Riviera meets the Paris–Marseille A7 Autoroute du Soleil 17 km (11 miles) west of Aix, while the A9 Languedocienne heads west through Nîmes towards Spain.

The main towns are all linked by trains and buses, though bus services tend to be poor outside towns. Arles and Aix-en-Provence make particularly good bases for getting around. Boat trips are organized from Arles and Stes-Maries-de-la-Mer in the Camargue, where a good way to see the countryside is to hire the native horses.

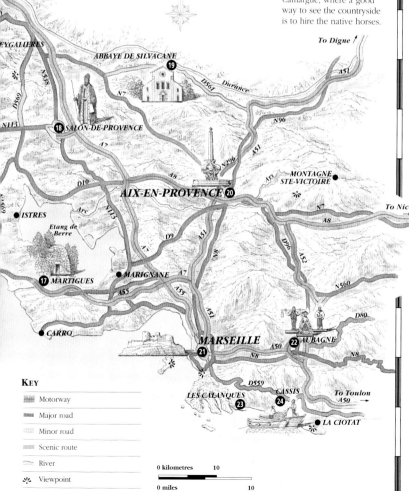

To Digne

ABBAYE DE SILVACANE ⑲

Durance

⑱ **SALON-DE-PROVENCE**

MONTAGNE STE-VICTOIRE

AIX-EN-PROVENCE ⑳

To Nice

● **ISTRES**

Etang de Berre

⑰ **MARTIGUES** ● **MARIGNANE**

● **CARRO**

MARSEILLE ㉑ ㉒ **AUBAGNE**

To Toulon

LES CALANQUES ㉓ ㉔ **CASSIS**

● **LA CIOTAT**

KEY

▬	Motorway
▬	Major road
▬	Minor road
▬	Scenic route
⌐	River
☼	Viewpoint

0 kilometres   10

0 miles   10

Part of the Chartreuse du Val-de-Bénédiction, Villeneuve

Villeneuve-lès-Avignon ❶

Road map B3. 🚶 12,500. 🚉 Avignon. 🚌 🚏 1 pl Charles David (04 90 25 61 33). 🛒 Thu.

THIS TOWN AROSE beside the Rhône, opposite Avignon (*see pp166–7*), and the connecting bridge, Pont St-Bénézet, was guarded by the **Tour de Philippe le Bel**, built in 1307. Its rooftop terrace, 176 steps up, gives a fine panorama of the papal city. Even better is the view from the two giant 40-m (130-ft) round towers at the entrance to the impressive 14th-century **Fort St-André**, which enclosed a small town, monastery and church.

Between these two bastions lies the 14th-century Eglise de Notre-Dame. In the **Musée Pierre de Luxembourg** is *The Coronation of the Virgin* (1453) by Enguerrand Quarton, widely regarded as the best work of the Avignon School.

This work was painted for the abbot of the **Chartreuse du Val-de-Bénédiction**, which was founded by Innocent VI, in 1356 and was once the largest charterhouse in France. There are three cloisters and a chapel dedicated to Innocent VI, decorated with frescoes by Giovanetti da Viterbo. Today it is used as a cultural centre for the area.

♣ **Fort St-André**
Villeneuve-lès-Avignon. 🎫 04 90 25 45 35. ⭕ daily. 🈲

🏛 **Musée Pierre de Luxembourg**
Rue de la République. 🎫 04 90 27 49 66. ⭕ mid-Jun–mid-Sep: daily; mid-Sep–mid-Jun: Tue–Sun. ● Feb, public hols. 🈲 &

⛪ **Chartreuse du Val-de-Bénédiction**
Rue de la République. 🎫 04 90 15 24 24. ⭕ daily. ● 1 Jan, 1 May, 1 & 11 Nov, 25 Dec. 🈲

Barbentane ❷

Road map B3. 🚶 3,300. 🚉 Avignon, Tarascon. 🚌 🚏 La Mairie (04 90 95 50 39).

MEMBERS OF AVIGNON's papal court liked to build summer houses in Barbentane, on the slopes beside the Rhône 10 km (6 miles) south of the city. One such was the handsome Renaissance Maison des Chevaliers with an arcaded gallery, opposite the 13th- to 15th-century Notre-Dame-de-Grace. Only the 40-m (130-ft) Tour Anglica remains of the town's 14th-century castle.

Just outside the medieval quarter is the **Château de Barbentane**, a finely decorated Italianate mansion, built in 1674 by the Barbentane aristocracy who still own it.

Close to the town is the **Provence Orchidée**, an important orchid-growing centre.

♣ **Château de Barbentane**
Barbentane. 🎫 04 90 95 51 07. ⭕ Easter–Jun, Oct: Thu–Tue; Jul–Sep: daily; Nov–Mar: Sun. ● 1 Jan, 1 Nov, 25 Dec. 🈲

Provençal doll and doll's carriage, Château de Barbentane

Abbaye de St-Michel de Frigolet ❸

Road map B3. 🎫 04 90 95 70 07. ⭕ daily. ● (cloisters) public hols. 🈲 (cloisters only). 🈲 obligatory for cloisters at 2:30pm Mon–Fri, 4pm Sun. &

THE ABBEY IS SITUATED south of St-Michel de Frigolet, in the unspoiled La Montagnette countryside. A cloister and small abbey church date from the 12th century, but in 1858 a Premonstratensian abbey was founded and one of the most richly decorated churches of that period was built. The whole interior is colourfully painted, with stars and saints on the pillars and ceiling. After a brief period of exile in Belgium early this century, the monks returned to Frigolet, and there are now 15 of them. There is a restaurant, accommodation in 40 rooms and the monks sell their traditional liqueur based on local herbs. *Frigolet* is Provençal for thyme.

The ceiling of the abbey church of St-Michel de Frigolet

Pont du Gard ❹

Road map A3. 🚌 *Nîmes*. 🚏 *rue du Moulin d'Aure, Remoulins (04 66 37 22 34).*

BUILT AROUND 19 BC, this bridge is part of the aqueduct which transported spring water from a catchment area near Uzès to the Romans in Nîmes *(see pp132–3)*. Bridges, ditches, tunnels and siphons were engineered to carry the 20 million litre (4.4 million gallon) daily water supply a distance of 50 km (31 miles). The Pont du Gard spans the Gardon valley and is the most important and spectacular section of the aqueduct. Huge

The Pont du Gard, the tallest of all Roman aqueducts at 48 m (158 ft)

Trademark graffiti left by 18th-century masons on the stones

limestone rocks, some as heavy as six tonnes, were driven into the base of the river Gardon. The slightly curved, slender structure helped resist river currents, and the protrusions helped guide and regulate the flow. The top level took the water, while the two lower ones were for general access. By the 1st century BC the population had declined, and the aqueduct fell into disuse. In the Middle Ages, the centre level was used as a walkway, then as a bridge for vehicles, but it soon deteriorated and the structure was not restored until the 19th century.

Protruding stones for supporting scaffolding during construction

THE REMAINS OF THE AQUEDUCT

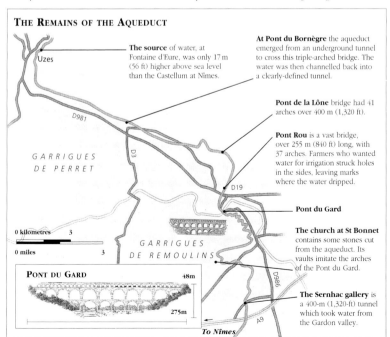

Uzes

D981

GARRIGUES DE PERRET

D3

0 kilometres   3

0 miles   3

GARRIGUES DE REMOULINS

PONT DU GARD   48m

275m

D19

D986

A9

To Nîmes

The source of water, at Fontaine d'Eure, was only 17 m (56 ft) higher above sea level than the Castellum at Nîmes.

At Pont du Bornègre the aqueduct emerged from an underground tunnel to cross this triple-arched bridge. The water was then channelled back into a clearly-defined tunnel.

Pont de la Lône bridge had 41 arches over 400 m (1,320 ft).

Pont Rou is a vast bridge, over 255 m (840 ft) long, with 37 arches. Farmers who wanted water for irrigation struck holes in the sides, leaving marks where the water dripped.

Pont du Gard

The church at St Bonnet contains some stones cut from the aqueduct. Its vaults imitate the arches of the Pont du Gard.

The Sernhac gallery is a 400-m (1,320-ft) tunnel which took water from the Gardon valley.

Nîmes ➎

Publicity poster for a Nîmes festival

A MAGNIFICENT CARVED BLACK BULL at the end of the avenue Jean-Jaurès highlights Nîmes' passion for bullfighting. Crowds fill Les Arènes, the Roman amphitheatre, for bullfights during the three annual *ferias (see pp30–31)*. Year round, the city's biggest draw is its fine Roman architecture, and it is a great city of the arts. The city's textile industry is famous for creating denim *(de Nîmes)*, the tough, material used for blue jeans and worn by the Camargue cowboys. Most shops stock Provençal fabrics *(see p219)*.

Exploring Nîmes

Nîmes' first inhabitants, Roman veterans from Augustus's 31 BC Egyptian campaign, introduced the city's coat of arms: a crocodile chained to a palm tree. Today, the logo is splashed on everything from bollards to road signs.

Nîmes' generous boulevards give it a wide-open feel. A renaissance of modern building, art and design, including the fine Carré d'Art, lends it a touch of class. Some of the new monuments, such as the Fontaine du Crocodile in the place du Marché, are becoming as well known as Nîmes' most familiar landmark, the Castellum.

The city's coat of arms: a crocodile and palm tree

with seating for 24,000, it is marginally smaller than Arles' amphitheatre *(see p146)*. It was built as a venue for gladiatorial combat, chariot racing and waterborne battles (it could be flooded).

After the collapse of Rome in 476, it became a fortress and knights' headquarters. Until its 19th-century restoration, it was used as home to 2,000 people in slum conditions. Today it is considered to be perhaps the best preserved of all Roman amphitheatres.

🏛 Les Arènes

Bd des Arènes. 【 04 66 76 72 77.
◯ daily. ● 1 Jan, 1 May, 25 Dec & on performance days. 🖼 ♿
Of all the city's Roman ruins, the most dramatic is the 1st-century amphitheatre. At 130 m (427 ft) by 100 m (328 ft) and

🏛 Porte d'Auguste

Bd Amiral Courbet.
With a central arch 6 m (20 ft) high and 4 m (13 ft) wide, this gate was built to take horsemen and carriages, since the main road from Rome to Spain, the Domitian Way, passed through the middle of Nîmes.

An ancient inscription tells visitors that the city walls were built in 15 BC and extended for nearly 6 km (4 miles).

🏛 Maison Carrée

Pl de la Maison Carrée. 【 04 66 36 26 76. ◯ daily. ● 1 May, 25 Dec.
The Maison Carrée ("square house") is the Roman world's best-preserved temple. Built by Augustus's son-in-law Marcus Agrippa, it is Hellenic with Corinthian columns around the main hall. Louis XIV's chief minister, Colbert, wanted it taken brick by brick to Versailles.

🏛 Carré d'Art

Pl de la Maison Carrée. 【 04 66 76 35 80. ◯ Tue–Sun. 🖼 ♿
On the opposite side of the square from the Maison Carrée and in stunning contrast to it, is the Carré d'Art. This modern art complex, finished in 1993, was designed by Norman Foster.

Norman Foster's Carré d'Art

🏛 Musée du Vieux Nîmes

Pl aux Herbes. 【 04 66 36 00 64.
◯ Tue–Sun. ● 1 Jan, 1 May, 1 & 11 Nov, 25 Dec. 🖼
The 17th-century Bishop's Palace just east of the cathedral houses this museum. The old-fashioned interior has been beautifully restored: the summer room has Directoire and Empire-style furnishings and Old Town views. In the wardrobe is a billiard table with inlaid work by the eldest Bernassau son from Nîmes.

🏛 Musée Archéologique et Musée d'Histoire Naturelle

13 bis bd Amiral Courbet. 【 04 66 67 25 57. ◯ Tue–Sun. ● 1 Jan, 1 May, 1 & 11 Nov, 25 Dec. 🖼
The ground-floor gallery of this museum has a number of pre-Roman carvings, including busts of Gallic warriors, friezes and also contemporary objects. Upstairs, Gallo-Roman tools

The Roman amphitheatre, today used for bullfights at festival times

and household utensils give a good idea of life at the time. There is also a range of glassware and bronze objects. The pottery collection includes the pre-Roman *Warrior of Grézan*. The atmospheric chapel in this one-time Jesuits' College is used for temporary displays.

🏛 Musée des Beaux-Arts

Rue Cité Foulc. **[** 04 66 67 38 21. **◻** Tue–Sun. **●** 1 Jan, 1 May, 1 & 11 Nov, 25 Dec. **◺** **&**
A diverse collection in the Fine Art Museum includes paintings by Boucher, Rodin and Watteau. The ground floor displays a large Roman mosaic, *The Marriage of Admetus*, which was found in Nîmes market-place.

Archaeological museum statue

🏛 Cathédrale Notre-Dame et St-Castor

Pl aux Herbes. **◻** daily.
Nîmes' cathedral, situated in the centre of the Old Town, dates from the 11th century but was extensively rebuilt in the 19th century. The west front has a partly Romanesque frieze that depicts dramatic scenes from the Old Testament.

🏛 Castellum

Rue de la Lampèze.
Between the Porte d'Auguste and the Tour Magne, set in the Roman wall, is the Castellum, a tower used for storing the water brought in from Uzès via the aqueduct at Pont du Gard *(see p131)*. The water was distributed in the town by means of a canal duct system.

🌷 Jardin de la Fontaine

Quai de la Fontaine.
The city's main leisure park lies at the end of the wide, villa-lined avenue Jean-Jaurès. It was named after an underground spring harnessed in the 18th century. The park's 2nd-century Temple of Diana, believed to have been part of a complex of baths, is today in ruins. Benedictine nuns lived there during the Middle Ages, and converted it into a church. The church was sacked in the Wars of Religion *(see pp46–7)*.

At the summit of the 114-m (374-ft) Mont Cavalier stands the 34-m (112-ft) octagonal Tour Magne. Of all the towers originally set in Nîmes' Roman

VISITORS' CHECKLIST

Road map A3. 🏘 *130,000.*
🚉 *Nîmes-Arles-Camargue.* 🚌 *bd Talabot.* 🚌 *rue Ste-Felicité.*
ℹ *6 rue Auguste (04 66 67 29 11).* 🚪 *daily.* 🎪 *Féria d'Hiver (Feb); Féria de Pentecôte (May); Féria des Vendanges (late Sep).*

wall, this is the largest and most remarkable. Dating from 15 BC, it is the earliest surviving Roman building in France. There are 140 steps leading to the top, from where there is a fine view of Mont Ventoux.

L'Obéissance Récompensée by Boucher, Musée des Beaux-Arts

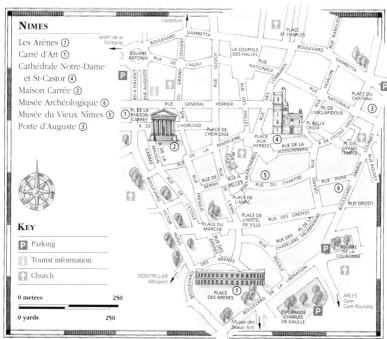

NIMES

Les Arènes ⑦
Carré d'Art ①
Cathédrale Notre-Dame et St-Castor ④
Maison Carrée ②
Musée Archéologique ⑥
Musée du Vieux Nîmes ⑤
Porte d'Auguste ③

KEY

P Parking

🛈 Tourist information

🛕 Church

0 metres   250
0 yards   250

Aigues-Mortes ⑥

ALONE, STURDY SENTINEL set among the salt marshes of the Camargue, Aigues-Mortes ("dead waters" in Provençal) looks today much as it must have done when it was completed, around 1300. Then, however, the Rhône had not deposited the silt which now landlocks the town. Canals brought the vast stone blocks to make its walls from the quarries of Beaucaire, and the town's founder, Louis IX set sail from under the shadow of Tour de Constance on his crusade of 1248 *(see pp42–3)*. Only the Hundred Years' War saw its ramparts breached: now its gates are always open to the besieging armies of admiring visitors.

Tour de la Poudrière
was the arsenal, where weapons and gunpowder were stored.

Porte de l'Arsenal

King Louis IX
Saint Louis, as he was to become, built Aigues-Mortes as his only Mediterranean sea port. People had to be bribed to come and settle in this inhospitable spot.

RUE DE L'ARSENAL
RUE HOCHE
RUE S ARSENAL
RUE ROGER
RUE ROUGET DE L'ISLE
SALENGRO
BOULEVARD GAMBETTA
RUE EM
RUE PAUL BERT
RUE BAUDIN
RUE DE

Porte de la Reine
was named for Anne of Austria, who visited the town in 1622.

Tour de la Mèche
or "wick tower" held a constant flame used to light cannon fuses.

Chapelle des Pénitents Blancs

Tour des Sels

★ **The Ramparts**
The 1,634-m (1-mile) long walls are punctuated by ten gates, six towers, arrow slits and overhanging latrines.

Chapelle des Pénitents Gris
Built from 1676–99, this chapel is still used by an order founded in 1400. Named for their grey cowls, they walk with their white-cowled former rivals in the Palm Sunday procession.

STAR SIGHTS

★ **Tour de Constance**

★ **The Ramparts**

Porte de la Marine
This was the main portside gate. Ships were moored by the Porte des Galions, *anchored to a vast metal ring known as an* organeau.

VISITORS' CHECKLIST

Road map A4. 5,800. av F Mistral. route de Nîmes. Porte de la Gardette (04 66 53 73 00). Wed & Sun. Festival St-Louis (medieval pageant & fireworks, late Aug).

Place St-Louis
This charming, leafy square, lined with cafés, is at the heart of town life. In its centre is a bronze statue of Saint Louis, on a base carved with the prows of crusader ships.

Notre-Dame des Sablons, "Our Lady of the Sands", was built before the town itself.

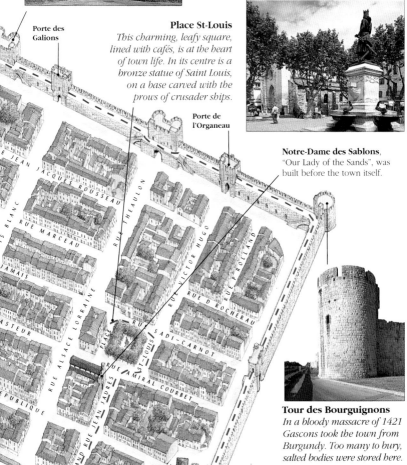

Porte des Galions

Porte de l'Organeau

RUE JEAN JACQUES ROUSSEAU

RUE MARCEAU

RUE THEAULON

RUE VICTOR HUGO

RUE P ROLLAND

RUE D ROCHERAU

RUE ALSACE LORRAINE

RUE SADI-CARNOT

PLACE ST-LOUIS

RUE AMIRAL COURBET

GRAND RUE JEAN JAURES

Porte de la Gardette

Tour des Bourguignons
In a bloody massacre of 1421 Gascons took the town from Burgundy. Too many to bury, salted bodies were stored here.

KEY

– – – Suggested route

0 metres 100

0 yards 100

★ **Tour de Constance**
This tower often held religious prisoners: first Catholic, then Calvinist, and then Huguenot women like Marie Durand, freed in 1768 after 38 years.

The Camargue

THIS FLAT, scarcely habited land is one of Europe's major wetland regions and natural history sites. Extensive areas of salt marsh, lakes, pastures and sand dunes, covering a vast 140,000 ha (346,000 acres), provide a romantic and haunting environment for the wildlife. Native horses roam the green pastures and are ridden by the traditional cowboys of the region, the *gardians, (see p20)* who herd the black bulls. Numerous sea birds and wildfowl also occupy the region, among them flocks of greater flamingoes. North of the reserve, rice is cultivated in paddy fields. Many of the thousands of visitors confine their exploration to the road between Arles and Saintes-Maries-de-la-Mer, and miss the best of the wild flora and fauna.

Gardians look after the horses and bulls

Camargue Bulls
Periodically, the herds of black bulls are rounded up by the gardians to perform in local bullfights. The larger bulls are sold to Spain.

Camargue Horses
These hardy animals are direct descendants of pre-historic horses. The foal's coat turns white between the age of four and seven.

Parc Ornithologique du Pont-de-Gau bird reserve *(see p138)* is where most birds in the Camargue live and where, twice a year, over 350 species of migrating birds stop off on their journey north or south.

CAMARGUE BIRDS
This region is a haven for bird spotters, particularly during the spring when migrant birds visit on their journey north. Resident birds include little egrets and marsh harriers. This is the only French breeding site of the slender-billed gull, and the red-crested pochard, rarely seen in Europe, also breeds here.

Little egret
(Egretta garzetta)

Slender-billed gull
(Larus genei)

Marsh harrier *(Circus aeruginosus)*

Collared pratincole
(Glareola pratincola)

Black-winged stilt
(Himantopus himantopus)

Red-crested pochard
(Netta rufina)

European Beavers

European beavers came close to extinction at the start of the 20th century, when they were hunted for their fur. These nocturnal animals were protected in 1905 and began to colonize the region in the 1970s.

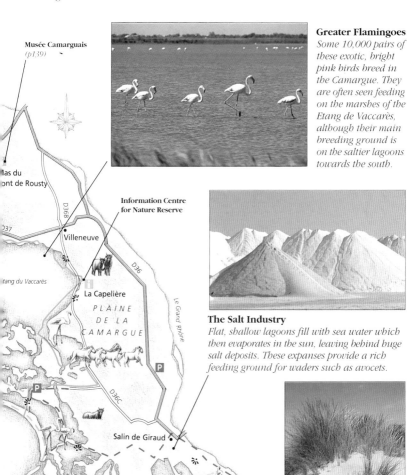

Greater Flamingoes

Some 10,000 pairs of these exotic, bright pink birds breed in the Camargue. They are often seen feeding on the marshes of the Etang de Vaccarès, although their main breeding ground is on the saltier lagoons towards the south.

The Salt Industry

Flat, shallow lagoons fill with sea water which then evaporates in the sun, leaving behind huge salt deposits. These expanses provide a rich feeding ground for waders such as avocets.

Dune Vegetation

The sand dunes form a line between the lagoons and salt marshes and the sea. Among the many wild flowers that grow here is sea chamomile.

Map labels:

Musée Camarguais *(p139)*

Mas du Pont de Rousty

D36B

D37

Villeneuve

Information Centre for Nature Reserve

D36

Etang du Vaccarès

La Capelière

Le Grand Rhône

PLAINE DE LA CAMARGUE

P

D36C

P

Salin de Giraud

KEY

—— Nature reserve boundary

— — Walking routes

— — Walking and cycling routes

0 kilometres 5

0 miles 5

Exploring the Camargue

Entrance
to Méjanes
bullring

THE UNIQUE CHARACTER of the Camargue has given rise to unusual traditions. The native white horses and black bulls are ranched by *manadiers* and herded, branded and tended by the region's cowboys, or *gardians*, whose small, low, whitewashed houses dot the landscape. Local bullfights are advertised in Saintes-Maries-de-la-Mer, the main tourist centre of the region and chief place to stay, also renowned for its gypsy population. It has a sandy beach and offers watersports and boat trips. Tourist offices throughout the area provide information on walks, but the best views are from the 7-km (5-mile) footway and cycle path along the Digues-de-la-Mer (sea dyke) from the town. Several sights within the Camargue have been turned into museums and exhibitions of local life and natural history. Several ranches and activity centres organize rides and riding holidays.

A bloodless Camargue bullfight in Méjanes

A place of pilgrimage

The three Marys who gave Saintes-Maries-de-la-Mer its name are Mary Magdalene, Mary Jacobea (the Virgin Mary's sister) and Mary Salome, mother of the apostles James and John. Set adrift after the Crucifixion with, among others, their servant Sara, Saint Martha and her brother Lazarus, they landed here in their boat. They built a shrine to the virgin, and while the others went to spread the word of the gospel, Mary Jacobea, Mary Salome and Sara stayed behind.

In winter, the town is an unpretentious, whitewashed, low-rise resort. It overflows during the May and October festivals, when Mary Salome and Mary Jacobea are celebrated, their statues marched

to the sea to be blessed. The larger festival is in May, when gypsies from all over the world come to pay homage to their patron saint, Sara, the richly dressed black Madonna who lies in the crypt of the 9th-century Eglise de Notre-Dame-de-la-Mer. An effigy is also paraded through the streets to the sea. Afterwards there are bullfights, horse races and flamenco dancing *(see pp34–5)*.

Throughout the centre of the town are cheery restaurants with checked tablecloths, and shops selling patterned skirts, shirts and scarves, lucky charms and Romany souvenirs. The prominent church is also worth visiting for the view from the rooftop walkway of its simple, fortified exterior. Just 40 m (44 yards) away from the

church, the Musée Baroncelli in the old town hall is devoted to zoology and archaeology.

Still in the Saintes-Maries area, 4.5 km (3 miles) north of the centre on the banks of the Etang de Ginès, lies the Parc Ornithologique du Pont-de-Gau, with a vast range of Camargue birdlife *(see p136)*.

🏛 Musée Baroncelli
Ancien Hôtel de Ville, rue Victor Hugo.
📞 04 90 97 87 60. 🕐 Apr–11 Nov:
Wed–Mon 🖭
The documents and artifacts relating to bull rearing and local life on display here were amassed by Marquis Folco de Baroncelli-Javon (1869–1943), a *manadier* who promoted the *gardian* life and the region's customs and traditions.

🏛 Le Centre de Ginès
Pont-de-Gau. 📞 04 90 97 86 32.
🕐 Apr–Sep: daily; Oct–Mar: Sat–Thu.
🌑 1 Jan, 1 May, 25 Dec.
This information centre offers wonderful views over the flat lagoon. Photographs and documents chronicle the history of the Camargue and its diverse flora and fauna.

🦅 Parc Ornithologique du Pont-de-Gau
Pont-de-Gau. 📞 04 90 97 82 62.
🕐 daily. 🌑 25 Dec. 🖭 🖭
Most of the birds that live in or migrate through the region are represented in this reserve. Huge aviaries house birds that might otherwise be hard to spot. Visitors are encouraged to follow the network of signposted paths to avoid damage or disturbance *(see p136)*.

Honey buzzard enclosure at the
Pont-de-Gau bird sanctuary

🏛 Musée Camarguais

Parc Naturel Régional de Camargue, Mas du Pont de Rousty. (On the D570, 10km south-west of Arles). ▮ 04 90 97 10 82. ⬜ Apr–Sep: daily; Oct–Mar: Wed–Mon. ⬛ 1 Jan, 1 May, 25 Dec. ▨ ♿

A traditional Provençal *mas* or farmhouse *(see pp20–21)*, that only a short time ago was part of a farm raising cattle and sheep, has been converted to accommodate a fascinating museum of the Camargue. The main part of the museum is housed in a huge sheep barn, built in 1815 and skilfully restored. Displays, including video footage and slide shows, provide an excellent introduction to traditional life in the Camargue and to the unique plant and animal life of the Camargue delta. Among the many subjects

Eglise de Notre-Dame-de-la-Mer, in Saintes-Maries-de-la-Mer

covered are the lives of the Camargue cowboys, and the *grand* and *petit* Rhône rivers which once flowed far to the east past Nîmes. Look out for displays on *Mirèio*, the master-work of poet and champion of the Provençal language, Frédéric Mistral, *(see p26)*, a local man who won the Nobel Prize for literature in 1904.

A signposted 3.5-km (2-mile) nature trail leads out from the museum to the Marré de la Grand Mare and back again by a pleasant circular route. Examples of traditional *mas* husbandry are marked on the way. An observation tower at the end of the walk gives great views over the surrounding countryside.

The fine Romanesque façade of the abbey church at St-Gilles-du-Gard

St-Gilles-du-Gard ⓼

Road map A3. 🏘 12,000. ▤ ▮ place F Mistral (04 66 87 33 75). ⬛ Thu & Sun.

CALLED the "Gateway to the Camargue", St-Gilles is famous for its **Abbaye de St-Gilles**. In medieval times the abbey was vast. The building was damaged in 1562 during the Wars of Religion and all that remains are the west façade, chancel and crypt. The carved façade is the most beautiful in all Provence. It includes the first sculpture of the Passion in Christendom, from the late 12th century.

Founded by Raymond VI of Toulouse, the abbey church was the Knights of St John's first priory in Europe. It soon became a key place on the pilgrimage route to Santiago de Compostela in Spain and a port of embarkation for the Crusades *(see pp42–3)*. The crypt houses the tomb of Saint Gilles, a hermit who arrived by raft from Greece.

The belltower of the original abbey contains *Le Vis*, a spiral staircase which is a master-piece of stonemasonry.

Beaucaire ⓽

Road map B3. 🏘 13,400. ▤ Tarascon. ▤ ▮ 24 cours Gambetta (04 66 59 26 57). ⬛ Thu & Sun.

THE BULLRING in Beaucaire occupies the site of one of the largest fairs in Europe. Held every July for the past seven centuries, it attracted up to a

quarter of a million people. A smaller version of the fair takes place today, with a procession through the town on 21 July. It was inaugurated by Raymond VI in 1217, who enlarged the **Château de Beaucaire**.

This was later used by the French kings to look down on their Provençal neighbours across the river. It was partly dismantled on the orders of Cardinal Richelieu but the triangular keep and enough of the walls remain to indicate its impressive scale. There is a Romanesque chapel within the walls and medieval spectacles, including displays of falconry, which are held for visitors between Easter and October.

The **Abbaye de St-Roman** is situated 5 km (3 miles) to the northwest of Beaucaire. Dating from the 5th century, it is the only troglodyte monastery in Europe.

⛪ Château de Beaucaire

Rue du Château. ▮ 04 66 59 47 61. ⬜ Wed–Mon. ⬛ public hols. ▨

The unique troglodyte Abbaye de Saint-Roman near Beaucaire

The legendary Tarasque, the terror of Tarascon

Tarascon ⑩

Road map B3. 🕮 11,300. 🚊 🚌
🅸 59 rue des Halles (04 90 91 03 52).
🚌 Tue.

THE GLEAMING WHITE vision of the **Château de Tarascon** is one of the landmarks of the Rhône. Little is left of the glittering court of Good King René who finished the building his father, Louis II of Anjou, began early in the 15th century (see pp46–7). Following René's death in 1480, Provence fell to France, and the castle became a prison until 1926. A drawbridge leads to the poultry yard and garrison quarters. Beside it rises the impressive main castle, centred on a courtyard from where two spiral staircases lead to royal apartments and other rooms in its sturdy towers. Prisoners' graffiti and some painted ceiling panels remain, but the only adornment is a handful of borrowed 17th-century tapestries which depict the deeds of Roman general Scipio (237–183 BC).
The **Collégiale Ste-Marthe**, nearby has a tomb in the crypt to the monster-taming saint. According to legend, St Martha (see p42) rescued the inhabitants from the Tarasque, a man-eating monster, half lion, half armadillo, which gave the town its name. The event is celebrated each June in the Fête de la Tarasque (see p31).
In the old town is the 16th-century Cloître des Cordeliers where exhibitions and concerts are held. On the arcaded rue des Halles is the 17th-century town hall, with an attractively carved façade and balcony.

The traditional life of the area and its hand-printed fabrics is seen in the **Musée Souleïado**. The ancient textile industry was revived in 1938, under the name *Souleïado*, which means "the sun passing through the clouds" in Provençal. In the museum are 40,000 woodblocks dating from the 18th century, still used for the company's colourful prints.
The **Maison de Tartarin** is a museum devoted to the tallstory telling Provençal "hero" of three comic novels by Alphonse Daudet (see p26).

🏰 **Château de Tarascon**
Bd de Roi René. 📞 04 90 91 01 93.
◻ Apr–Oct: daily; Nov–Mar: Wed–Mon. ⬤ 1 Jan, 1 May, 1 & 11 Nov, 25 Dec. 🎫
🏛 **Musée Souleïado**
39 rue Proudhon. 📞 04 90 91 08 80.
◻ Mon–Fri: guided tours by reservation only. ⬤ public hols. 🎫
🏛 **Maison de Tartarin**
55 bis bd Itam. 📞 04 90 91 05 08.
◻ mid-Mar–mid-Dec: Mon–Sat.
⬤ 1 May, 1 & 11 Nov. 🎫

The fairy tale Château de Tarascon, stronghold of Good King René

St-Rémy-de-Provence ⑪

Road map B3. 🕮 9,500.
🚊 Avignon. 🅸 pl Jean-Jaurès (04 90 92 05 22). 🚌 Wed.

ST-RÉMY IS IDEAL for exploring the Alpilles countryside which supplies the plants for its traditional *herboristeries*, or herb shops. The **Musée des Arômes de Provence**, in boulevard Mirabeau, displays implements of their craft and properties of the local flora.
St-Rémy's **Eglise St-Martin** contains an exceptional organ, and recitals are held here on Saturdays. Two of its most attractive 15th–16th-century mansions are now museums. The **Musée des Alpilles** has a fine ethnographic collection and the **Hôtel de Sade**, home of the infamous Marquis' forebears, contains some Roman remains from nearby Glanum.

Herbs and spices on sale in St-Rémy market, place de la République

This town was the birthplace of Nostradamus. The well-known 16th-century physician and astrologer was born in a house in the outer wall of the avenue Hoche, in the old quarter.
Le **Centre d'Art Présence Van Gogh** in the 18th-century Hôtel Estrine is a reminder of the great artist's association with St-Rémy. In May 1889, after he had mutilated his ear, he arrived at the **Clinique St-Paul**, which is situated between the town and the Roman remains at Glanum. The grounds and the 12th-century cloisters of the clinic can be visited, and the tourist office gives a map of some of the views Van Gogh painted while he stayed here.
Just behind the clinic is Le Mas de la Pyramide, a farmstead half-built into the rock, which has remained in the

The triumphal arch at Glanum, built in the reign of Augustus, a 15-minute walk from the centre of St-Rémy

same family for generations. It was formerly a Roman quarry, and the grounds contain an enormous ancient stone pillar.

The remains of the earliest Greek houses in Provence, from the 4th-century BC, are in **Glanum** *(see p40)*, a Greco-Roman town at the head of a valley in the Alpilles. Dramatic memorials, known as Les Antiques, stand on the roadside: a triumphal arch from 10 BC, celebrating Caesar's conquest of the Greeks and Gaul, and a mausoleum from about 30 BC.

🏛 **Musée des Arômes des Provence**
34 bd Mirabeau. 📞 04 90 92 48 70. ⭕ Easter–mid-Sep: daily; mid-Sep– Easter: Mon–Sat. ⬤ public hols.
🏛 **Musée des Alpilles**
Rue du Parage, place Favier. 📞 04 90 92 08 10. ⭕ Mar–Dec: daily. ⬤ 1 May, 25 Dec. 🖼
🏛 **Hôtel de Sade**
Rue du Parage. 📞 04 90 92 64 04. ⭕ Feb–Dec: Tue–Sun. ⬤ 1 Jan, 1 May, 25 Dec. 🖼
🏛 **Le Centre d'Art Présence Van Gogh**
8 rue Estrine. 📞 04 90 92 34 72. ⭕ Apr–Oct & Dec: Tue–Sun. 🖼
🏛 **Clinique St-Paul**
Av Vincent Van Gogh, St-Paul de Mausole. ⭕ daily. ♿
∩ **Glanum**
Rte de Baux. 📞 04 90 92 23 79. ⭕ daily. ⬤ 1 Jan, 1 May, 1 & 11 Nov, 25 Dec. 🖼

Les Alpilles ⑫

Road map B3. 🚂 Arles, Tarascon, Salon-de-Provence. 🚌 Les Baux-de-Provence, St-Rémy-de-Provence, Eyguières, Eygalières. ℹ Les Baux-de Provence (04 90 92 68 24).

ST-RÉMY-DE-PROVENCE is on the western side of the limestone massif of Les Alpilles, a 24-km (15-mile) chain between the Rhône and Durance. A high point is **La Caume**, at 387 m (1270 ft), reached from St-Rémy, just beyond Glanum.

East of St-Rémy, the road to Cavaillon runs along the north side of the massif, with a right turn to Eygalières. The painter Mario Prassinos (1916–85), whose work is displayed in

Notre-Dame-de-Pitié in St-Rémy, lived here. Just beyond the village is the 12th-century Chapelle St-Sixte.

The road continues towards Orgon where there are views across the Durance Valley and the Luberon. Orgon skirts the massif on the eastern side. A right turn leads past the ruins of Castelas de Roquemartine and Eyguières, a pleasant village with a Romanesque church. It is a two-hour walk to Les Opiés, a 493-m (1,617-ft) hill crowned by a tower. This forms part of the GR6 which crosses the chain to Les Baux, one of the best walking routes in Provence. From Castelas de Roquemartine the road heads back west towards Les Baux.

The chalky massif of Les Alpilles, "Little Alps", in the heart of Provence

A late 18th-century fresco showing the Baux warriors in battle against the Saracens in 1266

Les Baux-de-Provence ⑬

Road map B3. 🏛 460. 🚏 ℹ *Ilôt Post Tenebras Lux (04 90 54 34 39).*

LES BAUX SITS on a spur of the Alpilles (*bau* in Provençal means escarpment), with views across to the Camargue (see *pp136–9*). The most dramatic fortress site in Provence, it has nearly two million visitors a year, so it is best to avoid midsummer, or to go early in the morning. The town is pedestrianized with a car park beside the Porte Mage gate.

When the Lords of Baux built their fine citadel here in the 10th century, they claimed one of the three wise men, King Balthazar, as ancestor and took the star of Bethlehem as their emblem. Though fierce warriors, they originated the troubadour Courts of Love and wooed noble ladies with their poetry and songs. This became a medieval convention known as courtly love and paved the way for a literary tradition.

The citadel ruins lie on the heights of the escarpment. The entrance to the citadel is via the 14th-century Tour-de-Brau, which has been converted into the **Musée d'Histoire de la Citadelle**. A plateau extends to the end of the escarpment, where a monument stands in memory of the Provençal poet Charloun Rieu (1846–1924). In the town centre, two other museums of local interest are the **Fondation Louis Jou** and

Monument to poet Charloun Rieu

the **Musée des Santons**. Next door to the 12th-century Eglise St-Vincent is the Chapelle des Pénitents Blancs, decorated in 1974 by the local artist Yves Brayer. Just north of Les Baux lies the **Cathédrale d'Images**.

🏛 Musée de la Tour du Brau
Rue du Trencart. 📞 04 90 54 55 56. ⏰ *daily.* 🖼

On display in this small archaeological museum are objects that have been excavated in Les Baux and the surrounding area.

🏛 Fondation Louis Jou
Hôtel Brion, Grande Rue. 📞 04 90 54 34 17. ⏰ *daily by appointment only.* 🖼

Medieval books are housed here, along with a collection of prints and drawings by Dürer, Goya and Jou, the local engraver after whom the museum is named.

🏛 Musée des Santons
Place Louis Jou. 📞 04 90 54 34 39. ⏰ *daily.*

In the 16th-century old town hall, a Provençal crib scene has been created, representing the nativity at Les Baux. Handmade clay *santons* or figurines (see *p48*), representing saints and local figures, show the evolution of Provençal costume.

🏛 Cathédrale d'Images
Route de Val d'Enfer. 📞 04 90 54 38 65. ⏰ *Feb–Dec: daily.* 🖼 ♿

Located on the D27 road to the north of Les Baux and within walking distance of the main car park in Les Baux is the Val d'Enfer or the Valley of Hell. It was this jagged gorge, said to be inhabited by witches and spirits, that inspired Dante's poetry. It is also the site where bauxite was discovered in 1822 by the mineralogist Berthier, who named it after the town. It was in this big quarry that the Cathédral d'Images or Picture

View of the citadel and village of Les Baux

Palace was established. The imaginative slide show is projected not only onto the white limestone walls of the natural theatre, but also the floor and ceiling, creating a three dimensional effect. The 30-minute show, which has a different theme every Christmas, is accompanied by haunting music, and is an extraordinary audio-visual experience.

Les Baux's Chapelle des Pénitents, next to the Eglise St-Vincent

Fontvieille ⑭

Road map B3. 🏘 *3,700.* 🚌 🚉
ℹ 5 rue Marcel Honorat. 📞 *04 90 54 67 49.* 🛍 *Mon & Fri.*

FONTVIEILLE IS an agreeable country town in the flat fruit and vegetable lands of the irrigated Baux Valley. Half-way between Arles and Les Alpilles, the town makes an excellent centre from which to explore. Until the French Revolution in

1789, the town's history was bound up with the Abbaye de Montmajour. The oratories that stand at the four corners of the small town were erected in 1721 to celebrate the end of the plague (*see pp48–9*).

To the south on the D33, set on a stony hill is the Moulin de Daudet and further on at Barbegal are the remarkable remains of a Roman aqueduct and a series of 16 water mills.

Abbaye de Montmajour ⑮

Road map B3. Route de Fontvieille. 📞 *04 90 54 64 17.* ⏰ *Apr–Sep: daily; Oct–Mar: Wed–Mon.* 🔒 *public hols.* 🎫

STANDING OUT like Noah's ark on Mount Ararat, 5 km (3 miles) northwest of Arles, this Benedictine abbey was built in the 10th century. At the time, the site was was an island refuge in marshland. The handful of monks in residence spent all their spare time draining this area of marshland between the Alpilles chain and the Rhône.

The abbey is a massive and imposing place, though all the Baroque buildings were destroyed by fire 1726 and never restored. The original church is said to have been founded by Saint Trophime as a sanctuary from the Romans. It grew rich in the Middle Ages when thousands of pilgrims arrived at Easter to purchase pardons. After 1791, the abbey was broken up by two successive owners who bought it from the

The cloisters and keep of the Abbaye de Montmajour

state. The abbey was largely restored in the 19th century.

The **Eglise Notre-Dame** is one of the largest Romanesque buildings in Provence. Below, the 12th-century crypt has been skilfully built into the sloping hill. The cloister has double pillars ornamented with beasts and lies in the shadows of the 26-m (85-ft) tower, built in the 1360s. It is worth climbing the 124 steps to the tower platform to see the stunning, panoramic view across to the sea. Also carved into the hillside is the atmospheric **Chapelle de St-Pierre**. It was established at the same time as the abbey and is a primitive place of worship. There are a number of tombs in the abbey grounds, but the principal burial area is the 12th-century **Chapelle Ste-Croix**. It lies a few hundred yards to the east and is built in the shape of a Greek cross.

DAUDET'S WINDMILL

The Moulin de Daudet is one of the most famous literary landmarks in France. Alphonse Daudet was born in Nîmes in 1840 and made his name in Paris. The windmill is the setting of Daudet's *Letters from my Windmill*, stories about Provençal life, first published in 1860 and popular ever since. He observed the local characters and wrote about their lives with irony and pathos. He never actually lived in the mill, but made imaginative use of some of the resident miller's tales. When he stayed in Fontvieille he was a guest in the 19th-century Château de Montauban. He came to find respite from the capital, but returned there in order to write his stories. The restored mill can be visited, and there is a small museum dedicated to Daudet.

Street-by-Street: Arles ⑯

Many of the tourist sites in Arles bear the stamp of their Roman past, and all are within comfortable walking distance of the central place de la République. On its north side is the Hôtel de Ville, behind which is the place du Forum. This convivial square is the heart of modern life in Arles. Another place to sit at a café and observe the Arlésiens promenade is the boulevard des Lices, where the lively twice-weekly market is held. Some of the shops here and in nearby rue Jean-Jaurès sell bright Provençal fabrics. For museum-buffs, an inclusive ticket is available giving access to all the museums.

Les Thermes de Constantin are all that remain of Constantine's Palace, built in the 4th century AD.

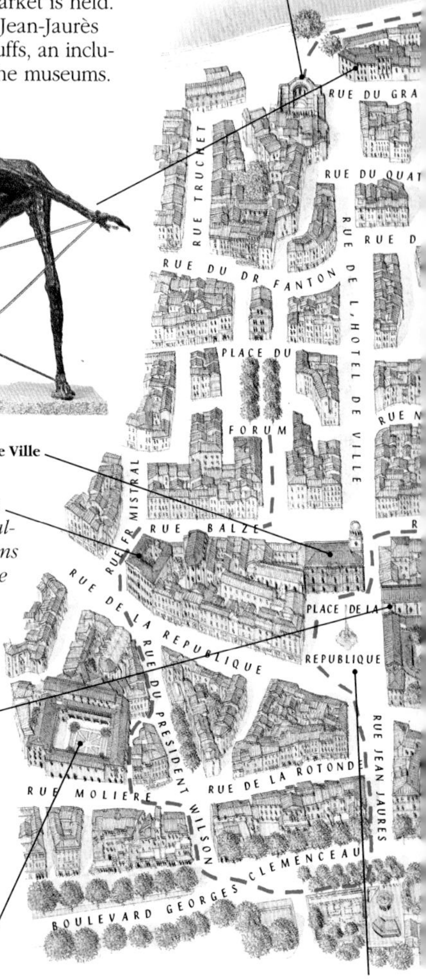

Musée Réattu
This museum on the banks of the Rhône houses 18th–19th-century and modern art, including this figure of Le Griffu *(1952) by Germaine Richier.*

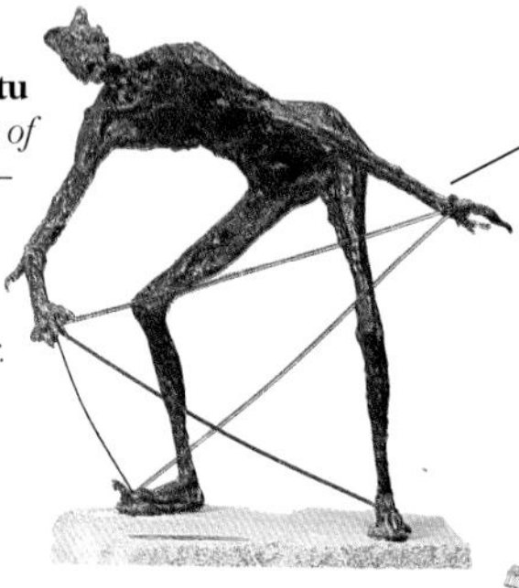

Hôtel de Ville

Museon Arlaten
The Hôtel de Laval-Castellane contains the largest folklore collection in Provence, a treasure house of local history.

★ **Eglise St-Trophime**
This fine Romanesque church has a 12th-century portal of the Last Judgment, *including saints and apostles.*

L'Espace Van Gogh, a cultural centre

STAR SIGHTS

★ **Les Arènes**

★ **Théâtre Antique**

★ **Eglise St-Trophime**

Egyptian Obelisk
An ancient obelisk with fountains at its base (one of which is shown here) stands in the place de la République. It came from the Roman circus across the Rhône.

★ Les Arènes
This is one of the largest, best-preserved Roman monuments in Provence. The top tier provides an excellent panoramic view of Arles.

VISITORS' CHECKLIST

Road map B3. ⚑ 52,000. ✈
Nîmes-Arles-Camargue. 🚌 🚌
av Paulin Talbot. 🛈 esplanade
C de Gaulle (04 90 18 41 20). 🚋
Wed, Sat. 🎭 Féria Pascale (Easter);
Fête des Gardians (1 May); Feria
des Fêtes d'Arles (early Jul). Feria
des Prémices du Riz (early Sep).

★ Théâtre Antique
Once a fortress, its stones were later used for other buildings. These last remaining columns are called the "two widows".

Notre-Dame-de-la-Major is dedicated to Saint George, patron saint of the Camargue *gardians* (cowboys).

Cloisters of St-Trophime
This sculpted capital is a fine example of the Romanesque beauty of the cloisters.

Map labels:
RUE DE GRILLE
IEURE
PTEMBRE
RUE BARBES
JISSES
RUE ARISTIDE BRIAND
RUE BALECHOU
ROND-POINT DES ARENES
RUE A TARDIEU
RUE DE LA BASTILLE
RUE DIDEROT
LA CALADE
UE DU CLOITRE
RUE PORTE DE LAURE
PLACE DE LA MAJOR
RUE DE LA MADELEINE
RUE GRAND COUVENT
MONTEE VAUBAN
BOULEVARD DES LICES

VAN GOGH IN ARLES

Vincent Van Gogh painted over 300 canvases in the 15 months he lived in Arles, but the town has none of his work. In belated appreciation of this lonely artist, the Hôtel-Dieu has been turned into L'Espace Van Gogh, with a library and exhibition space. Several sites are evocative of him, however; the Café Van Gogh in the place du Forum has been renovated to look as it did in his *Café du Soir*.

L'Arlésienne by Van Gogh (1888)

Exploring Arles

THE CITY OF ARLES was a Greek site expanded by the Romans into a "little Rome". Here, on the most southerly crossing point on the Rhône, they built shipyards, baths, a racetrack and an arena. Then the capital of the three Gauls – France, Spain and Britain – Arles remains one of the most distinctive towns in Provence with fine relics from its Gallo-Roman past. Cars should be parked outside the narrow lanes of the old town.

Sarcophagi on Les Alyscamps

♠ Les Arènes
Rond-point des Arènes. **℡** *04 90 49 36 86.* ☐ *daily.* ● *1 Jan, 1 Nov, 25 Dec & occasional days for bullfights.* 📷
The most impressive of the surviving Roman monuments, the amphitheatre is on the east side of the old town. It was the largest of the Roman buildings in Gaul. Slightly oval, it measures 136 m (446 ft) by 107 m (351 ft) and could seat 21,000. The floors of some of the internal rooms were decorated with mosaics, the better to wash down after bloody affrays. Today both Provençal and Spanish bullfights are held regularly in the arena.

View of Arles from the opposite bank of the Rhône

Just to the southwest of the amphitheatre is the elegant Roman **Théâtre Antique**, which has 12,000 tiered seats arranged in a hemisphere.

⛪ Musée de l'Arles Antique
Av de la Première Division Française Libre. **℡** *04 90 18 88 88.* ☐ *daily.* ● *1 Jan, 1 Nov, 25 Dec.* 📷 ♿
Built in 1994, this museum displays ancient artifacts from Arles and Christian and pagan art. Arles became Christian after Constantine's conversion in AD 312, and fine examples of Romano-Christian sculpture are here. Among the pagan art is a copy of the Venus of Arles and Roman mosaics.

♠ Cryptoporticus
Rue Balze. ☐ *daily.* 📷
These huge subterranean galleries (see p41), ventilated by air shafts, were part of the forum's structure. They were probably used for storing grain.

♠ Les Alyscamps
Av des Alyscamps. ☐ *daily.* 📷 ♿
For nearly fifteen centuries, from Roman to late Medieval times, Les Alyscamps was one of the largest and the most famous cemeteries in the Western world. Romans

Roman mosaic of *Europa and the Bull*, in the Musée de l'Arles Antique

avoided it at night, making it an ideal meeting place for early Christians, led by St Trophime. Christians were often buried by the tomb of Genesius, a Roman servant and beheaded Christian martyr.

♠ Eglise St-Trophime
Place de la République. ☐ *daily.* ♿
This is one of the most beautiful Romanesque churches in Provence. The portal and cloisters are exquisitely decorated with biblical scenes. St Trophime, thought to be the first bishop of Arles in the early 3rd century, appears with St Peter and St John on the carved northeast pillar.

⛪ Museon Arlaten
Hôtel Laval-Castellane, rue de la République. **℡** *04 90 96 08 23.* ☐ *Jul–Sep: daily; Oct–Jun: Tue–Sun.* ● *1 Jan, 1 May, 1 Nov, 25 Dec.* 📷
This folklore collection includes costumes, tableaux and artifacts in 32 rooms around a quadrangle. A treasure trove of information about local customs, superstitions and traditions, it was founded in 1896 by the poet Mistral (see p26), who refurbished the 16th-century Hôtel Laval-Castellane using his Nobel prize money.

⛪ Musée Réattu
10 rue du Grand-Prieuré. **℡** *04 90 96 37 68.* ☐ *daily.* ● *1 Jan, 1 May, 1 Nov, 25 Dec.* 📷
The local artist Jacques Réattu (1760–1833) and his contemporaries form the basis of this collection. A Picasso donation and a photographic display are among 20th-century works.

Martigues

Road map B4. 🚶 *45,000.* 🚉 🚌
🛈 *2 quai Paul Doumer (04 42 42 31 10).* 🐟 *Thu & Sun.*

THE ETANG DE BERRE, situated between Marseille and the Camargue, has the largest petroleum refinery industry in France, which dominates the landscape. On the inland side of the Canal de Caronte is the former fishing port and artists' colony of Martigues, which still attracts a holiday crowd.

Martigues lies on both banks of the canal and on the island of Brescon, where the Pont St-Sébastien is a popular place for artists to set up their easels. Félix Ziem (1821–1911) was the most ardent admirer of this "little Venice" *(see p24)* and his paintings can be viwed in the **Musée Ziem**, together with works by contemporary artists.

🏛 **Musée Ziem**
Bd du 14 juillet. 📞 *04 42 80 66 06.*
◯ *Jul–Aug: Wed–Mon; Sep–Jun: Wed–Sun pm.* ● *public hols.*

The Canal St-Sébastien, Martigues, known as the Birds' Looking-Glass

Salon-de-Provence

Road map B3. 🚶 *34,000.* 🚉 🚌
🛈 *56 cours Gimon (04 90 56 27 60).*
🐟 *Wed & Sun.*

KNOWN FOR ITS OLIVES (the olive oil industry was established in the 1400s) and soap, Salon-de-Provence is dominated by the castellated **Château de l'Empéri**. Once home of the archbishops of

The 12th-century Cistercian Abbaye de Silvacane

Arles, this now contains the Musée de l'Empéri, which has a large collection of militaria from Louis XIV to World War II.

The military tradition in the town is upheld by the French Air Force officers' college, La Patrouille Aérienne de France.

Near the château is the 13th-century **Eglise de St-Michel** and in the north of the old town is the Gothic **St-Laurent**, where the French physician and astrologer Nostradamus is buried. Nostradamus is Salon's most famous citizen. Here, in his adopted home, he wrote *Les Centuries*, his book of predictions, published in 1555. It was banned by the Vatican, as it foretold the diminishing power of the papacy. But his renown was widespread and in 1560 he was made Charles IX's physician.

Salon's four-day Gospel music festival in July echoes throughout the town, with concerts in the château, free street performances and song workshops.

Nostradamus, astrologer and citizen of Salon

♠ **Château de l'Empéri**
Monté du Puech. 📞 *04 90 56 22 36.*
◯ *Wed–Mon.* ● *1 Jan, 1 May, 25 Dec.* 🎫

Abbaye de Silvacane

Road map C3. 📞 *04 42 50 41 69.*
◯ *Apr–Sep: daily; Oct–Mar: Wed–Mon.* ● *1 Jan, 1 May, 25 Dec.* 🎫

LIKE HER TWO Cistercian sisters, Silvacane is a harmonious 12th-century monastery tucked away in the countryside. A bus from Aix-en-Provence runs regularly to Roque-d'Anthéron, the nearest village. The abbey was founded on the site of a Benedictine monastery, in a clearing of a "forest of reeds" *(silva canorum).* It adheres to the austere Cistercian style, with no decoration. The church, with nave, two aisles and a high, vaulted transept, is solid, bare and echoing. The cloisters, arcaded like a pigeon loft, are 13th century and the refectory 14th century. Shortly after the refectory was built, all the monks left and the church served the parish. After the Revolution, it was sold as state property and became a farm until transformed back into an abbey this century.

Aix-en-Provence ⑳

PROVENCE'S FORMER CAPITAL is an international students' town, with one of the region's most cosmopolitan streets of restaurants and bars, rue de la Verrerie. The university was founded by Louis II of Anjou in 1409 and flourished under his son, Good King René (see p46–7).

Another wave of prosperity transformed the city in the 17th century, when ramparts, first raised by the Romans in their town of Aquae Sextiae, were pulled down, and the mansion-lined cours Mirabeau was built. Aix's renowned fountains were added in the 18th century.

The cours Mirabeau, grandest of Aix's boulevards

Exploring Aix

North of the cours Mirabeau, sandwiched between the Cathédrale St-Sauveur and the place d'Albertas, lies the town's old quarter. Sights include the Musée des Tapisseries, housed in the former Bishop's palace, and the splendid 17th-century Hôtel de Ville. Built around a courtyard by Pierre Pavillon from 1655–1670, it stands in a square now used as a flower market. Nearby is the 16th-century clock tower.

Just outside the old town are the ancient Roman baths, the Thermes Sextius, and nearby is the 18th-century spa complex.

Aix's finest street, the cours Mirabeau, is named after the orator and revolutionary Comte de Mirabeau. At its western end is the Fontaine de la Rotonde and Général de Gaulle, a cast-iron fountain built in 1860. The north side is lined with shops, pâtisseries and cafés, the most illustrious being the 18th-century Les Deux Garçons (see p217).

Pavillon de Vendôme detail

The south side is lined with elegant hôtels: No. 4, Hôtel de Villars (1710); No. 10, the Hôtel d'Isoard de Vauvenargues, (1710), former residence of the Marquis of Entrecasteau who murdered his wife here; No. 19, Hôtel d'Arbaud Jouques (1730); No. 20, Hôtel de Forbin (1658); and Hôtel d'Espargnet at No. 38, once home to the Duchess of Montpensier, known as "La Grande Mademoiselle", niece of Louis XIII. South of the cours Mirabeau is the Quartier Mazarin built during the time of Archbishop Michel Mazarin. Aix's first Gothic church, St-Jean-de-Malte, now houses the Musée Granet.

🛡 Cathédrale St-Sauveur

24 pl des Martyrs-de-la-Résistance. ☎ 04 42 23 45 55. ◯ Mon–Sat.
The cathedral at the top of the old town creaks with history. The main door has solid walnut panels sculpted by Jean Guiramand of Toulon (1504). On the right there is a fine 4th–5th-century baptistry, with a Renaissance cupola standing on 2nd-century Corinthian columns. These are from a basilica which stood here beside the Roman forum. The jewel of the church is the triptych of *The Burning Bush* (1476, see pp46–7) by Nicolas Froment which hangs on the wall by the baptistry. South of the cathedral are the tiled Romanesque cloisters.

🏛 Musée des Tapisseries

28 place des Martyrs-de-la-Résistance. ☎ 04 42 23 09 91. ◯ Wed–Mon. ● 31 Dec–1 Jan, 1 May, 24–25 Dec. 🖼
Apart from magnificent 17th- and 18th-century Beauvais tapestries, the museum has opera costumes and stage designs from 1948 onwards, used in the annual Festival International d'Aix (see p31).

🏛 Musée du Vieil Aix

17 rue Gaston-de-Saporta. ☎ 04 42 21 43 55. ◯ Nov-Sep: Tue–Sun. ● 1 Jan, 1 May, 24–25 Dec, 31 Dec. 🖼
This eclectic collection of local memorabilia includes furniture, marionettes, a 19th-century *crèche parlante* and figures from the Corpus Christi parade commissioned by King René.

The 17th-century Hôtel de Ville, with the flower market in front

🏛 Muséum d'Histoire Naturelle

6 rue Espariat. ☎ 04 42 26 23 67. ◯ daily. ● 1 Jan, 1 May, 24–25 Dec, 31 Dec. 🖼
Located in the Hôtel Boyer d'Eguilles, designed by Pierre Puget and built in 1675, the museum has some fascinating collections of mineralogy and palaeontology. Dinosaur eggs which were found locally are a high point of the exhibits.

Cézanne's studio, filled with his furniture and personal belongings

VISITORS' CHECKLIST

Road map C4. 124,000.
av Victor Hugo. rue
Lapierre. 2 place du Général de
Gaulle (04 42 16 11 61). Tue,
Thu & Sat. Festival International
d'Aix (Jun–Jul).

Musée Granet

13 rue Cardinale. 04 42 38 14 70.
Wed–Mon. public hols.
The city's main museum is in an impressive 17th-century former priory of the Knights of Malta. François Granet (1775–1849) was a local painter, and bequeathed his collection of French, Italian and Flemish paintings to Aix. These include Ingres' *Portrait of Granet* and *Jupiter and Thetis*. There are also works by Granet himself and other Provençal painters, with eight canvases by Paul Cézanne. In addition there is archaeological material from Aquae Sextiae, Roman Aix.

Fondation Vasarely

1 av Marcel Pagnol. 04 42 20 01
09. daily. 1 Jan. 1 May, 25 Dec.
One of Aix's most distinctive landmarks, this series of black-and-white metal hexagons was designed by the king of Op Art Victor Vasarely in the mid-1970s to house his foundation. Alongside his monumental works, its exhibitions promote art in the city at a national and international level.

Atelier Paul Cézanne

9 av Paul Cézanne. 04 42 21 06 53.
daily. 1 Jan. 1 May, 25 Dec.
Ten minutes' walk uphill from the cathedral is the modest house of artist Paul Cézanne (*see p24*). The studio, designed by Cezanne himself, is much as he left it when he died in 1906. Here he painted *Les Grandes Baigneuses*, and from here you can see Montagne Ste-Victoire, a favourite subject.

Pavillon de Vendôme

34 rue Celony. 04 42 21 05 78.
Wed–Mon. 1 Jan, 1 May, 25
Dec.
One of the grandest houses in Aix, it was built for Cardinal de Vendôme in 1667 and enlarged in the 18th century. The main entrance door is supported by two figures of Atlantes (*see p48*), and the rooms are filled with Provençal furniture.

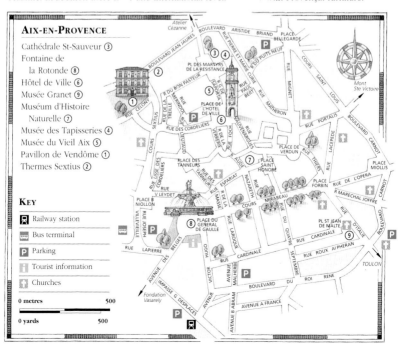

AIX-EN-PROVENCE

Cathédrale St-Sauveur ③
Fontaine de
    la Rotonde ⑧
Hôtel de Ville ⑥
Musée Granet ⑨
Muséum d'Histoire
    Naturelle ⑦
Musée des Tapisseries ④
Musée du Vieil Aix ⑤
Pavillon de Vendôme ①
Thermes Sextius ②

KEY

Railway station
Bus terrminal
Parking
Tourist information
Churches

0 metres   500
0 yards   500

Marseille ㉑

FRANCE'S PREMIER PORT and oldest major city is in a surprisingly attractive setting, centred on the Vieux Port, which fishing boats enter between the guardian forts of St-Jean and St-Nicolas. On the north side are the commercial docks and the old town, rebuilt after World War II. People have lived here for 26 centuries, its mixture of cultures being so varied that Alexandre Dumas called it "the meeting place of the entire world".

The Vieux Port looking south, with Notre-Dame-de-la-Garde on high

Exploring Marseille

Inland, running from the end of the port, is La Canebière – cannabis walk – a big, bustling boulevard which stretches from former hemp fields down to the port where the hemp was made into rope.

At the top of La Canebière is the Neo-Gothic church of St-Vincent-de-Paul. A left and a right turn lead to boulevard Longchamp, and a walk along its length brings you to the Palais Longchamp. This is not really a palace, but more an impressive folly in the form of a colonnade that fans out around a fountain and ends in two large wings. These wings support a natural history and a fine arts museum.

Behind the palace is the city's zoo. Beyond the grid of shopping streets to the south, the town rises towards the basilica of Notre-Dame-de-la-Garde, which provides an unparalleled view of the city.

If you visit the morning fish market on the quai des Belges, you can delight in Marseille's famed *bouillabaisse (see p205)* at one of the countless nearby fish restaurants. Just behind the quai des Belges, at the back of St-Ferréol, is the Jardin des Vestiges, where remains of the ancient Greek settlement from the 4th century BC have been recently discovered.

🏛 Vieille Charité
2 rue de la Vieille Charité. **[** 04 91 14 58 80. **⬤** Tue–Sun. **⬤** public hols.

The old town's finest building is the Vieille Charité, a large, well-restored hospice designed by Pierre Puget (1620–94), architect to Louis XIV. Begun in 1671, its original purpose was to house rural migrants. It is centred on a beautifully proportioned chapel with an oval dome, now used as an exhibition centre. The arcaded three-storey quadrangle was completed in 1749. The first floor has a small but rich collection of ancient Egyptian artifacts in the Musée d'Archéologie Méditerranéenne.

🏛 Cathédrale de la Major
Place de la Major. **[** 04 91 90 53 57. **⬤** Tue–Sun.

The old town descends on the west side to the Cathédrale de la Major, a Neo-Byzantine confection completed in 1893. Its crypt contains the tombs of the bishops of Marseille. Beside it, small and beautiful, is the 11th-century Ancienne Cathédrale de la Major, part of which was sacrificed in the building of the new cathedral. Inside are a reliquary altar of 1073 and a 15th-century altar.

🏛 Musée des Docks Romains
28 place Vivaux. **[** 04 91 91 24 62. **⬤** Tue–Sun. **⬤** public hols.

During post-war rebuilding the Roman docks were uncovered. A small museum, mainly displaying large storage urns once used for wine, grain and oil, occupies the site of the docks, now buried in the foundations of a residential block.

The Palais Longchamps, a 19th-century folly set around a fountain

Stall at the daily fish market, on the old port's quai des Belges

VISITORS' CHECKLIST

Road map C4. 800,500.
25 km (15 miles) NW Marseille.
place Victor Hugo. SNCM,
61 bd des Dames. 4 La Canebière (04 91 13 89 00). daily.
Fête de la Chandeleur (2 Feb).

Musée du Vieux Marseille

Maison Diamantée, 2 rue de la Prison.
04 91 55 10 19. until 2001
for renovation.

The quai du Port follows the
north side of the port past the
17th-century Hôtel de Ville.
Behind it lies the most interesting museum of the town's
history: the Musée du Vieux
Marseille, in the 16th-century
Maison Diamantée. The building takes its name from the
diamond-shaped stones in its
façade. It houses 18th-century
Provençal furniture, domestic
objects and *santons*.

Musée d'Histoire de Marseille

Centre Bourse, square Belsunce.
04 91 90 42 22. Mon–Sat.
public hols.

In the Centre Bourse shopping
centre is the Musée d'Histoire
de Marseille. Reconstructions
of the city at the height of the
Greek period make this a good
starting point for a tour. From
here there is acces to the
Jardin des Vestiges, with
remains of Greek fortifications
and ancient docks dating
from the 1st century AD.

Musée Cantini

19 rue Grignan. 04 91 54 77 75.
Tue–Sun. public hols.

The Musée Cantini is housed
in the 17th-century Hôtel de
Montgrand. Its collection of
20th-century art, given by the
sculptor Jules Cantini, includes
Fauve, Cubist and Surrealist
paintings.

Musée de la Faïence

157 av de Montredon. 04 91 62 21
82. Tue–Sun. public hols.

Marseille's fine new ceramic
museum, in the 19th-century
Chateau Pastré, has over
1,200 items of local, national
and European ceramics from
Neolithic times to today.

The imposing, heavily fortified
walls of the Basilique St-Victor

Basilique St-Victor

Place St-Victor. 04 96 11 22 60.
daily. for crypt.

Marseille's finest piece of religious architecture is St Victor's
basilica, between Notre-Dame
and the port. This religious
fortress belonged to one of
the most powerful abbeys in
Provence. It was founded in
the 5th century by a monk, St
Cassian, in honour of St Victor,
martyred two centuries earlier,
and was enlarged from the
11th to the 14th centuries.

There are crypts containing
catacombs, sarcophagi and
the cave of St Victor.

On 2 February each year St-
Victor becomes a place of pilgrimage. Boat-shaped cakes
are sold to commemorate the
legendary arrival in Provence
of the Stes-Maries (*see p41*).

Basilique de Notre-Dame-de-la-Garde

Rue Fort du Sanctuaire. 04 91 13
40 80. daily.

The basilica of Notre-Dame-
de-la-Garde, which dominates
the south of the town at 155 m
(500 ft), is a 19th-century Neo-
Byzantine extravaganza. It is
presided over by a golden
Madonna on a 46-m (150-ft)
bell tower. Much of the interior
decoration is by the Düsseldorf
School. Many come for the
incomparable view over the
city, while others come here
to leave votive offerings.

Musée Grobet-Labadié

140 bd Longchamp. 04 91 62 21
82. Tue–Sun. public hols.

To the north of the city, at the
top of boulevard Longchamp,
is the finest house in Marseille,
with one of the most unusual
interiors in the region. It was
built in 1873 for a Marseille
merchant, Alexandre Labadié.
The house and its collection
were given to the city in 1919
by his daughter, Marie-Louise.

The Musée Grobet-Labadié
has a fine furniture collection,
tapestries, 17th–19th century
paintings, and many objects
of interest, including unusual
musical instruments, among
them silk and ivory bagpipes.

Detail of *The Flagellation of Christ*,
in the Musée Grobet-Labadié

🏛 Musée des Beaux Arts

Palais Longchamp, 142 bd Longchamp.
📞 *04 91 14 59 30.* ⭕ *Tue–Sun.*
⬤ *public hols.* ♿

The museum contains works by the city's best known sons: the sculptor, painter and architect Pierre Puget (1620–94) and the caricaturist, sculptor and painter, Daumier (1808–79). Serre's paintings of Marseille's plague in 1721 *(see pp48–9)* are housed here and there is a large collection of Flemish, Italian and French painting, including works by Rubens, Carracci, Courbet and Ingres.

The Château d'If in the bay of Marseille, a prison in reality and fiction

Le Sacrifice de Noé by Pierre Puget in the Musée des Beaux Arts

⚓ Château d'If

📞 *04 91 59 02 30.* ⭕ *Apr–Sep: daily; Oct–Mar: Tue–Sun.* ♿

Fact, fiction and legend mingle in this island castle in the bay of Marseille. Up until the 16th century, it was a barren island, only visited by local fishermen. On a trip to Marseille in 1516, François I decided to make it a fortress to protect the port. It was completed in 1528, and turned into a political prison in 1580. Famous inmates have included Alexander Dumas' fictional Count of Monte Cristo, the legendary Man in the Iron Mask *(see p71)* and the real Comte de Mirabeau. Nine years before the château was built, the first rhinoceros ever to set foot in Europe was brought ashore here, and drawn by Albrecht Dürer *(see p47)*.

▦ Cité Radieuse

280 boulevard Michelet.
A landmark in modern architecture, the Cité Radieuse or Radiant City was opened in 1952. This vertical, concrete construction by Le Corbusier includes shops, social clubs schools and crèches *(see p23)*.

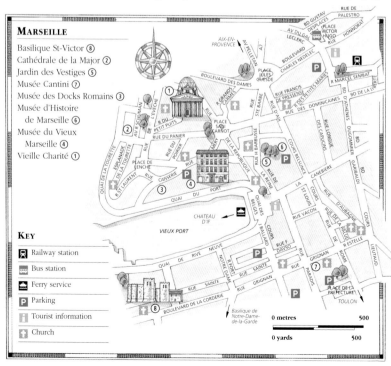

MARSEILLE

Basilique St-Victor ⑧
Cathédrale de la Major ②
Jardin des Vestiges ⑤
Musée Cantini ⑦
Musée des Docks Romains ③
Musée d'Histoire de Marseille ⑥
Musée du Vieux Marseille ④
Vieille Charité ①

KEY

🚉 Railway station
🚌 Bus station
⛴ Ferry service
🅿 Parking
ℹ Tourist information
✝ Church

0 metres   500
0 yards   500

Aubagne ㉒

Road map C4. 🚶 44,000. 🚉 🚌
🛈 av Antide Boyer (04 42 03 49 98).
🗓 Tue, Thu, Sat & Sun.

Marcel pagnol's life and work is the main attraction of this unprepossessing market town. It has a tradition of making ceramics and *santons (see p48)*. The tableaux can be seen in the Petit Monde de Marcel Pagnol display in the Syndicat d'Initiative.

Just outside the town is the headquarters of the French Foreign Legion, moved here from Algeria in 1962. The headquarters has a **Musée de la Légion Etrangère** with a selection of memorabilia on display from a variety of campaigns ranging from Mexico to Indochina.

🏛 **Musée de la Légion Etrangère**
Caserne Quartier Viénot. 📞 04 42 18 82 41. ◻ Jun–Sep: Tue–Sun (excl Fri pm); Oct–May: Wed, Sat & Sun. ♿ limited.

Les Calanques ㉓

Road map C4. 🚶 Marseille. 🚉 Marseille, Cassis. 🚌 Cassis. ⛴ Marseille. 🛈 Cassis (04 42 01 71 17).

Between marseille and Cassis the coast is broken up by *calanques* – enticing fjord-like inlets lying between vertical white cliffs. Continuing deep under the blue waters, they offer safe natural harbours and

Poster for Pagnol's film *Angèle*

fascinating aquatic life, with glorious views from the high clifftops *(see also pp28–29)*. Their precipitous faces provide a challenge to climbers.

Access to some inlets is by boat. From Cassis, it is possible to walk or drive to the nearest *calanque*, Port-Miou. Beyond it lies Port-Pin, with occasional pine trees and a shady beach, but the most scenic is En-Vau, which has a sandy beach and needle-like rocks rising from the sea. On the western side, the Sormiou and Morgiou inlets can be approached by road.

In 1991, a cave was found with its entrance 36 m (118 ft) beneath the sea at Sormiou. It is decorated with pictures of prehistoric animals resembling the ancient cave paintings at Lascaux in the Dordogne.

Bear in mind when visiting the area that the main car parks serving Les Calanques beaches are notorious for theft.

MARCEL PAGNOL

A plaque at No. 16 cours Barthélemy in Aubagne marks the birthplace of Pagnol, Provençal writer and film-maker. Born in 1905, he grew up in the village of La Treille, to the northwest. His insights into rural Provence enriched tales such as *Jean de Florette* and *Manon des Sources*. The Syndicat d'Initiative has a Circuit Marcel Pagnol, with road routes and walks which take in La Treille and other sites of Pagnol's inspiration.

Cassis ㉔

Road map C4. 🚶 8,000. 🚉 🚌
🛈 place Baragnon (04 42 01 71 17).
🗓 Wed & Fri.

A favourite summer resort of such artists as Derain, Dufy and Matisse, Cassis is a lovely little port, tucked into limestone hills. The Romans liked it, too, and built villas here, and when Marseille prospered in the 17th century a number of mansions were erected.

There is a charming **Musée Municipal** in the 1703 rectory with items dating back to the Greeks, some rescued from the seabed. It also shows Cassis to have been a substantial trading port up till World War II, when ships were destroyed by the Germans in the small harbour. There are works by the oriental and landscape painter Félix Ziem *(see p24)* and other early 20th-century artists who were inspired by the attractive town. It was also here that Winston Churchill learnt to paint.

Apart from Les Calanques, there are three good beaches to visit. The Plage de la Grande Mer is the best, and behind it, the promenade des Lombards heads under the red cliffs to the east of the town. A busy, prosperous fishing centre in the 19th century, Cassis is still known for its excellent seafood. The local delicacy is fresh sea urchins, enjoyed with a glass of white wine from Cassis.

🏛 **Musée Municipal**
Rue X-d'Authier. 📞 04 42 01 88 66.
◻ Wed, Thu & Sat pm only.
⬤ 1 Jan, 1 May, 25 Dec.

En-Vau, the most beautiful of Les Calanques, along the coast from Cassis

VAUCLUSE

AUCLUSE IS A *land of vines and lavender, truffles and melons, which many know about through the books of the English expatriate Peter Mayle, depicting village life in the Luberon, an idyllic countryside where Picasso spent his last years. Roussillon, set among ochre quarries, also became the topic of a book, when American sociologist Laurence Wylie experienced village life there in the 1950s.*

The jewel of Vaucluse is the fortified riverside city of Avignon, home to the popes during their "Babylonian exile" from 1309–77, and now host to one of the great music and theatre festivals of France. The popes' castle at Châteauneuf-du-Pape is now a ruin, but well worth a visit for the stupendous wines it produces. The Côtes-du-Rhône region is justly renowned, and its vineyards spread as far northeast as the slopes of the towering giant of Provence, Mont Ventoux.

The Roman legacy in Vaucluse is also remarkable. It is glimpsed in the great theatre and triumphal arch in Orange, and in the ruins of Vaison-la-Romaine which, unusually, were not built over by successive civilizations. Carpentras was also a Roman town, but its claim to fame is its possession of France's oldest synagogue. The story of the Jews, who were given papal protection in Vaucluse, is one of many religious histories which can be traced through the region. Another is the Baron of Oppède's brutal crusade against the Vaudois heretics in 1545, when many villages were destroyed.

Near Oppède, at Lacoste, a poppy-lined path leads to the château of France's notorious deviant, the Marquis de Sade. A more elevated writer was Petrarch, who lived in Fontaine-de-Vaucluse, where the Sorgue river emerges from a mysterious source.

Façade of vine-covered house at Le Bastidon, near the Luberon

◁ Fountain in village square, Châteauneuf-du-Pape

Exploring Vaucluse

Vaucluse, which takes its name from the Latin *vallis clausa* (closed valley), covers 3,540 sq km (2,200 sq miles). It is bordered by the Rhône on the west, the Durance in the south, and the foothills of the Alps to the east, and has a series of highland chains, dominated by the serene Mont Ventoux *(see p160)*. The extraordinary Dentelles pinnacles are in the west and to the south is the Vaucluse Plateau, where the river Sorgue flows in the beautiful and dramatic setting of Fontaine-de-Vaucluse.

SIGHTS AT A GLANCE

Abbaye de Sénanque **9**
Ansouis **19**
Apt **17**
Avignon pp166–8 **12**
Bollène **1**
Cadenet **18**
Caderousse **6**
Carpentras **8**
Cavaillon **15**
Châteauneuf-du-Pape **7**
Fontaine-de-Vaucluse **10**
Gordes **13**
La Tour d'Aigues **21**
L'Isle-sur-la-Sorgue **11**
Mont Ventoux **4**
Orange pp161–3 **5**
Pertuis **20**
Roussillon **14**
Vaison-la-Romaine **2**

Tours

Dentelles **3**
Petit Luberon pp170–71 **16**

KEY

▨	Motorway
▬	Major road
▨	Minor road
▨	Scenic route
⌐	River
☆	Viewpoint

The roofs and terraces of Gordes, crowned by the church and castle

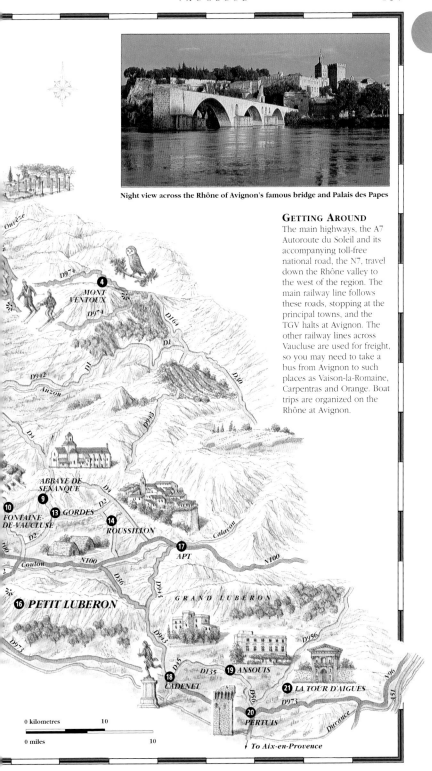

Night view across the Rhône of Avignon's famous bridge and Palais des Papes

GETTING AROUND

The main highways, the A7 Autoroute du Soleil and its accompanying toll-free national road, the N7, travel down the Rhône valley to the west of the region. The main railway line follows these roads, stopping at the principal towns, and the TGV halts at Avignon. The other railway lines across Vaucluse are used for freight, so you may need to take a bus from Avignon to such places as Vaison-la-Romaine, Carpentras and Orange. Boat trips are organized on the Rhône at Avignon.

0 kilometres   10

0 miles   10

To Aix-en-Provence

The Belvédère Pasteur garden in Bollène

Bollène **①**

Road map B2. 🚶 *14,000.* 🚗 🚌
🛈 *pl Reynaud de la Gardette (04 90 40 51 44).* 🕒 *Mon.*

DESPITE BEING spread along the A7 autoroute, Bollène is pleasant, with airy boulevards and walks beside the river Lez, where there is a camping site. The narrow streets of the old quarter lead to the 12th-century **Collégiale St-Martin**, with its timber saddleback roof and Renaissance doorway. Bollène became famous in 1882, when Louis Pasteur stayed here and developed innoculation against swine fever. The **Belvédère Pasteur** garden above the town has views over the Rhône valley to the Cévennes, the Bollène hydroelectric power station and Tricastin nuclear power plant. The **Chapelle des Trois-Croix** in the gardens has a small museum.

Just north of Bollène is the ghost village of Barri. Its trogolodyte houses, some still in use at the end of the last century, proved handy hiding places in World War II.

Vaison-la-Romaine **②**

Road map B2. 🚶 *5,600.* 🚌 🛈 *pl du Chanoine Sautel (04 90 36 02 11).* 🕒 *Tue.*

THE PAVEMENT CAFES in this attractive stone-and-red-roof town on the river Ouvèze are among Provence's most chic. The modern town sits beside the Roman town, opposite the hilltop Haute-Ville on the other side of the river. Vaison is a smart address for Parisians' second homes and, judging by the opulent remains left by the Romans, it has long been sought after. The Romans lived with the native Celtic Vocontii and the population was around 10,000. Two sites have been excavated, divided by the avenue Général-de-Gaulle. The upper site, known as the Puymin Quarter, has a Roman theatre, still used for Vaison's summer festival of music, theatre and dance. Its stage is cut out of rock, and the theatre seats up to 6,000. Many Roman remains come from the villa of a wealthy family, the House of the Messii, and an elegant,

Mosaic in the museum at Vaison-la-Romaine

colonnaded public building, Pompey's Portico. The site is dotted with copies of original statues that are now kept in the **Musée Theo Desplans**, and include a powerful nude of Hadrian and his well-draped empress, Sabina. Many statues were designed to have their heads replaced whenever there was a change of local officials. Other remains include a communal six-seater latrine and a 3rd-century silver bust which once stood in the hall of a patrician's house in La Villasse, the district on the other side of the avenue Général-de-Gaulle.

The Haute-Ville, which artists and craftspeople helped to re-populate, is reached by means of a Roman bridge, a single 56-ft (17-m) span used for more than 2,000 years until recent devastating floods necessitated huge repairs. Entrance is via a 14th-cen- tury fortified gate. The Romanesque church, built as a **cathedral**, has 7th-century columns in the apse, and a 12th-century cloister. At the summit is the ruined castle the victorious Counts of Toulouse built here in 1160.

🏛 **Roman City**
Fouilles de Puymin and Musée Theo Desplans, pl du Chanoine Sautel.
📞 *04 90 36 02 11.* ⏰ *Mar–Oct: daily; Nov–Feb: Wed–Mon.* ⬤ *1 Jan, 1 May, 25 Dec.* 🎫

Grounds of Roman house with 3rd-century silver bust, Vaison-la-Romaine

A Tour of the Dentelles ❸

DENTELLE MEANS "LACE", and the Dentelles de Montmirail is the name of the 15-km (9-mile) range of hills which form a lacework of delicate peaks. Not as high or rugged as they initially seem, the Dentelles have good paths and offer some of the most accessible, enjoyable mountain walks in Provence. The paths are bright with broom and flanked by pines, oaks and wild almond trees. When you have had your fill of the stunning scenery, enjoy fine Côtes-du-Rhône wines and delicious goat's cheese produced in the picturesque villages tucked into the folds of the Dentelles.

Muscat grapes outside Beaumes-de-Venise

Vaison-la-Romaine ①
A chic town, favoured by wealthy Parisians, Vaison is built on separate Roman and medieval sites. Among its many attractions are the cathedral with its 6th-century sarcophagus of healer St Quenin, and a Romanesque chapel.

Gigondas vineyard

Gigondas ⑥
The local red wine is highly regarded and its producers include the master-chef Roux brothers. The Counts of Orange built the 14th-century château.

Crestet

Séguret

DENTELLES DE MONTMIRAIL

Lafare

Montmirail

Malaucène ②
This former Huguenot strong-hold has a clock tower, originally built as a watchtower during the Wars of Religion *(see pp46–7).*

Le Barroux ③
Surrounded by olive and apricot trees, this tiny village is overlooked by a 12th-century château, once a stronghold of the lords of Baux. It has fine views.

Vacqueyras ⑤
The home of the famous troubadour, Raimbaud, who died on a Crusade, this village has a church with a 6th-century baptistry.

Beaumes-de-Venise ④
This is a town of many restaurants, and the home of Muscat, the town's famous fortified sweet white dessert wine, which can be enjoyed with lunch or dinner.

KEY

▬▬	Tour route
----	Other roads

0 kilometres 2

0 miles 2

TIPS FOR DRIVERS

Tour length: 50 km (30 miles).
Stopping off points: The hilltop village of Crestet; Lafare, a hamlet leading to the 627-m (2057-ft) Rocher du Turc; and Montmirail, a 19th-century spa resort visited by Mistral. (See also pp242–3.)

Mont Ventoux ➍

🛩 Avignon. 🚡 2,200. 🚌 Orange, Bédoin. ℹ Espace Marie-Louis Gravier, Bédoin (04 90 65 63 95).

T HE "GIANT OF PROVENCE" is the dominant feature west of the Alps, a limestone massif which reaches 1,909 m (6,233 ft). It is easy to reach the car park at the top, unless there is deep snow, which can last until April. The snowline starts at 1,300 m (4,265 ft), but the limestone scree of its summit forms a year-round white cap.

Until 1973 there was a motor race on the south side of Mont Ventoux, to the top: speeds reached up to 145 km/h (90 mph). A vintage car rally still takes place in Bédoin. The roads have gradually improved and the worst hairpins are now ironed out, but the mountain roads are often included as a gruelling stage on the Tour de France. Britain's cyclist Tommy Simpson suffered a fatal heart attack here in 1967.

It takes around five hours to walk to the summit of Mont Ventoux. Petrarch (see p45) made the first recorded journey from Malaucène on one May dawn in 1336. As there were no roads then, it took him a great deal longer.

The mountain is often windy and its name comes from the French word (vent) for wind.

Summit of Mont Ventoux during the Mistral season

Engraving of motor rally car ascending Mont Ventoux (1904)

When the northerly Mistral blows, it can almost lift you out of your boots. But the winds dry the moisture in the sky, painting it a deep blue colour and leaving behind incredibly clear vistas.

There are three starting points for a walking tour of the mountain: Malaucène, on the north slopes, Bédoin to the south and Sault to the east. Another direct route for hikers is from Brantes on the northeast side, up the Toulourenc valley. The first two towns both have tourist offices which organize guided hikes to see the sun rise at the summit. The 21-km (13-mile) road from Malaucène passes

Monument to cycling hero Tommy Simpson

the 12th-century Chap- elle Notre-Dame-du-Groseau and the Source Vauclusienne, a deep pool tapped for an aqueduct by the Romans. The ski centre at Mt Serein is based 5 km (3 miles) from the summit. A viewing table at the peak helps to discern the Cévennes, the Luberon and Ste-Victoire. Descending via Bédoin, the road passes the Col des Tempêtes, known for its stormy weather. The ski centre of Le Chalet-Reynard is at the junction leading to Sault and les Gorges de la Nesque, and St-Estève, once notorious for racing car accidents, has fine views over the Vaucluse.

PROVENÇAL FLOWERS

Because the temperature on Mont Ventoux drops between the foot and the summit by around 11° C (20° F), the vegetation alters from the lavender and peach orchards of the plain via the oak, beech and conifer woodlands to the arctic flowers towards the summit. June is the best month for flowers.

Early purple orchid
Orchis mascula

Alpine poppy
Papaver rhaeticum

Trumpet gentian
Gentiana clusii

Orange ❺

Road map 2B. 🏛 *27,000.* 🚉 🚌
🛈 *cours Aristide Briand (04 90 34 70 88).* 🚌 *Thu.*

THIS HISTORICAL TOWN contains two of the finest Roman monuments in Europe: The Théâtre Antique d'Orange is known for its world-famous concerts *(see pp162–3).* The Arc de Triomphe celebrates Julius Caesar's conquest of the Gauls and victory over the Greek fleet. Orange is also the centre for the Côtes-du-Rhône vineyards and produce such as olives, honey and truffles. Visitors can enjoy the area around the 17th-century Hôtel de Ville, where streets open on to peaceful, shady squares with café terraces.

Side-chapel altar in the Ancienne Cathédrale Notre-Dame, Orange

Roman Orange
When the first Roman army attempted to conquer Gaul, it was defeated near Orange with a loss of 100,000 men in 105 BC. When it came back three years later and triumphed, one of the first monuments built to show supremacy was the 22-m (72-ft) Arc de Triomphe on the via Agrippa between Arles and Lyons, today cast to one side.

The Old Town
Old Orange is centred around the 17th-century town hall and **Ancienne Cathédrale Notre-Dame**, with its crumbling Romanesque portal, damaged in the Wars of Religion *(see pp46–7).* The theatre's wall dominates the place des Frères-Mounet. Louis XIV described it as "the greatest wall in my kingdom". There is

an excellent view of the theatre, the city of Orange and the Rhône plain from **Colline St-Eutrope**. This is the site of the remains of the castle of the princes of Orange, who gave the Dutch royal family its title, the House of Orange, through marriage. The family also lent their name to states and cities around the world.

🎫 Arc de Triomphe
Av de l'Arc de Triomphe.
The monument has excellent decorations devoted to war and maritime themes. There is a modernistic quality, particularly visible in the trophies above the side arches. On the east face, Gallic prisoners, naked and in chains, broadcast to the world who was in charge. Anchors and ropes showed maritime superiority.
When Maurice of Nassau fortified the town in 1622 by using Roman buildings as quarries, the arch escaped this fate by being incorporated into the defensive walls as a keep.

🏛 Musée Municipal
Rue Madeleine Roc. 📞 *04 90 51 18 24.* ◯ *daily.* ● *1 Jan, 25 Dec.* 🈚
The exhibits found in the courtyard and ground floor reflect the history of Orange. They include more than 400 marble fragments which, when assembled, proved to be plans of the area, based on three

Stone carving of a centaur in the Musée Municipal, Orange

surveys dating from AD 77, and extending from Bollène to Auzon. Also in the museum are portraits of members of the Royal House of Orange and paintings by the British artist, Sir Frank Brangwyn (1867–1956). One room demonstrates how printed fabrics were made in 18th-century Orange.

🎫 Maison J-H Fabre
Harmas de J-H Fabre. 📞 *04 90 70 00 44.* ◯ *Wed–Sat & Mon.* ● *public hols.* 🈚
At Sérignan-du-Comtat, 8 km (5 miles) northeast of Orange is *L'Harmas*, the estate of the entomologist and poet Jean-Henri Fabre (1823–1915). His superb collection of insects and fungi, and the glorious surrounding botanical garden, attract visitors from all over the world.

Arc de Triomphe monument, representing Julius Caesar's conquests

Théâtre Antique d'Orange

ORANGE'S ROMAN THEATRE is one of the best
preserved of the entire Roman empire.
It was constructed in the reign of Augustus
(around 27–25 BC) against the natural height
of the Colline-St-Eutrope. Its stage doors
were hollow so that actors could stand in
front and amplify their voices; today other
acoustic touches make it ideal for concerts.
In Roman times the theatre was also used
for meetings and lectures. The *cavea*, or
tiered semicircle, held up to 10,000 spectators,
seated according to their social status. From
the 16th to 19th centuries, the theatre was
filled with squalid housing, traces of which
can still be seen.

Awning Supports
*Still visible on the exterior walls are corbels
which held the huge* velum-*bearing masts.*

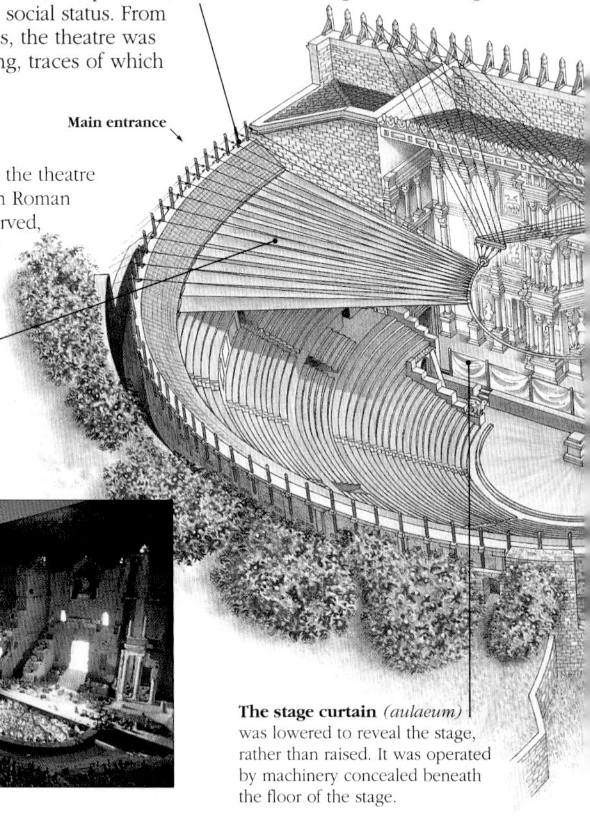

Main entrance

ROMAN THEATRE
This reconstruction shows the theatre
as it would have looked in Roman
times. Although well-preserved,
what remains is a shadow
of its past magnificence.

A canvas awning,
known as a *velum*,
protected the theatre-
goers from sun or rain.

The stage curtain *(aulaeum)*
was lowered to reveal the stage,
rather than raised. It was operated
by machinery concealed beneath
the floor of the stage.

Night Concerts
Cultural events such as Les
Chorégies d'Orange, *a festival
of opera, drama and ballet, once
frequented by Sarah Bernhardt,
have been held here since 1869
(see p31). The theatre is also a
popular rock concert venue.*

The Great Wall
*Built of red sandstone, this
massive construction is 103 m
(338 ft) long, 37 m (120 ft) high
and over 1.8 m (5 ft) thick.*

Emperor Augustus

This 3.5-m (11-ft) statue, with a hand raised in greeting, dominates the stage at the third level. At its base kneels a figure in breeches, possibly a defeated enemy. Other statues have been destroyed, but this copy was returned to the niche in 1951.

VISITORS' CHECKLIST

Place des Frères-Mounet.
📞 04 90 51 17 60. ⏰ Apr–Sep: 9am–6:30pm daily; Oct–Mar: 9am–noon, 1:30–5pm daily.
🚫 1 Jan, 25 Dec. 🎫 also valid for Musée Municipal (see p161).

Side rooms, or *parascaenia,* were where actors could rest, and props be stored, when not required on stage.

Stage Wall
The inner face of the stage wall (Frons Scanae) still bears fragments of marble friezes and mosaics. A frieze of centaurs framed the royal doorway in the centre.

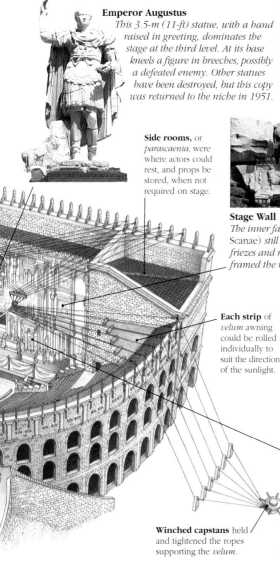

Each strip of *velum* awning could be rolled individually to suit the direction of the sunlight.

Marble Columns
The stage wall had three levels of between 76 and 122 marble columns, of which only two remain. The wall's many surfaces helped to break up sound waves, so that the actors could speak without their voices having an echo.

Winched capstans held and tightened the ropes supporting the *velum.*

The Great Roman Temple
From 1925–37, excavations took place to the west of the theatre, where 22 houses had been pulled down. They unearthed evidence of what seems to have been a group of Roman temples and a forum, baths or gymnasium. With the theatre, they would have formed an impressive social, religious and cultural centre.

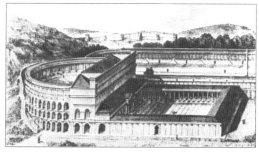

Romanesque church at Caderousse

Caderousse **6**

Road map B2. 🏠 2,300. **ℹ** La
Mairie (04 90 51 90 69). 🗓 Tue.

THIS BANKSIDE village lies at
a point where Hannibal is
said to have crossed the river
Rhône with his elephants on
his way to Rome in 218 BC.
For centuries, Caderousse has
stoically endured the floods of
the River Rhône, and plaques
on the town hall record the
high levels of floodwater. By
1856, the villagers had had
enough, and erected a dyke
which is still in place today.
Its four entry points can close
if floods should threaten again.
Caderousse has a Roman-
esque church, **St-Michel**, to
which the flamboyant Gothic
chapel of St-Claude was added
during the 16th century.

Châteauneuf-du-Pape **7**

Road map B3. 🏠 2,100. 🚉
🚊 Sorgues, then bus. **ℹ** place du
Portail (04 90 83 71 08). 🗓 Fri.

THE BEST-KNOWN of the Côtes-
du-Rhône wine labels takes
its name from an unassuming
yellowstone village on a small
hill, given over to cellars and
restaurants selling the products
of the local growers entitled
to the *appellation contrôlée*.
The **Musée du Père Anselme**
traces the history and current
state of the local viniculture.
   At the top of the village are
the ruins of the **Château des
Papes**, mostly burned down
in the 16th-century Wars of
Religion. From the remaining
walls there is a superb view
of Avignon and the vineyard-
lined clay fields where smooth
stones deposited by the Rhône
reflect the sun's heat onto 13
varieties of grapes. The château

was built in 1317 by John XXII,
an Avignon pope who planted
the first vineyards, but it took
some 400 years for the wine's
reputation to spread. Today,
there are 35 Châteauneuf-du-
Pape domaines. The nearby
town of Pernes-les-Fontaines
is known for its 36 fountains,
in particular the 18th-century
Fontaine du Cormoran. Until
1914, each of the fountains
had an individual keeper.

🏛 Musée du Père Anselme de Vignerons

Rte d'Avignon, Châteauneuf-du-Pape.
📞 04 90 83 70 07. 🗓 daily.
🚫 1 Jan, 25 Dec. 🚫

Carpentras **8**

Road map B3. 🏠 26,000. **ℹ** 170
allée Jean-Jaurès (04 90 63 57 88).
🗓 Tue, Fri.

AS THE CAPITAL of the Comtat
Venaissin, this market town
is in the centre of the Côtes-du-
Ventoux wine region. It has a
reputation for truffles and *berlingots*, stripy caramel sweets.
   Boulevards encircle the old
town, but the Porte d'Orange is
the only surviving part of the
medieval ramparts. In the
Middle Ages, the town had a
large Jewish community, and
their 15th-century **synagogue**
is the oldest in France, now
used by some 100 families.
While not openly persecuted
under papal rule, many Jews
changed faith and entered the
Cathédrale-St-Siffrein by its
15th-century south door, the
Porte Juive. The cathedral is in
the centre of the old town,
near a smaller version of

Orange's Arc de Triomphe.
In it are Provençal paintings
and statues by local sculptor
Jacques Bernus (1650– 1728),
and a small treasury.
   The *Hôtel-Dieu* has a fine
18th-century pharmacy, and
there are regional costumes in
the **Musée Comtadin**.

✡ Synagogue
Pl Maurice Charretier. **📞** 04 90 63 39
97. 🗓 Mon–Fri. 🚫 Jewish feast days.
✝ Cathédral St-Siffrein
Pl du Général de Gaulle. 🚫
🏛 Musée Comtadin
234 bd Albin-Durand. **📞** 04 90 63 04
92. 🗓 Wed–Mon. 🚫 public hols. 🚫

Pharmacy in the 18th-century
Hôtel-Dieu at Carpentras

Abbaye de Sénanque **9**

Road map C3. **📞** 04 90 72 05 72.
🗓 Mar–Oct: Sun pm–Sat; Nov–Feb:
pm only. 🚫

THE BEAUTIFULLY SITED Abbaye
de Sénanque, surrounded
by a tranquil sea of lavender, is
best approached from Gordes
(see p169). Often to be seen in
the fields are the monks, in
their brown or blue robes.
   Like the other abbeys that
make up the Cistercian triumvirate in Provence *(see p43)*,
Sénanque is harmonious and

Châteauneuf-du-Pape vineyards

unadorned. It was founded in 1148 by an abbott and 12 monks, and the building of the serene north-facing abbey church started 12 years later.

Some roofs of the building are still tiled with limestone slates called *lauzes*, also used for making traditional stone dwellings known as bories *(see p169)*. The abbey's simply designed interior has stone walls, plain windows and a barrel-vaulted ceiling.

Sénanque reached its zenith in the early 13th century, when the abbey owned several local farms. But new riches brought corruption in the 14th century, and by the 17th century, only two monks remained. By 1854 it had come under the control of the Iles de Lérins monks, some of whom remained there from 1927 to 1969. Then a wealthy industrialist formed the *Association des Amis de Sénanque* to restore the abbey. The monks have been living there since 1989, and some of their home produce is for sale.

Abbaye de Sénanque with lavender

Fontaine-de-Vaucluse ⑩

Road map B3. 🏠 580. 🚊 *Avignon.* 🅸 *chemin de la Fontaine (04 90 20 32 22).* 🛎 *Tue.*

T HE SOURCE OF the Sorgue river is one of the natural wonders of Provence. It begins underground, with tributaries that drain the Vaucluse plateau, an area of around 2,000 sq km (800 sq miles). In the closed valley above the town, water erupts from an unfathomable depth to develop into a fully

Fontaine-de-Vaucluse, where the Sorgue river begins

fledged river. Beside the river is the **Moulin à Papier Vallis Clausa**, which has produced handmade paper ever since the 14th century. It now sells maps, prints and lampshades.

The underground museum, **Le Monde Souterrain de Norbert Casteret** features this speleologist's findings over 30 years of exploring Sorgue's dams, caves and waterfalls. The **Musée de la Résistance**, which traces the movement from 1870–1940, is a reminder of the indomitability of the human spirit. The house the poet lived in for 16 years and wrote of his unrequited love for Laura of Avignon is now the **Musée Pétrarque**.

🎠 Moulin à Papier Vallis Clausa
Chemin de Gouffre. 🅲 *04 90 20 34 14.* 🔲 *daily.* 🌑 *1 Jan, 25 Dec.*
🏛 Monde Souterrain de Norbert Casteret
Chemin de la Fontaine. 🅲 *04 90 20 34 13.* 🔲 *Feb–11 Nov: daily.* 🎫 🅗
🏛 Musée de la Résistance
Chemin de la Fontaine. 🅲 *04 90 20 24 00.* 🔲 *mid-Apr–mid-Oct: Wed–Mon; mid-Oct–Dec & Mar–mid-Apr: Sat–Sun.* 🌑 *Jan, Feb, 1 May, 25 Dec.* 🎫 🅗
🏛 Musée Pétrarque
Rive gauche de la Sorgue. 🅲 *04 90 20 37 20.* 🔲 *mid-Apr–mid-Oct: Wed–Mon.* 🌑 *1 Jan, 25 Dec.* 🎫

L'Isle-sur-la-Sorgue ⑪

Road map B3. 🏠 *18,000.* 🚊 🚌 🅸 *pl de l'Eglise (04 90 38 04 78).* 🛎 *Thu & Sun (antiques and flea).*

T HIS ATTRACTIVE TOWN is a major haunt for antique hunters at weekends. It lies on the river Sorgue which once powered 70 watermills that pressed grain and oil. Today, six idle wheels remain. The town's 17th-century **Notre-Dame-des-Anges** is ornate inside. The tourist office is in an 18th-century granary, and the Hôpital, also 18th century, has a collection of Moustiers pottery jars in its pharmacy.

Water wheel near place Gambetta, l'Isle-sur-la-Sorgue

Street-by-Street: Avignon ⑫

St Jerome,
Petit Palais

BORDERED TO THE NORTH and west by the Rhône, the medieval city of Avignon is the chief city of Vaucluse and gateway to Provence. Its walls cover nearly 4.5 km (3 miles) and are punctuated by 39 towers and seven gates. Within the walls thrives a culturally rich city with its own opera house, university, several foreign language schools and numerous theatre companies. The streets and squares are often filled with buskers, and the Avignon festival in July, which includes theatre, mime and cabaret, has now become a major European event.

Chapelle St-Nicolas, named after the patron saint of bargemen, is a 16th-century building on a 13th-century base. Entrance is via Tour du Châtelet.

Porte du Rhône

★ Pont St-Bénézet
Begun in 1177 by shepherd boy Bénézet, this bridge is the subject of the famous rhyme Sur le Pont d'Avignon.

Conservatoire de Musique
The façade of this former mint, the Hôtel des Monnaies (1619), bears the arms of Cardinal Borghese.

RUE DE LIMAS

RUE GRANDE FUSTERIE

RUE DES GROTTES

RUE ST-ETIENNE

RUE DE LA BALANCE

RUE PETITE FUSTERIE

RUE RACINE

RUE FERRU

PLACE DE L'HORLOGE

Place de l'Horloge
The main square was laid out in the 15th century and is named after the Gothic clock tower above the town hall. Many of today's buildings date from the 19th century.

KEY

– – – Suggested route

0 metres	100
0 yards	100

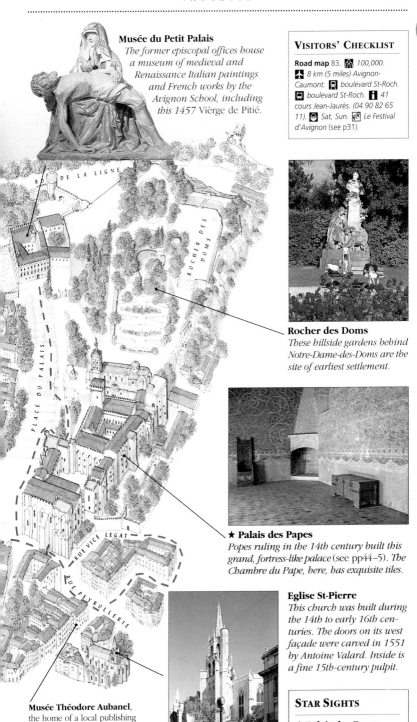

Musée du Petit Palais
The former episcopal offices house a museum of medieval and Renaissance Italian paintings and French works by the Avignon School, including this 1457 Vièrge de Pitié.

VISITORS' CHECKLIST

Road map B3. 🏃 100,000.
✈ 8 km (5 miles) Avignon-Caumont. 🚉 boulevard St-Roch.
🚌 boulevard St-Roch. 🛈 41 cours Jean-Jaurès. (04 90 82 65 11). 🛒 Sat, Sun. 🎭 Le Festival d'Avignon (see p31).

Rocher des Doms
These hillside gardens behind Notre-Dame-des-Doms are the site of earliest settlement.

★ **Palais des Papes**
Popes ruling in the 14th century built this grand, fortress-like palace (see pp44–5). The Chambre du Pape, here, has exquisite tiles.

Eglise St-Pierre
This church was built during the 14th to early 16th centuries. The doors on its west façade were carved in 1551 by Antoine Valard. Inside is a fine 15th-century pulpit.

Musée Théodore Aubanel, the home of a local publishing family since 1744, houses a museum of printing, Provençal furniture and literature.

STAR SIGHTS

★ **Palais des Papes**

★ **Pont St-Bénézet**

Exploring Avignon

MASSIVE RAMPARTS ENCLOSE one of the most fascinating towns in southern France. A stroll around the streets reveals *trompe l'oeil* windows and mansions such as King René's house in the rue du Roi-René. This street leads to the cobbled rue des Teinturiers, named after the town's dyers and textile-makers, where a bridge crosses the river Sorgue to the 16th-century Chapelle des Pénitents Gris.

Palais des Papes in Avignon glimpsed across the river Rhône

♣ Palais des Papes

Pl du Palais. **04 90 27 50 74.**
◯ *daily (times vary).* 🖉

These buildings *(see pp44–5)* give an idea of the grand life under the seven French popes who built a miniature Vatican during their rule here, lasting from 1309–77. They owned their own mint, baked a vast number of loaves every day, and fortified themselves against the French.

Entrance is by means of the Port des Champeaux, beneath the twin pencil-shaped turrets of the flamboyant Palais Neuf (1342–52), built by Clement VI, which extends south from the solid Palais Vieux (1334–42) of Benoit XII. In the new palace, the main courtyard, La Cour d'Honneur, is the grand central setting for the summer festival *(see p35).* La Chambre du Pape in the Tour des Anges opposite the entrance has exquisite tiles, and there are fine 14th-century deer-hunting scenes painted by Matteo Giovanetti and others in the adjoining Chambre du Cerf.

The Palais Vieux, centred on a cloister, has two square defence towers. The larger

Bird tile in the Chambre du Pape

rooms around it include the 45-m (148-ft) banqueting hall, Le Grand Tinel, and La Salle du Consistoire, centre of courtly activity, where pictures of all the popes are displayed. The chapel beside it has exquisite ceiling frescoes, painted by Giovanetti between 1344 and 1345.

♠ Cathédrale Notre-Dame-des-Doms

Pl du Palais. **04 90 86 81 01.** ◯ *daily.*
This building beside the Palais des Papes was begun in the 12th century. Since then it has been damaged and rebuilt several times. A gilded Madonna was added on to the tower as recently as the 19th century, and the original 12th-century altar is now located in the first side chapel, where two popes are entombed.

🏛 Musée du Petit Palais

Pl du Palais. **04 90 86 44 58.**
◯ *Wed–Mon.* ● *1 Jan, 1 May, 14 Jul, 1 Nov, 25 Dec.* 🖉
Set around an arcaded courtyard, the "little palace", built in 1318, was modified in 1474 to suit Michelangelo's patron and nemesis, Cardinal Rovere,

later Pope Julius II. It became a museum in 1958, and houses Avignon's medieval collection, which includes works by Simone Martini and Botticelli, as well as frescoes and sculptures from the Avignon School, and many French and Italian religious paintings.

🏛 Musée Angladon

5 rue Laboureur. **04 90 82 29 03.**
◯ *Wed–Sun, pm only.* 🖉 ♿
This museum cleverly combines modern technology with the intimacy of a private home for displaying this outstanding private collection of 18th- to 20th-century works of art.

🏛 Musée Théodore Aubanel

Pl St-Pierre. **04 90 86 35 02.** ◯ *by appt only.* ● *Sat, Sun.* 🖉 ♿
Former home home of the Aubanel publishing family, including poet Théodore Aubanel, a founder of the Félibrige *(see p26),* the museum houses collections of printing materials, Provençal literature and furniture.

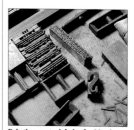

Printing materials in the Musée Théodore Aubanel

🏛 Musée Lapidaire

27 rue de la Republique. **04 90 85 75 38.** ◯ *Wed–Mon.* ● *1 Jan, 1 May, 25 Dec.* 🖉 ♿
Once a 17th-century Baroque Jesuit college, the museum has Celtic-Ligurian, Egyptian, Gallic and Roman artifacts, including masks from Vaison-la-Romaine and a 2nd-century Tarasque monster *(see p158).*

🏛 Musée Calvet

65 rue Joseph Vernet. **04 90 86 33 84.** ◯ *Wed–Mon.* ● *1 Jan, 1 May, 25 Dec.* 🖉 ♿
This evocative museum was visited by the French writer Stendhal, who left his inscription behind. The 19th–20th century collection has works

Gordes ⑬

Road map C3. 🔺 *2,000.* 🚪 *Le Château (04 90 72 02 75).* 🚌 *Tue.*

EXPENSIVE RESTAURANTS and hotels provide a clue to the popularity of this hilltop village, which spills down in terraces from a Renaissance château and the church of St-Firmin. Its impressive position is the main attraction, although its vaulted, arcaded medieval lanes are also alluring. The village has been popular with artists ever since the academic Cubist painter André Lhote began visiting in 1938.

The **Château de Gordes** was built in the 16th century on the site of a 12th-century fortress. One of the château's best features is an ornate 16th-century fireplace in the great hall on the first floor, decorated with shells, flowers and pilasters. In the courtyard there is an attractive Renaissance door. The building was bought and restored by the Hungarian-born Op Art painter Victor Vasarely (1908–97). In 1970 he opened a museum in the château and devoted it to his abstract

BORIES

The ancient dwellings known as *bories* were domed dry-stone buildings made from *lauzes* (limestone slabs), with walls up to 1.5 m (4 ft) thick. They dated from 3,500 BC and were regularly rebuilt, using ancient methods, until the last century when they were abandoned. Around 3,000 bories are still standing, many in fields where they were used for shelter or storing implements. Twenty have been restored in the Village des Bories, outside Gordes.

works. The museum is currently devoted to the works of Flemish painter, Pol Mara. Just outside Gordes is the **Village des Bories**, stone huts which are now a museum of rural life.

♣ Château de Gordes
🎫 *04 90 72 02 75.* 🕐 *Jul–Aug: daily, Sep–Jun: Wed–Mon.* ⬤ *1 Jan, 25 Dec.* ♿

🏠 Village des Bories
Route de Cavaillon. 🎫 *04 90 72 03 48.* 🕐 *daily.* 📷 ♿

The hilltop village of Gordes spilling down in terraces

Roussillon ⑭

Road map C3. 🔺 *1,200.* 🚪 *pl de la Poste (04 90 05 60 25).* 🚌 *Thu.*

THE DEEP OCHRES used in the construction of this hilltop community are stunning. No other village looks so warm and rich, so harmonious and inviting. Its hues, which seem to be the product of an artist's brush, come from at least 17 shades of ochre discovered in and around the village, notably in the dramatic former quarries of the enormous Chaussée de Géants (Giants' Causeway). The quarries are to the east of the village, a 45-minute walk from the information office. The Val des Fées (Valley of the Fairies) to the south contains breathtaking cliffs, in the centre of which are the Falaises de Sang (Cliffs of Blood). The superb panorama to the north can be seen from the Castrum, the viewing table beside the church, above the tables with umbrellas in the main square.

Before its recent housing boom, Roussillon was a typical Provençal backwater. During the early 1950s, an American sociologist, Laurence Wylie, moved to Roussillon, spent a year there with his family and wrote a book about village life, *Un Village du Vaucluse*. He concluded that Roussillon was a solidly "hard-working, productive community" for all its feuds and tensions. The playwright Samuel Beckett, who lived here during World War II, had a decidedly less favourable impression.

Triumphal arch behind Cavaillon

Cavaillon ⑮

Road map B3. 🏘 *25,000.* 🚉 🚌
ℹ *pl François Tourel (04 90 71 32 01).*
🗓 *Mon.*

PERHAPS THE BEST place to get
your bearings is the viewing
table outside the **Chapelle St-
Jacques** at the top of the town,
which renders the Luberon
range in perspective against
Mont Ventoux and the Alpilles
chain. In closer proximity are
the acres of fruit and vegetable
plots, for Cavaillon is France's
largest market garden, synonymous especially with melons.
Its local market competes with
the one in Apt for renown as
the most important in Vaucluse.

Colline St-Jacques was the
site of the pre-Roman settlement that, under Rome, was
moved down from its heights
and prospered. There is a 1st-
century Roman arch in place
François-Tourel nearby. Roman
finds have been collected in
the **Musée Archéologique**
in the Grand Rue, which leads
north from the church, a former cathedral dedicated to
its 6th-century bishop, Saint
Véran. The synagogue in place
Castil-Blaze dates from 1772,
although there has been one
on this site ever since the 14th
century. A small museum, the
Musée Juif Comtadin, com-
memorates its history.

🏛 **Musée Archéologique**
Hôtel Dieu, Porte d'Avignon. 📞 *04 90
76 00 34.* 🕐 *Mid-Apr–mid-Sep:
Thu–Mon* 🎫
🏛 **Musée Juif Comtadin**
Rue Hébraïque. 📞 *04 90 76 00 34.*
🕐 *mid-Arp–mid-Sep: Thu–Mon; mid-
Sep–mid-Apr: Mon, Wed–Fri.* ⬤ *1
Jan, 1 May, 25 Dec.* 🎫

A Tour of the Petit Luberon ⑯

THE PARC NATUREL REGIONAL covers 120,000 ha (463 sq
miles) of a limestone mountain range running east
from Cavaillon towards Manosque in the Alpes-de-
Haute-Provence. It embraces about 50 communities
and a past peppered with such infamous figures as
the Baron of Oppède and the Marquis de Sade. An unspoiled area, it is ideal for walking. Its two main centres
are Apt and Lourmarin. The D943 in the Lourmarin
Coomb valley divides the park: the Grand Luberon
(see p172) is to the east; and to the west is the Petit
Luberon, a land of limestone cliffs, hidden corries and
cedar woods, with most
towns and villages to the
north side of the range.

Oppède-le-Vieux ①
The dominating ruined castle belonged to Jean Maynier, Baron of
Oppède, whose bloody crusade
against the Luberon Vaudois in
1545 destroyed 11 villages.

**Cedar Forest Botanical Trail,
Bonnieux**

0 kilometres   2

0 miles   2

KEY

▨▨▨ Tour route

─ ─ ─ Other roads

LUBERON WILDLIFE

The Parc Naturel Régional is rich
in flora and fauna. The central
massif is wild and exposed on
the north side, sheltered and
more cultivated in the south. A
wide range of habitats exist in
a landscape of white chalk and
red ochre cliffs, cedar forests,
moorlands and river-hewn
gorges. Information is available
from La Maison du Parc in Apt
(see p172) which publishes
suggested walks and tours.

Monkey orchid (Orcis
simia) *is found on the
sunny, chalky grasslands.*

The rugged peaks of the Petit Luberon

Ménerbes ②
The stronghold of 16th-century
Calvinists, the village's defences
were recently tested by Peter
Mayle's book *A Year in Provence*,
which explored inhabitants' lives.

Bonnieux ④
The Musée de la Boulangerie
gives a history of bread making.
From here the two-hour Cedar
Forest Botanical Trail is
a pleasant, scenic walk.

Lacoste ③
Little remains of the Marquis
de Sade's château. Arrested
for corrupt practices in 1778,
he spent 12 years in prison
writing up his experiences.

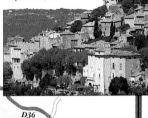

Abbaye St-Hilaire

D189   ②   D109   ③   ④   D3

D36

D943

MONTAGNE DU LUBERON

Lourmarin ⑤
The Countess of Agoult, whose family
owned the village château, bore the
composer Franz Liszt (1811-86) three
children: one married Richard Wagner.

⑤

AIX-EN-PROVENCE ↓

Wild boar (Sus scrofa, *known
as* sanglier *in French) is a hunt-
er's prize and a chef's delight.*

Eagle owl *(Bubo bubo, known
as* dugas *in Provençal) is judged
Europe's largest owl.*

Beaver *(Castor fiber, known as*
castor *in French) builds dams
on the Calavon and Durance.*

GRAND LUBERON

This spectacular range of mountains to the east of the Lourmarin Coomb rises as high as 1,125 m (3,690 ft) at Mourre Nègre. The fine view at the summit must be appreciated on foot, and takes several hours from where you leave the car at Auribeau. The area is out-standingly beautiful and ideal to escape from the crowds. The panorama from the top takes in Digne, the Lure mountain and Durance valley, the Apt basin, l'Etang de Berre and Mont Ventoux.

Apt ⓱

Road map C3. 🏔 11,500. 🚌 Avignon. 🚉 20 av Philippe de Girard (04 90 74 03 18). 🚌 Sat.

Apt IS THE NORTHERN entry to the Parc Naturel Régional du Luberon (see pp170–71). The Maison du Parc Naturel Régional du Luberon in the park, a restored 17th-century mansion, provides a full in-troduction to the area, with details of walks, *gîtes* and flora and fauna. It also has a **Musée de Paléontologie**, with fascinating examples of fossils found in the Luberon.

The busy old town of Apt, typical of the area, has a square for playing *boules*, fountains and plane trees. Surrounded by cherry orchards, it claims to be the world capital of crystal-lized fruit. It is also famous for truffles, lavender essence and pottery, and might have been known as a principal olive-growing area had the trees not all been completely

devastated by frost in 1953. The Saturday market offers a wide range of Provençal delicacies as well as en-tertainment, including jazz, barrel organ music and some stand-up comedy. Excursions can be made to the *Colorado de Rus-trel*, the best ochre quarry site by the River Dôa, to the northeast. Its many attractions include some unusual earth pillars, called the Cheminées de Fées.

The medieval **Cathédrale Ste-Anne** lies at the heart of Apt's old town. Legend has it that the veil of St Anne was brought back from Palestine and hidden in the cathedral by Auspice, who is thought to have been Apt's first bishop. Each year grapes are offered in celebration of her festival in July, and there is a procession from the cathedral through the town. When you enter the

14th-century priest's embroidery

cathedral, the first chapel on the left side, known as the Royal Chapel, com-memorates Anne of Austria. She paid a pilgrimage to Apt to pray for fertility and contributed the funds to finish the chapel which was finally completed around 1669–70. Inside the sacristy is the treasury con-taining the saint's shroud, and an 11th-century Arabic standard from the First Crusade (1096–9). In the apse is a 15th- to 16th-century window which depicts beautifully the tree of Jesse.

North of the church is the **Musée Archéologique**. The items displayed are a treasure trove of prehistoric flints, stone implements, Gallo-Roman carvings and jewellery and mosaics from that period. The second floor concentrates on local ceramics, such as the work of Apt ceramicist Léon Sagy (1865–1939).

🏛 **Cathédrale St-Anne**
Rue St-Anne. 📞 04 90 74 36 60. 🕐 Tue–Sat.
🏛 **Musée de Paléontologie**
60 place Jean-Jaurès. 📞 04 90 04 42 00. 🕐 Mon–Sat. ● Sat pm, public hols. 🈺
🏛 **Musée Archéologique**
27 rue de l'Amphithéâtre. 📞 04 90 74 00 34 ext 1133. 🕐 Jun–Sep: Sun pm–Mon, Wed–Sat; Oct–May: Wed–Fri pm only, Sat. ● public hols. 🈺

Jam label illustrating traditional produce of Apt

Cadenet 🔞

Road map C3. 🏘 *3,500.* 🚌
Avignon. 🚌 🛈 *pl Tambour d'Arcole
(04 90 68 38 21).* 🅿 *Mon & Sat
(marché paysan, Apr–Oct).*

Tucked underneath the hills in the Durance valley, Cadenet has 11th-century castle ruins and a 14th-century church with a fine square bell tower. Its font is made from a Roman sarcophagus. In the main square, which is used as the *marché paysan* (farmers' market), is a statue of the town's heroic drummer boy, André Estienne, who beat such a raucous tattoo in the battle for Arcole Bridge in 1796 that the enemy thought they could hear gunfire, and retreated.

**Drummer boy in
Cadenet town square**

Ansouis 🔞

Road map C3. 🏘 *900.* 🛈 *pl du
Château (04 90 09 86 98).* 🅿 *Thu.*

One of the most remarkable things about the Renaissance **Château d'Ansouis** is that it has been owned by the Sabran family, lords here since 1160. Theirs is a proven pedigree: in the 13th century, Gersende de Sabran and Raymond Bérenger IV's four daughters, Eleonore, Margaret, Sancy and Beatrice became queens of France, England, Romania and Naples respectively. In 1298, Elzéar de Sabran married Delphine de Puy, a descendant of the Viscount of Marseille. But she had already resolved to become a nun, so agreed to the marriage, but not to its consummation. Both were canonized in 1369. The castle's original keep and two of its four towers are still visible. It has a grand staircase and a guard room with 17th- to 19th-century armour. Its gardens include the Renaissance Garden of Eden, built on the former cemetery. One further stop is at the **Musée Extraordinaire de Georges Mazoyer**, an individual mix of the artist's work, Provençal furniture and a recreated underwater cave, all in 15th-century cellars.

🏰 **Château d'Ansouis**
🅲 *04 90 09 82 70.* 🕐 *Oct–Jun:
Wed–Mon pm; Jul–Sep: daily.*
🚫 *1 Jan, 1 May, 25 Dec.* 🖽
🏛 **Musée Extraordinaire de
Georges Mazoyer**
Rue du Vieux Moulin. 🅲 *04 90 09
82 64.* 🕐 *Wed–Mon pm only.* 🖽

Pertuis 🔞

Road map C3. 🏘 *17,000.* 🚌 🛈 *Le
Donjon, place Mirabeau (04 90 79 15
56).* 🅿 *Wed & Sat (marché paysan), Fri.*

Once the capital of the Pays d'Aigues, present-day Pertuis is a quiet town, whose rich and fertile surrounding area was gradually taken over by Aix-en-Provence. Pertuis was the birthplace of the philandering Count of Mirabeau's father, and the 13th-century clock tower is to be found in place Mirabeau.

The **Eglise St-Nicholas**, re-built in Gothic style in the 16th century, has a 16th-century triptych and two 17th-century marble statues. To the south-west is the battlemented 14th-century **Tour St Jacques**.

**Triumphal arch entrance to La
Tour d'Aigues' Renaissance château**

La Tour d'Aigues 🔞

Road map C3. 🏘 *3,800.* 🚌 *to
Pertuis.* 🛈 *Château de la Tour
d'Aigues (04 90 07 50 29).* 🅿 *Tue.*

Nestling beside the Luberon, and surrounded by vineyards and orchards, this town takes its name from a 10th-century tower. The 16th-century castle completes the triumvirate of Renaissance châteaux in the Luberon (the others are Lourmarin and Ansouis). Built on the foundations of a medieval castle by Baron de Cental, its massive portal is based on the Roman arch at Orange *(see p161).* The castle was damaged in the French Revolution (1789–94) and is now being restored. The **Musée de l'Histoire du Pays d'Aigues et Musée des Faïences**, in its cellars, tell the region's story.

🏛 **Musée de l'Histoire du
Pays d'Aigues et Musée des
Faïences**
Caves du Château, La Tour d'Aigues.
🅲 *04 90 07 50 33.* 🕐 *daily.* ◗
*Sep–Jun: Tue pm & Sat–Sun am; 20
Dec–4 Jan.* 🖽

Duchess's bedroom in the Château d'Ansouis

ALPES-DE-HAUTE-PROVENCE

I N THIS, THE MOST UNDISCOVERED REGION *of Provence, the air is clearer than anywhere else in France, which is why it was the chosen site for France's most important observatory. But the terrain and the weather conditions can be severe. Inaccessibility to areas has restricted development and the traditional, rural way of life is still followed.*

Irrigation has helped to improve some corners of this mountainous land. The Valensole plain is now the most important lavender producing area of France. Peaches, apples and pears have been planted in orchards only recently irrigated by the Durance, the region's main river, which has been tamed by dams and a hydro-electric power scheme. These advances have created employment and helped bring prosperity to the region. Another modern development is the Cadarache nuclear research centre, situated just outside Manosque. The town's population has grown rapidly to 19,000 inhabitants, overtaking the region's capital, Digne-les-Bains. Famous for its lavender and healthy living, Digne is a handsome spa town that has attracted visitors for more than a century and now hopes to enhance its appeal through its devotion to sculpture, which fills the streets. The region's history and architecture have also been greatly influenced by the terrain and climate. Strategically positioned citadels crown mountain towns such as Sisteron, which was won over by Napoleon in 1815, and the frontier town of Entrevaux. The design of towns and buildings has remained practical, in keeping with the harsh winter and strong Mistral winds. Undoubtedly, the beauty of the region is seen in the high lakes and mountains, the glacial valleys and the colourful fields of Alpine flowers.

Bundles of cut lavender drying in fields near the Gorges du Verdon

◁ **Olive groves on the hills outside the fortified town of Entrevaux**

Exploring Alpes-de-Haute-Provence

THIS REMOTE AND RUGGED AREA in the north of Provence covers 6,944 sq km (2,697 sq miles) of mountainous landscape. Its main artery is the Durance river which is dotted with dams, gorges and lakes – a haven for mountaineers and canoeists. One tributary is the Verdon, which runs through the stunning Gorges du Verdon, Europe's answer to the Grand Canyon. The scenery becomes wilder and more rugged in the northeast, with Mont Pelat at the heart of the Parc National du Mercantour. Further south lie the plains of Valensole, which colour the landscape in July when the abundant lavender blossoms.

Fields of lavender on the Valensole plains

SIGHTS AT A GLANCE

Annot ⑱
Barcelonnette ③
Castellane ⑯
Colmars ⑤
Digne-les-Bains ⑥
Entrevaux ⑲
Forcalquier ⑨
Gréoux-les-Bains ⑪
Les Penitents des Mées ⑦
Lurs ⑧
Manosque ⑩
Mont Pelat ④
Moustiers-Ste-Marie ⑮
Riez ⑬
St-André-les-Alpes ⑰
Seyne ②
Sisteron ①
Valensole ⑫

Tour
Gorges du Verdon (see pp184–5) ⑭

KEY

Motorway

Major road

Minor road

Scenic route

River

☀ Viewpoint

A quiet Provençal-style bar in the mountain town of Castellane, situated in the picturesque old quarter

GETTING AROUND

The Durance river provides the point of entry into the region. The A51 autoroute from Aix-en-Provence follows the river to Sisteron, known as the "gateway to Provence". National roads continue to follow the Durance, to Lac de Serre-Ponçon in the north, then east along the Ubaye to Barcelonnette. The the region's capital, Digne-les-Bains, is well-connected by national roads, but otherwise there are only minor roads. The regions railway line also follows the Durance, connecting Sisteron and Manosque with Aix-en-Provence.

To Briançon

Lac de Serre-Ponçon

3 BARCELONNETTE

SEYNE 2

4 MONT PELAT

PARC NATIONAL DU MERCANTOUR

5 COLMARS

6 DIGNE-LES-BAINS

ST-ANDRÉ-LES-ALPES 17

18 ANNOT

19 ENTREVAUX **To Nice**

Lac de Castillon

15 MOUSTIERS-STE-MARIE

16 CASTELLANE

Lac de Ste-Croix

14 GORGES DU VERDON

0 kilometres 10

0 miles 10

The dramatic Rocher de la Baume, just outside the town of Sisteron

Sisteron ❶

Road map D2. 🚶 *7,000.* 🚗 🚌
🛈 *Hôtel de Ville, pl Republique (04
92 61 12 03).* 🚌 *Wed & Sat.*

Approaching sisteron from
the north or south, it is
easy to see its strategic importance. The town calls itself the
"gateway to Provence", sitting
in a narrow valley on the left
bank of the Durance river, surrounded by olive groves. It is a
lively town, protected by the
most impressive fortifications
in Provence. However, it has
suffered for its ideal military
position, most recently in heavy
Allied bombardment in 1944.
    The **citadelle**, originally built
in the 13th century, dominates
the town and gives superb
views down over the Durance.
From May to September a
small train takes visitors from
the town hall to the citadel, but
it is only a short distance to
walk. These defences, though
incomplete, are a solid assembly of keep, dungeon, chapel,
towers and ramparts, and offer
a fine setting for the Nuits de la
Citadelle, the summer festival
of music, theatre and dance.

A traditional Provençal farmhouse just outside the village of Seyne

The church in the main square,
Notre-Dame des Pommiers,
is an example of the Provençal
Romanesque school, dating
from 1160. To the left of the
church, follow signs to the Old
Town, where small boutiques,
cafés and bars line the narrow
alleyways called *andrônes*.
    Rocher de la Baume on
the opposite bank is a popular
practice spot for mountaineers.

♣ **La Citadelle**
04200 Sisteron. ☎ *04 92 61 27 57.*
🕐 *Apr–mid-Nov: daily.* 🖼

Sisteron citadel, strategically positioned high above the Durance valley

Seyne ❷

Road map D2. 🚶 *1,200.* 🚌
🛈 *place d'Armes (04 92 35 11 00).*
🚌 *Tue & Fri.*

The small mountain village of
Seyne dominates the Vallée
de la Blanche, sitting 1,210 m
(3,970 ft) above sea level.
Horses and mules graze in the
nearby fields, and there is a
celebrated annual horse and
mule fair. Beside the main road
is **Notre-Dame de Nazareth**,
a 13th-century Romanesque
church with Gothic portals,
sundial and large rose window.
The path by the church leads
up to the **citadelle**, built by
Vauban in 1693, which encloses
the still-standing 12th-century
watchtower. The town is also
a centre for winter sports, with
facilities nearby at St-Jean, Le
Grand Puy and Chabanon.

Barcelonnette ❸

Road map E2. 🚶 *3,500.* 🚌
🛈 *place Frédéric Mistral (04 92 81
04 71).* 🚌 *Wed & Sat.*

In the remote Ubaye Valley,
surrounded by a demi-halo
of snowy peaks, lies Provence's
northernmost town. It is a flat,
open town of cobbled streets,
smart cafés and restaurants and
quaint gift shops, selling specialities such as strawberry and
juniper liqueurs. The town was
named in 1231 by its founder
Raymond-Bérenger V, Count
of Barcelona and Provence,
whose great-grandfather of the
same name married into the
House of Provence in 1112.

NAPOLEON IN PROVENCE

In his bid to regain power after his exile on Elba, Napoleon knew his only chance of success was to win over Sisteron. On 1 March, 1815, he secretly sailed from the island of Elba, landing at Golfe-Juan with 1,026 soldiers.

He hastily started his journey to Paris via Grenoble, making his first stop at Grasse, where the people shut their doors against him. Abandoning carriages, cannon and horses, Napoleon and his troops scrambled along mule-tracks and across difficult terrain, surmounting summits of more than 3,000 ft (1,000 m). At Digne, he lunched at the Hôtel du Petit Paris before spending the night at Malijai château where he waited for news of the royalist stronghold of Sisteron. He was in luck. The arsenal was empty and he entered the town on 5 March – a plaque on rue Saunerie honours the event. The people were, at last, beginning to warm to him.

The dramatic *Napoleon Crossing the Alps*, painted by Jacques Louis David in 1800

One of the distinctive Mexican-style villas in Barcelonnette

The town's Alpine setting gives it a Swiss flavour, but it also has added Mexican spice. The Arnaud brothers, whose textile business in Barcelonnette was failing, emigrated to Mexico and made their fortune. Others followed, and on their return in the early 20th century, they built grand Mexican-style villas which encircle the town.

Housed in one of the villas is the three-storey **Musée de la Vallée de l'Ubaye**, where the Mexican connection is explained in detail through illustrations and costumes.

During the summer there is an information point below the museum, for the Parc National du Mercantour. The park stretches along the Italian border and straddles the Alpes Maritimes region in the south

(see p97). As well as being a haven for birds, wildlife and fauna, the park has two important archaeological sites.

🏛 **Musée de la Vallée de l'Ubaye**
10 av de la Libération. 📞 04 92 81 27 15. ⬛ Wed–Sat pm; school hols: daily. 🎫

Mont Pelat ❹

🚉 Digne-les-Bains, Thorame-Verdon.
🚌 Barcelonnette, Colmars, Allos. 🛈 le Presbytère, Allos (04 92 83 02 81).

THIS IS THE LOFTIEST peak in the Provençal Alps, rising to a height of 3,050 m (10,017 ft) and all around are mountains and breathtaking passes, some

of them closed by snow until June. Among them are the Col de Cayolle (2,327 m/7,717 ft) on the D2202 to the east, and the hair-raising Col d'Allos (2,250 m/7,380 ft) on the D908 to the west. South of Mont Pelat, in the heart of the Parc National du Mercantour, is the beautiful 50-ha (124-acre) Lac d'Allos. It is the largest natural lake in Europe at this altitude. The setting is idyllic, ringed by snowy mountains, its crystal-clear waters swimming with trout and char. Another record-breaker is Cime de la Bonette, on the D64 northeast of Mont Pelat, at 2,862 m (9,390 ft) the highest pass in Europe. It has what is perhaps the most magnificent view in all this abundant mountain scenery.

Cime de la Bonette, the highest mountain pass in Europe

Colmars ❺

Road map 2E. 🏛 *400*. 🚌 ℹ️
*Ancien Auberge Fleurie (04 92 83 41
92).* 🕑 *Tue & Fri.*

Colmars is an unusually
complete fortified town,
nestling between two medieval
forts. You can walk along the
12-m (40-ft) ramparts, which
look across oak-planked roofs,
patched in places with sheet
steel. The town is named after
the hill on which it is built,
collis Martis, where the Romans
built a temple to the god Mars.
Vauban, the military engineer,
designed its lasting look. On
the north side, an alley leads
to the 17th-century **Fort de
Savoie**, a fine example of
military architecture. From the
Porte de France a path leads
to the ruined Fort de France.

Situated among wooded hills
Colmars is popular in summer,
when time is spent relaxing on
wooden balconies, known as
solarets (sun-traps), or strolling
along alpine paths, soaking up
the beautiful views. Signposts
lead from the town to the
Cascade de la Lance, a waterfall half-an-hour's walk away.

The fortified town of Colmars, flanked by two compact forts

♠ **Fort de Savoie**
04370 Colmars. 📞 *04 92 83 46 88.*
🕑 *Sep– Jul by appointment only;
Jul–Aug: am daily.* 📷 📹 *obligatory.*

Digne-les-Bains ❻

Road map 2D. 🏛 *17,500.* 🚌 🚉
ℹ️ *pl de Tampinet (04 92 36 62 62).*
🕑 *Wed & Sat.*

The capital of the region
has been a spa town since
Roman times, primed by
seven hot springs. It
still attracts those seeking various cures, who
visit the Etablissement
Thermal, a short drive
southeast of the town.
Health seems to radiate
from Digne's airy
streets, particularly
from the boulevard
Gassendi, named after
the local mathematic-
ian and astronomer
Pierre Gassendi (1592–
1655). This is where
the town's four-day
lavender carnival rolls

out in August *(see p35)*, for
Digne styles itself the *"capitale
des Alpes de la Lavande"*. In
recent years, the town has promoted itself as a key centre for
modern sculpture, which
liberally furnishes the town.

The **Musée Municipal** is
found in the old town hospice
and houses 18th- and 19th-cen-
tury French, Italian and Dutch
paintings, a collection of local
art and Pierre Gassendi's
scientific instruments. Among
portraits of Digne's
famous is Alexandra
David-Néel, one of
Europe's most intrepid
travellers, who died in
1969 aged 101. Her
house, *Samten-Dzong*
(fortress of meditation)
is now the **Fondation
Alexandra David-Néel**
and includes a Tibetan
centre and museum.

At the north end of
the boulevard Gassendi
is the 19th-century
Grande Fontaine and

Street sculpture in Digne

just beyond this lies the oldest
part of Digne-les-Bains, now
a residential suburb. The most
impressive architectural site is
the cathedral of **Notre-Dame-
du-Bourg**. It is the largest
Romanesque church in Haute
Provence, built between the
years 1200 and 1330.

Another place to visit is the
**Jardin Botanique des
Cordeliers**. This enchanting
walled garden in a converted
convent houses a large and
varied collection of plants and
herbs with medicinal qualities
and samples of local flora.

🏛 **Musée Municipal**
64 bd Gassendi. 📞 *04 92 31 45
29.* 🕑 *Tue–Sun.* 🕐 *until summer
2000, public hols* 📷 ♿
🏛 **Fondation Alexandra
David-Néel**
27 av Maréchal Juin. 📞 *04 92 31 32
38.* 🕑 *daily.* 🕐 *public hols.* 📷 *4
per day (3 from Oct–Jun).*
♣ **Jardin Botanique des
Cordeliers**
Couvent des Cordeliers, Collège Maria
Borrély. ℹ️ *for information.* 🕑
Tue–Sat. 🕐 *public hols.* ♿

Les Penitents des Mées **➐**

Road map 3D. 🚉 *Marseille.* 🚌 *St-Auban.* 🚌 *Les Mées.* ℹ️ *Château Arnoux (04 92 64 02 64).*

ONE OF THE MOST spectacular geological features in the region is Les Pénitents des Mées, a serried rank of columnar rocks more than 100 m (300 ft) high and over a mile (2 km) long. The strange rock formation is said to be a cowled procession of banished monks. In local mythology, monks from the mountain of Lure took a fancy to some Moorish beauties, captured by a lord during the time of the Saracen invasion in the 6th century. Saint Donat, a hermit who inhabited a nearby cave, punished their effrontery by turning them into stone.

The small village of Les Mées is tucked away at the north end. Walk up to the church of St-Roch for a clear view of the rocks' strange formation of millions of pebbles and stones.

The curiously-shaped Penitents des Mées, dominating the area

Lurs **➑**

Road map 3D. 🚉 *320.* 🚌 *La Brillane.* ℹ️ *04700 Lurs (04 92 79 10 20).*

THE BISHOPS of Sisteron and the Princes of Lurs were given ownership of the fortified town of Lurs in the 9th century, under the command of Charlemagne. Earlier this century, the small town was virtually abandoned, and was only repopulated after World War II, mainly by printers and graphic artists, who keep their trade in the forefront of events with an annual competition.

The narrow streets of the old town, entered through the Porte d'Horloge, are held in by the medieval ramparts. North of the partially ruined Château of the Bishop-Princes is the beginning of the 300-m (900-ft) **Promenade des Evêques** (Bishops' walk), lined with 15 oratories leading to the chapel of Notre-Dame-de-Vie. It is worth visiting purely for the stupendous views over the sea of poppy fields and olive groves of the Durance valley.

Head north out of Lurs on the N96, to the 12th-century **Prieuré de Ganagobie**. The church contains beautifully restored red-, black- and white-tiled mosaics, inspired by oriental and Byzantine design and imagery. Offices are held several times a day by the monks – visitors may attend.

⌂ Prieuré de Ganagobie
N96, 04310. 📞 *04 92 68 00 04.* ⌂ *Tue–Sun pm.*

Floor mosaic of the church of the 12th-century Prieuré de Ganagobie

LE TRAIN DES PIGNES

An enjoyable day out is to be found on the Chemin de Fer de Provence, a short railway line that runs from Digne-les-Bains to Nice. It is the remaining part of a network that was designed to link the Côte d'Azur with the Alps, built between 1891 and 1911. Today the Train des Pignes, a diesel train, usually with two carriages, runs four times a day throughout the year. It is an active and popular service, used by locals going about their daily business as much as by tourists. It rattles along the single track at a fair pace, rolling by the white waters of the Asse de Moriez and thundering over 16 viaducts, 15 bridges and through 25 tunnels.

The train journey is an excellent way of seeing the surrounding countryside. The most scenic part is when it leaves the main towns and heads into uninhabited countryside, for instance, between St-André-les-Alps and Annot, where the *grès d'Annot* can be seen clearly *(see p187)*. The journey takes about three hours and can be broken anywhere along the way. Entrevaux *(see p187)* is a good place to stop, half-way between the two towns.

The vaulted scriptorium of the Couvent des Cordeliers in Forcalquier

Forcalquier ❾

Road map C3. 🏘 *4,200.* 🚉 ℹ️ *pl du Bourguet (04 92 75 10 02).* 🚌 *Mon.*

Crowned by a ruined castle and domed chapel of the 19th-century Notre-Dame-de-Provence, Forcalquier is an intriguing shadow of its former self. Its ancient heart lies in the old town, redolent of its glorious days as an independent state and capital of the region.

Streets that once rang with trade and troubadours are now silent, although the weekly market is a lively affair, filled with lavender and honey stalls and artists selling their wares.

There are some fine façades in the old town, but only one remaining gate, the Porte des Cordeliers. The **Couvent des Cordeliers** nearby dates from 1236 and is where the local lords have been entombed. The carefully restored cloisters, library, scriptorium and refectory can all be visited.

The **Observatoire de Haute Provence** to the south of the town was sited here after a study in the 1930s to find the town with the cleanest air. The Centre d'Astronomie nearby is a must for star-gazers.

🏛 **Couvent des Cordeliers**
Bd des Martyres. 🕿 *04 92 75 02 38.* 🕐 *May–Jun & mid-Sep–Oct: Sun pm & public hols; Jul–mid-Sep: daily.* 📷 🎫 *(obligatory).*

🏛 **Observatoire de Haute Provence**
St-Michel l'Observatoire. 🕿 *04 92 70 64 00.* 🕐 *Wed pm.* 📷 🎫 *only.* ♿

Manosque ❿

Road map C3. 🏘 *19,100.* 🚉 🚉 ℹ️ *pl du Docteur Joubert (04 92 72 16 00).* 🚌 *Sat.*

France's national nuclear research centre, Cadarache, has brought prosperity and traffic to Manosque, an industrial town which has

sprawled beyond its original hill site above the Durance. The centre is pedestrianized, with two 12th-century gates, Porte Saunerie and Porte Soubeyran. The shoe shop in rue Grande was once the atelier of writer Jean Giono's father *(see p26)*. The **Centre Jean Giono** tells the story of his life. The town's adoptive son is the painter Jean Carzou, who decorated the interior of the **Couvent de la Présentation** with apocalyptic allegories of modern life.

🏛 **Centre Jean Giono**
1 bd Elémir Bourges. 🕿 *04 92 70 54 54.* 🕐 *Tue–Sat.* 📷 ● *public hols.*

🏛 **Couvent de la Présentation**
9 bd Elémir Bourges. 🕿 *04 92 87 40 49.* 🕐 *Fri–Sun.* 📷

Gréoux-les-Bains ⓫

Road map D3. 🏘 *1,700.* 🚉 ℹ️ *5 av des Marronniers (04 92 78 01 08).* 🚌 *Tue & Thu.*

The cleansing thermal waters of Gréoux-les Bains have been enjoyed since antiquity, when baths were built by the Romans in the 1st century AD. The waters can still be enjoyed at the Etablissement Thermal, situated on the east side of the village along the D952, where bubbling, sulphurous water arrives at the rate of 100,000 litres (22,000 gallons) an hour.

Like most spa towns, Gréoux flourished in the 19th-century and has retained a restful air.

LAVENDER AND LAVENDIN

The famous flower of Provence colours the Plateau de Valensole every July. Lavender began to be cultivated in the region in the 19th century and provides the world with around 80 per cent of its needs. Harvesting continues until September and is mostly mechanized although, in some areas, it is still collected in cloth sacks slung over the back. After two or three days' drying,it is sent to a distillery.

These days the cultivation of a hybrid called lavendin has overtaken traditional lavender. Lavender is now used mainly for perfumes and cosmetics, lavendin for soaps.

Harvesting the abundant lavender in Haute Provence

The sweeping fields of the Plateau de Valensole, one of the largest lavender-growing areas of Provence

A ruined castle of the Templars is on a high spot and an open-air theatre is in the grounds. The **Crèche aux Santons**, just outside Gréoux, is well worth a visit for its display of clay *santons* and *son-et-lumière* shows.

⚜ Crèche aux Santons
36 av des Alpes. **(** *04 92 77 61 08.*
◯ *Mar–Dec: Tue–Sun.* 🎦 ⚿

Corinthian columns front the Gallo-Roman baths in Gréoux-les-Bains

Valensole ⓬

Road map D3. 🏠 *2,200.* 🚌
ℹ *Av Segond (92 74 90 02).*
🚊 *Sat.*

THIS IS THE CENTRE of France's most important lavender-growing area. It sits on the edge of the Valensole plains with a sturdy-towered Gothic church at its height. Admiral Villeneuve was born here in 1763, the unsuccessful adversary of Admiral Nelson at the Battle of Trafalgar. Signs for locally made lavender honey are everywhere and just outside the town is the **Musée**

Vivant de l'Abeille. This is an interactive museum explaining the life of the honey bee, with demonstrations, photographs and videos. In the summer, you can visit the beehives and see the beekeepers at work.

🏛 Musée Vivant de l'Abeille
Route de Manosque. **(** *04 92 74 85 28.* ◯ *May–Aug: Tue–Sat; Sep–Apr: Tue–Sun.* ⬤ *public hols.* ⚿

Riez ⓭

Road map D3. 🏠 *1,700.* 🚌
ℹ *4 allée Louis Gardiol (04 92 77 99 09).* 🚊 *Wed & Sat.*

AT THE EDGE of the sweeping Valensole plateau is this unspoiled village, filled with small shops selling ceramics and traditional *santons*, honey and lavender. Its grander past is reflected in the Renaissance façades of the houses and mansions in the old town. This is entered through the late-13th-century Porte Aiguière, which leads on to the peaceful, tree-lined rue Droite, with the finest examples of Renaissance architecture at numbers 27 and 29.

The most unusual site is the remains of the 1st-century AD Roman temple dedicated to Apollo. It stands out of time and place, in the middle of a field by the river Colostre; this was the original site of the town where the Roman colony, *Reia Apollinaris,* lived. On the other side of the river is a rare example of Merovingian architecture, a small baptistry dating from the 5th century.

Just south of the old town is the small **Musée Nature en Provence**, which traces the geological history of Provence, with an exhibition of over 3,000 fossils, minerals and rocks. The highlight of the museum is a remarkably preserved fossil of a wader bird dating back 35 million years.

🏛 Musée Nature en Provence
4 allée Louis Gardiol. **(** *04 92 77 99 09.* ◯ *Jun–Sep: Mon–Sat; Oct–May: Tue–Sat.* ⬤ *public hols.* 🎦 ⚿

Fossil of a wader bird, housed in the Musée Nature en Provence in Riez

Tour of the Gorges du Verdon ⑭

THE BREATHTAKING CHASM of the Gorges du Verdon is one of the most spectacular natural phenomena in France. The Verdon river, a tributary of the Durance, cuts into the rock up to 700 m (2,300 ft) deep. A tour of the gorges takes at least a day and this circular route encompasses its most striking features. At its east and west points are the historic towns of Castellane, the natural entry point to the gorges, and Moustiers-Ste-Marie. Parts of the tour are particularly mountainous, so drivers must be aware of hairpin bends and narrow roads with sheer drops. Weather conditions can also be hazardous and roads can be icy until late spring.

Hikers in one of the deep gorges

Moustiers-Ste-Marie ④
Set on craggy heights, the town is famed for its *faience (p186)*.

Flowered-façade in Moustiers

KEY

▬▬ Tour route

═══ Other roads

᠅ Viewpoint

Aiguines ③
The beautifully restored 17th-century château crowns the small village, with fine views down to the Lac de Ste-Croix.

0 kilometres 2
0 miles 2

TIPS FOR DRIVERS

Tour length: 113 km (72 miles).
Stopping-off points: La Palud-sur-Verdon has several cafés and a good place to stop for lunch is Moustiers-Ste-Marie. For an over-night stop, there are a number of hotels and camp sites in the town of Castellane. (See also pp242–3.)

The azure-blue waters of the enormous Lac de Ste-Croix

OUTDOOR ACTIVITIES

The Verdon gorges have offered fantastic opportunities for the adventurous since Isadore Blanc (1875–1932) made the first complete exploration in 1905. Today's activities include hiking, climbing, canoeing and white-water rafting *(see pp224–5)*. Boating needs to be supervised as the river is not always navigable and the powerful water flow can change dramatically.

White-water rafting down the fast-flowing Verdon river

Gorge explorer, Isadore Blanc

Point Sublime ⑥
This is one of the best viewing points. Signposted walks lead down to the canyon floor, but a torch is required to walk through the long tunnels.

Castellane ①
An ancient clock tower and gate remain in the Old Town of Castellane, a popular tourist centre *(p186)*.

La Palud-sur-Verdon ⑤
Organized walking excursions start at the village of La Palud, the so-called capital of the Gorges.

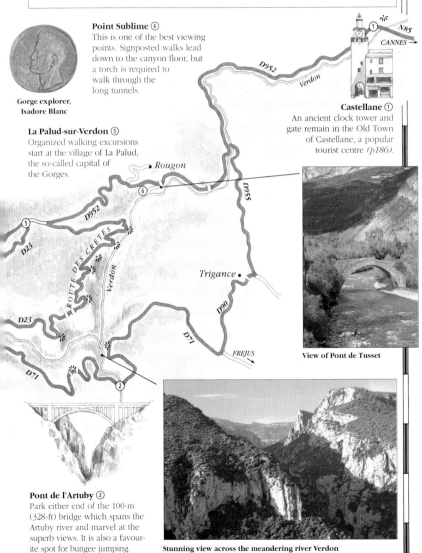

View of Pont de Tusset

Pont de l'Artuby ②
Park either end of the 100-m (328-ft) bridge which spans the Artuby river and marvel at the superb views. It is also a favourite spot for bungee jumping.

Stunning view across the meandering river Verdon

Moustiers-Ste-Marie ⑮

Road map 3D. 👥 *580.* 🚗 ℹ️ *Hôtel Dieu, rue de la Bourgade (04 92 74 67 84).* 🥖 *Fri am.*

T HE SETTING OF the town of Moustiers is stunning, high on the edge of a ravine, beneath craggy rocks. Situated in the town centre is the parish church, with a three-storey Romanesque belfry. Above it, a path meanders up to the 12th-century chapel of Notre-Dame-de-Beauvoir. The view across to the Gorges du Verdon *(see pp184–85)* is magnificent.

Across the ravine, where the river Rioul crashes through, is a heavy iron chain, 227 m (745 ft) in length, suspended over the valley. Hanging from the centre is a five-pointed, golden star. Although it was renewed in 1957, it is said to date back to the 13th century, when Baron Blacas hoisted it up in thanks for his release from captivity during the Seventh Crusade of St Louis *(see p42)*.

Moustiers is a popular tourist town, the narrow streets crowded in summer. This is due not only to its dramatic setting, but also to its ceramics. The original Moustiers ware is housed in the **Musée de la Faïence**, set in a cavernous crypt built by monks. Modern reproductions can be bought in the many studios and shops.

🏛 Musée de la Faïence
Moustiers St Marie. 📞 *04 92 74 61 64.* ⏰ *Apr–Oct: Wed–Mon; Nov–Mar Sat–Sun pms only; school hols: Wed–Mon pms only.* 📷

Notre-Dame-du-Roc chapel, perched high above the town of Castellane

Castellane ⑯

Road map 3D. 👥 *1,300.* 🚗 ℹ️ *rue Nationale (04 92 83 61 14).* 🥖 *Wed & Sat.*

T HIS IS ONE of the main centres for the Gorges du Verdon, surrounded by campsites and caravans. Tourists squeeze into the town centre in summer and, in the evenings, fill the cafés after a day's hiking, climbing, canoeing and white-water rafting. It is a well-sited town, beneath an impressive 180-m (600-ft) slab of grey rock. On top of this, dominating the skyline, is the chapel of **Notre-Dame-du-Roc**, built in 1703. A strenuous, 20-minute walk from behind the parish church to the top is rewarded with superb views.

Castellane was once a sturdy fortress and repelled invasion several times. The lifting of the siege by the Huguenots in 1586 is commemorated every year with firecrackers at the Fête des Pétardiers on January 31.

The town's fortifications were completely rebuilt in the 14th century after most of the town, dating from Roman times, crumbled and slipped into the Verdon valley. Most social activity takes place in the main square, place Marcel-Sauvaire, which is lined with small hotels that have catered for generations of visitors.

All that remains of the ramparts is the Tour Pentagonal and a small section of the old wall, which lie just beyond the 12th-century St-Victor, on the way up to the chapel.

MOUSTIERS WARE

The most important period of Moustiers faïence was from its inception in 1679 until the late 18th century, when a dozen factories were producing this highly-glazed ware. Decline followed and production came to a standstill in 1874, until it was revived in 1925 by Marcel Provence. He chose to follow traditional methods, and output has continued ever since.

The distinctive glaze of Moustiers faïence was first established in the late 17th century by Antoine Clérissy, a monk from Faenza in Italy. The first pieces to be fired had a luminous blue glaze and were decorated with figurative scenes, often copied from engravings of hunting or mythological subjects. In 1738, Spanish glazes were introduced and brightly coloured floral and fauna designs were used.

A number of potters continue the tradition, with varying degrees of quality, and can be seen at work in their *ateliers.*

A tureen in Moustiers' highly glazed faïence ware

The narrow streets of Moustiers

St-André-les-Alpes ⑰

Road map 3D. 🏠 *850.* 🚉 🚌
🛈 *place Marcel Pastorelli (04 92 89 02 39).* 🗓 *Wed & Sat.*

LYING AT THE north end of the Lac de Castillon, where the river Isolde meets the river Verdon, is St-André. It is a popular summer holiday and leisure centre, scattered around the sandy flats on the lakeside. The lake is man-made, formed by damming the river by the 90-m (295-ft) Barrage de Castillon and is a haven for swimming and watersports.

Inland, the scenery is just as picturesque, surrounded by lavender fields and orchards. Hang-gliding is so popular in the area that one of the local producers advertises its wine as "the wine of eagles".

Annot ⑱

Road map 3E. 🏠 *1,000.* 🚉
🛈 *place de la Marie (04 92 83 23 03).*
🗓 *Tue.*

THE TOWN OF ANNOT, on the Train des Pignes railway line *(see p181)*, has a distinct Alpine feel. Annot lies in the the Vaïre valley, crisscrossed by icy waters streaming down from the mountains. The surrounding scenery however, is a more unfamiliar pattern of jagged rocks and deep caves.

Vast sandstone boulders, known as the *grès d'Annot*, are strewn around the town, and local builders have con-

The steep path of zigzag ramps leading to the citadel of Entrevaux

structed houses against these haphazard rocks, using their sheer faces as outside walls. The Vieux Ville lies behind the main road, where there is a Romanesque church. The tall buildings that line the narrow streets have retained some of their original 17th- and 18th-century carved stone features.

Every Sunday in summer, a 1909 Belle Epoque steam train chugs its way from Puget-Théniers to Annot, a pleasant way for visitors to enjoy the unspoiled countryside.

Entrevaux ⑲

Road map 3E. 🏠 *800.* 🚉 🚌 🛈
Porte Royale (04 93 05 46 73). 🗓 *Fri.*

IT IS CLEAR TO SEE why Entrevaux is called a "fairytale town", as you cross the drawbridge and enter through the Porte Royale. The dramatic entrance is flanked by twin towers, the Porte de France and the Porte d'Italie, and from here you enter the Ville Forte. A good time to visit is early-August, when the town holds its biennial music festival *(see p31)*. The next is in 2001.

Fortified in 1690 by the military engineer Vauban (1633–1707), Entrevaux became one of the strongest military sites on the Franco-Savoy border. Even the 17th-century cathedral was skilfully incorporated into the turreted ramparts.

Unlike most military strongholds, the citadel was not built on top of a hill, but strategically placed on a rocky outcrop. A steep, zigzag track leads to the citadel, 135 m (440 ft) above the village. The 20-minute climb to the top, past basking lizards, should not be made in the midday heat.

Houses in the town of Annot built against huge sandstone rocks

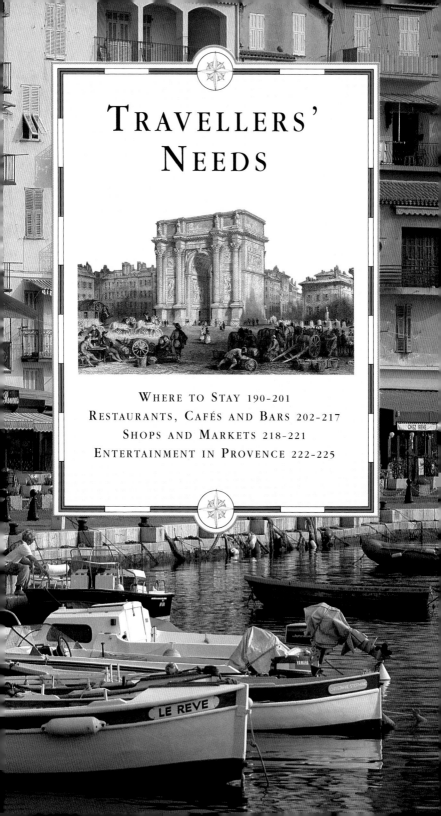

TRAVELLERS'
NEEDS

WHERE TO STAY 190-201

RESTAURANTS, CAFÉS AND BARS 202-217

SHOPS AND MARKETS 218-221

ENTERTAINMENT IN PROVENCE 222-225

WHERE TO STAY

THE DIVERSITY of Provence is reflected in the wide range of hotels it has to offer. Accommodation varies from luxurious palaces like the Carlton in Cannes to simple country cottages where a warm welcome, peaceful setting and often excellent cuisine are more customary than mod cons.

A broad range of hotels from all price categories has been selected across the length and breadth

Négresco doorman

of Provence. The hotel listings on pages 196–201 are arranged by *département* and town according to price, and have been selected for offering interesting accommodation and good value for money. There is also a selection of the very best hotels in Provence on pages 194–5. Self-catering holidays are a popular and inexpensive option and information is given on renting a rural home or *gîte* and camping.

WHERE TO LOOK

THERE IS NO shortage of hotels in Provence and the Côte d'Azur. Ever since the crusades of the Middle Ages, the medieval villages and ports have accommodated travellers, to varying degrees of luxury.

Some of the most attractive and best value coastal accommodation is found along the shores of the Var between Toulon and St-Tropez. The glamour and glitz come further east – the coast from Fréjus to Menton is predictably extravagant, but it is possible to find accommodation to suit all budgets and tastes, from the exclusive Eden Roc, favourite of filmstars on Cap d'Antibes, to the 15th-century townhouse of the Café des Arcades in Biot.

Inland, the major towns and cities of Provence offer a good variety of hotels, from the luxurious mansions of Aix-en-Provence and Arles to the more simple hostelries of the Luberon and the Var. Most villages offer at least one small hotel. Pleasant surprises are to be found – the dreamy ideal of a converted farmhouse or medieval priory lost in the midst of vibrant lavender fields is very much a reality if you know where to look.

If you are seeking tranquillity, travel north to the wilds of Haute Provence where several châteaux and *relais de poste* (post-houses and coaching inns) provide excellent accommodation and regional cuisine in rustic surroundings.

Those seeking a country idyll should head to the hills and valleys of the Central Var, the Luberon National Park or the foothills of Mont Ventoux. More refined bases include the university town of Aix, the papal capital of Avignon or the Roman town of Arles. Much-maligned Marseille does in fact make an exciting, cosmopolitan base, offering excellent hotels and restaurants.

HOTEL PRICES

SINGLE OCCUPANCY rates are usually the same as two sharing – prices are normally per room, not per person. Tax and service are included in the price, with the exception of full board *(pension)* and half board *(demi-pension),* and rates posted are exclusive of breakfast. You are not required to take breakfast and should stipulate if you want it.

Rooms with a shower tend to be 20 per cent cheaper than those with a bath. In more remote areas, half board may

The palatial Carlton Hotel in Cannes *(see p196)*

be obligatory and is often necessary in places where the hotel has the only restaurant. In high season, popular coastal hotels may give preference to visitors who want half board.

Prices drop considerably in Provence in low season (Oct–Mar). Many hotels close for five months of the year, reopening for Easter. During festivals *(see pp30–35)*, prices can rival high-season tariffs. In low season, discount packages are common along the Côte d'Azur. It is worth checking with travel agents or contacting the hotels directly as many of the biggest and most famous hotels offer dramatic discounts – even the palaces of the Riviera need to fill their rooms in winter.

The elegant reception area of the Grand Hôtel du Cap-Ferrat *(see p197)*

Hôtel de Paris entrance *(see p197)*

HOTEL GRADINGS

FRENCH HOTELS are classified by the tourist authorities into five categories: one to four stars, plus a four-star deluxe rating. A few very basic places are unclassified. These ratings give an indication of the level of facilities you can expect but offer little idea of cleanliness, ambience or friendliness of the owners. Some of the most charming hotels are blessed with few stars, while the higher ratings often turn out to be impersonal business hotels.

FACILITIES AND MEALS

FACILITIES WILL VARY greatly depending on the location and rating of each hotel. In remoter areas most hotels have adjoining restaurants, and nearly all feature a breakfast

room or terrace. Many three-star hotels have swimming pools which can be a godsend in the summer. Parking is readily available at country hotels. Some city hotels have underground or guarded parking – in the larger cities like Marseille and Nice this is becoming a necessity as car crime is an increasing problem. Most hotels will have telephones in the bedrooms. Televisions are rarer, especially outside towns. Double beds *(grands lits)* are common, but it is advisable to specify you want one.

Many Provençal hotels are converted buildings and, while this adds a definite charm, it can mean enduring eccentric plumbing, erratic electricity and ceilings that go bump in the night. Some hotels are near a main road or town square – choosing a room at the back is usually all that is required for a peaceful night.

Many hotels use the time-honoured French bolster – a long cushion which many find uncomfortable – if you desire a pillow, ask for *un oreiller*. You have to ask specifically for a room with a bath or toilet – a *cabinet de toilette* simply has a basin and bidet.

Traditional French breakfasts are common in Provence and in summer are often enjoyed outside. Evening meals are served daily until about 9pm, except Sunday when dining rooms are often closed – check before you arrive. Check-out time is about noon – if you stay any longer you will have to pay for an extra day.

BOOKING

IN HIGH SEASON it is imperative to book well in advance, especially for any popular coastal hotels. During peak season, proprietors may ask for a deposit. Tourist offices *(see p229)* are useful if you want personal descriptions and recommendations of places. Tourist offices will also book for you. Outside peak season (Jun–Sep) you may be able to turn up on the day, but it is always wise to phone ahead to make sure the establishment is open.

The exclusive Eden Roc *(see p196)*

CHILDREN

FAMILIES WITH young children can often share a room at no extra cost, since prices are per room and not per person. Few hotels will refuse children although some insist they must be well behaved. Numerous country hotels boast modern annexes with bungalow apartments specifically designed for visiting families, often only a few steps away from the swimming pool.

The extensive formal grounds of Le Château de Roussan *(see p200)*

THE CLASSIC FAMILY HOTEL

IF YOU ARE TRAVELLING on a budget, the friendly, family-run hotel is ideal. These establishments are found in virtually every village and the atmosphere is extremely informal, with children, cats and dogs running in and out. It is likely to be the focal point of the village, with the dining room and bar open to non-residents.

The annual *Logis de France* guide, available from the **French Government Tourist Office**, lists these one- and two-star restaurants-with-rooms *(auberges)*, often specializing in regional cuisine. Most are basic roadside inns, with only a few listed in the main towns and cities, but off the beaten track you can find charming converted farm-houses and inexpensive seaside hotels.

THE MODERN CHAIN HOTEL

OUTSIDE THE MAIN motorway routes there are few chain hotels in Provence. For those wishing to break their journey or seeking inexpensive accommodation on the outskirts of towns, the chains **Campanile**, **Formule 1** and **Ibis** offer modern and comfortable rooms. They are a safe and practical bet if nothing else is available, and can be booked directly over the phone by credit card. However, they do lack the charm and intimacy of an authentic Provençal hotel. Often you can find accommodation in the town itself or the surrounding countryside for an equivalent price, albeit with a less sanitized decor.

Other modern chains are geared to the business traveller and are found in most major towns. **Sofitel, Novotel** and **Mercure** all have hotels in Aix, Nice, Marseille and Avignon. For more information, phone the French Government Tourist Office.

DIRECTORY

CHAIN HOTELS

Campanile
📞 *01 64 62 46 46 Paris.*

Formule 1
📞 *020-8507 0789 (UK, for brochure).*
📞 *08 36 68 56 85 France.*

Ibis, Novotel, Sofitel, Mercure
📞 *020-8283 4500 UK.*
📞 *01 60 87 90 90 Paris.*

BED AND BREAKFAST

France Accueil Contacts
3 rue de Colonel Moll, 75017 Paris.
📞 *01 45 00 45 51.*
FAX *01 44 17 90 84.*

France-Lodge
41 rue La Fayette, 75009 Paris.
📞 *01 53 20 09 09.*
FAX *01 53 20 01 84.*

HOSTELS

CROUS
39 av G Bernanos, 75005 Paris.
📞 *01 40 51 37 10.*

FUAJ (Fédération Unie des Auberges de Jeunesse)
27 rue Pajol, 75018 Paris.
📞 *01 44 89 87 27.*
FAX *01 44 89 87 49.*

YHA (Youth Hostel Association, UK)
8 St Stephens Hill, St Albans, Herts AL1 2DY.
📞 *(01727) 855215.*
FAX *(01727) 844126.*

American Youth Hostel Association
1108 K St NW, Washington, DC 20005..
📞 *(202) 783 0717.*

SELF-CATERING/ EFFICIENCIES

Brittany Ferries
For brochure with gîtes.
📞 *(0990) 360360 UK.*

Maison des Gîtes de France
59 rue St Lazare, 75009 Paris.
📞 *01 49 70 75 75.*
FAX *01 42 81 28 53.*

CAMPING

Camping and Caravaning Club
📞 *(01203) 694995.*
FAX *(0203) 694886.*

Eurocamp
📞 *(01606) 787878.*
FAX *(01606) 787034.*

Fédération Française de Camping-Caravaning
78 rue de Rivoli, 75004 Paris.
📞 *01 42 72 84 08.*
FAX *01 42 72 70 21.*

DISABLED TRAVELLERS

Association des Paralysés de France
17 bd Auguste Blanqui,

75013 Paris.
📞 *01 40 78 69 00.*

CNFLRH
236 bis rue de Tolbiac, 75013 Paris.
📞 *01 53 80 66 66.*
FAX *01 53 80 66 67.*

Mobility International USA
PO Box 3551, Eugene, Oregon 97403.
📞 *(503) 343 1248.*

RADAR
Unit 12, 12 City Forum, 250 City Road, London EC1V 8AF.
📞 *0171-250 3222.*

FURTHER INFORMATION

French Government Tourist Office
UK: 178 Piccadilly, London W1V 0AL.
📞 *020-7399 3500.*
FAX *020-7493 6594.*

US: 610 Fifth Avenue, New York, NY 10020.
📞 *(900) 990 0040.*

BED AND BREAKFAST

I N RURAL AREAS, some cottages, farms and private houses offer bed and breakfast. These *chambres d'hôte* come in all shapes and sizes and will provide dinner on request. They are listed separately in tourist office brochures and many are inspected and registered by the **Gîtes de France** organization; look out for their distinctive *chambre d'hôtes* road signs. Two privately-run bed and breakfast agencies are **France Accueil Contacts** and **France-Lodge**.

Gîtes de France road sign

HOSTELS

F OR THE SINGLE traveller this is the cheapest accommodation. A membership card, purchased from the **Youth Hostel Association** in your country, is required. In summer, you can stay in university rooms; contact **CROUS**, the Centre Régional des Oeuvres Universitaires. For the regions' main youth hostels see p237.

SELF-CATERING

P ROVENCE IS a popular self-catering destination and many companies specialize in renting anything from rural farm cottages to beach apartments. One of the best organizations is **Gîtes de France**, with its headquarters **Maison des Gîtes de France** in Paris, which provides detailed lists of accommodation to rent by the week in each *département*.

Often the owners live nearby and are always welcoming, but rarely speak much English. Don't expect luxury from your *gîte* as facilities are basic, but it is a great way to get a better insight into real Provençal life.

CAMPING

L ONG A POPULAR pastime in Provence, camping remains an invitingly cheap and atmospheric way of seeing the area. Facilities vary, from a basic one-star farm or vineyard site to the camping metropolises of the Riviera, complete with water fun parks and satellite TV. **Eurocamp** specializes in family holidays. Luxury tents are preassembled at the campsite of your choice and everything is ready on arrival. Organized children's entertainment and baby-sitting are available on site. Some campsites will not accept visitors unless they have a special *camping carnet*, available from the AA, RAC and clubs such as the **Fédération Française de Camping-Caravaning**.

DISABLED TRAVELLERS

D UE TO THE venerable design of most Provençal hotels, few are able to offer unrestricted wheelchair access. Larger hotels have lifts and hotel staff will go out of their way to aid disabled guests. The **Association des Paralysés de France** publishes a guide to accessible accommodation. Other useful sources of information are the **Comité Nationale Française de Liaison pour la Réadaptation des Handicapés (CNFLRH)** and **Radar (Royal Association for Disability and Rehabilitation)**.

USING THE LISTINGS

The hotels on pages 196–201 are listed according to area and price category. The symbols summarize the facilities at each hotel.

🛏 all rooms/number of rooms with bath or shower
24 24-hour room service
TV TV in all rooms
✦ rooms with good views
▤ air-conditioning in all rooms
🏊 hotel swimming pool or beach
🧒 children's facilities
♿ wheelchair access
⬆ lift
P hotel parking available
🌳 grounds or terrace
🍴 restaurant in hotel
★ highly recommended
💳 credit cards accepted
AE American Express
MC Mastercard
DC Diners Club
V Visa

Price categories for a standard double room (not per person) with shower for one night, including tax and service, but not breakfast.
Ⓕ Under F200
ⒻⒻ F200–400
ⒻⒻⒻ F400–600
ⒻⒻⒻⒻ F600–1,200
ⒻⒻⒻⒻⒻ Over F1,200.

Camping in Provence, a popular accommodation alternative

Provence's Best: Hotels

N O OTHER REGION OF FRANCE can boast such a range of accommodation as Provence. The listings on pages 196–201 have been compiled to give you as wide a choice as possible to suit your budget and preferences. All the establishments included meet exacting requirements but certain hotels stand out, whether for character, comfort or simple good value. Those shown here have been selected as among the best in their particular style and price range.

Le Beffroi
Antique furniture, beamed ceilings and chandeliers are among the elegant features of Vaison's Belfry. (See p201.)

L'Europe
Napoleon stayed here in 1799, and it is still Avignon's most exclusive hotel, with beautifully preserved period furniture and fine Gobelin tapestries. (See p201.)

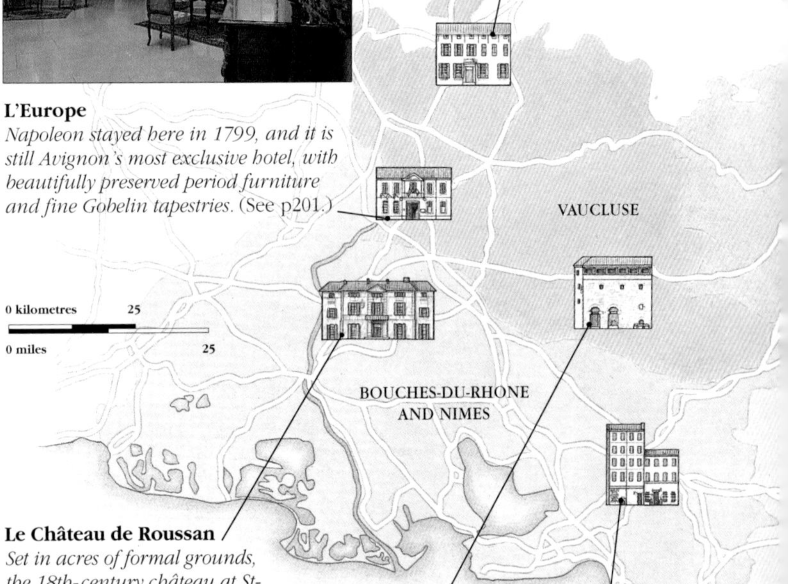

VAUCLUSE

0 kilometres   25

0 miles   25

BOUCHES-DU-RHONE
AND NIMES

Le Château de Roussan
Set in acres of formal grounds, the 18th-century château at St-Rémy has been owned by the Roussan family for over a century. (See p200.)

Moulin de Lourmarin
A former olive mill is now an enchanting hotel-restaurant, offering comfort and charm. (See p201.)

Hôtel des Augustins
In the heart of Aix, this 12th-century priory combines lovingly restored original features with luxury mod cons. (See p199.)

Auberge du Vieux Fox
This delightful hotel, in the small, peaceful village of Fox-Amphoux, was once a hostelry for the Knights Templar. (See p198.)

L'Hermitage
Perched above the harbour at Monte-Carlo, this lavish establishment was built in 1899 and has been superbly renovated in authentic Belle Epoque style. (See p197.)

ALPES-DE-HAUTE-PROVENCE

THE RIVIERA AND THE ALPES MARITIMES

THE VAR AND THE ILES D'HYERES

Le Négresco
Nice's white Belle Epoque palace is a Riviera landmark, attracting the world's rich and famous. (See p197.)

Le Bellevue
As its name suggests, the views from this small, simple family-run hotel are lovely, over the terracotta rooftops of Bormes-les-Mimosas to the sea. (See p198.)

RIVIERA AND THE ALPES MARITIMES

ANTIBES

L'Auberge Provençale

Road map E3. 61 place Nationale, 06600. **[** 04 93 34 13 24. **FAX** 04 93 34 89 88. **Rooms:** 7. 🛏 🖩 🍴 🍽
AE, MC, V. **(F)(F)**

A large, welcoming house under the plane trees of Antibes' main square, this *auberge* lives up to its name with rustic Provençal furniture and canopied beds. The bedrooms are simple, comfortable and clean.

BEAULIEU

Le Select Hôtel

Road map E3. Pl Charles-de-Gaulle, 06310. **[** 04 93 01 05 42. **FAX** 04 93 01 34 30. **Rooms:** 20. 🛏 📺 🍽
MC, V. **(F)(F)**

Conveniently situated just up from the station, the Select offers small simple rooms and a *pension* atmosphere. The rooms at the back tend to be rather stuffy in summer so ask for one overlooking the square, site of Beaulieu's daily market.

Hôtel Métropole

Road map E3. 15 bd Maréchal Leclerc, 06310. **[** 04 93 01 00 08. **FAX** 04 93 01 18 51. **Rooms:** 40. 🛏 24 📺
🍽 🖩 🌊 🌊 P 🛢 🍴 ★ 🍽
AE, MC, DC, V. **(F)(F)(F)(F)(F)**

The palatial Métropole combines a *fin-de-siècle* Italianate style with ultra-modern facilities and a relaxed atmosphere. Without a doubt, the hotel's centrepiece is its majestic terrace restaurant, which overlooks the Mediterranean. It serves excellent regional cuisine. There is also a heated sea-water swimming pool.

BIOT

Galerie des Arcades

Road map E3. 16 place des Arcades, 06410. **[** 04 93 65 01 04. **FAX** 04 93 65 01 05. **Rooms:** 12. 🛏 🌊 🍴
★ 🍽 AE. **(F)(F)**

This 15th-century inn is a quirky haven of tranquillity, hidden away in the quiet place des Arcades. The bedrooms are small but undeniably atmospheric. The top-floor rooms have terraces with views over the hills to the sea. The hotel bar also serves as the breakfast room and restaurant, which you share with local painters and their dogs.

CAGNES-SUR-MER

Hôtel le Minaret

Road map E3. 3 av Serre, 06800. **[** 04 93 20 16 52. **FAX** 04 92 13 05 56. **Rooms:** 20. 🛏 📺 🌊 🛢 P
🍽 MC, V. **(F)(F)**

A minute's walk from the beach and close to the town centre, this peaceful hotel has a shaded garden full of mimosa and orange trees. Rooms overlook the sea or the garden and many have terraces or balconies.

CANNES

Hôtel Molière

Road map E4. 5–7 rue Molière, 06400. **[** 04 93 38 16 16. **FAX** 04 93 68 29 57. **Rooms:** 42. 🛏 📺 🍴 🌊 🛢
🍽 AE, MC, V. **(F)(F)(F)**

This 19th-century town house is a mere five minutes' walk from the sea, with bright and comfortable rooms and terraces overlooking the floral garden. It is very popular in season and often full, so book well in advance for the Film Festival.

Carlton Inter-Continental

Road map E4. 58 la Croisette, 06400. **[** 04 93 06 40 06. **FAX** 04 93 06 40 25. **Rooms:** 338. 🛏 24 📺 🍴
🌊 🌊 🌊 P 🛢 🍴 ★ 🍽 AE, MC, DC, V. **(F)(F)(F)(F)(F)** *(see pp68–9).*

Home to stars during the Film Festival and business people the rest of the year, the Carlton rivals Le Négresco *(see p197)* as the jewel in the crown of the Riviera. Rooms are predictably luxurious with those at the front boasting balconies that overlook the sea and the Iles de Lérins. There is no garden, but the hotel's private beach allows you to book in direct from your yacht.

CAP D'ANTIBES

La Gardiole

Road map E3. 74 Chemin de la Garoupe, 06600. **[** 04 93 61 35 03. **FAX** 04 93 67 61 87. **Rooms:** 20. 🛏
🌊 🛢 🍴 🍽 AE, MC, V.
(F)(F)(F)

Amid the exclusive pine woods of Cap d'Antibes, this small, pink villa is a surprisingly affordable retreat. The decor is traditional and simple – tiled floors, white walls and beamed ceilings. All the bedrooms are bright and airy and vary in price according to size. The large terrace provides welcome shade in the summer-time beneath a spreading wisteria.

Eden Roc

Road map E3. Bd Kennedy, 06600. **[** 04 93 61 39 01. **FAX** 04 93 67 76 04. **Rooms:** 134. 🛏 24 📺 🍴
🌊 🌊 P 🛢 🍴 ★ **(F)(F)(F)(F)(F)**

Built in 1870, Eden Roc was the inspiration for F Scott Fitzgerald's *Tender is the Night*. It was a mecca for 1930s' socialites: Charlie Chaplin, Hemingway and the Fitzgeralds all stayed here. Today it welcomes the likes of Clint Eastwood, Bill Cosby and Arnold Schwarzenegger. Set in idyllic grounds, the palatial hotel is now the most exclusive on the Riviera, and perhaps in France.

EZE

Château Eza

Road map F3. Rue de la Pise, 06360. **[** 04 93 41 12 24. **FAX** 04 93 41 16 64. **Rooms:** 10. 🛏 24 📺 🍴
P 🛢 🍴 ★ 🍽 AE, MC, DC, V.
(F)(F)(F)(F)(F)

This remarkable building is a collection of medieval houses perched high at the summit of Eze's "eagle's nest". Once home to Prince William of Sweden, it has been converted into a luxury hotel. The château's splendid rooms have Persian rugs and huge marble bathrooms.

JUAN-LES-PINS

Hôtel des Mimosas

Road map E3. Rue Pauline, 06160. **[** 04 93 61 04 16. **FAX** 04 92 93 06 46. **Rooms:** 34. 🛏 24 📺 🌊
P 🛢 🍽 AE, MC, V. **(F)(F)(F)**

This 19th-century town house on a quiet road is attractively designed and warmly welcoming. Rooms are modern and spacious, most with their own balconies. The salons are equally comfortable, mixing traditional decor with Art Nouveau. Gardens are kept shady by leafy palms which complete the blissful picture of peace and tranquillity.

MENTON

Le Magali

Road map F3. 10 rue Villarey, 06500. **[** 04 93 35 73 78. **FAX** 04 93 57 05 04. **Rooms:** 40. 🛏 📺 🍴 🌊 P 🛢
🍴 AE, MC, DC, V. **(F)(F)**

The best of the surprisingly low-quality hotels in Menton, Le Magali offers air-conditioned rooms, fading decor and a tranquil garden with lemon trees. Several rooms have garden-side balconies.

MONACO

L'Hermitage

Road map F3. Square Beaumarchais, Monte-Carlo, 98000. 🄲 00 377 92 16 40 00. **FAX** 04 92 16 38 52. **Rooms:** 227. 🖶 24 TV 🍽 🍴 🛗 P 🅿️ 🍽 ★ 🅰 AE, MC, V. Ⓕ Ⓕ Ⓕ Ⓕ Ⓕ

The vast cream Belle Epoque palace at the heart of Monte-Carlo is one of Europe's most splendid hotels. This haven of opulence is as impressive today as when it opened at the turn of the century. It is known for its lofty glass-domed Winter Garden foyer, sumptuous pink-and-gold restaurant and the marble terrace.

Hôtel de Paris

Road map F3. Pl du Casino, Monte-Carlo 98000. 🄲 00 377 92 16 30 00. **FAX** 04 92 16 38 49. **Rooms:** 250. 🖶 24 TV 🍽 🍴 🛗 P 🅿️ 🍽 🅰 AE, MC, DC, V. Ⓕ Ⓕ Ⓕ Ⓕ Ⓕ

The superbly superior Hôtel de Paris is indicative of the opulent history of the area. Everyone has stayed here, from pop star Michael Jackson to Queen Victoria. Prices are as rich as the furnishing, worth it if only for a once-in-a-lifetime experience.

NICE

La Belle Meunière

Road map F3. 21 av Durante, 06000. 🄲 04 93 88 66 15. **Rooms:** 17. 🖶 🅿️ 🅰 AE, MC, DC, V. Ⓕ Ⓕ

One of Nice's most popular inexpensive hotels, this is near the train station with a private car park. This charming house is ever-welcoming, as is the friendly patron. The bedrooms are simple and spacious.

Hôtel Windsor

Road map F3. 11 rue Dalpozzo, 06000. 🄲 04 93 88 59 35. **FAX** 04 93 88 94 57. **Rooms:** 57. 🖶 24 🍽 🍴 🛗 ★ 🅰 AE, MC, DC, V. Ⓕ Ⓕ Ⓕ

Behind the unimposing grey façade hides an exotic hotel in the heart of Nice. Oriental furnishing marks the entrance hall, which leads to a tropical garden complete with a palm-fringed pool. Further facilities include an English-style pub and a Thai-style lounge. Bedrooms are decorated with dreamy frescoes.

La Pérouse

Road map F3. 11 quai Rauba Capeu, 06000. 🄲 04 93 62 34 63. **FAX** 04 93 62 59 41. **Rooms:** 64. 🖶 TV 🍽 🍴 🛗 P 🅿️ 🅰 AE, MC, DC, V. Ⓕ Ⓕ Ⓕ Ⓕ

At the eastern end of the Baie des Anges, La Pérouse enjoys the most impressive and most painted view in Nice – the long, luxurious sweep of the promenade. Matisse stayed here, as did Dufy, who captured the view from his window in a number of canvases. Rooms with a sea view have small terraces where you can paint your masterpiece or sip an aperitif as the sun sets.

Le Négresco

Road map F3. 37 promenade des Anglais, 06000. 🄲 04 93 16 64 00. **FAX** 04 93 88 35 68. **Rooms:** 141. 🖶 24 TV 🍽 🍴 🛗 P 🅿️ 🍽 ★ 🅰 AE, MC, DC, V. Ⓕ Ⓕ Ⓕ Ⓕ Ⓕ (see pp94–5).

The most famous luxury hotel on the Riviera has been carefully renovated and retains its unique Belle Epoque grandeur. The furnishings, atmosphere and service are stylish and delightfully ostentatious, as one would expect from this *monument historique*. Le Négresco offers a stay never to be forgotten.

ST-JEAN-CAP-FERRAT

Clair Logis

Road map F3. 12 av Centrale, 06230. 🄲 04 93 76 04 57. **FAX** 04 93 76 11 85. **Rooms:** 18. 🖶 TV 🚹 P 🅿️ ★ 🅰 AE, MC, DC, V. Ⓕ Ⓕ Ⓕ

The Riviera's hidden gem, this small turn-of-the-century villa lies in lush grounds of orange trees, palms and bougainvillea. Each room has been spaciously refurbished and named after a flower, from mimosa to jasmine. Four bedrooms have large balconies and there is a ground-floor annex suitable for families.

La Voile d'Or

Road map F3. Port de St-Jean, 06230. 🄲 04 93 01 13 13. **FAX** 04 93 76 11 17. **Rooms:** 45. 🖶 24 TV 🍽 🍴 🛗 P 🅿️ 🍽 ★ 🅰 AE, MC, V. Ⓕ Ⓕ Ⓕ Ⓕ Ⓕ

Set by the tranquil port of St-Jean, this luxury hotel is a romantic place of hanging gardens and parasoled terraces. Both the decor and service are quietly lavish and there are two salt-water pools. Rooms looking onto the garden are not as expensive as those on the port-side. The restaurant is highly recommended.

Grand Hôtel du Cap Ferrat

Road map F3. Bd Géneral de Gaulle, 06230. 🄲 04 93 76 50 50. **FAX** 04 93 76 50 76. **Rooms:** 53. 🖶 24 TV 🍽 🍴 🛗 P 🅿️ 🍽 ★ 🅰 AE, MC, DC, V. Ⓕ Ⓕ Ⓕ Ⓕ Ⓕ

At the southern tip of Cap Ferrat lies this sumptuous palace, concealing some of the world's most expensive real estate. Its luxurious rooms have been lovingly restored in a grand Mediterranean style, set in tropical garden surroundings. A funicular railway transports guests down to a terrace restaurant and Olympic-size sea-water pool, where Charlie Chaplin taught his children to swim.

ST-PAUL-DE-VENCE

Le Hameau

Road map E3. 528 route de la Colle, 06570. 🄲 04 93 32 80 24. **FAX** 04 93 32 55 75. **Rooms:** 17. 🖶 🍽 🍴 🖶 P 🅿️ ★ 🅰 MC, V. Ⓕ Ⓕ Ⓕ

Above the main road, five minutes' walk from the village, is this finely designed collection of terracotta-roofed villas. Rooms are countrified in style with wooden-beamed ceilings, red tiled floors and historic furniture. Many bedrooms have a small terrace or balcony. Terraces of orange and lemon trees descend from the hotel, proffering superb views up to the village and down to the sea. Rooms near the main road can be noisy.

VENCE

La Roseraie

Road map E3. Av Henri Giraud, 06140. 🄲 04 93 58 02 20. **FAX** 04 93 58 99 31. **Rooms:** 14. 🖶 TV 🍽 🍴 P 🅿️ ★ 🅰 AE, MC, V. Ⓕ Ⓕ Ⓕ

Following various articles in French and American magazines, this smart Belle Epoque town house is now far and away Vence's most sought-after hotel. The rooms are small but lovingly decorated with traditional Provençal fabrics and furniture. The enticing garden is shaded by two palm trees and breakfast is served under a venerable magnolia.

VILLEFRANCHE

Hôtel Welcome

Road map F3. Quai Amiral Courbet, 06230. 🄲 04 93 76 27 62. **FAX** 04 93 76 27 66. **Rooms:** 32. 🖶 TV 🍽 🍴 🛗 🅰 AE, MC, DC, V. Ⓕ Ⓕ Ⓕ

This sizeable, ochre-painted hotel looks down over the picturesque port of Villefranche. Rooms overlooking the bay offer truly excellent views across to the wealthy woods of Cap Ferrat, while the town-side vista is less attractive. Facilities are modern and the classy restaurant serves excellent local cuisine.

For key to symbols *see p193*

THE VAR AND THE ILES D'HYERES

LES ARCS

Logis du Guetteur

Road map D4. Pl du Château, 83460. **(** 04 94 99 51 10. **FAX** 04 94 99 51 29. **Rooms:** 12. ⛺ 📺 🖥 🅿 🔌 ⓘ ★ AE, MC, V. €€€€

The medieval hotel is visible from far off – a castle tower dominating the small village. Exposed stonework and weighty wooden doors combine with comfortable, modern furnishing. Views from the ramparts are epic, sweeping across the valley of the Argens to the pine forests of the Massif des Maures.

BORMES-LES-MIMOSAS

Le Bellevue

Road map D4. Pl Gambetta, 83230. **(** 04 94 71 15 15. **FAX** 04 94 71 55 96 04. **Rooms:** 12. ⛺ 🖥 🔌 ⓘ ★ 🅿 MC, V. €

A small, family-run hotel with spacious bedrooms and wrought iron balconies, the Bellevue offers stunning views over terracotta roofs to the Iles de Porquerolles. Room ten is the largest, with an en suite bathroom and double French windows shaded by two large palm trees.

Le Grand

Road map D4. 167 route du Baguier, 83230. **(** 04 94 71 23 72. **FAX** 04 94 71 51 20. **Rooms:** 60. ⛺ 24 🖥 👤 🐾 🅿 🔌 ⓘ 🍴 MC, V. €€

Bormes' Grand hotel commands the grandest of locations in the Massif des Maures, crowning the village hillside above the Mediterranean. Its décor is faded 1930s. The once opulent rooms are a little ragged, but the spectacular setting, sun-soaked terrace and friendly service make this a memorable stay.

LA CADIERE D'AZUR

Hostellerie Bérard

Road map C4. Rue Gabriel-Péri, 83740. **(** 04 94 90 11 43. **FAX** 04 94 90 01 94. **Rooms:** 38. ⛺ 📺 🖥 ▤ 🖥 👤 🅿 🔌 ⓘ ★ 🖥 AE, MC, V. €€€

The medieval village centre's old convent is now an *auberge*, with a heated pool, shady terrace, gardens, a good restaurant and lovely views. Rooms, far from austere cells, are comfortable and spacious.

COGOLIN

Au Coq Hôtel

Road map E4. Place de la République, 83310. **(** 04 94 54 13 71. **FAX** 04 94 54 03 06. **Rooms:** 25. ⛺ 📺 🅿 🔌 ⓘ 🖥 MC, V. €€

In the centre of the bustling village of Cogolin, this delightful pink hotel is ideally situated, only ten minutes' drive from St-Tropez and near the beaches of Cavalaire *(see pp28–9)*. Rooms are spacious and there is a terrace garden in which to worship the glorious Tropezienne sun.

COTIGNAC

Lou Calen

Road map D4. 1 cours Gambetta, 83850. **(** 04 94 04 60 40. **FAX** 04 94 04 76 64. **Rooms:** 18. ⛺ 🅿 🔌 ⓘ 🍴 ★ 🖥 AE, MC, DC, V. €€€€

Lou Calen is a large, authentic Varois town house, situated next to the main fountain in the village. The rustic rooms are a pleasing jumble of paintings, antiques and vases of fresh flowers. The shady garden at the back of the hotel is perfect for refined al fresco eating.

FAYENCE

Moulin de la Camandoule

Road map E3. Chemin de Notre-Dame des Cyprès, 83440. **(** 04 94 76 00 84. **FAX** 04 94 76 10 40. **Rooms:** 11. ⛺ 📺 🖥 ▤ 🅿 🔌 ⓘ 🍴 ★ 🖥 MC, V. €€€€

In the valley beneath the village of Fayence, this converted 15th-century olive mill proffers peace and quiet amid vines and olive trees as well as a swimming pool and carefully renovated rooms. Remnants of the olive pressing process abound, including a large millwheel alongside the restaurant. The delicious cuisine complements the rustic setting, serving authentic Provençal dishes.

FOX-AMPHOUX

Auberge du Vieux Fox

Road map D4. Pl de l'Eglise, 83670. **(** 04 94 80 71 69. **FAX** 04 94 80 78 38. **Rooms:** 8. ⛺ 🖥 🅿 🍴 ★ 🖥 AE, MC, V. €

This was once a staging post for the Knights Templar *(see p123)*, as the building's proximity to the small village church indicates. Sections of the hotel date back to the 11th century – although the rooms are small, the ancient features and sweeping views from Fox-Amphoux's craggy hilltop are recompense enough.

GRIMAUD

Côteau Fleuri

Road map E4. Pl des Pénitents, 83310. **(** 04 94 43 20 17. **FAX** 04 94 43 33 42. **Rooms:** 14. ⛺ 🖥 🔌 ⓘ 🖥 AE, MC, V. €€

High on the western edge of the village, this grey-stone inn boasts grandiose views over the Massif des Maures. Summer meals take place on a pretty garden terrace. The food served is truly excellent.

LES ILES D'HYÈRES

Le Manoir

Road map D5. Port-Cros, 83400. **(** 04 94 05 90 52. **FAX** 04 94 05 90 89. **Rooms:** 23. ⛺ 🖥 🔌 ⓘ 🍴 🖥 MC, V. €€€€

A hotel situated on this island paradise is a rare commodity. Le Manoir is a simple yet seductive 19th-century manor house, offering a warm welcome and delicious food among the eucalyptus groves. It's wise to reserve; *demi-pension* is required.

ST-PIERRE-DE-TORTOUR

Auberge St-Pierre

Road map D4. St-Pierre, 83690. **(** 04 94 70 57 17. **FAX** 04 94 70 59 04. **Rooms:** 16. ⛺ 🖥 ▤ 🅿 🔌 🍴 🖥 V. €€€

Peace and quiet broken only by the sound of sheep is a characteristic of this 16th-century farmhouse. In the dining room a fountain trickles hypnotically while the terrace is the place where you can enjoy views across the countryside of the Haut Var. Invigorating outdoor activities' including tennis, archery, swimming and fishing are all available on site. The extensive grounds also contain a fully working farm.

ST-TROPEZ

La Ponche

Road map E4. 3 rue des Remparts, 83990. **(** 04 94 97 02 53. **FAX** 04 94 97 78 61. **Rooms:** 18. ⛺ 24 📺 🖥 ▤ 👤 🅿 🔌 🍴 ★ 🖥 AE, MC, V. €€€€

Situated behind the small port and beach of La Ponche, this cluster of one-time fishermen's cottages is St-Tropez's most enchanting hotel. Mme Duckstein has run her bohemian nook since 1937 – artist Pablo Picasso was a regular at the small bar. The bedrooms are large and artfully chic, including two that are suitable for families.

SEILLANS

Hôtel des Deux Rocs

Road map E3. Pl Font d'Amont, 83440. ⌐ 04 94 76 87 32. FAX 04 94 76 88 68. **Rooms:** 14. 🛏 🚻 ⭐ 🍽 MC, V. ⒻⒻⒻ

This large old Provençal house is situated on a small square in the upper village. The decoration is local, dominated by antiques and lovely traditional fabrics. The rooms vary in size and in the amount of light they receive. Those situated at the front are larger and brighter. In summertime, meals are served around the square's fountain.

BOUCHES-DU-RHONE AND NIMES

AIX-EN-PROVENCE

Le Prieuré

Road map C4. Rte de Sisteron, 13100. ⌐ 04 42 21 05 23. FAX 04 42 21 60 56. **Rooms:** 23. 🛏 🍽 P 🚻 🍽 MC, V. ⒻⒻⒻ

Le Prieuré is a converted 17th-century priory located in a quiet suburb of Aix. The rooms are large and comfortable. Ask for one that overlooks both the pond that ripples with fish and the stretching alleys of plane trees. In the summertime, breakfast is served on a pleasant terrace above the immaculately kept formal gardens where monks used to keep their bees.

Hôtel des Augustins

Road map C4. 3 rue de la Masse, 13100. ⌐ 04 42 27 28 59. FAX 04 42 26 74 87. **Rooms:** 29. 🛏 TV 🍽 🚻 🍽 ⭐ 🍽 AE, MC, DC, V. ⒻⒻⒻⒻ

Once through the front doors, you enter a hushed world of discretion and attentiveness that is entirely appropriate for a converted 12th-century priory. Stained glass and vaulted ceilings add a distinctive ecclesiastical refinement to the very spacious rooms, which all boast luxurious bathrooms, complete with pleasantly un-religious jacuzzis.

ARLES

Hôtel Calendal

Road map B3. 22 pl du Docteur-Pomme, 13200. ⌐ 04 90 96 1189. FAX 04 90 96 05 84. **Rooms:** 27. 🛏 TV 🍽 P 🚻 🍽 AE, MC, DC, V. ⒻⒻ

Situated close to the Roman arena, this relaxing hotel has large, simple, well-furnished rooms. Car-parking is available behind the hotel. The greatest attraction is undoubtedly the enticing garden where breakfast and drinks are served beneath cool, spreading palm trees.

Hôtel d'Arlatan

Road map B3. 26 rue du Sauvage, 13200. ⌐ 04 90 93 56 66. FAX 04 90 49 68 45. **Rooms:** 48. 🛏 TV 🍽 P 🚻 🍽 AE, MC, DC, V. ⒻⒻⒻⒻ

The former residence of the Comtes d'Arlatan dates from the 16th century. It is among the area's most beautiful historic hotels. Glass panels in the salon floor offer glimpses of Roman foundations. The house also has a compact walled garden and stone terrace where breakfast is served in summer.

Nord Pinus

Road map B3. 14 place du Forum, 13200. ⌐ 04 90 93 44 44. FAX 04 90 93 34 00. **Rooms:** 25. 🛏 🚻 TV 🍽 P 🚻 🍽 ⭐ AE, MC, DC, V. ⒻⒻⒻⒻ

This classified national monument is the most intriguing luxury hotel that you will find in Arles. It was the favourite of Frédéric Mistral, whose statue it faces. Today you are likely to encounter top class matadors and opera singers. A sense of history is balanced by tastefully renovated rooms with all mod cons. The salons are full of heavy, dark furniture, bullfighting posters, trophies and the stuffed, mounted heads of unfortunate bulls.

LES-BAUX-DE-PROVENCE

Le Benvengudo

Road map B3. Vallon de l'Arcoule, 13520. ⌐ 04 90 54 32 54. FAX 04 90 54 42 58. **Rooms:** 20. 🛏 TV 🍽 🚻 P 🚻 🍽 AE, MC, V. ⒻⒻⒻⒻ

Le Benvengudo lies in the scenic valley below the rock of Les Baux. The charming ivy-covered hotel is good value for money, with its large garden, swimming pool and tennis court. The rooms are comfortable and sumptuously decorated; some have private terraces.

CASSIS

Les Jardins de Cassis

Road map C4. Rue A Favier, 13260. ⌐ 04 42 01 84 85. FAX 04 42 01 32 38. **Rooms:** 36. 🛏 P 🚻 🍽 AE, MC, DC, V. ⒻⒻⒻⒻ

Accommodation is limited in the crowded, picturesque port of Cassis. Reserve well in advance for a room in this fine Provençal-style hotel. Its rooms are pleasant, and although not on the sea, there is a swimming pool sunk into a garden of lemon groves and bougainvillea.

FONTVIEILLE

Le Régalido

Road map B3. Rue F Mistral, 13990. ⌐ 04 90 54 60 22. FAX 04 90 54 64 29. **Rooms:** 15. 🛏 TV 🍽 P 🚻 🚻 ⭐ 🍽 AE, MC, DC, V. ⒻⒻⒻⒻⒻ

This converted olive mill near the main street in sleepy Fontvieille is the most welcoming and luxurious hotel in the area. Rooms are tastefully decorated and inviting. The beautifully kept flower garden, with palm and fig trees, is a delight.

MARSEILLE

Le Ruhl

Road map C4. 269 Corniche Kennedy, 13007. ⌐ 04 91 52 01 77. FAX 04 91 52 49 82. **Rooms:** 15. 🛏 TV 🍽 🚻 🚻 🍽 AE, MC, V. ⒻⒻⒻ

You can't miss the Ruhl while going east from Marseille on the Corniche road – it hoves into view like the white prow of an ocean liner. The sea-going impression continues with "cabin" doors featuring portholes; the decor of its classy fish restaurant is nautical. Choose a room at the front despite possible traffic noise – sunset views across the bay to Chateau d'If from the large terraces make the choice worthwhile.

Hôtel Mercure Beauvau

Road map C4. 4 rue Beauvau, 13100. ⌐ 04 91 54 91 00. FAX 04 91 54 15 76. **Rooms:** 71. 🛏 🚻 TV 🍽 🍽 🚻 P 🍽 AE, MC, DC, V. ⒻⒻⒻⒻ

The revamped Beauvau smiles once more over Marseille's Vieux Port. Occupying the best location in the city and boasting comfy air-conditioned rooms, it is an ideal base. Rooms are soundproofed – which is essential, since Marseille's most famous street, La Canebière, and fish market are right next door.

MAUSSANE-LES ALPILLES

L'Oustaloun

Road map B3. Place de l'Eglise, 13520. ⓒ 04 90 54 32 19. **FAX** 04 90 54 45 57. **Rooms:** 10. 🚗 📺 🅿️ 🍽 ★ 🅴 AE, MC, V. ⒻⒻ

Stone walls, wooden beams and red tiles feature strongly in this 16th-century town house, situated on Maussanne's main square. The hotel has been lovingly restored – simple rooms are beautified with antiques. Meals are served in the vaulted 16th-century dining room.

NÎMES

Plazza

Road map A3. 10 rue Roussy, 30000. ⓒ 04 66 76 16 20. **FAX** 04 66 67 63 99. **Rooms:** 28. 🚗 📺 🕭 🗐 🖳 🅿️ 🅴 AE, MC, DC, V. ⒻⒻ

Situated in a quiet back street near the Porte d'Auguste, the Plazza has been completely renovated to provide comfort and mod cons with a slightly 1930s feel. Facilities include cable TV and protected car-parking. Fourth-floor room patios have rooftop views of the city.

Imperator Concorde

Road map A3. Quai de la Fontaine, 30900. ⓒ 04 66 21 90 30. **FAX** 04 66 67 70 25. **Rooms:** 60. 🚗 📅 📺 🗐 🖳 🅿️ 🍽 🅴 AE, MC, DC, V. ⒻⒻⒻⒻ

Nîmes' grandest hotel stands in its own gardens close to the Jardin de la Fontaine. The rooms are a good size, yet still cozy and comfortable. The restaurant, l'Enclos de la Fontaine, opens onto the garden and serves innovative cuisine.

ST-RÉMY-DE-PROVENCE

Le Château de Roussan

Road map B3. Rte de Tarascon, 13210. ⓒ 04 90 92 11 63. **FAX** 04 90 92 50 59. **Rooms:** 21. 🚗 🕭 🕭 🅿️ 🖳 🍽 ★ 🅴 AE, MC, V. ⒻⒻⒻ

Opinions are divided on this atmospheric 18th-century château, set in beautiful and extensive formal grounds. Some love it, others feel it has become too shabby. Visit for its character and setting, but not if you expect sanitized luxury and all mod cons. The ancient farmhouse in the grounds once belonged to Nostradamus (see p46).

Domaine de Valmouriane

Road map B3. Petite route des Baux, 13210. ⓒ 04 90 92 44 62. **FAX** 04 90 92 37 32. **Rooms:** 14. 🚗 📅 📺 🕭 🗐 🚹 🕭 🅱 🅿️ 🖳 🍽 ★ 🅴 AE, MC, DC, V. ⒻⒻⒻⒻ

This luxurious country mas, set in vineyards and pine woods, is a welcome retreat. The immaculate decor incorporates Provençal fabrics and marble bathrooms. In winter life revolves around the open fire in the billiard room, while in summer the swimming pool, tennis courts and stone terrace offer relaxation.

SAINTES-MARIES-DE-LA-MER

Hôtel de Cacharel

Road map A4. Rte de Cacharel, 13460. ⓒ 04 90 97 95 44. **FAX** 04 90 97 87 97. **Rooms:** 15. 🚗 🕭 🕭 🅿️ 🖳 🅴 MC, V. ⒻⒻⒻⒻ

Gardians, the famous cowboys of the Camargue, used to inhabit this historic ranch in the heart of the marshes. The hotel is surprisingly comfortable with large rooms and relaxing salons. Horse riding and bull-watching are available on site.

Mas de la Fouque

Road map A4. Route du Petit Rhône, 13460. ⓒ 04 90 97 81 02. **FAX** 04 90 97 96 84. **Rooms:** 14. 🚗 📺 🕭 🗐 🕭 🅿️ 🍽 🅴 AE, MC, DC, V. ⒻⒻⒻⒻⒻ

At the heart of the Camargue, this hotel offers all possible comforts. The rooms are well designed, with wooden beamed ceilings and tiled floors. Bedrooms have balconies built over the lagoon. There is also a pool, golf, tennis and a herd of white horses for excursions among the bulls and flamingos.

SALON-DE-PROVENCE

L'Abbaye de Ste-Croix

Road map B3. Route de Val de Cuech, 13300. ⓒ 04 90 56 24 55. **FAX** 04 90 56 31 12. **Rooms:** 24. 🚗 📺 🅿️ 🕭 🕭 🅴 AE, MC, DC, V. ⒻⒻⒻⒻ

Views from this 12th-century abbey are almost enough on their own to merit a visit, and the interior retains a distinctly medieval charm – some of the rooms are vast, while others are more cosy, having been converted from the original monks' cells. The extensive grounds feature groves of olive trees and a swimming pool.

VILLENEUVE-LÈS AVIGNON

Hôtel de l'Atelier

Road map B3. 5 rue de la Foire 30400. ⓒ 04 90 25 01 84. **FAX** 04 90 25 80 06. **Rooms:** 19. 🚗 📺 🚹 🅿️ 🕭 🅴 AE, DC, MC, V. ⒻⒻ

This is a beautiful 16th-century village house offering quiet, comfortable rooms filled with antique furniture. The lounge is dominated by a huge stone fireplace. Breakfast is served on the patio and guests can enjoy the flower-filled roof terrace.

La Magnaneraie

Road map B3. 37 rue Camp-de-Bataille, 30400. ⓒ 04 90 25 11 11. **FAX** 04 90 25 46 37. **Rooms:** 28. 🚗 📅 📺 🗐 🕭 🕭 🅿️ 🕭 🍽 ★ 🅴 AE, MC, DC, V. ⒻⒻⒻⒻ

Divided between a former silkworm nursery with old-fashioned rooms, and a modern annex that is well-suited for families, La Magnaneraie offers a warm welcome and fine cuisine; the owner, Monsieur Prayal, is a Maître Cuisinier de France. Life centres on the pool in summer.

VAUCLUSE

AVIGNON

Ferme Jamet Domaine de Rhodes

Road map B3. Chemin de Rhodes, 84000. ⓒ 04 90 86 88 35. **FAX** 04 90 86 17 72. **Rooms:** 4. 🚗 🕭 🕭 🅿️ 🕭 🅴 MC, V. ⒻⒻⒻ

Ivy covers this large 16th-century farmhouse, set in verdant grounds on the scenic island of Barthelasse, five minutes' drive from the centre of Avignon. The hotel consists of three bungalows and three apartments in the main house. The decor is simple, with a strong emphasis on Provençal materials.

Saint-Roch

Road map B3. 9 rue Paul-Mérindol, 84000. ⓒ 04 90 16 50 00. **FAX** 04 90 82 78 30. **Rooms:** 27. 🚗 📺 🅿️ 🕭 🕭 🅴 MC, V. ⒻⒻ

Located just outside Porte St-Roch close to the railway station, this is the best of Avignon's budget hotels. Inside are cool, terracotta floors, exposed stonework and spacious bedrooms, while the large garden provides pleasant shade in summer.

L'Europe

Road map B3. 12 pl Crillon, 84000.
【 *04 90 14 76 76.* **FAX** *04 90 85 43 66.* **Rooms:** *47.* 🛏 24 TV 🍽 🛄 ↕ P 🅰 🚻 ★ 🌿 *AE, MC, DC, V.* ⓕⓕⓕⓕ

L'Europe has been Avignon's most refined hotel since Napoleon first stayed here in 1799. The elaborate carriage gateway leads into a peaceful terrace where a fountain greets guests. Inside, the monumental hallway sets the mood. Bedrooms are elegant and Gobelin tapestries hang in the sumptuous salon.

LE BARROUX

Hôtel les Géraniums

Road map B2. Pl de la Croix, 84330.
【 *04 90 62 41 08.* **FAX** *04 90 62 56 48.* **Rooms:** *22.* 🛏 🚻 P 🅰 🚻 🌿 *AE, MC, DC, V.* ⓕⓕ

In the countryside on the edge of Mont Ventoux, just outside the historic village of Le Barroux, this ancient stone house is a peaceful hideaway. The interior boasts wonderful, large bathrooms. The most notably comfortable rooms are located in the modern annex. A terrace offers expansive views across the beautiful Ventoux hills.

GORDES

Les Romarins

Road map C3. Route de Sénanque, 84220. 【 *04 90 72 12 13.* **FAX** *04 90 72 13 13.* **Rooms:** *10.* 🛏 TV 🍽 🖼 P 🚻 ↕ 🅰 & 🌿 *AE, MC, V.* ⓕⓕⓕ

Overlooking the village, the rooms in this 18th-century country house are comfortably furnished in a traditional style, with open fires and *faïence*-tiled bathrooms. Breakfast is served on the terrace and the garden boasts its own drystone *borie*. Don't miss a dip in the swimming pool.

LOURMARIN

Hostellerie le Paradou

Road map C3. Combe de Lourmarin, D943, 84160. 【 *04 90 68 04 05.* **FAX** *04 90 08 54 94.* **Rooms:** *8.* 🛏 🖼 P 🅰 🚻 🌿 *MC, V.* ⓕⓕⓕ

Hidden from the main road beneath the gorges of Lourmarin, this friendly hotel enjoys a utopian setting. The sleepy terrace leads to meadows that overlook the peaceful village.

Moulin de Lourmarin

Road map C3. Rue de Temple, 84160. 【 *04 90 68 06 69.* **FAX** *04 90 68 31 76.* **Rooms:** *20.* 🛏 24 TV 🖼 🍽 🚻 🛏 P 🅰 🚻 ★ 🌿 *AE, MC, DC, V.* ⓕⓕⓕⓕⓕ
See also **Restaurants**, *p215.*

One of the most enchanting luxury hotels of the area, this used to be Lourmarin's olive mill. It has been refurbished with immense panache. Provençal meets Art Nouveau in its tasteful decoration, while the pleasantly cavernous restaurant serves superb Luberon specialities. The top-floor bedrooms have small terraces with scenic views across to the château and surrounding hills.

PERNES-LES-FONTAINE

Mas de la Bonoty

Road map B3. Chemin de Bonoty, 84210. 【 *04 90 61 61 09.*
FAX *04 90 61 35 14.* **Rooms:** *8.* 🛏 🖼 🍽 P 🅰 🚻 🌿 *AE, MC, V.* ⓕⓕ

Surrounded by lavender fields and olive groves, this converted farmstead enjoys a perfect Provençal setting beneath the slopes of Mont Ventoux. Rooms are spacious and modern, with rustic furniture and tasteful regional fabrics.

ROUSSILLON

Le Mas de Garrigon

Road map C3. Route de St-Saturnin Apt, 84220. 【 *04 90 05 63 22.*
FAX *04 90 05 70 01.* **Rooms:** *9.* 🛏 TV 🖼 🍽 P 🚻 🌿 *AE, MC, DC, V.* ⓕⓕⓕⓕ

Set in pine forests in a tucked away corner of Upper Provence, this *mas* is an ideal place for a quiet retreat. In the evenings, classical music plays in the salons and each room has a private terrace that looks onto the blue, enticing swimming pool.

SÉGURET

Domaine de Cabasse

Road map B2. Rte de Sablet, 84100.
【 *04 90 46 91 12.* **FAX** *04 90 46 94 01.* **Rooms:** *12.* 🛏 TV 🖼 P 🚻 🅰 🚻 🌿 *AE, MC, V.* ⓕⓕⓕ

This Côtes-du-Rhône vineyard of Cabasse offers comfortable rooms, with views across the winelands of Séguret, and a swimming pool. The restaurant is very good, serving local delicacies. Not surprisingly, it has an impressive wine list.

VAISON-LA-ROMAINE

Le Beffroi

Road map B2. Rue de l'Evêché, 84100.
【 *04 90 36 04 71.* **FAX** *04 90 36 24 78.* **Rooms:** *22.* 🛏 🖼 🚻 🅰 🚻 ★ 🌿 *AE, MC, DC, V.* ⓕⓕⓕ

Le Beffroi is a 16th-century inn on one of the narrow streets in the upper village. The elegantly decorated salons boast period furniture, chandeliers and paintings; the bedrooms present stylish, modern fittings beneath medieval beams.

ALPES-DE-HAUTE-PROVENCE

CHÂTEAU-ARNOUX

La Bonne Etape

Road map D2. Chemin du Lac, 04160. 【 *04 92 64 00 09.*
FAX *04 92 64 37 36.* **Rooms:** *18.* 🛏 24 TV 🖼 🍽 🚻 🛏 P 🅰 🚻 ★ 🌿 *AE, MC, DC, V.* ⓕⓕⓕⓕ
See also **Restaurants**, *p215.*

This 18th-century *relais de poste* has spacious, individually designed bedrooms adorned with antiques. The Gleize family's service is attentive – they have been running the hotel for four generations.

FORCALQUIER

Hostellerie des Deux Lions

Road map C3. 11 pl du Bourget, 04300. 【 *04 92 75 25 30.* **FAX** *04 92 75 06 41.* **Rooms:** *15.* 🛏 TV P 🚻 🌿 *AE, MC, V.* ⓕⓕ

On the corner of the main square, the Deux Lions has been a staging post since the 17th-century. A warm welcome and spacious rooms are its main attractions. Rooms at the front of the hotel can be noisy in the day, but rarely at night.

REILLANNE

Auberge de Reillanne

Road map C3. D214, 04110.
【 *04 92 76 45 95.* **Rooms:** *7.* 🛏 🖼 P 🅰 🚻 🌿 *MC, V.* ⓕⓕ

A beautiful bastide in the eastern Luberon, surrounded by vines and fields, this *auberge* is simple yet wonderfully alluring. Ancient books attractively line the ancient shelves and antiques fill the characterful rooms.

RESTAURANTS, CAFÉS AND BARS

ONE OF THE JOYS of this sun-drenched region is the abundance of fresh, enticing food on offer. The coast of Provence is famous for its seafood restaurants – these are best in the coastal towns of Marseille and Nice, but generally do not come cheap.

Les Routiers
road sign

For traditional Provençal fare, it is advisable to head inland to the villages of the Var and northern Vaucluse. In the valleys of Haute Provence, the cuisine is more simple, but delicious – local game and the much-loved truffle.

Life in the south revolves around meals and villages and towns come to a standstill during the main midday meal and dinner. Lunch is served from noon until 2pm with dinner from 7:30pm until about 10pm, while cafés and bars in towns tend to stay open later (see pp216–17). The restaurants on pages 210–15 have been carefully selected for their excellence of food, decor and ambience, covering all price ranges, with a small selection of the very best Provence has to offer on pages 208–9.

TYPES OF RESTAURANT

IN THE COUNTRY, you may eat at a *ferme auberge*, a small, basic inn attached to a farm or wine estate. Here you will enjoy good, inexpensive meals, often made with fresh farm produce, eaten with the host's family as part of your room and board. Many country restaurants are attached to hotels but serve a predominantly non-residential clientele. These establishments are good value for money and are often the focus of local social activity.

In towns, there is the usual mixture of Americanized fast food joints and more traditional French restaurants. The larger towns such as Aix, Nice and Avignon provide a wide range of restaurants, including some of the best outside Paris.

For those on the move, look out for the distinctive red and blue Les Routiers sign – this is a long established organization that recommends anything from large family restaurants to

smaller brasseries, serving good quality, inexpensive food in a friendly, relaxed atmosphere.

In Provence, as in the rest of France, the decor of a restaurant is very much secondary to the quality of the food. This said, there are many places that offer charming medieval interiors or superb views.

In spite of recent legislation requiring restaurants to provide their clientele with a non-smoking section, a laissez-faire attitude prevails. If you are sensitive to smoke, ask for a table near the window or door.

HOW MUCH TO PAY

PRICES IN PROVENCE are generally lower than those in urban France. Most restaurants offer fixed-price menus which are invariably better value than à la carte. Lunch is always good value – you can enjoy a large repast with wine for under F70. Inland you can dine very well for under F200 a head while, on the coast, the

Les Deux Garçons in Aix (see p217)

profusion of restaurants means that prices are kept competitively lower. In the deluxe dining rooms of the Côte d'Azur and the Riviera, you can expect to spend at least F400 a head, although the food will usually be of outstanding quality.

Restaurants are obliged by law to post menu prices outside. These generally include service, but a tip is expected for good service – up to five per cent of the bill. The most widely accepted credit card is Visa, linked to the French Carte Bleue. American Express is becoming increasingly popular, as is the case with Diners Club. Traveller's cheques and Eurocheques are virtually unheard of for settling bills.

MAKING RESERVATIONS

FOR THE UP-MARKET PALACES of the Côte d'Azur and Riviera, reservations are often mandatory. In season, it may be necessary to reserve a table in

Relaxing in the popular Café de Paris in St-Tropez (p216–17)

the smallest restaurants. In rural areas it is normally possible to find a table – the owner will simply add one to the terrace or extend his or her establishment further into the street.

DRESS CODE

THE FRENCH are generally well-turned out, even when dressed casually, and visitors should aim for the same level of presentable comfort when eating out. Beach clothes are not acceptable, except in cafés and bars. The listings on pages 210–15 indicate which restaurants require formal dress.

READING THE MENU

MENUS USUALLY comprise three courses. The waiter will take your choice of *entrée* (first course) and main course. Dessert is ordered afterwards. More expensive menus are often four courses, with cheese eaten before the dessert, while some country restaurants serve six course extravaganzas, which can take several hours to eat.

The *entrée* usually includes salads, pâté, Provençal soups and often shellfish. Main dishes are predominantly a choice of lamb, chicken or fish – game is widely available in season.

Coffee is always served after, not with, dessert – you will need to specify whether you want it *au lait* (with milk).

Breakfast for two in a local café

CHOICE OF WINE

WINE IS so much a part of everyday life in Provence that you will find a good range at even the smallest establishments *(see pp206–7)*. The price may be off-putting as all restaurants put a large mark-up on wine (up to 300 per cent).

The elegant Colombe d'Or restaurant in St-Paul-de-Vence *(see p211)*

Most wine is produced locally and usually served in carafes. Ordering a *demi* (50 cl) or *quart* (25 cl) is an inexpensive way of sampling the region's finest wines. French law divides the country's wines into four classes, in ascending order of quality: Vin de Table, Vin de Pays, Vin Délimité de Qualité Supérieure (VDQS) and Appellation d'Origine Contrôlée (AOC). If in doubt, order the house wine *(la réserve)* – few owners will risk their reputation on an inferior quality wine as this is their personal choice.

VEGETARIAN FOOD

UNIQUELY VEGETARIAN restaurants are hard to find, as this concept has yet to filter down to the carnivorous South. Most establishments will offer salads, omelettes or soup, or dishes from the *entrée* menu. Some can rustle up a concoction of Provençal vegetables if given enough warning.

CHILDREN

MEALS IN PROVENCE are very much a family affair and children are welcome in most places. However, special facilities like high chairs or baby seats are rarely provided. Few establishments have a specific children's menu but many will be happy to provide smaller dishes at reduced rates.

WHEELCHAIR ACCESS

WHEELCHAIR ACCESS to many restaurants is restricted. In summer, this will be less of a problem at establishments with outside terraces; even so, when booking ahead, ask for a conveniently situated table.

USING THE LISTINGS

Key to the symbols in the listings on pages 210–15.

▢ open
🍴 fixed-price menu(s)
👶 children's portions
Ⅴ vegetarian or
vegetarian options
▦ outdoor eating
♿ wheelchair access
👔 jacket and tie required
🚭 non-smoking section
🍷 excellent wine list
★ highly recommended
▨ credit cards accepted
AE American Express
MC Mastercard
DC Diners Club
V Visa

Price categories for a three-course evening meal for one, including a half-bottle of house wine, cover charge, tax and service:
Ⓕ Under F150
ⒻⒻ F150–250
ⒻⒻⒻ F250–350
ⒻⒻⒻⒻ F350–500
ⒻⒻⒻⒻⒻ Over F500.

What to Eat in Provence

Goat cheese from Banon

Sᴏᴍᴇ ᴏꜰ ᴛʜᴇ ʙᴇꜱᴛ chefs in France's culinary history have come from Provence – a glance at any market stall can tell you why. The menus of today still faithfully reflect a passion for regional produce: fish from local waters, lamb from the salt flats of the Camargue, seasonal fruit and vegetables, and wild mushrooms from the forests of the Var. The dishes shown here are typical of regional menus. Try any one for a true flavour of Provence, from simple street food like *socca* to the budget-breaking masterpiece of *bouillabaisse*.

Olive oil   **Provençal herbs**

Olives and herbs, along with garlic and tomatoes, are the indispensable ingredients of traditional Provençal cuisine.

Pan bagnat *("soaked bread") is a crusty roll, stuffed with tuna, olives, peppers, onions and salad steeped in olive oil, then pressed so that the flavours blend.*

Socca *is a huge pancake made of chickpea flour, sprinkled with olive oil and black pepper and served in crisp, hot slices.*

Pissaladière, *the Provençal pizza, is topped with olives, onion purée and anchovies. Every* boulangerie *sells it.*

Tapenade

Brandade de morue

PROVENÇAL PURÉES

Salt cod is the basis of *brandade de morue*, blended with cream, olive oil, potatoes and garlic. Anchovies appear in both *anchoïade* and *tapenade*, the latter combined with capers, tuna and olives. They are served as appetizers with toast or raw vegetables.

Anchoïade

Aïoli *is a garlic mayonnaise served with side dishes of salt cod, boiled eggs, snails and regional vegetables.*

Salade Niçoise *comes in many guises but usually includes tuna, lettuce, olives, green beans, eggs, tomato, potatoes and anchovies.*

Soupe au pistou *is a rich vegetable and pulse-based soup flavoured with* pistou, *a sauce of basil, garlic and olive oil.*

Mesclun *is a mixture of green salad leaves, usually including rocket, lamb's lettuce, chervil and endive.*

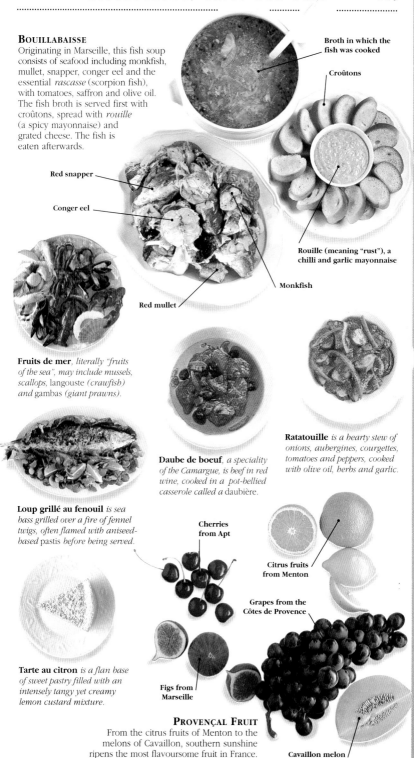

BOUILLABAISSE
Originating in Marseille, this fish soup consists of seafood including monkfish, mullet, snapper, conger eel and the essential *rascasse* (scorpion fish), with tomatoes, saffron and olive oil. The fish broth is served first with croûtons, spread with *rouille* (a spicy mayonnaise) and grated cheese. The fish is eaten afterwards.

Broth in which the fish was cooked

Croûtons

Rouille (meaning "rust"), a chilli and garlic mayonnaise

Red snapper

Conger eel

Monkfish

Red mullet

Fruits de mer, *literally "fruits of the sea", may include mussels, scallops,* langouste *(crawfish)* and gambas *(giant prawns).*

Loup grillé au fenouil *is sea bass grilled over a fire of fennel twigs, often flamed with aniseed-based* pastis *before being served.*

Daube de boeuf, *a speciality of the Camargue, is beef in red wine, cooked in a pot-bellied casserole called a* daubière.

Ratatouille *is a hearty stew of onions, aubergines, courgettes, tomatoes and peppers, cooked with olive oil, herbs and garlic.*

Tarte au citron *is a flan base of sweet pastry filled with an intensely tangy yet creamy lemon custard mixture.*

Cherries from Apt

Citrus fruits from Menton

Grapes from the Côtes de Provence

Figs from Marseille

Cavaillon melon

PROVENÇAL FRUIT
From the citrus fruits of Menton to the melons of Cavaillon, southern sunshine ripens the most flavoursome fruit in France.

What to Drink in Provence

THE REGION COVERED by this book could not encompass a more varied and enticing range of wines. To the north, the stony, heat-baked soil of the southern Rhône nurtures intense, spicy red wines, the best of which is Châteauneuf-du-Pape. In the south, the Mediterranean coast produces a range of lighter, fresh and fruity whites and rosés, as well as some delicious red wines. Especially good are the dry white wines of seaside Cassis and reds or rosés from the tiny fine wine pocket of Bandol. In the past, some Provençal wines had a reputation for not "travelling" well, but the introduction of modern wine-making techniques and more suitable grape varieties are fast improving quality. Here, we suggest a selection of wines to look out for on local menus.

Two bottle styles distinctive of the region's wines

WHITE WINES

THE RHONE produces several fine, rich, buttery whites from grapes such as Viognier. The more accessible, and less expensive, alternatives listed below are perfect with the region's delicious seafood.

A fine white Châteauneuf-du-Pape

White Côtes-du-Rhône

RECOMMENDED WHITES

- **Clos Ste-Magdeleine**
  Cassis
- **Châteaux Val Joanis**
  Côtes du Luberon
- **Domaine St-André-de-Figuière**
  Côtes de Provence
- **Domaines Gavoty**
  Côtes de Provence

WINE AREAS OF PROVENCE
Wine-producing areas are concentrated in the southwest of the region, where vineyards cluster on the rocky hillsides (*côtes*). Les Arcs is a good base for a Côtes de Provence wine tour (*see pp108–9*).

ORANGE · Gigondas
· Beaumes-de-Venise
Lirac
Tavel · Châteauneuf-du-Pape
· AVIGNON
· NIMES
· Les Baux-de-Provence
· ARLES
Rhône
AIX-EN-PROVENCE
· Palette
MARSEILLE
Cassis
Bando[l]

ROSÉ WINES

PROVENÇAL ROSÉ is no longer just a sweetish aperitif wine in a skittle-shaped bottle. Grape varieties like Syrah give a full flavour and more body. Tavel is a typical example – dry and weighty enough to accompany Provençal flavourings such as garlic and herbs. Bandol's *vin gris* is also highly regarded.

Pale rosé (*gris*) from Bandol

RECOMMENDED ROSÉS

- **Château Romassan**
  Bandol
- **Commanderie de Bargemone**
  Côtes de Provence
- **Commanderie de Peyrassol**
  Côtes de Provence
- **Domaine la Forcadière**
  Tavel
- **Domaines Gavoty**
  Côtes de Provence

Terraced vineyards on the coast above Cassis

RED WINES

AT ITS BEST, Châteauneuf-du-Pape produces heady, intense wines to accompany the most robust meat dishes. Bandol also makes superb, long-lived red wines. For a lighter alternative, choose a Provençal or Côtes-du-Rhône red. Wines from one of the named Rhône villages should be of superior quality – or seek out reds from reliable producers in, for example, Les Baux-de-Provence, or the Côtes du Luberon.

Fine red wine from Les Baux

A spicy Châteauneuf-du-Pape

A jewel in Côtes du Luberon's crown

RECOMMENDED REDS

- *Château de Beaucastel*
  Châteauneuf-du-Pape
- *Château du Trignon*
  Sablet, Côtes-du-Rhône
- *Château Val Joanis*
  Côtes du Luberon
- *Domaine de Pibarnon*
  Bandol
- *Domaine des Alysses*
  Coteaux Varois
- *Domaine Font de Michelle*
  Châteauneuf-du-Pape
- *Domaine Tempier*
  Bandol

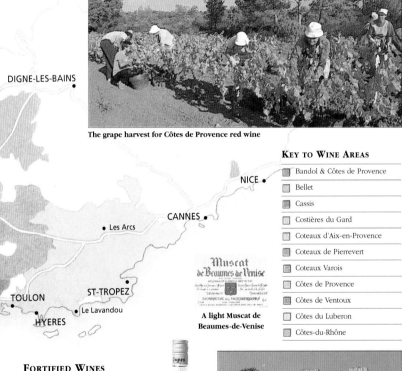

DIGNE-LES-BAINS

The grape harvest for Côtes de Provence red wine

NICE

CANNES

Les Arcs

TOULON ST-TROPEZ

Le Lavandou

HYERES

A light Muscat de Beaumes-de-Venise

KEY TO WINE AREAS

- Bandol & Côtes de Provence
- Bellet
- Cassis
- Costières du Gard
- Coteaux d'Aix-en-Provence
- Coteaux de Pierrevert
- Coteaux Varois
- Côtes de Provence
- Côtes de Ventoux
- Côtes du Luberon
- Côtes-du-Rhône

FORTIFIED WINES

DESPITE THE misleading name, *vins doux naturels* (naturally sweet wines) are sweet wines fortified with spirit. They are delicious as a chilled apéritif, with desserts or instead of an after-dinner liqueur. Most are based on the exotically scented Muscat grape, and range from cloyingly sweet to lusciously fragrant. An unusual alternative is red Rasteau, a port-like wine based on the Grenache grape.

Typical Muscat bottle shape

The stony, sun-reflecting soil of the Rhône valley

Provence's Best: Restaurants

THERE IS AN ENORMOUS CHOICE of restaurants in
Provence, ranging from simple country inns,
thronged with locals, to the gastronomic temples of
the coast. Cosmopolitan cities like Marseille and Nice
offer an even wider choice, particularly Italian, North
African and Vietnamese cuisine. The restaurants here
are just a few Provençal favourites, selected from the
listings on pages 210–15, as being among the very
best in their particular field.

Hiély-Lucullus
*A wine list offering some of the
region's most exalted names
enhances the classic cuisine of
Avignon's gastronomic
stalwart. (See p214.)*

Prévot
*The regional Cavaillon
melon is one of the many
local delicacies on the menu
at Jean-Jacques Prévot's chic
restaurant. (See p214.)*

0 kilometres   25

0 miles   25

Oustaù de Baumanière
*The food is as breathtaking
as the bird's-eye views from
Les Baux's gastronomic
mecca. (See p213.)*

VAUCLUSE

**BOUCHES-DU-RHONE
AND NIMES**

L'Aix Quis
*Previously Les Frères Lani, this
restaurant changed hands in 1996.
The new owners have maintained
the high standards set by the Lani
brothers. (See p213.)*

Le Miramar
*From the bewildering array of fish restaurants
in Marseille, the Miramar is the place to enjoy
the ultimate bouillabaisse. (See p214.)*

La Bonne Etape
Classic Provençal flavours are reinterpreted to great effect by chef Jany Gleize, whose family has run this hotel-restaurant in Château-Arnoux for four generations. (See p215.)

Le Louis XV
The imaginative menus of Alain Ducasse, one of France's most revered young chefs, have raised this Monte-Carlo institution to new heights of acclaim. (See p210.)

Le Moulin de Mougins
The chef, Roger Vergé, invented the phrase "cuisine of the sun" to describe his approach to Provençal cooking. (See p210.)

THE RIVIERA AND THE ALPES MARITIMES

ALPES-DE-HAUTE-PROVENCE

L'Acchiardo
There are no frills here, just good value, superb cuisine and a great atmosphere, in the heart of the Old Town of Nice. (See p211.)

THE VAR AND THE ILES D'HYERES

La Palme d'Or
You don't have to be a movie star to partake of Cannes' most glitzy and memorable dining experience. (See p210.)

La Pesquière/ Le Mazagran
This friendly family-run pair of restaurants straddles the charming place de la Ponche in the oldest part of St-Tropez. (See p212.)

RIVIERA AND THE ALPES MARITIMES

BAR-SUR-LOUP

L'Amiral

Road map E3. 8 place Francis-Paulet.
(04 93 09 44 00. **○** noon–2:30pm,
7–9pm Thu–Tue. **†●| 🖩 ★**
⊘ MC, V. **Ⓕ**

This impressive 18th-century town house once belonged to Admiral de Grasse. Today gendarmes and shop-keepers lunch in the simple dining room, with fine views down to the valley. The daily menu is spot on for freshness and value, with lamb, duck and fish dishes. Reservations are recommended for the evening.

BIOT

Auberge du Jarrier

Road map E3. 30 pass de la Bourgade.
(04 93 65 11 68. **○** noon–2pm,
7:15–9:30pm Wed–Sun, 7:15–9:30pm
Mon. **†●| 🏃 🖩 ⚡ ⊘** AE, MC,
V. **ⒻⒻⒻ**

Tucked away from the main street, this is one of the best value gastro-nomic restaurants on the Riviera. It offers a wide range of delicate sea-food dishes and intriguing cheeses. The terrace is a delight on summer evenings; the cooking seductive. It is best to reserve for dinner a week in advance in season.

CAGNES-SUR-MER

Auberge du Port

Road map E3. 95 bd de la Plage.
(04 93 07 25 28. **○** noon–2:30pm,
7–10:30pm daily. **†●| 🏃 🖩 ⚡**
⊘ AE, MC, DC, V. **ⒻⒻ**

Opposite the harbour, the friendly Auberge du Port specializes in fish and local Niçois dishes. The scarlet façade gives way to a more prosaic interior but there are tables on the terrace in summer. The restaurant is on the main road but this doesn't matter once you have chilled Côtes-de-Provence rosé and a plate of *sole meunière* on the table.

Le Cagnard

Road map E3. Rue Sous-Barri.
(04 93 20 73 21. **○** mid-Dec–Oct:
noon–2pm, 7:30–10:30pm Fri–Wed.
†●| 🖩 ⚡ ⊘ AE, MC, DC, V.
ⒻⒻⒻⒻ

This superb restaurant is housed in a skilfully converted medieval inn in the ramparts of the village. The

dining room has been built in the castle guard room and there are spectacular views from the terrace down over the rooftops to the coast. The cuisine is equally as impressive, offering a mostly classic menu with delicacies such as roast pigeon with morels and *foie gras.*

CANNES

La Mère Besson

Road map E4. 13 rue des Frères-Pradignac. **(** 04 93 39 59 24. **○**
12:15–2pm, 7:30–10:30pm Tue–Sat,
7:30 – 10:30pm Mon. **V 🏃 🖩 &**
⚡ ⊘ AE, DC, MC,V. **ⒻⒻ**

If you want to escape from the glamour and glitz for a while, then visit this popular, friendly bistro, which offers reasonable prices. It's a great place to relax and absorb the atmosphere and enjoy home-style Provençal dishes. *Aïoli* with fresh cod is a favourite, as are the snails and traditional *estouffade* (stew).

La Palme d'Or

Road map E4. 73 la Croisette.
(04 92 98 74 14. **○** 12:30–2pm,
7:30–10:30pm Wed– Sun,
7:30–10:30pm Tue (15 Jun–15 Sep).
†●| V 🏃 🖩 & T ⚡ 🍷 ★
⊘ AE, MC, DC, V. **ⒻⒻⒻⒻⒻ**

This is the restaurant of the stars, whose photographs decorate the entrance. Created by prize-winning chef Christian Willer, the menus are packed with seafood, *foie gras,* snails and lamb. Try Mel Gibson's favourite dish – fresh lobster rissoles with Provençal-style mushrooms.

EZE

La Bergerie

Road map F3. RN7. **(** 04 93 41 03
67. **○** 7–10:30pm daily (Sat, Sun
only in winter). **†●| & 🖩 ⚡ ⊘**
AE, MC, V. **ⒻⒻ**

In winter by the open fire, or in summer on the terrace, La Bergerie is always welcoming and offers top-class Provençal food. The *gigot d'agneau* (leg of lamb) *aux fines herbes* and seafood tagliatelle are excellent, as is the local wine.

JUAN-LES-PINS

La Terrasse

Road map E4. Hôtel Juana, La Pinède,
Av Gallice. **(** 04 93 61 20 37. **○** Jul
& Aug: 12:30–2pm, 7:30– 10:30pm
daily; Apr–Jun & Sep–Oct: 12:30–
10:30pm Thu–Tue. **†●| V & 🏃 🖩**
T 🍷 ⊘ AE, MC, V. **ⒻⒻⒻⒻ**

This is undoubtedly the best restaurant in Juan-les-Pins. The terrace overlooks lush gardens, and the glass roof opens for a view of the stars. Specialities of the house include cannelloni with clams and pink roasted crayfish with risotto and asparagus.

MENTON

Auberge Pierrot-Pierrette

Road map F3. Place de l'Eglise, Monti.
(04 93 35 79 76. **○** May–Nov:
12:30–2pm, 7:30–10pm Tue–Sun.
†●| 🖩 & ⚡ ⊘ MC, V. **ⒻⒻ**

This country restaurant is a 5-km (3-mile) drive from Menton. It offers pleasant rustic ambience and high quality rural produce, such as rabbit cooked with fresh rosemary, *écre-visse* (crawfish) and home-made ravioli. The views are spectacular.

MONACO

Le Périgordin

Road map F3. 5 rue des Oliviers.
(00 377 93 30 06 02. **○** noon–
2:30pm, 8pm–10pm (flexible) Mon–
Fri, Sat pm. **†●| & 🖩 🏃 ⚡**
⊘ AE, MC, DC, V. **ⒻⒻ**

In a small side street, two minutes' walk from the casino, the friendly Périgordin serves specialities from the Périgord region, including duck and *foie gras* – rich and flavourful food at affordable prices. Don't be put off by the rather tacky exterior.

Le Louis XV

Road map F3. Pl du Casino, Monte-Carlo. **(** 04 92 16 30 01. **○** noon–
2pm, 8–10pm Thu–Mon (and Wed in
summer). **†●| V & T ⚡ 🍷**
⊘ AE, MC, DC, V. **ⒻⒻⒻⒻ**
See also **Where to Stay**, p197.

The dining room here never disap-points – oppulent surroundings, attentive service and outstanding cuisine. This was a favourite of Edward VII, whose mistress was served a *crêpe* which was accident-ally set alight. The Prince suggested they name the new dessert after his companion, hence *crêpe suzette.*

MOUGINS

Le Moulin de Mougins

Road map E3. Notre-Dame de Vie.
(04 93 75 78 24. **○** noon–2:30pm,
7:30–10:30pm Tue–Sun, 7:30–
10:30pm Thu. **†●| V 🖩 & 🍷**
🍷 ★ ⊘ AE, MC, DC, V.
ⒻⒻⒻⒻ

Provençal Master-Chef Roger Vergé lost one of his three Michelin stars, but still stays ahead of the competition. Free tables are a rarity in May as this is a film stars' favourite spot during the Cannes Film Festival.

NICE

L'Acchiardo

Road map F3. 38 rue Droite. **☎** 04 93 85 51 16. ◯ noon–1:30pm, 7–9:30pm Mon–Fri, noon–1.30pm Sat. ★ Ⓕ

This remains a bustling temple of Niçois ambience and cuisine – one of the few authentic bar-restaurants left in Vieux Nice. Dishes like *escalope maison* are simple and good; expect Nice's best *soupe de poisson*. Jean Acchiardo's service is affable.

Le Grand Pavois

Road map F3. 11 rue Meyerbeer. **☎** 04 93 88 77 42. ◯ noon–2:30pm, 7–10:30pm daily. ¶Ⓖ⛄🎽💺 Ⓔ MC, V. ⒻⒻⒻ

Widely thought to be Nice's top fish restaurant, Le Grand Pavois has unstylish decor but excellent à la carte menus of *dorade* (sea bream) and *bouillabaisse*. Lobster and *langoustines* (scampi) also figure regularly.

Le Chantecler

Road map F3. Le Négresco, 37 promenade des Anglais. **☎** 04 93 16 64 00. ◯ 12:30–2:30pm, 7:30–10:30pm daily. ¶Ⓖ🎽💺🎽Ⓟ ★ Ⓔ AE, MC, DC, V. ⒻⒻⒻⒻⒻ See also **Where to Stay**, p197.

Long the bastion of gastronomy in Nice, Le Chantecler retains the high standards established when Russian Princes came to dine here in the last century. The lunch *menu plaisir* offers roast fillet of salmon and *canard col-vert* (duck); the *menu de la mer* provides a banquet of seafood. The desserts are tempting and wine list is exceptional.

PEILLON

Auberge de la Madone

Road map F3. Peillon Village. **☎** 04 93 79 91 17. ◯ noon–2pm, Thu–Tue evenings by reservation only. ¶Ⓖ🎽🎽🎽💺 ★ Ⓔ MC, V. ⒻⒻⒻ

This excellent restaurant in the hilltop village behind Nice is often very crowded with the well-heeled of the area. The terrace, set among olive trees, provides a really most delightful setting for local dishes such as *rascasse* and *tourtou des pénitents* (crab with almonds).

ROQUEBRUNE-CAP-MARTIN

Les Deux Frères

Road map F3. Place des Deux Frères. **☎** 04 93 28 99 00. ◯ noon–2:30pm, 7:30–10pm Sat–Wed, 7:30–10pm Fri. ¶Ⓖ🎽🎽💺🎽 Ⓔ AE, MC, DC, V. ⒻⒻⒻ

For those who admire great views and lovely food, Les Deux Frères will not disappoint. The menus are Provençal in flavour, with lamb and duck featuring strongly. In summer, tables are placed out in the square, which affords a truly stunning view over the skyscrapers of Monaco to the Mediterranean.

ST-JEAN-CAP-FERRAT

Le Saint Jean

Road map F3. Place Clemenceau. **☎** 04 93 76 04 75. ◯ noon–2pm daily , 7–10pm Thu–Mon. ¶Ⓖ🎽 Ⓔ AE, MC, V. Ⓕ

This eponymous restaurant is a real find among the world's most expensive real estate, specializing in simple, high class food – pizzas cooked over wood, pastas and fish at extremely affordable prices. The first-floor terrace is perfect for balmy summer evenings.

ST-PAUL-DE-VENCE

La Colombe d'Or

Road map E3. Pl du Géneral de Gaulle. **☎** 04 93 32 80 02. ◯ 12:30–2pm, 7:30–10pm daily. 🎽💺🎽🎽 Ⓔ AE, MC, DC, V. ⒻⒻⒻⒻ

An old farmhouse that was once populated by the Impressionists is now a hotel-restaurant, frequented by film stars and models. The well-prepared food is full of flavour – traditional meat and fish dishes with a good choice of Côtes-de-Provence wine. The dining room is adorned with Picasso and Matisse originals and the terrace is decorated with murals by Léger. In winter, log fires crackle in the comfortable salons.

STE-AGNÈS

Le Sarrasin

Road map F3. 40 rue de Sarrasin. **☎** 04 93 35 86 89. ◯ 8am–10pm Tue–Sun daily. ¶Ⓖ💺🎽 ★ Ⓔ AE, MC, V. Ⓕ

This simple, family-run restaurant, perched just behind Menton in the Alpine foothills, is famous for its very generous portions, easy-going atmosphere and spectacular views. The cuisine is a combination of Italian and Provençal – six courses are the norm, including delicious *raviolis maison* and *torte aux épinards* (spinach tart). The service is efficient and friendly, although Sundays can be hectic, when much of Italy crosses the border for lunch.

TOUËT-SUR-VAR

Auberge des Chasseurs

Road map F3. Av Général de Gaulle. **☎** 04 93 05 71 11. ◯ noon–2pm, 7–9pm Wed–Mon. ¶Ⓖ💺🎽 ★ Ⓔ AE, DC, MC, V. ⒻⒻ

This is an adorable little restaurant covered in climbing vines, situated in the woods of the Var. The mountains soaring above the Var valley are renowned as hunting grounds, and l'Auberge des Chasseurs excels at turning locally caught game and fish into appetizing dishes. Trout, rabbit and *sanglier aux pruneaux* (wild boar with prunes) feature.

VENCE

Auberge des Seigneurs

Road map E3. Place du Frêne. **☎** 04 93 58 04 24. ◯ 12:30–2:30pm Wed–Sun, 7:30–10pm Tue–Sun. ¶Ⓖ Ⓔ AE, DC, MC,V. ⒻⒻ

Come with an appetite to this fine medieval *auberge* complete with a roaring open fire. The menu offers succulent dishes including freshly caught blue trout and tender lamb which are cooked before you on a spit. Local artists used to pay for meals with their works of art, some of which adorn the dining room.

VILLEFRANCHE

Le Carpaccio

Road map F3. Promenade des Marinières. **☎** 04 93 01 72 97. ◯ noon–3pm, 7–11pm daily. 🎽💺🎽 Ⓔ AE, V. ⒻⒻⒻ

The Rolls Royces and Bentleys at the end of Villefranche's quay in summer have brought their owners to appreciate Carpaccio's wonderful setting, its prompt, attentive service and its high quality food. *Carpaccio* (thinly sliced raw beef) is the speciality and the seafood and massive salads are prepared to perfection. On warm summer days the terrace is packed with customers admiring the fabulous views across the bay to St-Jean-Cap-Ferrat; during winter months, the cleverly lit interior is equally agreeable.

THE VAR AND THE ILES D'HYERES

COLLOBRIÈRES

La Petite Fontaine

Road map D4. 1 pl de la République.
【 04 94 48 00 12. ⏰ noon–1:30pm,
7:30–9pm Tue–Sat, noon–1:30pm Sun.
🍽️👤 Ⓕ

Right in the heart of the Massif des
Maures, this secluded restaurant is
surrounded by a necklace of imposing hills. It serves delicious local
specialities. Dishes include chicken
and garlic fricassée, young rabbit
in white wine and breast of duck,
all washed down with the only
wine, that of the local co-operative.

FAYENCE

Le France

Road map E3. 1 grand rue du Château.
【 04 94 76 00 14. ⏰ 7–10pm daily
(Jul–Aug), noon–2pm Tue–Sun, 7–
0:30pm Tue–Sat (Sep–Nov, Feb–Jun).
🍽️👤 🈲 👥 🅼 MC, V. ⒻⒻ

A grand family dining room with a
lovely terrace makes this a pleasant
place to stop for lunch or spend a
relaxed evening. The more ambit-
ious *menu gastronomique* includes
breast of duck with mushrooms.

Le Castellaras

Road map E3. Route de Seillans.
【 04 94 76 13 80. ⏰ noon–2pm,
7:30–10pm Mon–Wed. 🍽️ Ⓥ 👥
👤 🈲 🅼 AE, MC, V. ⒻⒻⒻ

Just north of Fayence's centre, this
stone *mas* (villa) has fine views and
a shaded terrace. The food is a mix
of inventive and traditional – lamb
fillet is served with tarragon sauce,
and the menu features *feuilleté de
cuisses de grenouilles à la crème de
ciboulette* (frogs' legs wrapped in a
fine pastry with cream and chives) –
frogs being a local speciality.

LA CADIÈRE D'AZUR

Hostellerie Bérard

Road map D4. Rue Gabriel-Péri.
【 04 94 90 11 43. ⏰ noon–2pm,
7:30–10pm Tue–Sun. 🍽️ 🈲 👤
👥 ★ 🈲 AE, MC, V.
ⒻⒻⒻⒻ

This 10th-century convent is now
a renowned restaurant, with a view
over the Bandol vineyards that is
unforgettable. René Berard's area of
expertise is fish and shellfish – the
mussel soup flavoured with saffron

is dreamily smooth and the sea bass
in pastry is mouthwatering. Food
is accompanied by delicious Bandol
wine. There is even an enticing
swimming pool in which to work
up a healthy appetite.

LA GARDE-FREINET

Auberge Sarrasin

Road map E4. D 558. 【 04 94 43 67
16. ⏰ noon–2pm, 7–10pm daily.
🍽️👤 🈲 👥 ★ 🈲 MC, V. Ⓕ

If passing through the Massif des
Maures, there is no better place to
stop than this cosy front-room restaurant, where a fire roars in winter
and prettily arranged flowers adorn
the tables in summer. The excellent
cassoulet Provençal (white beans,
pork and white wine) and *oeuf à la
Provençale* are not to be missed.

LA MÔLE

Auberge de la Môle

Road map D4. RN 98. 【 04 94 49 57
01. ⏰ noon–2:30pm, 8–11pm
Tue–Sun. 🍽️ Ⓥ 👥 🈲 👤 ★
ⒻⒻⒻ

In the square of the tiny village of
La Môle, this intimate restaurant is
well worth the diversion from the
coast. Passing through the local bar,
you reach an ancient dining room
dominated by an open fireplace.
Monsieur Raynal wines and dines
his guests with charm. The excellent
food is characterized by regional
fare – duck, lamb, terrines, salads,
cheese and numerous desserts.

LES ILES D'HYERES

Mas du Langoustier

Road map D5. Ile de Porquerolles.
【 04 94 58 30 09. ⏰ May–Oct.
🍽️ 🈲 👤 👥 Ⓥ 🈲 AE, MC,
DC, V. ⒻⒻⒻ

This is the place for some of the
best food on the island. Diners are
met at the port (there are no cars on
Porquerolles) and driven to the
hotel-restaurant on the island's
western tip. The menu is strong on
seafood – try the warm salad of
langoustine roasted with grapefruit,
olives and celery.

ST-TROPEZ

Le Baron

Road map E4. 23 rue de l'Aioli.
【 04 94 97 06 57. ⏰ Apr–Oct:
8am–8pm daily. 👥 🈲 AE, MC,
V. ⒻⒻ

Situated at the foot of the citadel,
Le Baron serves a good-value lunch
menu and a more expensive dinner
menu. The interior is elegant and
the food is beautifully presented.
At lunchtime, dishes include
bavette à l'échalotte (beef and
shallots). For dinner you can try
scampi flavoured with pesto, or *filet
de chapon farci* (capon stuffed with
pork, vegetables and herbs).

L'Echalotte

Road map E4. 35 rue Allard. 【 04
94 54 83 26. ⏰ noon–2pm, 7–
11:30pm daily (Oct-Jun: Fri–Wed). 🍽️
👥 🈲 👤 ★ 🈲 AE, MC, V.
ⒻⒻ

An elegant, honey-coloured façade
fronts a snazzily sharp young restaurant that is a great favourite with
the trendier jet set in St-Tropez. The
food is, perhaps surprisingly, not
dictated by fashion, and it has a
deserved reputation as consistently
delicious. The menu offers Provençal specialities, such as *courgettes
farcies* (courgettes filled with vegetables and herbs). The grilled steak
with shallots is always a popular
choice for the many regulars.

La Pesquière/
Le Mazagran

Road map E4. 1 rue des Remparts.
【 04 94 97 05 92. ⏰ noon–midnight
daily (Jun–Sep), noon–3pm, 7pm–midnight (Oct–May). 🍽️ 🈲 👤 👥 👥
★ 🈲 MC, V. ⒻⒻ

This busy, family-run pair of
restaurants is situated in the oldest
part of town, one on each side of
the place de la Ponche, with
fantastic views out over the bay to
Ste-Maxime. The mesclun salad is
highly recommendable, and so is
the aïoli and fresh pasta. You might
like to round off the meal with a
mouthwatering warm apple tart.

TOULON

La Chamade

Road map D4. 25 rue de la Comédie.
【 04 94 92 28 58. ⏰ noon–1:30pm,
7:30–9:30pm Mon–Fri, 7:30–9:30pm
Sat (Sep–Jul). 🍽️ 👥 🈲 AE, MC, V.
ⒻⒻ

In the centre of Toulon, a number
of small dining rooms provide an
intimate setting for delicious food.
A single fixed-price menu offers a
choice of three appetizers, main
courses and deserts. Dishes on
offer depend on locally available
produce and change with the
seasons, but you can expect such
delights as stuffed courgette
flowers, sea bass with a buttery
basil sauce, and fresh roasted figs.

BOUCHES-DU-RHONE AND NIMES

AIGUES-MORTES

La Camargue

Road map A3. 19 rue de la République.
█ 04 66 53 86 88. ◯ noon–2pm,
8–11pm daily. ¶◑ 🍴 🅑 🄴 MC, V.
Ⓕ Ⓕ

It is rumoured that the folk band the Gypsy Kings frequent this restaurant, but even in their absence this is the liveliest place in town. Flamenco guitars strum in the background as you dine in the garden in summer, enjoying local fish, seafood and grilled meat dishes.

AIX-EN-PROVENCE

L'Hacienda

Road map C4. 7 rue Mérindol.
█ 04 42 27 00 35. ◯ noon–2pm
Tue–Sun, 8–11pm Tue–Sat. ¶◑ Ⓥ
🍴 🄴 🄴 MC, V. Ⓕ

Opposite a quiet square with its requisite Aixois fountain, L'Hacienda is eternally crowded, especially at lunchtimes when shopkeepers and office workers pack into the green dining rooms. Food is traditional and enjoyable – *foie gras canard*, fish and lamb. The restaurant also serves a tasty *table de la mer* – fresh seafood straight from the sea.

L'Aix Quis

Road map C4. 22 rue Leydet.
█ 04 42 27 76 16. ◯ noon–2pm,
7:30–10pm Mon–Sat. ¶◑ 🄴 🄴 ★
🄴 MC, V. Ⓕ Ⓕ Ⓕ

Inventive and stylish fish and meat dishes are the trademarks of this modern restaurant (previously Les Frères Lani) that is becoming the culinary headquarters of Aix. New owners took over from the Lani brothers in early 1996, but the high standards they set have not fallen.

Chez Gu et Fils

Road map C4. 3 rue F Mistral.
█ 04 42 26 75 12. ◯ noon–3pm,
8–10:30pm Mon Fri, noon–2pm Sun.
¶◑ 🄴 MC, V. Ⓕ Ⓕ Ⓕ

Being mentioned in Peter Mayle's *A Year in Provence* seems to have sent prices rocketing, although this small bistro just off the cours Mirabeau still offers tasty Provençal dishes as well as fresh pasta and pizza. Traditional dishes include *gigot d'agneau* (lamb) with fresh thyme, hot oysters and a top class tagliatelle carbonara.

Relais Ste-Victoire

Road map C4. Beaureceuil.
█ 04 42 66 94 98. ◯ noon–2pm,
7:30–9:30pm Tue–Sat, noon–2pm Sun.
¶◑ 🄴 🄴 🄴 🄴 AE, MC, V. Ⓕ Ⓕ Ⓕ

Do as many Aixois do and head out of the town for Sunday lunch in the peaceful countryside at the foot of Montagne Ste-Victoire. This converted *mas* offers excellent regional cuisine. The idyllic terrace offers wonderful views across to Cézanne's favourite mountain.

ARLES

Vitamine

Road map B3. 16 rue du Docteur
Fanton. █ 04 90 93 77 36. ◯ noon–3pm Mon–Fri , 7–10pm Mon–Sat.
Ⓥ 🄴 🄴 🄴 🄴 MC, V. Ⓕ

The colourful Vitamine is enjoyable and good value and a haven for vegetarians. Choose from 50 different salads and numerous pasta dishes served in an informal atmosphere. The dining room is small, so come early or reserve.

Le Vaccarès

Road map B3. 1st Floor, rue Favorin.
█ 04 90 96 06 17. ◯ noon–2pm,
7–9:30pm Tue–Sat, noon–2pm Sun.
¶◑ 🄴 🄴 🄴 AE, MC, V. Ⓕ Ⓕ Ⓕ

Delectable versions of Provençal fare grace this popular eating place. The freshest ingredients are used in dishes like medallions of lamb with rosemary and *broufado* (marinated beef).

Lou Marquès

Road map B3. Bd des Lices.
█ 04 90 93 43 20. ◯ noon–1:30pm,
7:30–9:30pm daily. ¶◑ 🄴 🄴 🄴
🄴 🄴 AE, MC, DC, V. Ⓕ Ⓕ Ⓕ Ⓕ

This gastronomic restaurant, located in the Jules César hotel, is one of the finest in Arles. Pascal Renaud delights in transforming regional dishes into haute cuisine. Try, for example, the John Dory with sweet peppers and squid. The garden and terrace are ideal for al fresco dining.

LES-BAUX-DE-PROVENCE

Le Riboto de Taven

Road map B3. Le Val d'Enfer. █ 04
90 54 34 23. ◯ Jul–Sep: noon–2pm,
7:30–9:30pm Thu–Tue (other months:
7:30–9:30pm Thu–Mon). ¶◑ 🄴
🄴 🅑 🄴 AE, MC, DC, V.
Ⓕ Ⓕ Ⓕ Ⓕ

In summer you can sit on the terrace of this nineteenth-century farmhouse and enjoy the beautifully-kept garden as you eat. The fine cooking makes great use of heady provençal herbs, with specialities such as turbot with rosemary, caramelised fennel tart, and *fricassée* of mussels with basil.

Oustaù de Baumanière

Road map B3. Le Val d'Enfer. █ 04
90 54 57 27. ◯ noon–2:30pm, 7:30–9:30pm daily. ¶◑ Ⓥ 🄴 🅑 🄴 🄴
🄴 AE, MC, DC, V. Ⓕ Ⓕ Ⓕ Ⓕ Ⓕ

Two Michelin stars, a breathtaking view over Les Baux and a memorable menu distinguish the famous Oustaù. Jean-André Charial's delicious food mixes ancient Provençal dishes and nouvelle cuisine. The patron takes great pride in the wine cellar and the choice is outstanding.

CARRY-LE-ROUET

L'Escale

Road map C4. Promenade du Port.
█ 04 42 45 00 47. ◯ noon–2pm,
8–10pm Tue –Sun, 8–10pm Mon.
¶◑ 🄴 🅑 🄴 ★ 🄴 AE, MC, V.
Ⓕ Ⓕ Ⓕ Ⓕ

Chef Gérard Clor champions local produce. His dining room overlooks the small port of Carry, set among parasol pines on the Côte Bleue. The restaurant's unrivalled specialities include braised turbot, and apples with sautéed sea urchin.

FONTVIEILLE

La Régalido

Road map B3. Rue Mistral.
█ 04 90 54 60 22. ◯ noon–1:30pm,
7:30–9pm Wed–Sun, 7:30–9pm Mon
& Tue. ¶◑ Ⓥ 🅑 🄴 🄴 AE, MC,
DC, V. Ⓕ Ⓕ Ⓕ Ⓕ

This gastronomic restaurant serves top-notch fresh seafood, such as a gratin of mussels with spinach. The unmistakably Provençal flavour makes light-fingered use of garlic, olive oil and fresh herbs. Meals are enjoyed on the terrace.

MARSEILLE

Le Roi du Couscous

Road map C4. 63 rue de la République. █ 04 91 91 45 46. ◯ noon–3pm, 7–11pm Tue–Sun. Ⓕ

Couscous is the speciality of this lively North African restaurant, just north-west of the Vieux Port. There are no frills here – just good food and an animated atmosphere.

Chez Madie

Road map C4. 138 quai du Port.
[04 91 90 40 87. ⬜ noon–2pm,
8–11pm, Mon–Sat. ⬛ ⬛ ⬛ ★
⬛ AE, MC, DC, V. Ⓕ Ⓕ

Towards the northwestern end of
the Vieux Port, Chez Madie is a
Marseillais institution. It is perhaps
the best provider of fish dishes. Try
well-priced *bouillabaisse*, *bourride*
(fish stew with *aïoli*) or *dorade*
(sea bream) *aux fines herbes*.

Les Arcenaulx

Road map C4. 25 cours d'Estienne
d'Orves. [04 91 59 80 30. ⬜ noon–
2:30pm, 8–11:30pm Mon–Sat. ⬛
⬛ ⬛ ⬛ AE, MC, DC, V. Ⓕ Ⓕ

Northeast of the Vieux Port is the
heart of Marseille's nightlife – cours
d'Estienne d'Orves and cours Julien
house innumerable bars, clubs and
restaurants. Les Arcenaulx serves
excellent Provençal dishes – such as
young rabbit and aubergine tart –
within a venerable former library.

Le Miramar

Road map C4. 12 quai du Port.
[04 91 91 10 40. ⬜ noon–2pm
Tue–Sat, 7:30–10pm Mon–Sat. ⬛ ⬛
⬛ ★ ⬛ AE, MC, DC, V. Ⓕ Ⓕ Ⓕ Ⓕ

The grandiose Miramar has long
been the doyen of the Vieux Port
restaurants. Here *bouillabaisse* is
perhaps the most authentic in town,
but at a price. There is also a large
selection of shellfish, such as sea
urchins with quail eggs and ginger
cream. A small terrace offers views
up to Notre-Dame-de-la-Garde.

Le Petit Nice

Road map C4. Corniche JF Kennedy.
[04 91 59 25 92. ⬜ 12:30–2pm,
7:30–10pm daily (winter: Tue–Sat).
⬛ ⬛ ⬛ ⬛ ★ ⬛ AE, MC, V.
Ⓕ Ⓕ Ⓕ Ⓕ Ⓕ

This superb restaurant is in the
Belle Epoque villa of the Passédat
Hotel. Views from the terrace are
memorable, especially at sunset.
The cuisine is equally impressive.
The lobster terrine and sea bream
with fresh ginger and cumin is
faultlessly prepared. The wine
cellar is outstanding.

MAUSSANE-LES-
ALPILLES

La Petite France

Road map B3. 55 av Vallée des Baux.
[04 90 54 41 91. ⬜ noon–2pm,
7:30–9:30pm Fri–Tue, 7:30–9:30pm
Thu. ⬛ ⬛ ⬛ ⬛ MC, V.
Ⓕ Ⓕ Ⓕ Ⓕ

On the D17 running west to Fontvieille, this small restaurant can be
a gastronomic stopover between
Les Baux and Arles. *Crépinettes de
caille farcie* (stuffed quail), *foie gras*
and truffles star on the two menus
of regional dishes. There is even a
menu for junior gastronomes.

NÎMES

Au Flan Coco

Road map A3. 31 rue du Mûrier
d'Espagne. [04 66 21 84 81. ⬜
noon– 3pm Mon–Sat, 7pm–midnight
Sat. ⬛ ⬛ ⬛ ⬛ ⬛ MC, V. Ⓕ

Lunch is a delight in this miniscule
restaurant run by two *traiteurs* next
door to their shop. The food comes
fresh from the market and is made
before your eyes. On warm days
the green marble tables tumble out
onto the street.

Enclos de la Fontaine

Road map A3. Quai de la Fontaine.
[04 66 21 90 30. ⬜ noon–2pm,
7:30–9:45pm daily. ⬛ ⬛ ⬛ ⬛
⬛ ★ ⬛ AE, MC, DC, V. Ⓕ Ⓕ Ⓕ

In the classical Impérator Concorde
hotel, favourite of the world's top
matadors, Nîmes' finest restaurant
serves classical dishes alongside
more inventive fare, such as veal
with fresh fig *beignets* (fritters). The
courtyard is often crowded, especially during the famous *ferias*.

ST-RÉMY-DE-
PROVENCE

Le Jardin de Fréderic

Road map B3. 8 bd Gambetta.
[04 90 92 27 76. ⬜ noon–2pm,
7:30–9:30pm Thu–Tue (Mar–Jan).
⬛ ⬛ ⬛ ⬛ MC, V. Ⓕ Ⓕ

Close to the centre of town, *Le
Jardin de Fréderic* is a small, family-
run restaurant cooking local dishes
such as onion tart, and poached
turbot with sorrel. In summer, tables
are set up in front of the villa.

VAUCLUSE

AVIGNON

Fourchette

Road map B3. 17 rue Racine.
[04 90 85 20 93. ⬜ 12:30–2pm,
7:30–9:30pm Mon–Fri. ⬛ ⬛ ★
⬛ MC, V. Ⓕ Ⓕ

This is the offspring of Avignon's
gastronomic heavyweight Le Hiély-
Lucullus. In this smaller and more
relaxed version, the food is not as
expensive but it is just as good –
feuilleté de rascasse (scorpion fish
in flaky pastry) and warm quail
and duck salad. Luscious desserts
cap a mouthwatering experience.

Le Petit Bedon

Road map B3. 70 rue Joseph-Vernet.
[04 90 82 33 98. ⬜ noon–1pm,
7:30–10pm Tue–Sat. ⬛ ⬛ ⬛ ⬛
⬛ AE, MC, DC, V. Ⓕ Ⓕ

Le Petit Bedon serves large amounts
of Provençal food at fair prices. It is
a perennial favourite of professors
and their students. The kitchen is
renowned for subtle regional dishes
like monkfish with Gigondas and
ris de veau à la moutarde (sweet-
breads with mustard).

Hiély-Lucullus

Road map B3. 5 rue de la République.
[04 90 86 17 07. ⬜ 12:15–
1:30pm, 7:30–9pm Wed–Sun, 7:30–
9:30pm Mon & Tue. ⬛ ⬛ ⬛
⬛ MC, V. Ⓕ Ⓕ

A first-floor restaurant on the town's
main street, this has served Avignon
gastronomes for over 60 years. The
decor is less than spectacular, but
do not be put off – the food quality
remains as high as ever. First rate
specialities abound, for example
foie gras flan with morels and iced
meringue and almonds.

Christian Etienne

Road map B3. 10 rue du Mons.
[04 90 86 16 50. ⬜ noon–1:30pm,
7:30–9:30pm Mon–Sat (winter: Tue–
Sat). ⬛ ⬛ ⬛ ⬛ AE, MC, DC, V.
Ⓕ Ⓕ Ⓕ Ⓕ

Christian Etienne specializes in exciting Provençal dishes. He creates
mouthwatering feasts with local fish,
rabbit, lamb and the classic Provençal vegetables. The restaurant is
ideally located opposite the Palais
des Papes, in an imposing 12th-
century building.

CAVAILLON

Prévot

Road map B3. 353 av Verdun.
[04 90 71 32 43. ⬜ noon–2pm,
7:15–9:30pm Tue–Sat, 12:30–3pm
Sun. ⬛ ⬛ ⬛ ⬛ ⬛ ⬛ ★ ⬛
AE, MC, DC, V. Ⓕ Ⓕ Ⓕ

It may well come as a surprise to
discover such a gastronomic temple
in a small market town but, as Jean-
Jaques Prévot will tell you, Cavaillon
is the Eden of France. The small
dining room is decked out with
tapestries, gold mirrors and chandeliers. Edible wonders include *rouget
farci* (mullet), *artichaut soufflé*
and, of course, sweet Cavaillon
melons, the chef's pride and joy.

CHÂTEAUNEUF-DU-PAPE

La Mère Germaine

Road map B3. Pl de la Fontaine.
【 04 90 83 54 37. ⭘ 🚹 noon–2pm Thu–Tue, 7–9pm Thu–Mon.
🍴🎫👤🍷🍽 MC, V. ⓕⓕⓕ
Recently taken over by Frédéric Albar, La Mère Germaine still offers delectable dishes – veal kidneys with freshwater crayfish and morels – accompanied by a dazzling display of Châteauneuf-du-Pape wines. A brasserie has been added for more modest consumption.

GIGONDAS

Les Florets

Road map B2. Route des Dentelles.
【 04 90 65 85 01. ⭘ noon–2pm, 7:30–9pm Thu–Tue. 🍴🎫👤🚹🍷🍽 AE, MC, DC, V. ⓕⓕ
This spacious dining room is very often full of locals savouring the well-presented regional food that is served with the fine wines of Gigondas. Dinner is served in summer on the leafy terrace overlooking the Dentelles de Montmirail.

LOURMARIN

Moulin de Lourmarin

Road map C3. Rue Temple. 【 04 90 68 06 69. ⭘ noon–2pm Thu–Mon, 7–10pm Wed–Mon. 🍴🎫👤🚹🍷🍽★ AE, MC, DC, V. ⓕⓕⓕⓕ See also **Where to Stay**, p201.

The millstones are still intact in this converted olive mill, where luxury and excellent food have earned it a second Michelin star. Four extravagant menus cover a wide price range. Edouard Loubet excels with his superb venison and *effilochée d'aile de raie* (skate).

OPPÈDE-LE-VIEUX

Oppidum

Road map A3. Place de la Croix.
【 04 90 76 84 15. ⭘ 7–10pm (reservations only). 🍴🎫👤🍽 AE, MC, DC, V. ⓕ

In the medieval village square, this 15th-century dining room welcomes locals and tourists alike with simple yet extremely enjoyable food. The menu is happily dominated by local produce. There is a commendable selection of regional cheese and wine. There is also a *salon de thé*.

ORANGE

Le Yaca

Road map B2. 24 pl Sylvain. 【 04 90 34 70 03. ⭘ noon–2pm daily, 7–10pm Wed–Mon, (Thu–Mon winter). 🍴🎫👤🚹🍽 MC, V. ⓕ
This is a great place for a simple but delicious meal. The dining room is pretty, with stone walls and exposed beams. A variety of set menus offer the best value for money and plenty of choice. Dishes include leg of lamb with a cheesy crust and olive purée, and a home-made chicken liver *terrine*.

ROUSSILLON

Le Bistro de Roussillon

Road map C3. Place de la Marie.
【 04 90 05 74 45. ⭘ noon–2:30pm, 7–11pm Tue–Thu. 🍴👤🎫👤🍽 MC, V. ⓕⓕ
This stylish bistro tries to combine Parisian bar food with Provençal atmosphere and, for the most part, succeeds. You can lunch on inexpensive *pieds et paquets* (mutton and tripe), or on *daube Provençale* (meat braised in wine with olives and seasonal vegetables).

SÉGURET

La Table du Comtat

Road map B2. Hôtel la Table du Comtat. 【 04 90 46 91 49. ⭘ 12:30–2pm, 7:30–9pm daily (closed Tue D winter). 🍴🎫👤🍷🍽 AE, MC, DC, V. ⓕⓕⓕ
Truffles, pigeon and wild boar grace a menu of local produce that is expertly crafted by Master Chef Franck Gomez. The sweeping view over the Comtat Venaissin is splendid, and the cellar of Côtes du Rhône provides a fitting accompaniment.

ALPES-DE-HAUTE-PROVENCE

CHÂTEAU-ARNOUX

La Bonne Etape

Road map D2. Chemin du Lac. 【 04 92 64 00 09. ⭘ noon–1:30pm, 7:30–9:30pm daily. 🍴👤🚹🍷★🍽 AE, MC, DC, V. ⓕⓕⓕ See also **Where to Stay**, p201.

A place of pilgrimage in the otherwise nondescript town of Château-Arnoux, La Bonne Etape has long

featured on the gastronomic map of Provence. Tapestries and paintings hang in the dining room; a small salon offers an ancient fireplace. The flavour is Provençal with expertly crafted specialities such as salmon and oregano terrine.

DIGNE-LES-BAINS

Le Grand Paris

Road map D2. Hôtel du Grand Paris, 19 bd Thiers. 【 04 92 31 11 15. ⭘ noon–2:30pm, 7:30–9:30pm daily. 🍴🎫👤🍷🍽 AE, MC, DC, V. ⓕⓕⓕⓕ
In the venerable surroundings of this former 17th-century convent, the best restaurant in Digne serves traditional dishes, such as poached salmon and roasted duck breast with shallots. The menus are wholesome but they can sometimes lack a little imagination.

MANOSQUE

Le Petit Pascal

Road map C3. 17 promenade Aubert-Millot. 【 04 92 87 62 01. ⭘ noon–2pm, 7–9pm Thu–Sat, noon–2pm Mon–Wed. 🍴🚹👤 ⓕ
This hole-in-the-wall is Manosque's favourite lunchtime eatery. It is a one-woman show, where the jovial *patronne* cooks copious portions of steak, veal and *anchoiade* (anchovy purée on toast). The place is often filled with ravenous farmers and the town's police force.

Hostellerie de la Fuste

Road map C3. Le Village. 【 04 92 72 05 95. ⭘ noon–2pm, 7–9pm daily (closed Tue D winter). 🍴🎫🍽 AE, MC, DC, V. ⓕⓕⓕ
The award-winning chef of this converted *auberge* is an expert in creating traditional regional dishes. One of the reasons for this is that all the herbs and vegetables are home-grown. Fresh fish and meat dishes are popular and there is a good choice of cheese and desserts.

MOUSTIERS-STE-MARIE

La Treille Muscat

Road map D3. Place de l'Eglise.
【 04 92 74 64 31. ⭘ noon–2pm, 7:30–9pm daily. 🎫🍷🍽 MC, V. ⓕⓕⓕ
Gastronomic Provençal cuisine is the order of the day here – *pistou* of summer vegetables, *confit* of rabbit with ratatouille and seafood with Antibes sauce – plus an excellent range of regional wines.

Cafés, Bars and Casual Eating

I N RURAL AREAS the world over the local bar is the centre of village life, and nowhere is this more true than in Provence. Everywhere you go you will find lively watering holes, often with outside terraces or gardens. Most bars and cafés double as lunchtime restaurants, serving straightforward daily specials at reasonable prices. Snacks are not really a part of French life but nearly all bars will make you a traditional *baguette* sandwich or a *croque monsieur* (toasted ham and cheese sandwich). Drinking is a subject close to Provençal hearts – *pastis*, the aniseed spirit synonymous with Marseille, is the region's lifeblood. In many country towns, you will see the locals sitting outside sipping *pastis* from the early morning onwards, along with strong black coffee. Lunchtime tipples include ice-cold rosé, the perfect accompaniment to a sun-filled day.

CAFÉS

T HERE IS LITTLE distinction between cafés and bars in Provence and most serve alcohol all day. In the country, village cafés will often close around 8pm. In larger towns, many places stay open much later – popular Marseillais and Niçois bars close when the last person leaves. Many stay open all night, serving breakfast to the diehards as dawn breaks. Many cafés are also *tabacs* (tobacconists) selling cigarettes, tobacco, sweets and stamps.

While most Provençal cafés are simple places, where decor is restricted to the local fire brigade calendar and fashion to a hunting jacket and boots, there are several stylish exceptions. No visit to Aix is complete without an hour or two spent sipping coffee on the cours Mirabeau, one of the places in Provence to see and be seen. On the Côte d'Azur, chic cafés abound. The **Café Carlton** in Cannes is the place to spot visiting film stars during the festival. In Nice, the cafés on the cours Saleya are the hub of day and nightlife, while Monaco boasts the crème de la crème, the **Café de Paris**.

WHAT TO EAT

M OST PROVENÇAL cafés serve breakfast although, in village establishments, this will just be a couple of slices of *baguette* and coffee. More elaborate affairs are served in towns, with fresh orange juice, hot croissants and jam.

Café lunches usually include a *plat du jour* (dish of the day) and a dessert, along with a quarter litre of wine. These can be great bargains, costing little more than 50F. For more basic lunches, sandwiches, omelettes and salads can be ordered. Evening meals are usually the reserve of restaurants, although in rural areas, the local bar will also serve dinner, normally a varient on the lunchtime menu.

WHAT TO DRINK

S INCE ROMAN DAYS, when the legionnaires introduced wine to the region, drinking has been a favoured pastime in Provence. Cold beer seems to surpass the fruit of the vine in the hearts of most farmers, as village bars are filled with locals downing *pressions* (half-pint glasses of beer). More potent tipples include *pastis,* a 90 per cent proof nectar flavoured with aniseed, vanilla and cinnamon, and *marc*, a brandy distilled from any available fruits. Soft drinks such as *un diablo* (fruit syrup mixed with lemonade) and *orange pressé* (freshly squeezed orange juice) are also popular. As in most Mediterranean lands, coffee is a way of life – *un café* is a cup of strong and black expresso. If want white coffee you need to ask for *un café crème*. For filter or instant coffee order *un café filtre* or *un café américain*. Tea will always be served black unless you ask for milk or lemon. Herbal teas are also available, known as *tisanes* or *infusions*.

BARS

I N MOST TOWNS you will find a handful of bars that only serve beer and miscellaneous alcohol, rather than the more diverse range offered by cafés. These bars are lively in true Mediterranean style. Student centres such as Nice, Marseille and Aix contain British-style pubs, offering a large selection of European bottled and draught beer. Some have live bands, such as **Chez Wayne**, and **De Klomp** in Nice and **Pub Z** in Avignon.

More upmarket bars are found in the plush hotels of the Côte d'Azur. Here, in Belle Epoque splendour, you can sip champagne listening to jazz piano, string quartets or opera singers. Among the most impressive are the bars of the Carlton and Martinez hotels in Cannes, Le Négresco in Nice, **Somerset Maugham** at the Grand Hôtel in St-Jean-Cap-Ferrat and the Hermitage in Monte-Carlo (*see* Where to Stay, pp196–201).

PICNIC AND TAKE-AWAY FOOD

Y OU ARE NEVER FAR from food in Provence. The traditional street food of Provence is the *pan bagnat*, a thick bun filled with crisp salade Niçoise and doused in olive oil. Pizza is a local favourite, and every small town has its pizza van, where your choice is cooked to order. A particularly Provençal form of pizza is *pissaladière*, an onion pizza coated with anchovies and olives. In Nice, the number one snack is *socca*, thick crêpes made from chickpea flour (*see* pp204–5).

The French love picnics and the Provençaux are no exception. French alfresco eating is complex – families set out tables, chairs, barbecues and portable fridges. To service this penchant for portable food, Provençal villages have specialist shops offering ready-to-eat food. *Boulangeries* and *patisseries* serve everything from fresh croissants to quiches and a dazzling array of cakes and tarts. Nearly all *patisseries* provide freshly made *baguette* sandwiches.

In the main towns, specialist butchers called *traîteurs* provide ready-made dishes, such as salads, cold meats and roast chicken, sold in cartons according to weight. **Au Flan Coco** in Nîmes and **Bataille** in Marseille are fine examples. Most supermarkets also have similar delicatessen counters. *Charcuteries* specialize in pork dishes, particularly pâtés and sausages. For traditional spicy sausages much prized in the Camargue, head to the **Boucherie Milhau** in Arles.

The best place to buy picnic food is the local market. Every town in Provence has its market, some daily, like Aix-en-Provence, some just once or twice a week. No Provençal picnic is complete without French bread – the *baguette* is the mainstay of the country and Provence is no exception. The only difference is that the region boasts numerous local breads, incorporating traditional ingredients. *Pain aux olives* is found almost everywhere, often in the form of *fougasse*, a flat, lattice-like loaf. Alternatively, this may contain anchovies (*pain aux anchois*), or spinach (*pain aux épinards*) and there is a sweet version flavoured with almonds. Wholemeal or brown bread is an anathema to the traditional Provençaux, although many bakeries now produce it – ask for *pain aux ceréales*. The nearest to healthy bread is *pain de campagne*, a sturdier *baguette* made with unrefined white flour. One of the finest *boulangeries* in the region is **Espuno**, in the old quarter of Nice, where the same recipes have been used for generations.

Boulangeries are found in every village and usually have a good selection of *patisseries*, cakes and tarts. Provençal ingredients are combined to make these delights, such as honey, almonds and fruit – try those at **Béchard** in Aix-en-Provence. For those with an even sweeter tooth, these same ingredients are used in the handmade chocolates and candied fruit. *Calissons* (an almond-paste sweet) and *suce-miel* (honey-based candy) are very popular. Two of the best shops are **Puyricard** in Aix and **Auer** in Nice.

DIRECTORY

CAFÉS

Aix-en-Provence
Les Deux Garçons
53 cours Mirabeau.
04 42 26 00 51.

Cannes
Cafe Carlton
58 la Croisette.
04 93 06 40 21.

Eze
Château Eza
Rue de la Pise.
04 93 41 12 24.

Monaco
Café de Paris
Le Casino, place du Casino.
00 377 92 16 20 20.

Nice
Le Grand Café de Turin
5 place Garibaldi.
04 93 62 29 52.

Nîmes
Café Napoléon
46 boulevard Victor Hugo.
04 66 67 20 23.

St-Paul-de-Vence
Café de la Place
Place du Général de Gaulle.
04 93 32 80 03.

St-Tropez
Café des Arts
Place des Lices.
04 94 97 02 25.

Le Café de Paris
Quai de Suffren.
04 94 97 00 56.

Senequier
Quai Jean Jaurès.
04 94 97 00 90.

BARS AND PUBS

Aix-en-Provence
Le Richelm
24 rue Verrerie.
04 42 23 49 29.

Avignon
Pub Z
58 rue Bonneterie.
04 90 85 42 84.

Cannes
L'Amiral
Hôtel Martinez,
73 boulevard la Croisette.
04 92 98 73 00.

Juan-les-Pins
Le Festival
146 boulevard Wilson.
04 93 61 04 62.

Pam-Pam
137 boulevard Wilson.
04 93 61 11 05.

Marseille
L'Ascenseur
57 rue Jules Moulet.
04 91 33 86 31.

Bistrot Thiars
Place Thiars.
04 91 33 07 25.

Monaco
Bar du Soleil
Le Casino, place du Casino.
00 377 92 16 63 59.

Flashman's
7 avenue Princesse Alice.
00 377 93 30 09 03.

Nice
Chez Wayne
15 rue de la Préfecture.
04 93 13 46 99.

De Klomp
6 rue Mascoinat.
04 93 92 42 85.

Hole in the Wall
3 rue d'Abbaye.
04 93 80 40 16.

Les Trois Diables
2 cours Saleya.
04 93 62 47 00.

Nîmes
La Petite Bourse
2 boulevard Victor Hugo.
04 66 67 44 31.

St-Jean-Cap-Ferrat
Somerset Maugham
Grand Hôtel de Cap-Ferrat,
71 boulevard Général de Gaulle.
04 93 76 50 50.

Villefranche
Chez Betty
2 avenue Maréchal Foch.
04 93 01 70 91.

PICNIC AND TAKE-AWAY FOOD

Aix-en-Provence
Béchard
12 cours Mirabeau.

Puyricard
Rue Rifle-rafle.

Arles
Boucherie Milhau
11 rue Réattu.

Marseille
Bataille
18 rue Fontange.

Le Four des Navettes
136 rue Sainte.

Nice
Espuno
35 rue Droite.

Auer
7 rue St-François-de-Paule.

Nîmes
Au Flan Coco
31 rue du Mûrier
d'Espagne.

SHOPS AND MARKETS

SHOPPING IN PROVENCE is one of life's great delights. Even the tiniest village may be home to a craftsman potter or painter, or you may arrive on market day to find regional produce – artichokes, asparagus, wild mushrooms – still fresh with the dew from the surrounding fields. Larger towns are packed with individual boutiques selling anything from dried flowers to chic baby clothes, and the fashion-conscious will always be

Provençal olive oil

able to find an avenue or two of famous names in which to window-shop. If the idea of cramming fresh foodstuffs into your luggage to take back home proves too daunting, Provence has perfected the fine art of packaging its produce, with the bottles, jars and boxes often works of art in themselves. This section provides guidelines on opening hours and the range of goods with a Provençal flavour to be found in the many stores and markets.

OPENING HOURS

FOOD SHOPS OPEN at around 7am and close at noon for lunch, a break which may last for up to three hours in Provence. After lunch most stay open until 7pm, sometimes even later in big towns such as Nice and Marseille. Bakers often stay open until 1pm or later, serving tasty lunchtime snacks. Most supermarkets and hypermarkets stay open throughout lunchtimes.

Non-food shops are open 9am–6pm Mon–Sat, but some may close for lunch. Many are closed on Monday mornings.

Food shops and newsagents open on Sunday mornings but almost every shop is closed on Sunday afternoon. Small shops may close for one day a week out of high season.

LARGER SHOPS

HYPERMARKETS (*hypermarchés* or *grandes surfaces*) can be found on the outskirts of every sizeable town: look out for the signs indicating the *Centre Commercial*. Among the largest are Casino, Auchan and Carrefour. Discount petrol is usually sold: you may have to pay in cash.

Department stores, or *grands magasins*, including Monoprix and Prisunic, are usually found in town centres. More up-market stores such as Printemps and Galeries Lafayette are found both in towns and at out-of-town complexes.

Sweetly-scented dried flowers in a St-Tropez shop window

SPECIALIST SHOPS

ONE OF THE GREAT pleasures of shopping in Provence is that specialist food shops still flourish despite the new large supermarkets. The bread shop (*boulangerie*) is usually combined with the *pâtisserie* selling cakes and pastries. The cheesemonger (*fromagerie*) may also be combined with a shop selling other dairy produce (*laiterie*), but the *boucherie* (butcher) and the *charcuterie* (delicatessen) tend to be separate shops. A *traiteur* sells prepared foods. For dry goods and general groceries, go to an *épicerie fine*. Cleaning products and household goods are sold at a *droguerie* and hardware at a *quincaillerie*. Booksellers (*librairies*) in the main towns sometimes sell English books. For addresses, see page 235.

A Provençal olive merchant and his wares

MARKETS

THIS GUIDE GIVES the market days for every town featured. To find out where the market is, ask a passer-by for *le marché*. Markets are morning affairs, when the produce is super-fresh – by noon the stall-holders will already be packing up and the best bargains will have been sold out hours ago. By French law, price tags must state the origin of all produce: *pays* means local.

Les marchés de Provence were immortalized in song by Gilbert Bécaud, and rightly so. In a country famed for its markets, these are among the best. Some are renowned – cours Saleya (*see p84*) in Nice and the food and flower markets of Aix (*see p148*), for example, should not be missed. Others take more searching out, such as the truffle markets of the Var. Try Aups (*see p104*) on a Thursday during truffle season, from November to February.

The flower, fruit and vegetable market in cours Saleya, Nice

Bags of dried herbs on display in the market of St-Rémy-de-Provence

REGIONAL SPECIALITIES

THE SUNSHINE of Provence is captured in its distinctive, vividly coloured fabrics, known as *indiennes*. Many shops sell them by the metre; others, such as **Mistral** and **Souleïado** also make them up into items as diverse as soft furnishings, cowboy shirts and boxer shorts.

Throughout Provence, working olive mills churn out rich, pungent oil, which is also used to make the chunky blocks of soap, *savon de Marseille*. Tins and jars of olives, often scented with *herbes de Provence*, are widely available, as are bags of the herbs themselves. Bags of lavender, and honey from its pollen, are regional specialities; local flowers appear in other forms too, from dried arrangements to scented oils, or perfumes from Grasse *(see p67)*.

Traditional sweets *(confiseries)* abound, using regional fruits and nuts: almond *calissons* from Aix, fruity *berlingots* from Carpentras and candied *fruits confits* are just a few.

LOCAL WINES

PROVENCE IS NOT one of the great wine regions of the world, but its many vineyards *(see pp206–7)* produce a wide range of pleasant wines and you will see plenty of signs inviting you to a *dégustation* (tasting). You will usually be expected to buy at least one bottle. Wine cooperatives sell the wines of numerous smaller producers. Here you can buy wine in five- and ten-litre containers

(en vrac). This wine is "duty free" but, with vineyards such as Châteauneuf-du-Pape and Beaumes-de-Venise, wise buyers will drink *en vrac* on holiday and pick up bargains in fine wine to bring home.

Marseille's aperitif *pastis* is an evocative, if acquired, taste.

Works by local artists sold on the harbour at St-Tropez

ARTS AND CRAFTS

MANY OF THE CRAFTS now flourishing in Provence are traditional ones that had almost died out 50 years ago. The potters of Vallauris owe the revival in their fortunes to Picasso *(see pp72–3)* but, more often, it is the interest of visitors that keeps a craft alive. From the little pottery *santons* of Marseille to the flutes and tambourines of Barjols, there is plenty of choice for gifts and mementos. Many towns have unique specialities. Biot is famous for its bubbly glassware, Cogolin for pipes and carpets and Salernes for hexagonal terracotta tiles.

Liquorice-flavoured aperitif from Marseille

DIRECTORY

REGIONAL SPECIALITIES

Avignon
Souleïado
5 rue Joseph Vernet.
📞 04 90 86 47 67.
One of several branches.

Grasse
Moulin à huile
138 route de Draguignan.
📞 04 93 70 21 42.

Parfumerie Fragonard
20 bd Fragonard.
📞 04 93 36 44 65.

Parfumerie Galimard
73 route de Cannes.
📞 04 93 09 20 00.

Nice
Alziari
14 rue St-François-de-Paule.
📞 04 93 85 76 92.
Olive press: olives, oil, soap.

Nîmes
Mistral
2 bd des Arènes.
📞 04 66 21 69 57.
One of several branches.

St-Rémy-de-Provence
Santoline, l'Herbier de St-Remy
34 bd Victor Hugo.
📞 04 90 92 11 96.

ARTS AND CRAFTS

Biot
Verrerie de Biot
See p74.

Cogolin
Fabrique de Pipes Courrieu
58 av Georges Clémenceau.
📞 04 94 54 63 82.

Manufacture de Tapis
6 bd Louis Blanc.
📞 04 94 55 70 65.

Marseille
Ateliers Carbonel
47 rue Neuve Ste-Catherine.
📞 04 91 54 26 58.
Santon workshop and museum.

Vallauris
Roger Collet
Montée Ste-Anne.
📞 04 93 64 65 84.

What to Buy in Provence

BEST BUYS TO BE FOUND in Provence are those that
reflect the character of the region – its geographical
blessings of bountiful produce and its historic traditions
of arts and crafts. While the chic boutiques of St-Tropez
or Cannes may rival Paris in predicting the latest fashion
trend, your souvenirs of Provence should be far more
timeless. The evocative scents, colours and flavours
they offer will help to keep your holiday memories alive
throughout the darkest winter months, and longer – at
least until your next visit.

*Lavender, one of the
perfumes of Provence*

THE SCENTS OF PROVENCE

Provençal lavender is used to perfume a
wide range of goods, but most popular
are pretty fabric bags full of the dried
flowers. Bath times can be
heady with the scent of
local flowers and herbs,
captured in delightful
bottles, and Marseille's
famous olive oil soaps.

Olive oil savons de Marseille

**Orange water
from Vallauris**

**Linden-scented
bubble bath**

**Dried lavender, packed
in Provençal fabrics**

**Mallow-scented
bubble bath**

Glassware
*Glassblowing is a
modern Provençal
craft. At Biot (see
p74) you can watch
glassblowers at work,
as well as buy examples
of their art to take home.*

Pottery
*Look for traditional
tiles, cookware and
storage jars made
from terre rouge,
formal china of
Moustiers faïence
(see p186) or art-
works of grès clay.*

Terracotta Santons
*Provençal Christmas cribs are peopled with
these gaily painted traditional figures. Most
crafts shops offer a good choice of characters.*

Olive Wood
As rich in colour and texture as its oil, the wood of the olive can be sculpted into works of art or turned into practical kitchenware.

Hunting Knives
The huntsmen's shops of Provence are an unexpected source for the perfect picnic or kitchen knife, safe yet razor sharp.

Provençal Fabrics
Using patterns and colours dating back for centuries, these traditional prints are sold by the metre or made up into fashionable items.

THE FLAVOURS OF PROVENCE
No-one should leave Provence without at least a jar of olives or a bottle of olive oil, but consider also easy-to-pack tins, jars and boxes of preserved fruits, scented honey or savoury purées – prettily packaged, they make ideal gifts.

Crystallized chestnuts or *marrons glacés*

Almond sweetmeats, the speciality of Aix-en-Provence

Goat's milk cheese, wrapped in chestnut leaves

A spicy garnish for fish soups

Green olives with Provençal herbs

Virgin olive oil

Puréed salt cod or *brandade de morue*

Almond and orange conserve

Lavender honey and hazelnut *confit*

ENTERTAINMENT IN PROVENCE

THERE ONCE WAS a time when Provence was seen as a cultural backwater, where nothing much happened except wine harvests and Mistral gales. In recent years, however, the region has been transformed and barely a month goes by without some major festival *(see pp30–35)*. Concerts take place all year round, with first-class opera in Marseille, St-Tropez and Nice and rock concerts at Toulon.

Actor at the Avignon festival

Nightlife tends to be restricted to the coastal resorts, like Juan-les-Pins and St-Tropez where clubs and bars stay open all night. In winter, things are quieter, but the small bars of Marseille and Nice remain open and full of life. Provence's most common entertainment is free – locals spend much of their time enjoying the sunshine and fresh air, walking and playing *pétanque*, the Provençal form of bowls.

PRACTICAL INFORMATION

INFORMATION ABOUT what's on in Provence tends to be fairly localized, with tourist offices providing listings of various events. Marseille has its own free magazine, *Taktik*, which gives outlines of the best of each week's events and is available from the main tourist offices.

BUYING TICKETS

DEPENDING ON the event, most tickets can be bought at the door, but for blockbuster concerts, particularly during the summer months, it is best to reserve in advance. Tickets can be purchased at the **FNAC** chains in major towns, or at the **Virgin Megastore** in Marseille.

Theatre box-offices are open from approximately 11am – 7pm seven days a week and most will accept credit card bookings over the telephone.

If you haven't booked in advance, tickets to popular concerts can be bought from touts at the venue doors on

the night – these will be more expensive than the set price. Be warned that cases of counterfeit tickets are not uncommon.

THEATRE

MARSEILLE IS the centre of theatre in Provence and boasts one of France's top theatrical companies, the **Théâtre de la Criée**. Various smaller companies stage some of the most innovative plays in Europe, many of which end up in Paris. Avignon is also famous for its **Théâtre des Carmes**, the main venue for the **Festival d'Avignon** *(see p35)*. There is also a "fringe" to rival Edinburgh's, the **Avignon Public Off**, which has its own directors and box office.

DANCE

LIKE THEATRE, dance is at its best in Marseille, where an eclectic mixture of nationalities and styles has led to highly original and powerful produc-

tions. Companies such as the **Théâtre du Merlan** and **Bernadines** often take their productions to Paris. The National Ballet Company is based at the opera house in Marseille and run by the dancer Marie-Claude Pietra Galla.

OPERA AND CLASSICAL MUSIC

Classical cello

MUSIC IS EVERYWHERE in Provence, from small village churches to the Belle Epoque opera houses of Marseille, Toulon and Nice. The **Opéra de Nice** is recognized as one of the best in France and there is usually no problem getting tickets. The orchestra from Monte-Carlo plays with the world's most illustrious conductors. The annual **Festival International de la Musique**, based in Toulon, runs from late May to mid-July and attracts many top orchestras and performers.

ROCK AND JAZZ

ONCE A ROCK AND POP desert, Provence is now enjoying something of a renaissance with Toulon's **Zenith-Oméga**, a main venue on most major world tours. For really big stadium shows, such as U2 and The Rolling Stones, Marseille's soccer stadium, **Stade-Vélodrome**, is preferred.

The Nice **Festival du Jazz** in the arena of Cimiez *(see p84)* is one of the world's best. It was here that Miles Davis gave one of his last performances among the Roman walls and

Miles Davis playing at the Nice Festival du Jazz in the arena of Cimiez

olive groves. In recent years, top names have been favouring the **Jazz à Juan** festival in Juan-les-Pins, which has seen Ray Charles and the jazz debut of violinist Nigel Kennedy.

DISCOTHEQUES AND NIGHTCLUBS

DURING THE SUMMER, the main towns of Provence boogie all night. The music is far from trend-setting, usually following styles set the previous year in New York and London, but the dancers are chic and the prices high. A handful of clubs such as **Jimmy'Z** in Monaco and **Les Caves du Roi** in St-Tropez cater for the jet-set, while those like **Whisky à Gogo** in Juan-les-Pins and **Le Blitz** in Cannes serve a much younger crowd.

CINEMA

IT WAS IN THE SMALL PORT of La Ciotat that Louis Lumière shot the world's first motion picture, and Marcel Pagnol laid the foundations for modern French cinema from his studios in Marseille. Every small town has its cinema. In the bigger towns films in their original language are often shown – look for the code VO (*Version Original*). Dubbed films are coded VF (*Version Française*).

GAMBLING

THE RIVIERA is famed for its opulent casinos. If you are 21 and over you can play in most resorts. The most popular casino on the coast is in

The Open Tennis Championships in Monte-Carlo

Monaco, **Le Casino** where you have to pay a 50F entrance fee before you start gambling. Other casinos worth visiting for architecture and atmosphere are Cannes' **Casino Croisette** and **Casino Ruhl** in Nice. If you are not a high-roller, there is always the dazzling array of slot-machines, ever ready to take your coins.

View over the harbour in Monaco to the glittering casino

SPECTATOR SPORTS

WITH ITS SUPERB weather and glamorous reputation, the regions of Provence and the Côte d'Azur are ideal venues for some of France's top sporting events. The gruelling Tour de France passes through the region each July, while the Monte-Carlo and Nice tennis tournaments attract top players. The Grand Prix at Monaco (*see p30*) at the end of May is one of the highlights of the Formula 1 motor racing season. Horse-racing enthusiasts can visit the race track at Cagnes-sur-Mer between December and March.

Provence boasts two of the top soccer teams in France – *Olympique de Marseille*, back at the top after being demoted in disgrace over allegations of match rigging, and *Monaco*, known as the millionaires' club. Rugby is becoming increasingly popular in Provence, with top-class clubs in Nice and Toulon.

nîmes feria 9

BULLFIGHTING

Perhaps the most dramatic sporting occasions in Provence are the annual *férias* or bullfighting festivals. The traditional bullfight of Provence is the *course à la cocarde*, which starts with an *abrivado* when the bulls are chased through the town to the local arena. The bull enters the ring with a red *cocarde* or rosette tied to its horns, which the *razeteurs* or matadors try to snatch, providing riveting but goreless entertainment. At the end of the season the bullfighter with the most rosettes receives fame and adulation, as well as cash.

Increasingly, bullfights will end in death in the full-blooded Spanish-style *corrida*, but this is usually in the main arenas in Nîmes and Arles (*see p30*), and will always be advertised first. In one session there are usually six bullfights, of which two may be advertised as *mise à morte* (to the death).

Bullfighting poster for the 1992 Nîmes *féria* by Francis Bacon

PARTICIPANT SPORTS

THE VAST EXPANSE of varied countryside and coastline of the region provides endless possibilities for the athletically inclined. Watersports are very popular; a new organization, **France-Station-Voile,** links six Provençal resorts, offering week-long sailing courses. Sailing boats can be rented from most towns. Windsurfing is another favourite pastime and boards can be rented at any beach along the Côte d'Azur – many experienced windsurfers congregate at Brutal Beach just off Cap Sicié, west of Toulon. Below the surface, numerous scuba-diving clubs offer *baptêmes de mer,* courses for first-time Jacques Cousteaus. Some of the best diving in the Mediterranean is found off Ile de Port-Cros in the Var. Inland,

the rivers and lakes are home to dedicated kayakists and canoeists – in particular, the white water of the Verdon and the calmer flow of the Gard.

The Gorges du Verdon *(see pp184–5)* offer superb rock climbing, as do the spectacular Calanques near Marseille *(see p153).* Soaring above are hang-gliders and *parapentistes,* the practitioners of paragliding, a growing sport in Provence. Horse riding is the speciality of the Camargue, where you can ride alongside Camarguais cowboys, the famous *gardians.*

More sedate activity can be found on Provence's 20 or so golf courses, offering a variety of handicaps and beautiful settings, while every town and village has its own tennis courts. Many of them are the traditional Mediterranean clay courts. Walking and hiking are

the predominant activities for the region – the countryside is traversed by long-distance, marked paths called *Grandes Randonnées* (GRs for short). This complex network of paths takes in some of the most beautiful scenery in Provence, covering great distances, in-land across the Alps, or along the coastline; you can actually walk from Nice to Amsterdam.

One sport enjoyed by all is *pétanque,* the Provençal form of *boules.* The game has its origins, as legend states, in the small coastal town of La Ciotat, just outside Marseille. From dawn to dusk, locals gather in the town square to play their national game, sometimes with surprising competitiveness.

During the winter, the southern Alps are home to skiers at top resorts such as **Auron** and **Isola 2000** *(see p96).*

DIRECTORY

TICKET SALES

FNAC
Avignon
19 rue de la République.
[04 90 14 35 35.

Marseille
Centre Commercial Bourse.
[04 91 39 94 00.

Nice
30 avenue Jean Médecin.
[04 92 17 77 74.

Virgin Megastore
Marseille
75 rue St-Ferréol.
[04 91 55 55 00.

THEATRE AND DANCE

Avignon
Avignon Public Off
BP 5, 75521 Paris.
[01 48 05 20 97.

Festival d'Avignon
8 bis rue de Mons.
[04 90 27 66 50.

Théâtre des Carmes
6 place des Carmes.
[04 90 82 20 47.

Marseille
Bernardines
17 bd Garibaldi.
[04 91 24 30 40.

Théâtre de la Criée
30 quai de Rive-Neuve.
[04 91 54 70 54.

Théâtre du Merlan
Avenue Raimu.
[04 91 11 19 21.

Nice
Théâtre de l'Alphabet
10 bd Carabacel.
[04 93 13 08 88.

Théâtre du Cour
Cours Saleya.
[04 93 80 12 67.

Théâtre de la Semeuse
Rue du Château.
[04 93 62 31 00.

OPERA AND CLASSICAL MUSIC

Aix-en-Provence
Espace Forbin
3 place John Rewald.
[04 42 21 69 69.

Marseille
Opéra Municipal
Place Ernest Reyer.
[04 91 55 00 70.

Nice
CEDAC de Cimiez
49 av de la Marne.
[04 93 53 85 95.

Forum Nice Nord
10 bd Comte de Falicon.
[04 93 84 24 37.

Opéra de Nice
4 rue St-François-de-Paule.
[04 92 17 40 00.

Toulon
CNCDC Châteauvallon
[04 94 22 74 00.

Festival International de la Musique
[04 94 93 18 53 00.

Grand Opéra-Théâtre
Bd de Strasbourg.
[04 94 92 70 78.

ROCK MUSIC

Marseille
Espace Julien
39 cours Julien.
[04 91 24 34 14.

Stade Vélodrome
Bd Michelet.
[04 91 76 56 09.

Toulon
Zenith-Oméga
Bd commandant Nicolas.
[04 94 22 66 77.

JAZZ

Aix-en-Provence
Hot Brass
Route d'Eguilles-Célony.
[04 42 21 05 57.

Le Scat
11 rue de la Verrerie.
[04 42 23 00 23.

Juan-les-Pins
Festival du Jazz
Maison du Tourisme,
11 pl de Gaulle, Antibes.
[04 92 90 53 00.

Marseille
Le Zouk-Times
40 rue Plan Fourmiguier,
quai de Rive-Neuve.
[04 91 54 36 36.

Le Pêle-Mêle
45 cours d'Estienne d'Orves.
[04 91 54 85 26.

Nice
Bar des Oiseaux
5 rue St-Vincent (jazz and café-théâtre).
[04 93 80 27 33.

Festival du Jazz
Office du Tourisme,
5 prom des Anglais.
04 92 14 48 00.

DISCOTHEQUES AND NIGHTCLUBS

Aix-en-Provence
La Chimère Café
15 rue Bruyès.
04 42 38 30 00 (main gay bar and disco).

Avignon
Les Ambassadeurs Club
27 rue Bancasse.
04 90 86 31 55.

Cannes
Le Blitz
22 rue Macé.
04 93 39 05 21.

Disco 7
Rue Rouguière.
04 93 34 09 04.

Jimmy'Z
Casino Croisette,
Palais des Festivals.
04 93 68 00 07.

Hyères
L'Alligator
13 rue Garrel.
04 94 65 41 58.

Le Rêve
Avenue Badine.
04 94 58 00 07.

Juan-les-Pins
Le Village
1 boulevard de la Pinede.
04 92 93 9000.

Whisky à Gogo
Rue Jacques Leonetti.
04 92 93 90 00.

Marseille
L'Ascenseur
22 place Thiars.
04 91 33 13 27.

Club 116
5 rue Chantier.
04 91 33 77 22.

Monaco
Jimmy'Z
26 avenue Princesse Grace.
00 377 92 16 22 77.

Le Box
39 avenue Princesse Grace.
00 377 93 30 15 22.

St-Raphaël
Le Paname
159 rue de la Garonne.
04 94 95 37 49.

Actoria Studio
29 rue Alphonse Karr.
04 93 82 37 66.

St-Tropez
Les Caves du Roi
Palace de la Côte d'Azur,
avenue Paul Signac.
04 94 97 16 02.

Papagayo
Residence du Nouveau
Port.
04 94 54 88 18.

CINEMA

Aix-en-Provence
Le Mazarin
6 rue Laroque.
04 42 26 99 85.

Avignon
Utopia Cinema
4 rue Escalier Sainte Anne.
04 90 82 65 36.

Marseille
Breteuil
120 boulevard de Notre-
Dame.
04 91 37 88 18.

Monaco
Cinéma d'Eté
Avenue Princesse Grace.
00 377 93 25 86 80.
(Open-air in summer.)

Nice
Cinémathèque
3 esplanade Kennedy.
04 92 04 06 66.

Mercury Cinéma
16 place Garibaldi.
04 93 55 37 81.

Nîmes
Le Sémaphore
25a rue Porte de France.
04 66 67 88 04.

GAMBLING

Cannes
Casino Croisette
Palais des Festivals.
04 93 38 12 11.

Monaco
Le Casino
Place du Casino.
00 377 92 16 21 21.

Nice
Casino Ruhl
Promenade des Anglais.
04 93 87 95 87.

BULLFIGHTING

Arles
Arènes d'Arles
Rond-Point des Arènes.
04 90 49 36 86

Nîmes
Les Arènes
Blvd des Arènes.
04 66 76 72 77.

GOLF

Avignon
Golf Grand Avignon
Les Chênes Verts, Vedene.
04 90 31 49 94.

Cannes
Golf de Cannes
route du Golf, Mandelieu.
04 93 49 55 39

Marseille
Golf de la Salette
Impasse des Vaudrans.
04 91 27 12 16.

KAYAKING

Joinville-le-Pont
**Fédération Française de
Canoë-kayak**
87 quai de la Marne.
01 45 11 08 50.

SAILING AND WINDSURFING

Cannes
Cannes-Station-Voile
9 rue Esprit Violet.
04 92 18 88 88.

Juan-les-Pins
Nautic 2000
Port Gallice.
04 93 61 20 01.

Paris
**Fédération Française de
Voile**
29 rue Sèvres, 75006.
01 45 44 04 78.

SCUBA DIVING

Marseille
**Fédération d'Etudes et
de Sports Sous-Marins**
24 quai de Rive-Neuve.
04 91 33 99 31.

Nice
Centre Inter de Plongée
2 ruelle des Moulins.
04 93 55 59 50.

PARASCENDING

Nice
**Fédération Française de
Vol Libre**
4 rue de Suisse.
04 93 88 62 89.

HORSE RIDING

Marseille
**Centre Equestre de la
Ville de Marseille**
33 Traverse Carthage.
04 91 73 72 94.

SKIING

Auron
Office du Tourisme
04 93 23 02 66.

Isola 2000
Office du Tourisme
04 93 23 15 15.

TENNIS

Marseille
Tennis Municipaux
Allées Ray-Grassi.
04 91 71 00 78.

Nice
League de la Côte d'Azur
66 route de Grenoble,
04 93 18 00 95.

SPORTS CENTRES

Avignon
Parc des Sports
Avenue Pierre de
Coubertin.
04 90 87 45 51.

Marseille
Palais des Sports
81 rue Raymond-Teissère.
04 91 17 30 40.

Nice
Palais des Sports
Esplanade de Lattre de
Tassigny.
04 93 80 80 80.

SURVIVAL
GUIDE

PRACTICAL INFORMATION 228-237
TRAVEL INFORMATION 238-245

PRACTICAL INFORMATION

IN PROVENCE, AS ELSEWHERE in France, the peak holiday period is from mid-June to the end of August. The coast is particularly busy during this period. Since the beginning of the century, famous Hollywood names have flocked to the region's beaches, followed by the masses, and so the summer holiday industry was born. Today, although sometimes expensive compared to other French regions, Provence offers accommodation ranging from top hotels to small camp sites. There are activities to suit all tastes, from skiing

National logo for tourist information

in winter to sun and sand in summer. It has some of the world's best modern art collections, fine Roman ruins, ancient festivals, excellent food and wine and breathtaking scenery. Tourist offices are invaluable for providing local information and advice about where to stay. The main branches are listed opposite *(see also* Where to Stay *p192)*. The pace of life in Provence is very relaxed, with no trade between noon and 3pm. So be patient, and note their old maxim: "Slow in the mornings, and not too fast in the afternoons."

Enjoying the beach in Nice

WHEN TO GO

DURING HIGH SEASON in Provence, local businesses in tourist areas can make their whole year's profit. Along the coastal roads, camp sites, restaurants and hotels may be crowded, and prices can rise by as much as 30 per cent. French school holidays run from the first week in July to the first week in September. To avoid the crowds, head for the hills of the Var and Vaucluse or the wilds of upper Provence.

Provence is at its best in May and September, when the weather is still hot, but crowds are at their smallest. Flowers bloom in May, and grapes are harvested in September. The winter months can also offer some stunning sunny days, but beware of the bitterly cold Mistral wind that can mercilessly sweep

the region. Skiing is possible between mid-November and the start of April *(see p96).*

Most attractions stay open all year, although hours may shorten out of season. Many towns time their festivals in order to attract off-season tourists – from the Nice carnival to the Lemon festival in Menton.

TOURIST INFORMATION

MOST BIG TOWNS have either a *Syndicat d'initiative* or an *Office du Tourisme*, while in smaller villages, the town hall provides details. Tourist offices will supply free maps, accommodation information (which can include booking hotels) and festival timings. You can also obtain details in advance from French government tourist offices before leaving your own country.

OPENING TIMES

THIS GUIDE SHOWS opening times for each of the sights listed. Most businesses open from 8 or 9am until noon, and from 2 or 3pm until 6pm. Banks are open from 8:30am–noon and 1:30–4:30pm, Monday to Friday. The lunch break is sacred throughout the region, although larger department stores, supermarkets, tourist offices and some sights may remain open all the time.

Restaurants are generally closed for one day a week, which is normally Monday.

Off season, much of seaside Provence closes down. Be sure to telephone ahead to check what is open, as many hotels and restaurants may shut for several months of the year. Transport services may also be restricted out of season.

Tourist information office at Villecroze

Entertainment at Avignon festival

SIGHTSEEING

IN FRANCE, MANY museums close for lunch – normal opening hours are from 9am until noon and from 2pm until 5:30pm. They usually close for one day each week, national museums closing on Mondays and municipal museums on Tuesdays. Many museums also close throughout the month of November. Opening hours tend to vary according to season. Generally, museums are open for longer hours from May to September.

Museum admission charges range from F10 to F40. Passes for more than one museum or monument tend to be relatively rare items.

Provençal museum tickets

Normally, you will need to buy separate tickets for each sight within a town. One of the few exceptions to this rule is Arles, which offers a discounted pass allowing entry to the majority of its museums. There are usually some discounts available for students who have ISIC cards, and for anyone aged under 18 and over 65. Most museums offer free or discounted entry for everyone on Sundays.

While churches normally offer free admission, small charges may be levied for those who wish to visit cloisters and chapels.

DISABLED ACCESS

THE NATURE OF Provence's old, narrow streets and ancient architecture can make it a difficult area for disabled travellers to get around. Wheelchair access is often limited and many hotels and restaurants are poorly equipped. But the newer museums offer special services and facilities for disabled visitors. For more information about facilities before departure, contact:

Marseille
Service Municipal pour Handicapés et Inadaptés,128 avenue du Prado.
🕻 04 91 81 58 80.

Nice
Association HORUS (Society for the Blind), 31 bd Stalingrad.
🕻 04 93 89 77 75.
GIHP (Physically Handicapped).
🕻 04 93 26 44 24.

Paris
Comité National Français de liaison pour la Réadaptation des Handicapés 236 bis rue Tolbiac, Paris 75013.
🕻 01 53 80 66 66.

ENTERTAINMENT INFORMATION

THERE ARE SEVERAL sources of entertainment information in Provence. The large English-speaking community has its own radio station and newspaper. Riviera Radio, which broadcasts from Monte-Carlo in English, is a mini-BBC for the south of France, found on 106.3 FM and 106.5 FM. The *Riviera Reporter* is a monthly English-language newspaper which contains information on local issues and events. Local French papers can also provide details of festivals, sporting events and the weather. *Le Provençal* serves western Provence, and *Nice Matin* and its derivatives cover eastern Provence. Some cities have their own publications listing events, such as Taktik in Marseille. Tourist offices usually provide this informantion **Sign for a** too. Some tobacconists **tobacconist** or *tabacs*, sell newspapers and magazines.

Personal Security and Health

O N THE WHOLE, Provence is a safe place for visitors. As in all Mediterranean countries it is necessary to take precautions, especially in the larger cities. Extra caution is required along the Côte d'Azur, especially in Nice, which has a higher crime rate than Marseille. Rural areas, however, are usually very safe. Car crime is prevalent along the coast – so never leave valuables in a vehicle. In Nice and Marseille, it is wise to avoid bands of innocent-looking children who may in fact be skilled in the art of pickpocketing. Consular offices can be a good source of help in an emergency *(see p231)*.

Policeman   Fireman

PERSONAL PROPERTY

T AKE GREAT CARE of your personal property at all times. In big cities, try not to carry valuables with you. You should always make sure you are covered by adequate insurance. Choose travellers' cheques as the safest form of money.

Pickpockets are a problem in the tourist meccas of the Côte d'Azur and in towns such as Avignon and Marseille. In Nice, bag snatching is becoming a threat (more so than in Marseille), but mugging is still far from common. Try not to park your car in remote areas, and use underground or covered car parking where possible. In towns,

the multi-storey car parks are kept under surveillance by video cameras. Parking there will remove the risk of being towed away to a police pound, which is a greater everyday threat than most car crime.

Avoid taking valuables to the beach, or keep them with you. It is not advisable to sleep on beaches: robberies and attacks have been known to occur.

In the event of a theft, go to the nearest police station, or *gendarmerie*, taking identity papers (and vehicle papers, if relevant). The report process (a *PV* or *procès-verbal*) may

Ambulance

Fire engine

Police car

take time, but you will need a police statement for any insurance claim. If your passport is stolen, contact the police and your nearest consulate.

PERSONAL SAFETY

A NY CRIMINAL INCIDENT, however minor, is distressing to deal with. Some train routes, for example the Marseille–Barcelona line and also the Marseille–Ventimiglia, have dubious reputations. Keep the compartment door closed and valuables close to you. Vehicles have been reported vandalized on motorail trains.

In recent summers, road pirates have operated, ramming tourist cars on motorways to make them stop. There are police stations at almost all of the motorway exits. If in trouble, keep on until the next exit.

LEGAL ASSISTANCE

I F YOUR insurance policy is comprehensive, including a service in France such as Europ Assistance or Mondial Assistance, they will be able to help with legal advice on claims, such as accident procedure. If not, you should call your nearest consulate office.

INTERPRETERS

I F YOU ARE in a situation that requires an interpreter, contact **Société Française des Traducteurs Professionels** via Minitel *(see p235)*.

OUTDOOR HAZARDS

FOREST FIRES are a major risk in Provence. Every summer thousands of hectares are destroyed in this way. High winds and dry forests mean fire spreads rapidly, so be vigilant with cigarette butts. Camp fires are banned in the region. If you do witness a fire, contact the emergency services at once and keep well away: fire direction can change in an instant.

The Mediterranean is safe for swimming, although currents can be strong off Cap d'Antibes and the Camargue. Pollution is a minor problem around some of the major ports, although some beaches display European blue flags as a sign of cleanliness.

Fire hazard poster

If you go out walking in the mountains, beware that weather conditions can change very quickly. In winter, it is best to advise local authorities of your projected route. In summer, pack warm clothes and some provisions in case of sudden storms. Altitude sickness can occur in the southern Alps, so go up slowly, pausing regularly to acclimatize.

In the mountains behind Nice and Cannes, you may see a plain, grey-brown Montpellier snake. Despite its size (it grows to around 1.5 m/5 ft), it is very shy and will probably flee. Vipers also live in the region.

During the hunting season – from September to February, particularly Sundays – dress in brightly-coloured clothes when out walking. Signs on trees usually denote hunting areas.

MEDICAL TREATMENT

ALL EUROPEAN UNION nationals are entitled to French Social Security coverage, but treatment must be paid for in cash and hospital rates can vary. Reimbursements may be received if you have obtained an E111 form from post offices in the UK before travel. The process for claims is long and complicated, so it is best to purchase your own insurance.

French pharmacists can diagnose health problems and suggest appropriate treatments. They can be recognized by the green cross outside.

PUBLIC TOILETS IN PROVENCE

Modern automatic toilets are now found in many towns in Provence. Do not let children under 10 use these on their own as the automatic cleaning function can be dangerous. The best alternative is to use the toilets in the cafés or restaurants where you are a customer, or go to a large department store. Traditional *pissoirs* and keyhole toilets, still found in more rural areas, are not always very clean. Toilet facilities are provided on the *autoroute* at drive-in rest areas every 20 km (12 miles).

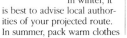

1 Put the amount indicated in the slot.

2 Press the button to open sliding door.

3 The light shows vacant or engaged.

DIRECTORY

EMERGENCY NUMBERS

Centre Anti-Poison (Marseille)
  04 91 75 25 25.

Fire (Sapeurs Pompiers)
  18.

Police (Gendarmerie)
  17.

Ambulance (SAMU)
  15.

TRANSLATION SERVICES

Société Française des Traducteurs Professionels
  Minitel 3615 SFT.

HOSPITAL EMERGENCIES

Avignon
Hôpital de la Durance,
305 rue Raoul Follereau.
  04 90 80 33 33.

Marseille
La Conception,
147 boulevard Baille.
  04 91 38 30 00.

Nice
Hôpital St-Roch,
5 rue Pierre-Devoluy.
  04 92 03 77 77.

CONSULATES

Australia
4 rue Jean Rey, 75015 Paris.
  01 40 59 33 00.

Ireland
Boulevard John Kennedy,
Antibes.
  04 93 61 50 63.

UK
24 avenue du Prado,
Marseille.
  04 91 15 72 10.

USA
12 boulevard Paul Peytral,
Marseille.
  04 91 54 92 00.

31 rue Maréchal Joffre, Nice.
  04 93 88 89 55.

Banking and Local Currency

I N PROVENCE, AS ELSEWHERE in France, the banks usually offer the best rates of exchange, along with American Express and Thomas Cook. Privately-owned *bureaux de change* are common in tourist areas, especially along the coast, but tend to have more variable rates. Take care to check the commission and minimum charges before completing a transaction. Travellers' cheques are the safest form of money. Credit cards can be used to draw money from automatic teller machines, but check the charges levied by your credit card company for this service.

CHANGE
CAMBIO-WECHSEL

Bureau de change sign

BANKING HOURS

B ANKS IN BIG TOWNS usually open from 8:30am–noon and from 1:30–4:30pm, Monday to Friday. Over public holiday weekends, they are often closed from Friday noon until Tuesday morning.

USING BANKS

T HERE IS NO LIMIT to the amount of money you may bring into France, but if you want to take back more than F50,000 to the UK, you should declare it on arrival. Most banks have a *bureau de change*, offering the best rates but also charging commission. Even in remoter areas, many banks now have automatic teller machines that take cards in the Visa/Carte Bleue or Eurocard/Mastercard groups. To take out money, you need to tap in a PIN code. Instructions are given in French, English and German. ATMs may run out of notes before the weekend. You can withdraw up to F2,000 a day on Visa at the foreign counter of any bank that displays the Visa sign. You will need your passport. Eurocheques, which are written in local currency for the exact amount of a purchase up to F1,400, are being phased out by many banks so do not rely on them as your sole source of funds.

TRAVELLERS' CHEQUES AND CREDIT CARDS

T RAVELLERS' CHEQUES can be obtained from American Express, Thomas Cook or your bank. American Express cheques are widely accepted in France, and if they are exchanged at an Amex office no commission is charged.

The most common credit cards in France, accepted even at motorway tolls, are Carte Bleue/Visa and Eurocard/Mastercard. Many Provençal businesses do not accept the American Express card.

French credit cards are now "smart cards", meaning they contain a microchip capable of storing data – the *puce*. Retailers have machines which read both new smart cards and older magnetic strips. If your conventional card cannot be read in the smart card slot, you will be told you have a *puce morte*. Persuade the cashier to swipe the card through the magnetic reader *(bande magnétique)*. You may also have to tap in your PIN code and press the green key *(validez)* on a small keypad.

THE EURO

T HE EURO BECAME legal tender in 11 European Union countries including France on 1 January 1999. Only paper or electronic transactions may be made in Euros until 1 Jan 2002, as notes and coins will not come into circulation until then. From that date, national currencies will be completely replaced by the Euro, which can then be used in any of the 11 Member States.

Eurocheque logo

DIRECTORY

BUREAUX DE CHANGE

Cannes
Office Provençal, 17 av Maréchal Foch. [C 04 93 39 34 37.

Marseille
Change de la Canebière, 39 la Canebière. [C 04 91 13 71 26.

Monaco
Compagnie Monégasque de Change, av Quarantaine.
[C (00 377) 93 25 02 50.

Nice
Office Provençal, 64 av Jean Médecin. [C 04 93 13 45 44.

FOREIGN BANKS

Cannes
American Express
8 rue des Belges. [C 04 93 38 15 87.

Barclays
8 rue Frédéric Amoutetti.
[C 04 92 99 68 00.

Lloyds
130 rue d'Antibes.
[C 04 92 98 35 00.

Marseille
American Express
39 la Canebière. [C 04 91 13 71 21.

Barclays
34 la Canebière. [C 04 91 13 61 61.

Monaco
American Express
35 bd Princesse Charlotte.
[C (00 377) 93 25 74 45.

Barclays
31 av de la Costa.
[fi (00 377) 93 15 35 35.

Lloyds
11 bd des Moulins.
[C (00 377) 92 16 58 58.

Nice
American Express
11 promenade des Anglais.
[C 04 93 16 53 46.

Barclays
2 rue Alphonse Karr.
[C 04 93 82 68 09.

LOST CARDS AND TRAVELLERS' CHEQUES

Visa/Mastercard/Carte Bleue.
[C 02 54 42 12 12.
American Express (Cards)
[fi 01 47 77 72 00.
American Express (Cheques)
Freecall [C 0800 90 86 00 (from France only).

CURRENCY

THE OUTGOING FRENCH UNIT of currency is the franc. It is generally indicated by the letter F or by FF, to distinguish it from the Belgian or Swiss franc, written BEF and FS respectively.

The franc sign appears either before or after the amount. There are 100 centimes to the franc, but their value is so insignificant that 1-centime coins are no longer in circulation.

Bank Notes
French bank notes come in the denominations F20, F50, F100, F200 and F500. They increase in size in proportion to their value.

F500 note

F200 note

F100 note

F50 note

F20 note

F20

F10

F5

F2

F1

50 centimes

20 centimes

10 centimes

5 centimes

Coins
Coins (shown here actual size) come in the following denominations: 5, 10, 20 and 50 centimes; F1, F2, F5, F10 and F20. The 5-, 10- and 20-centime coins are brass. The 50-centime, F1, F2 and F5 coins are silver-alloy.

Communications

Sign for public telephone

FRENCH TELECOMMUNICATIONS are among the most advanced in the world. The national agency is called France Télécom, while postal services are run by La Poste. Public telephones are relatively widespread throughout Provence. Most take a telephone card *(télécarte)* which can be purchased at local shops. Post offices, or *bureaux de postes*, are identified by the blue-on-yellow La Poste sign. La Poste was formerly known as the PTT, so road signs may indicate PTT. Foreign newspapers are available in most large towns, and an English-language radio station and newspaper operate on the Côte d'Azur.

Mail boxes throughout France are a distinctive yellow

USING A PHONECARD TELEPHONE

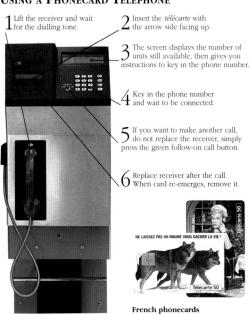

1 Lift the receiver and wait for the dialling tone.

2 Insert the *télécarte* with the arrow side facing up.

3 The screen displays the number of units still available, then gives you instructions to key in the phone number.

4 Key in the phone number and wait to be connected.

5 If you want to make another call, do not replace the receiver, simply press the green follow-on call button.

6 Replace receiver after the call. When card re-emerges, remove it.

French phonecards

TELEPHONING IN FRANCE

NEARLY ALL FRENCH public phone boxes now take telephone cards *(télécartes)*. A few also take F1, F2, F5 and F10 coins. Telephone cards are sold in units of either 50 or 120 and can be purchased at both post offices and *tabacs* (tobacconists) and at some newsagents. Pay-phones in cafés are coin-operated and take a minimum of F2.

Home Direct calling service, or *pays direct*, lets you make the call via an operator in your country, paying with a telephone chargecard, credit card or by reversing charges. In some cases, you can also call a third country (with AT & T, for example). Reverse charge calls are known as PCV. Most phone boxes can receive incoming calls – the box telephone number is displayed above the telephone unit. Main post offices offer long distance calling facilities from booths *(cabines)*. You then pay at the cashier. This is much cheaper than hotels for international calls – hotels tend to add a large surcharge. The Minitel electronic telephone directory can be used free in post offices *(see* How to Key in to Minitel*)*.

SENDING A LETTER

POSTAGE STAMPS *(timbres)* are sold singly or in *carnets* of ten. Common postage stamps are also sold at *tabacs*.

Post office hours vary. The minimum hours are around 9am to 5pm from Monday to Friday with a two-hour lunch break from noon to 2pm. On Saturdays they are open from 9am until noon. In some larger towns, the main post office may remain open every weekday from 8am until 7pm.

Letters and parcels can be sent worldwide (although delivery times may take longer than you are used to). Letters are dropped into yellow mail boxes which often have three slots – one for the town you are in; one for the surrounding *département* (Provence is divided into five *départements*, listed under *Postcodes*, right); and one for other destinations *(autres destinations)*.

For a small collection fee you can also receive or send mail care of post offices in France *(poste restante)*. The sender should write the recipient's name in block letters, followed by "Poste Restante", then the postcode and the name of the town to which it is to be sent.

Standard issue stamps and a small book of stamps called a *carnet*

Postcodes

ALL FRENCH ADDRESSES have five-digit postcodes. The first two digits represent the region's *département*. If 000 follows, this indicates the main town. The last two digits of the Marseille postcodes indicate the city's *arrondissements*.

Département Codes

Alpes-de-Haute-Provence	04
Alpes Maritimes	06
Bouches-du-Rhône	13
Var	83
Vaucluse	84

Other Services

AT POST OFFICES you can also consult the telephone directories *(annuaires)*, buy phonecards, send or receive money orders *(mandats)* and telephone all over the world. You can also make use of the fax and telex services. A huge amount of information is available when you use the Minitel electronic directory, which is rapidly re- placing paper directories. This can be used free of charge at many post offices.

Foreign Newspapers

ENGLISH LANGUAGE papers which can be bought on the day of publication are the *Financial Times*, the *Guardian* and the *International Herald Tribune*, with its digest of North American news and sport. In Nice, English newspapers such as *The Times*, the *Daily Telegraph* and the *Daily Mail* are often available for sale on the same day at the airport. Most other English newspapers as well as Swiss,

Useful Dialling Codes

- All Provence numbers start with 04. Ile de France is 01; the northwest is 02; the northeast 03; and the southwest 05.
- All Monaco numbers are prefixed 00 377 when calling from outside the Principality.
- For **operator service**, dial 13.
- For **Home Direct**, dial 0800 99, wait for tone, then dial 00.
- To make direct **international calls**, dial 00 first.
- The **country codes** for the following are: Australia: 61; Canada and USA: 1; Eire: 353; New Zealand: 64; UK: 44. Always omit the initial 0 of the country's area code.
- For all **telegrams**, dial 3655.

Italian, German and Spanish titles, are sold the day after issue. The *European* newspaper is published on Fridays.

The English-speaking population of Provence has its own radio station and newspaper which provides local information. (See *Entertainment Information*, p229).

A range of newspapers available in Provence

Television and Radio

THE SUBSCRIPTION channel Canal+ broadcasts ABC American evening news at 7am daily. Sky News and CNN are available in many hotels. The Franco-German channel ARTE broadcasts programmes

and films from all over the world, often in the original language with French subtitles. Listings indicate *vo* or *vf (version originale, version française)* for non-French films.

Riviera Radio broadcasts in English throughout the South of France on 106.3 and 106.5 FM stereo from Monte-Carlo. It offers news in English from the BBC and 24-hour music and current affairs, which includes BBC World Service programmes. *France Musique* is France's round-the-clock classical music station (92.2 FM in Nice and 94.7 in Marseille). *France Info* is a national rolling news station (105.2–105.8 FM).

English-Language Bookshops

Aix-en-Provence
Paradox, 15 rue du 4 Septembre.
📞 04 42 26 47 99.

Cannes
Cannes English Bookshop,
11 rue Bivouac Napoléon.
📞 04 93 99 40 08.

Marseille
Fuéri-Lamy, 26 rue Paradis.
📞 04 91 33 57 91.

Monaco
Scruples, 9 rue Princesse Caroline.
📞 (00 377) 93 50 43 52.

Nice
The Cat's Whiskers, 30 rue Lamartine.
📞 04 93 80 02 66.

Villeneuve-lès-Avignon
Centre Franco-Américain de Provence,
10 montée de la Tour.
📞 04 90 25 93 23.

How to Key in to Minitel

Minitel provides a vast range of services through a screen and keyboard connected to the telephone line. To use the system, press the telephone symbol and enter the Minitel number and code. For directory information, press the telephone symbol and key in 11. When beeping starts, press *Connexion/Fin*. Specify the service or name of supplier required. Enter town or area and press *Envoi* to start. To disconnect, press *Veille* or *Connexion/Fin*. Charges are displayed on the screen.

CUSTOMS AND IMMIGRATION

CURRENTLY THERE are no visa requirements for European Union nationals or for tourists from the United States, Canada, Australia or New Zealand staying in France for under three months. After that, a *carte de séjour* is required. Visitors coming from other countries should ask for visa information from the French authorities in their own country before departure.

TAX-FREE GOODS

IF YOU ARE RESIDENT outside the European Union you can reclaim the sales tax TVA (VAT) that you pay on French goods if you spend more than F1,200 in one shop, obtain a *détaxe* receipt, and take your purchases out of the country within six months. The *détaxe* form should be handed in at customs when leaving the country and the refund will be sent on to you.

Exceptions for *détaxe* rebate are food and drink, medicines, tobacco, cars and motorbikes, though tax can be reimbursed for bicycles bought in France.

DUTY-PAID LIMITS

There are no longer any restrictions on the quantities of duty-paid and VAT-paid goods you are allowed to take from one European Union country to another, as long as they are for your own use and not for resale. You may be asked to prove goods are for your personal use if they exceed the suggested amounts: 10 litres of spirits, 90 litres of wine, 110 litres of beer and 800 cigarettes.

DUTY-FREE LIMITS

FOR TRAVEL WITHIN the EU duty free was abolished in June 1999. For non-EU nationals arriving in the EU the following may be imported: up to 2 litres of wine, and a litre of sprits or 2 litres of drink less than 22˚ proof; 50g of perfume; 500g of coffee; 100g of tea; and up to 200 cigarettes. Visitors

under 17 may not import or export duty-free tobacco or alcohol, even as gifts.

COUNTERFEITS

IT IS ILLEGAL to import, export or even to possess certain counterfeit goods in France.

Locally purchased regional wine, on which duty has been paid

IMPORTING OTHER GOODS

IN GENERAL, personal goods (such as a car or a bicycle) may be imported to France duty-free and without any paperwork as long as they are obviously for personal use and not for resale. The brochure called *Bon Voyages* clarifies this and is available from the

Paris perfumes, available tax-free

Centre des Renseignements des Douanes. Customs offices can also give advice and information, although it is likely to be in French. Special rules apply, both within and without the EU, for the import and export of plants, animals, art objects, medicines and weapons. Consult your own, or French, customs.

ETIQUETTE

IN ALL YOUR dealings with customs, in duty-free shops, and in businesses outside the airport, remember: the people of Provence are traditionally welcoming but the French rituals of politeness apply in Provence more than anywhere. When introduced to someone, it is correct to shake hands. In shops, be prepared to say *bonjour* before asking what you want, then *merci* when you receive your change and *au revoir, bonne journée* when you depart. The usual greeting among friends of either sex is generally two or three kisses on the cheek.

While the larger tourist resorts can appear to be impersonal, in the smaller communities, any efforts by English speakers to make enthusiastic use of their French and to show a real interest in the area will be met with encouragement.

Student travellers and locals converse in the Old Town of Nice

STUDENT INFORMATION

International Student Identity Card

STUDENTS WITH a valid International Student Identification Card (ISIC card) benefit from discounts of between 25 and 50 per cent at museums, theatres, cinemas and at many of the public monuments when you produce the card. The region's principal university is Aix-en-Provence/Marseille, and the campuses are shared between the two cities. Other large universities are located in Avignon and Nice. The BIJ and CIJ (the Bureau Information Jeunesse/Centre Information Jeunesse) in each town both provide a great deal of information about student life, and contain a list of inexpensive accommodation.

PROVENCE TIME

PROVENCE is one hour ahead of Greenwich Mean Time (GMT). It is in the same time zone as Italy, Spain and other western European countries. There are some standard time differences between Provence and other major cities of the world, which can vary according to local summer alterations to the time. These changes are as follows: for London: minus 1 hour from GMT; New York: minus 6 hours; Dallas: minus 7 hours; Los Angeles: minus 9 hours; Perth: plus 7 hours; Sydney: plus 9 hours; Auckland: plus 11 hours; and Tokyo: plus 8 hours.

The French use the 24-hour military clock (am and pm are not used): after midday, just continue counting 13, 14 and so on to provide the 24-hour clock time. For example, 1pm = 13:00.

ELECTRICAL ADAPTORS

THE VOLTAGE in France is 220 volts. Plugs have two small round pins; the heavier-duty installations have two large round pins. Some of the upmarket hotels offer built-in adaptors – for shavers only. Multi-adaptors, useful because they have both large and small pins, can be bought at most airports before departure, and standard adaptors purchased from department stores.

French two-pin electrical plug

RELIGIOUS SERVICES

PROVENCE is a strong Catholic region, with many religious festivals and services dating back 500 years. Immigrants have brought religious diversification. Regular services in English are held at the Anglican churches in Nice and Marseille.

CONVERSION CHART

Imperial to metric
1 inch = 2.54 centimetres
1 foot = 30 centimetres
1 mile = 1.6 kilometres
1 ounce = 28 grams
1 pound = 454 grams
1 pint = 0.6 litre
1 gallon = 4.6 litres

Metric to imperial
1 millimetre = 0.04 inch
1 centimetre = 0.4 inch
1 metre = 3 feet 3 inches
1 kilometre = 0.6 mile
1 gram = 0.04 ounce
1 kilogram = 2.2 pounds
1 litre = 1.8 pints

DIRECTORY

CUSTOMS INFORMATION

Centre des Renseignements des Douanes
84 rue d'Hauteville,
75498 Paris Cedex 10..
📞 01 53 24 68 24.

Nice
18 rue Tonduti de l'Escarène.
📞 04 93 13 78 13.

Marseille
48 bd Schuman.
📞 04 91 14 14 91.

STUDENT INFORMATION

Aix-en-Provence
BIJ, 37 bis bd Aristide-Briand.
📞 04 42 23 18 45.

Marseille
CIJ, 96 la Canebière.
📞 04 91 24 33 50.

Nice
CIJ, 19 rue Gioffredo.
📞 04 93 80 93 93.

YOUTH HOSTELS

Aix
3 av Marcel Pagnol,
Jas de Bouffan.
📞 04 42 20 15 99.

Avignon
(Villeneuve-lès-Avignon)
7 bis chemin de la Justice.
📞 04 90 25 46 20.

Marseille
Château de Bois-Luzy,
allée des primevères.
📞 04 91 49 06 18.

Quartier Bonneveine,
impasse du Dr Bonfils.
📞 04 91 73 21 81.

Nice
Mt Alban, route Forestière
du Mt Alban.
📞 04 93 89 23 64.

Clairvallon, 26 av Scudéri.
📞 04 93 81 27 63.

Espace Magnan
(groups of at least 20 in winter) 31 rue Louis-de-Coppet.
📞 04 93 86 28 75.

PLACES OF WORSHIP

Catholic
Cathédrale Sainte-Réparate
Pl Rossetti,
Nice.
📞 04 93 62 34 40.

Basilique Notre-Dame de la Garde
pl Colonel Eden,
Marseille.
📞 04 91 13 40 80.

Anglican
Nice Anglican Church
57 rue de Buffa,
Nice.
📞 04 93 87 19 83.

Eglise Anglicane de Marseille
18 rue Jeune Anacharsis,
Marseille.
📞 04 91 55 57 38.

Jewish
Grande Synagogue
7 rue G Deloye,
Nice.
📞 04 93 92 11 38.

Temple Israëlite de Sainte Marguerite (Algerian)
205 bd Ste Marguerite,
Marseille.
📞 04 91 75 63 50.

Islamic
Mosque de la Capelette
68 rue Alfred Kertel,
Marseille.
📞 04 91 25 95 57.

TRAVEL INFORMATION

SITUATED AT THE CROSSROADS between France, Spain and Italy, Provence is well served by international motorway and rail links. Nice airport is the most modern and the busiest of French airports outside Paris, handling 4 million visitors annually. Marseille airport also welcomes daily direct flights from major European cities, as well as weekly direct flights from New York. For travelling across France, the TGV train is swift *(see p240),* while the motorail journey from channel ports takes 12 hours but is effortless and dispenses with motorway tolls. The motorways are excellent, but can become crowded in mid-summer.

Air France Boeing 737

ARRIVING BY AIR

THE TWO MAIN AIRPORTS in Provence are comfortably modern – Marseille, Marignane, and Nice, Côte d'Azur, which has recently enjoyed a face-lift. **Marseille Provence** has two terminals with national and international flights. It serves mainly business travellers and is more expensive to fly to, but is handy for destinations that are right in the centre of Provence, such as Avignon and Aix-en-Provence.

Airport taxis to the centre of Marseille cost around F235 (F285 at night and on Sundays). There is also an airport bus to the main train station in Marseille (St-Charles) every 20 minutes. Car hire companies at the airport include Avis, Budget, Citer, Ada, Europcar and Hertz.

Airport trolley slot machine

Nice, Côte d'Azur has two terminals. The east terminal (one) takes international flights, Air Littoral and TAT, while the west terminal (two) serves domestic flights only. Taxis to the centre cost F120–F140. Airport buses run to the Gare Routière station every 10 minutes, and bus No. 23 goes to Gare SNCF every 10 minutes. There are hourly buses to Cannes and buses every 90 minutes to Monaco and Menton. Heli-Inter offers helicopter transits every 20 minutes to Monte-Carlo, and several times a day to St-Tropez during the summer. The car hire companies at Nice airport include Ada, Avis, Budget, Europcar and Hertz.

Other Provençal airports with some international flights include Montpellier, Nîmes and Toulon.

AIRPORT INFORMATION

Avignon
☎ 04 90 81 51 15.
Airport to city 10 km (6 miles).
Taxi F120.

Marseille Provence
☎ 04 42 14 14 14.
Airport to city 25 km (17 miles).
Shuttle bus F46, taxi F250.

Montpellier Mediterranée
☎ 04 67 20 85 00.
Airport to city 7 km (4 miles).
Shuttle bus F30, taxi F80–100.

Nice, Côte d'Azur
☎ 04 93 21 30 12.
Airport to city 6 km (4 miles).
Shuttle bus F22, taxi F130.

Nîmes/Arles/Camargue
☎ 04 66 70 06 88.
Airport to city 8 km (5 miles).
Shuttle bus F28, taxi F130.

Toulon
☎ 04 94 00 83 83.
Airport to city 18 km (11 miles).
Shuttle bus F55, taxi F250.

The main international terminal at Nice, Côte d'Azur airport

AIRLINE DETAILS

PROVENCE is perhaps the most easily accessible place by air in France after Paris. The vast majority of large European cities have direct daily flights. The British carriers – British Airways, Air UK, Easyjet and British Midland – all run daily flights that depart for Nice from London Heathrow, London Gatwick or Luton. The French national airline, Air France, has daily flights to and from Nice to Britain, Spain, Germany, Italy (via Lyon), North Africa and the Middle East (via Paris). Air Liberté (part of BA) and AOM operate frequent flights between Paris and Provence.

There is a daily Delta flight scheduled from Nice to New York and also from New York to Nice (Apr–Oct).

From all other international departure points it is necessary to change planes in Paris to reach Provence. There are no direct flights from New Zealand, but Lufthansa has flights from most major French cities, via Frankfurt, to Auckland.

AIRLINE TELEPHONE NUMBERS

For France dialling codes see p235.

Air Canada
Paris (01 44 50 20 20.

Air France
(08 02 80 28 02.

Air UK
Reservations: Paris
(01 44 56 18 18.

AOM
(08 03 00 12 34.

British Airways
France (0802 802 902.
UK (0345-222 111.
US (1-800-AIRWAYS.

British Midland
Paris (01 48 72 55 65.
Nice (04 41 91 87 04.

Delta
Paris (01 47 68 92 92.
Freecall (US) (0800 35 40 80.

Easyjet
Nice (04 93 21 30 12.
UK (01582-702900.

Departure hall at Marseille airport

FARES AND DEALS

AIRLINE FARES to Provence are at their highest over the Easter period and in the peak season in July and August.

For flights only, Apex fares from London Heathrow are relatively inexpensive but they have to be booked well in advance. They cannot be changed or cancelled without a penalty and contain minimum and maximum stay clauses.

There are many flight deals to Nice both out of season and during the summer when the charter companies operate. Look around for the best offers at reputable discount agencies.

DISCOUNT TRAVEL AGENCIES

Aix
Council Travel
12 rue Victor-Leydet. (04 42 38 58 82.

Marseille
Voyages Wasteels
67 la Canebière. (04 95 09 30 20.

UK
Trailfinders
215 Kensington High St, London
W8 6BD.
(0171-937 5400.

US
Council Travel
205 East 42nd Street,
New York, NY 10016.
((212) 661 1450.

Nouvelles Frontières
12 East 33rd Street, New York,
NY 10016.
((212) 779 0609.

FLY-DRIVE AND FLY-RAIL PACKAGE HOLIDAYS

AIR FRANCE and the French railways offer combined fares for flight and train. You fly into Paris and then catch the train south. Good deals are available for the main destinations such as Avignon, Arles and Marseille.

There are also companies offering tailor-made package holidays in Provence, with flight, car hire and accommodation included in the cost.

TAILOR-MADE PACKAGE HOLIDAYS

Allez France Holidays (UK)
27 West St, Storrington RH20 4DZ.
(01903-742345.

Can Be Done Ltd
(for travellers with disabilities)
7–11 Kensington High St,
London W8 5NP.
(020-8907 2400.

Carpe Diem in France (US)
2601 Elliott Ave, Suite 3117, Seattle,
WA 98121.
((888) 374 4637.

FLIGHT TIMES

ON LONG-HAUL flights you will need to change planes in Paris or London. Approximate flight times from major cities are as follows:

London: 1 hour, 55 minutes.
Dublin: 2 hours, 20 minutes.
Toronto: 9 hours.
New York: 8 hours.
Sydney: 26 hours.

Getting Around by Train

SNCF logo

TRAVELLING TO PROVENCE by train is fast and efficient. The French state railway, Société Nationale des Chemins de Fer (**SNCF**), is one of Europe's best equipped and most comfortable. The train journey from Paris to Avignon is almost as quick as by air – the TGV (Train à Grande Vitesse) takes only 4 hours. With the channel tunnel (chunnel) open, travel to Provence from the UK is faster than before, though much of this route is not high speed.

MAIN ROUTES

THE MAIN TRAIN routes to Provence from Northern Europe pass through Lille and Paris. In Paris you may have to transfer to the Gare de Lyon – the main Paris station serving the south of France. Tickets from London to Nice, Avignon and Marseille, on the chunnel, hovercraft or ferry, are all available from the **Rail Europe** office in London. The chunnel connects at Lille with TGVs to the rest of France. For sea passengers, there is a daily direct sleeper from Calais to Nice.

From southern Europe, trains run to Marseille from Barcelona in Spain (6½ hours) and Genoa in Italy (3 hours).

Within Provence and the Côte d'Azur, the coastal route between Nice and Marseille is often crowded, so it is best to reserve tickets in advance on this and other *Grandes Lignes*. In the Var and Haute Provence, railway lines are scarce, but SNCF run bus services. The private rail service **Chemins**

de Fer de Provence runs the Train des Pignes *(see p181)*, a 151-km (90-mile) ride from Nice, through the scenic Var valley to Digne-les-Bains.

BOOKING FROM ABROAD

BOOKINGS BY POST, telephone or fax for all tickets to and within France can be made in the UK and US through Rail Europe. Rail Europe will also give information on prices and departure times. Reservations made abroad can be difficult to change once you are in France – you may have to pay for another reservation, or claim a refund on your return.

BOOKING IN FRANCE

TICKET COUNTERS at all the stations are computerized. There are also automatic ticket and reservation machines (with English instructions) on the concourse of main stations. If you have a credit card with a PIN number, you can check times and fares and make reservations using the Minitel

system *(see p235)*. For travel by TGV, a reservation is compulsory but can be made as little as five minutes before the train leaves. Costs rise considerably at peak times. The new international ticket and reservation system at Lille Europe station is connected by computer to most European travel agents and stations, allowing direct booking on services throughout the continent and the UK.

Automatic ticket machine

FARES AND BOOKING

TGVS HAVE TWO price levels for 2nd class, normal and peak, and a single level for 1st class. The cost of the obligatory seat reservation is included in the ticket price. Tickets for other trains can be subject to a supplement and

The orange TGV to Provence is slowly being replaced by a silver train

THE TGV TRAIN

Trains à Grande Vitesse, or high-speed trains, travel at up to 300 km/hr (185 mph) and can go faster. There are four versions of TGV serving all areas of France and some European destinations. The white and yellow Eurostar runs between Paris, Brussels and London. For Provence, take the train from Paris Gare de Lyon, Grenoble, Geneva or Lausanne. The trains' speed, comfort and reliability make them relatively expensive. You must always reserve a seat in advance.

do not include the 20F reservation charge.

Discounts of 25 per cent are available for people travelling with children (*Découverte Enfant+*), for young people (*Découverte 12–25*), for the over-60s (*Découverte Senior*), for two people travelling together (*Découverte à Deux*), for return trips including a Saturday night (*Découverte Sejour*) and for advance booking (*Découverte J8* and *J30*).

For those spending a bit more time on French railways, the SNCF issues a *Carte Enfant+* and a *Carte Senior* giving reductions of up to 50 per cent.

Rail passes bought outside the country for use in France include Eurodomino tickets which allow three, five or ten days' travel a month (with a reduction for those under 26).Inter-Rail cards allow unlimited travel in European countries excluding the one of issue. Eurail passes are available to non-European residents and, in North America, France Railpass offers yet more permutations.

A high-speed silver TGV or Train à Grande Vitesse

TYPES OF TRAIN

NOT ALL TRAINS in France are TGVs. *Train Rapide National* (TRN), still known as Corail, are less swift, but serve more stations and more routes. *Train Express*

Regional (TER), often only a carriage or two long, serve local routes. The overnight train from London to Nice is a *train auto couchette* (sleeper) service only. You must buy a *couchette* or berth, a fold-down bunk in a compartment of four or six. It is best to keep valuables with you. A compartment with twin berth and private washroom is a more expensive option. Not all trains contain restaurant cars or bars, even on long journeys. Check timetables for details. All TGVs have bars with light meals, and you can reserve an at-seat meal service in advance in first class.

Other services offered by SNCF include reserving a car, bike or hotel room at your station of arrival.

Rail traveller with luggage trolley

TIMES AND PENALTIES

TIMETABLES CHANGE twice yearly and leaflets for main routes are free. The Provence-Alpes-Côte d'Azur region has an all-inclusive Transports Express Régionaux timetable, which includes coach travel.

You must time-punch your ticket in the orange machine at the platform entrance or pay a penalty on the train. Trains in France are very rarely late.

MOTORAIL

MOTORAIL SERVICES carry cars, motorbikes and passengers overnight from Calais, Dieppe, Lille and Paris to Provence. The journey from the channel ports takes 12 hours 30 minutes, and is not cheap, but is a practical, stress-free way to avoid the long drive south and the motorway tolls. The service runs to Avignon, Marseille and Nice and seasonally to Fréjus/St-Raphaël. Debate always reigns on the merits and costs of road versus rail, but ultimately it comes down to personal choice. Information and bookings are available via Rail Europe in London.

DIRECTORY

INFORMATION AND RESERVATIONS

Eurostar
[*01233 617 575.*

Rail Europe
179 Piccadilly, London,
W1V 0BA.
[*0990 848 848.*
FAX *020--7633 9900.*

Rail Europe Inc.
2100 Central Avenue,
Suite 2000, Boulder,
CO 80301.
[*(800) 848 7245.*

Inter-Rail Bookings SNCF
Paris [*08 36 35 35 35.*
Minitel *36 15 SNCF.*

PRIVATE RAILWAY

Chemins de Fer de Provence
[*04 93 88 34 72.*

STATIONS IN PROVENCE

Aix
Reservations:
[*08 36 35 35 35.*

Arles
[*04 90 99 35 23.*

Nîmes
Reservations:
[*08 36 35 35 35.*

Toulon
Reservations:
[*08 36 35 35 35.*

MOTORAIL STATIONS IN PROVENCE

Avignon
[*08 36 35 35 35.*

Fréjus
[*08 36 35 35 35.*

Marseille
[*04 91 08 50 50.*
Reservations:
[*08 36 35 35 35.*

Nice
Reservations:
[*08 36 35 35 35.*

Getting Around by Road

FRANCE IS A MOTORIST'S PARADISE and the main route to Provence is via an excellent, if expensive, autoroute (motorway) network. Provence is ideal for touring, with some of the most beautiful road routes in the world, including the stunning Grande Corniche above Nice, and the hilltop lanes of the Luberon *(see pp170–71).* Popular routes, especially the motorway and coastal roads along the Côte d'Azur, can be busy in high season.

For the truly adventurous, the Route Napoléon leads from Grenoble south across the Alps to Digne, and continues to Grasse. From Grasse, take the scenic D3 then D2210 for Nice and environs, or carry on into Cannes.

Three of the most widely used car rental firms in France

GETTING TO PROVENCE

IF YOU ARE taking your own car to Provence, it is advisable to obtain a green card (a free extension of an existing policy from some insurers). Without it you are covered third party only in France, regardless of whether you have comprehensive cover in your own country. The AA, RAC and Europ Assistance have special policies. It is compulsory to take your car's original registration document, a current insurance certificate and a valid driving licence. A sticker showing the country of registration should be displayed close to the rear number plate. The headlights of right-hand drive cars must be adjusted – kits are available at most ports.

The quickest route south is the Autoroute du Soleil, the A6 motorway from Paris to Lyon, followed by the A7 to Marseille. Travellers from the UK and northern Europe will have difficulty avoiding Paris. Motorways skirt the city centre, leading from the northern A1 to the southern A6. If you can, avoid the Paris rush hour.

From Spain, the A8 motorway leads directly to Marseille and goes on to Nice and Italy.

In high season, the motorways get very crowded and if you have time it may be worth taking some more minor (and attractive) roads. Try turning off the main road at Montélimar to travel to the Luberon via Nyons and Vaison-la-Romaine. Or exit at Avignon, and head into the Luberon and on to Var.

CAR RENTAL

IT IS WORTH contacting a number of car-rental firms before you go, as there are numerous special offers for cars pre-paid in the UK and USA. In France, **Rent A Car** is good value.

Fly-drive options work well for small groups. SNCF offers train and car-rental deals with collection from main stations.

For more than three weeks, the best option is the short-term purchase and buy back service (TT leasing) offered by Citroën, Peugeot and Renault from Nice airport.

USING THE AUTOROUTE TOLL

When you join an autoroute, collect a ticket from the machine. This identifies your starting point on the autoroute. You do not pay until you reach an exit toll. You are charged according to the distance travelled and the type of vehicle used.

Motorway Sign
These signs indicate the name and distance to the next toll booth. They are usually blue and white; some show the tariff rates for cars, motorbikes, trucks and caravans.

Tollbooth with Attendant
When you hand in your ticket at a staffed tollbooth, the attendant will tell you the cost of your journey on the autoroute and the price will be displayed. You can pay with coins, notes, credit cards or with a Eurocheque in French francs. A receipt is issued on request.

Automatic Machine
On reaching the exit toll, insert your ticket into the machine and the price of your journey is displayed in French francs. You can pay either with coins or by credit card. The machine will give change and can issue a receipt.

RULES OF THE ROAD

REMEMBER TO DRIVE on the right. The *priorité à droite* rule applies, meaning that you must give way to any vehicle coming out of a side turning on the right, unless otherwise signposted. However, the *priorité à droite* rule no longer applies at roundabouts, meaning you have to give way to cars already on the roundabout. Flashing headlights mean the driver is claiming right of way.

Seatbelts are compulsory for front and back seats. Overtaking when there is a single solid centre line is heavily penalized.

SPEED LIMITS AND FINES

THE SPEED LIMITS in Provence are as follows:
• **Motorways** 130 km/hr (80 mph)
• **Dual carriageways** 110 km/hr (68 mph); 50 km/hr (30 mph) in towns
• **Other roads** 90 km/hr (56 mph).

Instant fines are issued for speeding and drink-driving.

The A6 from Paris to Lyon is the quickest route south

FAST THROUGH ROUTES

THERE ARE THREE main motorways in Provence: the A7 from Lyon to Marseille, the A9 from Orange to Barcelona, and the A8 from Marseille to Menton. The new A54 cuts across the Camargue from Aix-en-Provence via Arles to Nîmes. The A8 is the most expensive stretch of toll motorway in France, but allows you to drive from Nice to Aix-en-Provence in under two hours.

No entry for any vehicles

Sign indicating one-way system

VOUS N'AVEZ PAS LA PRIORITÉ

Give way at roundabout

Right of way ends, give way to right

COUNTRY ROUTES

ONE OF THE PLEASURES of touring Provence is turning off the main routes onto small country roads. The RN and D *(Route Nationale* and *Départmentale)* roads are a good alternative to motorways. *Bison futée* ("crafty bison") signs indicate alternative routes to avoid heavy traffic, and are especially helpful during the French holiday periods, appropriately known as the *grands départs*. The worst weekends are in mid-July, and at the beginning and end of August when French holidays start and finish.

MAPS

THE BEST GENERAL map of Provence is the Michelin yellow map No. 245, at a scale of 1:200,000. IGN (Institut Géographique National) maps are more detailed. Town plans are usually provided free by local tourist offices. In large towns you may need a more detailed map, published by Michelin or **Plans-Guides Blay**. In the UK, **Stanfords** is famous for its range of maps.

Some of the national and regional maps available

PARKING

Parking in the big towns, particularly along the coast, is strictly regulated. If you are illegally parked, you may be towed away instantly to the police pound to face a fine of up to F1,000. Most Provençal towns now have pay and display machines *(horodateurs)*. Many places offer free parking from noon to 2pm – ticket machines automatically allow for this. Parking is often time limited. Even if you are legally parked, you may find yourself hemmed in when you return: the French usually honk their horns to attract the guilty party.

An *horodateur*, or pay-and-display machine

PETROL

Petrol is relatively expensive in France, especially on autoroutes. Large supermarkets and hypermarkets sell petrol at a discount. A map issued by French Government Tourist offices *(see p229)* indicates the cheaper petrol stations situated up to 2 km (just over a mile) from motorway exits. Unleaded petrol is found in most stations. Diesel is also common and is the cheapest fuel in France, thanks to lobbying by truck drivers. LPG gas is available, often on motorways. A map of locations can be obtained from any LPG station in France.

Mountain bikes are ideal for exploring the Provençal countryside

CYCLING

Cycling is one of the most pleasant ways to see Provence. Although the French are cycling enthusiasts, at the moment there are few cycle lanes in towns in Provence. However, some towns, such as Arles, Avignon and Nîmes, have specified cycle routes. You can take bikes on certain trains – check the timetable first for the bike symbol. You can also hire bicycles at a number of stations. Rental shops are common, especially in the Luberon and in towns around the Camargue, which rent out mountain bikes *(VTT)*. Bicycle theft is common along the Côte d'Azur – make sure you are fully insured before you go.

A taxi meter showing a 14-franc fare, or *prix à payer*

TAXIS

Prices vary from one part of Provence to another. The charges are predictably highest along the Côte d'Azur, where prices of F200 for a 20-minute ride are not uncommon. Elsewhere the pick-up charge is usually around F14, and F3:80 or more for every kilometre.

An extra charge will be made for any luggage. All taxis must use a meter, or a *compteur*. Hailing a taxi is not customary in Provence – you must go to a taxi rank or book by phone.

HITCHHIKING

Hitchhiking is possible in France, although officially it is frowned upon. You are not supposed to hitch on the motorways and if you do will be cautioned by the police. There is a hitchhiking service which puts you in touch with cars heading south from Paris: 🄲 01 53 20 42 42. For region-to-region lifts: 🄲 01 53 20 42 43.

COACH AND BUS TRAVEL

Coach travel used to be the cheapest way of getting to Provence, but reductions in air fares have now made it a less competitive option. The journey time to Nice from London with **Eurolines** takes almost 24 hours, compared to a 2-hour flight. Coaches depart twice a week in the summer from London to St-Raphaël and Nice, and twice a week all year to Avignon and Marseille. **Intercars'** services also leave from Madrid, Spain to Nice, and from Portugal (Porto, Lisbon, Faro) to Nice and Marseille. A 36-hour service departs from Nice and Marseille to Tangiers.

Big towns have a bus station but, otherwise, the bus services are surprisingly limited. SNCF runs bus services in northern Provence, and private companies run along the major motorways between towns and on some minor routes, such as the coastal road between Toulon and St-Tropez *(see also p243)*. Local bus services are notoriously erratic.

Eurolines long-haul coach

Travelling by Boat

There are few more enticing sights than the glittering Mediterranean of the southern Provençal coast. Almost every city along this stretch of water has a port with boats for hire. Ferry and boat companies operating to offshore islands are easy to find, and there are trips to Corsica from Marseille and Nice throughout the year. For water-lovers, **Kuoni** tour operators offer cruises. The other main waterways in Provence are the Rhône and Durance rivers. Houseboat and barge holidays tend to centre on the Rhône and Camargue, and there are a number of Rhône river sightseeing tours.

Sailing out of a rocky inlet on the Provençal coast

MEDITERRANEAN PORTS

Car ferries depart all year round from Marseille and Nice to Corsica (Bastia, Ajaccio and Ile Rousse), operated by **SNCM Ferryterranée**. Summer ferries run from Marseille to Propriano, and from Toulon to Ajaccio, Bastia and Propriano, often crossing overnight. SNCM has one or two weekly sailings from Marseille and Toulon to Sardinia. There are crossings to North Africa every week from Marseille to Tunis or Algiers, and to Oran weekly in high season.

Regular ferries and boats to nearby islands operate from Bandol to the Ile de Bendor; from Tour Fondu to Porquerolles; and from Port d'Hyères and Le Lavandou to Le Levant and Port-Cros.

CRUISES AND RIVER TRIPS

The Mediterranean is famous as a cruise destination, and numerous companies operate on the south coast of France, stopping at St-Tropez, Villefranche and Monaco. **Crown Blue Line** has a good range of boats for hire for a leisurely river trip. Day cruises to the Iles d'Hyères sail from Quai Stalingrad at Toulon.

Some of the smaller, local boats moored in St-Tropez

Le Cygne offers 7-hour trips to Aigues-Mortes, and **La Camargue au Fil de l'Eau** runs daily cruises in a converted *peniche* – a traditional river cargo boat. **Mireio** runs dinner, dance or lunch cruises from Avignon to Arles. Barge or houseboat holidays can be planned and booked by **Rive de France**.

SAILING

The Provençal coastline is hugely popular for sailing. Over 70 ports welcome yachts, and mooring charges vary. The Côte d'Azur ports are particularly expensive. There are boats for hire at almost every city port, and many of the clubs teach sailing.

A privately owned motorboat from Cannes

General Index

Page numbers in **bold** type refer to
main entries.

A

A la Reine Jeanne
　(Aix-en-Provence) 219
Abbaye de Montmajour 143
L'Abbaye de St-Croix
　(Salon-de-Provence) 200
Abbaye de Sénanque 22, **164–5**
Abbaye de Silvacane 43, **147**
Abbaye de St-Michel de Frigolet 130
Abbaye du Thoronet 22, 102, **108**
L'Acchiardo (Nice) 209, **211**
L'Action Enchaînée (Maillol) 64
Actoria Studio (Nice) 225
Addresses, postcodes 235
Aga Khan 50
Agay 124
L'Age de l'Harmonie (Signac) 121
Agoult, Countess of 171
Agrippa, Marcus 132
Aigues-Mortes 23, 42, **134–5**
　restaurants 213
Aiguines
　Gorges du Verdon tour 184
Air Canada 239
Air France 238, 239
Air UK 238–9
Air travel 238–9
Airports 238
Aix-en-Provence 15, 127, 128, **148–9**
　architecture 21
　bookshops 235
　cafés and bars 217
　entertainment 224, 225
　festivals 31
　history 46, 48, 49
　hotels 199
　map 149
　railway station 241
　restaurants 213
　Roman remains 40
　shops 219
　student information 237
　tourist office 229
　travel agencies 239
　youth hostels 237
Albert, Prince of Monaco 91
Albert I, Prince of Monaco 92,
　94
Aldebert, Abbot 71
Allez France Holidays 239
Alpes d'Azur, skiing 96
Alpes-de-Haute-Provence 33, **175–87**
　Exploring Alpes-de-Haute-
　Provence 176–7
　festivals 35
　hotels 201
　restaurants 215
Alpes Maritimes 61–99
　Exploring the Riviera and the Alpes
　Maritimes 62–3
　festivals 34

Alpes Maritimes (cont.)
　hotels 196–7
　restaurants 210–11
Les Alpilles 16, **141**
Alziari (Nice) 219
Les Ambassadeurs (Avignon) 225
Ambulances 230, 231
American Express 232
L'Amiral (Bar-sur-Loup) 210
L'Amiral (Cannes) 217
Anne, St 172
Anne of Austria 134, 172
Annot 187
The Annunciation (Master of Aix)
　47
Ansouis 173
Anthropométrie (Klein) 85
Antibes 62, 72
　hotels 196
Anvers, Matthieu d' 64
AOM 239
Apt 172
Aqueduct, Pont du Gard 131
Aragon, Louis 83
Arcades 19
Les Arcs 107, 206
Les Arcenaulx (Marseille) 214
Architecture 20–23
Arènes d'Arles 225
Les Arènes (Nîmes) 225
Arles 144–6
　airport 238
　cafés and bars 217
　entertainment 225
　Festival Queen 15
　festivals 30, 31, 32
　history 48
　hotels 199
　medieval remains 42
　railway station 241
　restaurants 213
　Roman remains 40, 41
　Street-by-Street map 144–5
L'Arlésienne (Van Gogh) 145
Arnaud brothers 179
Artists 24–5
Arts and crafts 219
Artuby Gorges 105
Association des Paralysés de
　France 192
Association HORUS 229
Assumption Day 31
Atelier Carbonel (Marseille) 219
Atelier de Ségriès (Moustiers-Ste-
　Marie) 219
Au Coq Hôtel (Cogolin) 198
Au Flan Coco (Nîmes) 214, 217
Aubagne 153
Aubanel, Théodore 167, 168
Auberge des Chasseurs
　(Touët-sur-Var) 211
Auberge du Jarrier (Biot) 210
Auberge de la Madone
　(Peillon) 211

Auberge de la Môle (La Môle) 212
Auberge du Port (Cagnes-sur-
　Mer) 210
Auberge Pierrot-Pierette (Menton) 210
L'Auberge Provençale (Antibes) 196
Auberge de Reillane (Reillane) 201
Auberge St-Pierre (St-Pierre-de-
　Tortour) 198–9
Auberge Sarrasin (La Garde-
　Freinet) 212
Auberge des Seigneurs (Vence) 211
Auberge du Vieux Fox (Fox-
　Amphoux) 195, 198
Auer (Nice) 217
Augustus, Emperor 40, 89, 132
　statue of 163
Aundi, Antoine 72
Aups 104
Aurelian Way 111, 124, 125
Auron 96
　entertainment 225
Autoroute (traffic information) 243
Autoroutes 242
Autumn in Provence 32
Avignon 157, 166–9
　airport 238
　cafés and bars 217
　entertainment 224, 225
　festivals 31, 35
　history 49
　hospitals 231
　hotels 200–201
　Papal Avignon 44–5, 58
　railway station 241
　restaurants 214
　shops 219
　Street-by-Street map 166–7
　tourist office 229
　youth hostels 237
Avignon School 25, 46, 130, 167,
　168
Avis 243

B

Bac, Ferdinand 99
Bacon, Francis 223
Bandol 112
　beaches 29
　festivals 33
　wine 206
Bank notes 233
Banks 232
Bar des Oiseaux (Nice) 224
Bar du Soleil (Monaco) 217
Bar-sur-Loup, restaurants 210
Barbarossa 113
Barbentane 130
Barcelonnette 178–9
Barclays Bank 232
Bardot, Brigitte 15, 54, 55, 68, 122
Bargème 44, 105
Bargemon 19, **106**
Barjols 104

Le Baron (St-Tropez) 212
Baroncelli-Javon, Marquis Folco de 138
Le Barroux
    hotels 201
    Tour of the Dentelles 159
Bars 216–17
Le Bastidon 155
Bastille Day 31
Bataille (Marseille) 217
Les-Baux-de-Provence 19, **142–3**
    festivals 33
    hotels 199
    restaurants 213
    wine 207
Baux, Lords of 127, 142
Beaches 28–9
Beaucaire 139
Beaulieu 88
    entertainment 225
    hotels 196
Beaumes-de-Venise
    Tour of the Dentelles 159
Beauvoir, Simone de 75
Beavers 137
Bécaud, Gilbert 218
Béchard (Aix-en-Provence) 217
Beckett, Samuel 76, 169
Bed and breakfast 192, 193
Le Beffroi (Vaison-la-
    Romaine) 194, **133**
Bel-Air (St-Jean-Cap-Ferrat) 217
Bell towers, wrought-iron 21
Belle Epoque 50–51
La Belle Meunière (Nice) 197
Le Bellevue (Bormes-les-
    Mimosas) 195, **198**
Bellot, Jacques 75
Belmondo, Jean-Paul 15
Belsunce, Jean, Bishop of Marseille 49
Ben 54
Benedict XII, Pope 44, 168
Benedict XIII, Anti-Pope 45
Bénézet 166
Bennett, Gordon 88
Le Benvengudo (Les-Baux-de-
    Provence) 199
La Bergerie (Eze) 210
Bernassau 132
Bernhardt, Sarah 162
Bernus, Jacques 164
Berri, Claud 15
Berthier 142
Bertone, Honoré 95
Beuil 64
Bicycles 244
Biot 74
    hotels 196
    restaurants 210
    shops 219
Birds 16–17, **136**
Le Bistro de Roussillon (Roussillon) 215
Bistrot Thiars (Marseille) 217
Bizet, Georges 26
Blacas, Baron 186

Blanc, Isadore 185
Blanqui, Louis-Auguste 64
Le Blitz (Cannes) 225
Blue Line Camargue (Saint-Gilles) 245
Bogarde, Dirk 27
Bokelman, Christian, *Monte-Carlo
    Casino Interior* 50–51
Bollène 158
Bonaparte, Lucien 110
Bonaparte, Princess Pauline 66
Bonaparte family 94
Bonnard, Pierre 24, 78, 85
    Nu Devant la Cheminée 120
    Paysage en Cannet 76
La Bonne Etape (Château-Arnoux)
    201, 209, 215
Bonnieux
    hotels 201
    Tour of the Petit Luberon 170–71
Bookshops 235
Borghese, Cardinal 166
Bories 20, 38–9, **169**
Bormes-les-Mimosas 116–17
    festivals 33
    hotels 198
    restaurants 212
Borsalino 15
Botticelli, Sandro 168
Boucher, François, *L'Obéissance
    Récompensée* 133
Boucherie Milhan (Arles) 217
Bouches-du-Rhône 126–53
    Exploring 128–9
    festivals 34–5
    hotels 199–200
    restaurants 213–14
Boules 13
Le Box (Monaco) 225
Brangwyn, Sir Frank 161
Braque, Georges 73, 75
    Les Oiseaux Noirs 77
    Les Poissons 76
Brassaï 66
La Bravade (St-Tropez) 30
Brayer, Yves 142
Bréa, François 98
Bréa, Louis 72, 94
    Chapelle de la Miséricorde
        altarpiece (Nice) 81
    Crucifixion 25
    Lucéram altarpiece 95
    La Pietà 90
    St-Nicolas 90
    screen in Eglise St-Jean-Baptiste
        (Les Arcs) 107
    La Vièrge au Rosaire 74
Bréa school 25, 65, 89
Breakfast 216
Brecht, Bertolt 112
Breteuil (Marseille) 225
Brignoles 109
British Airways 239
British Midland 239
Broders, Roger 28

Brougham, Lord 68
Bruni, Carla 68
Budget (car rental) 243
Bullfighting 30, 223, 225
    Arles 146
    Méjanes 138
    Nîmes 132
Bulls, Camargue 136
Bureaux de change 232
Burgess, Anthony 27
Burning Bush Triptych (Froment)
    46–7, 148
Buses 238, 243, **244**
Butterflies 16

C

Cadenet 173
Caderousse 164
La Cadière d'Azur
    hotels 198
    restaurants 212
Caesar, Julius 40, 125
    Arc de Triomphe (Orange) 161
    triumphal arch (Glanum) 22
Café des Arts (St-Tropez) 217
Café Carlton (Cannes) 217
Café Napoléon (Nîmes) 217
Café de Paris (Monaco) 217
Le Café de Paris (St-Tropez)
    202, 217
Café de la Place (St-Paul-de-Vence)
    217
Cafés 216–17
Le Cagnard (Cagnes-sur-Mer) 210
Cagnes-sur-Mer 78
    festivals 30
    hotels 196
    restaurants 210
Les Calanques 16, 28, **153**
Calder, Alexander, *Les Renforts* 76
Camargue 52, **136–9**
    airport 238
    beaches 28
    birds 136
    map 136–7
    wildlife 16, 58
La Camargue (Aigues-Mortes) 213
Camargue, Côté Soleil (Ziem) 24
Camoin, Charles
    *Open Window on the Harbour at
        St-Tropez* 119
    *St-Tropez, la Place des Lices et le
        Café des Arts* 120
Campanile 192
Camping 192, **193**
Camping and Caravanning Club
    192
Campus Travel (London) 239
Camus, Albert 27
Canal du Midi 48
Canavesio, Giovanni 74, 95, 97
Can Be Done Ltd 239

Cannes 68–9
  banks and *bureaux de change* 232
  beaches 29
  bookshops 235
  cafés and bars 217
  entertainment 225
  festivals 30, 32
  hotels 196
  railway station 241
  restaurants 210
  tourist office 229
Cannes Film Festival 30, 53, 55, 68
Cantini, Jules 151
Canyon du Verdon 105
Cap d'Antibes 72
  hotels 196
Cap Camarat 117
Cap Ferrat 85
Cap Sicié 28
Capa, Robert 82
Capitole (Nice) 225
Caprais, St 70
Carcès
  Côtes de Provence tour 108
Carlone, Giovanni 85
  La Chute de Phaëton 78
Carlton Inter-Continental (Cannes)
  51, 190, **196**
Carnaval de Nice 33, 34
Carnival 14
Caroline, Princess of Monaco 91
Le Carpaccio (Villefranche) 211
Carpeaux, Jean Baptiste 94
Carpentras 48, 49, **164**
Carracci, Annibale 152
Carry-le-Rouet, restaurants 213
Cars 242–4
  ferries 245
  fly-drive package holidays 239
  Motorail 241
  motorways 242
  Musée de l'Automobiliste
    (Mougins) 66
  parking 230, 244
  petrol 244
  renting 238, 242, 243
  rules of the road 243
  safety 230
  speed limits and fines 243
Carzou, Jean 74, 182
Cascade de Courmes 65
Casinos **223**, 225
  Monaco 50–51, **94**, 225
Cassian, St 151
Cassis 153
  hotels 199
  wine 207
Castellane 176, **186**
  Gorges du Verdon tour 185
Le Castellaras (Fayence) 212
Casteret, Norbert 165
Castles *see* Châteaux and castles
Catherine de' Médici 67
La Caume 141

Cavaillon 14, **170**
  restaurants 214
Caves
  Les Calanques 153
  Grotte Cosquer 38
  Grotte de l'Observatoire (Monaco)
    38, 39, 94
  Grottes de St-Cézaire-sur-Siagne
    64–5
  Grottes Troglodytes (Villecroze)
    104, 105
  Grottes du Vallenot (Roquebrune)
    98
  Le Monde Souterrain de Norbert
    Casteret (Fontaine-de-Vaucluse) 165
  paintings 38
Les Caves du Roi
  (St-Tropez) 225
Cazin, Jean-Charles 117
CEDAC de Cimiez (Nice) 224
Cedonius, St 110
Celts 38, 39
Cental, Baron de 173
Centre Anti-Poison (Marseille) 231
Centre Equestre de la Ville
  de Marseille 225
Centre Inter de Plongée (Nice)
  225
Centre des Renseignements des
  Douanes (Paris) 237
César 85
Cézanne, Paul 24, 50, 104
  Atelier de Cézanne (Aix-en-
    Provence) 149
Chagall, Marc 25
  Chapelle Ste-Roseline mosaic (Les
    Arcs) 107
  grave 75
  Musée Chagall (Nice) 85
  La Vie 76
Chain hotels 192
La Chamade 212
Chambres d'hôte 193
Chanel, Coco 52, 98
Le Chantecler (Nice) 211
Chapels 19
Char, René 26
Charanton, Enguerrand 130
Charlemagne, Emperor 181
Charles II, Count of Provence 110
Charles III, Prince of Monaco 92
Charles V, Emperor 46, 47
Charles V (Titian) 47
Charles IX, King 147
Charles of Anjou 43
Charles the Bald 42
Charles du Maine, Count of
  Provence 46
Chartreuse de la Verne
  Massif des Maures tour 117
Château-Arnoux
  hotels 201
  restaurants 215
Château Eza (Eze) **196**, 217

Le Château de Roussan (St-Rémy-de-
  Provence) 192, 194, **200**
Châteauneuf-du-Pape 13, 155, **164**
  festivals 30
  restaurants 215
  wine 164, 206, 207
Châteaux and castles 18
  Ansouis 173
  Barbentane 23, 130
  Beaucaire 139
  La Citadelle (Sisteron) 178
  de l'Empéri (Salon-de-Provence) 147
  Fort St-André (Villeneuve-lès-
    Avignon) 130
  Gordes 169
  Grimaldi (Cagnes) 78–9
  d'If (Marseille) 152
  Palais des Papes (Avignon) 168
  Tarascon 46, 47, **140**
  Fort de Savoie (Colmars) 180
  Palais du Monaco (Monaco) 94
  Palais Lascaris (Nice) 85
  Roquebrune 98
Chemins de Fer de Provence **181**, 241
Cheques 232
Chéret, Jules 85
Le Cheval Blanc (Nîmes) 200
Chez Betty (Villefranche) 217
Chez Gu et Fils (Aix-en-Provence)
  213
Chez Madie (Marseille) 214
Chez Wayne (Nice) 217
Children
  in hotels 191
  in restaurants 203
La Chimère Câfé
  (Aix-en-Provence) 225
Chorégies d'Orange 31
Christian Etienne (Avignon) 214
Christianity 40, 42
Christmas 14, 33
Churches 237
  admission charges 229
Churchill, Winston 53, 98, 153
La Chute de Phaëton (Carlone) 78
Cians, river 64
Cigarettes, duty-free and duty-paid
  limits 236
Cime de la Bonette 179
Cinema 15, **223**, 225
  Cannes Film Festival 30, 53, 55, 68
Cinéma d'Eté (Monaco) 225
Cinema Utopia (Avignon) 225
Cinémathèque (Nice) 225
Ciriani 146
Cistercians 43, 108, 147, 164–5
Clair Logis (St-Jean-Cap-Ferrat) 197
Classical architecture 23
Classical Provence 48–9
Clemenceau, Georges 107
Clement VI, Pope 44, 45, 168
Clement VII, Anti-Pope 44, 45
Clérissy, Antoine 186
Clews, Henry 124
Climate in Provence 30–33

Clothes, dress code in
  restaurants 203
Club 116 (Marseille) 225
CNFLRH 192
Coaches 243, 244
Cocteau, Jean 53, 78, **99**
  Chapelle St-Pierre (Villefranche) 88
  Musée Jean Cocteau (Menton) 99
  Noce imaginaire 24
Cogolin
  hotels 198
  Massif des Maures tour 117
  shops 219
Coins 233
Colbert, Jean Baptiste 132
Col de la Bonette 17
Colette 27
Les Collettes (Cagnes-sur-Mer) 196
Collobrières
  Massif des Maures tour 116
  restaurants 212
Colmars 180
La Colombe d'Or (St-Paul-de-
  Vence) 203, **211**
Comité National pour la Réadaption
  des Handicapés 229
Communications 234–5
Comps-sur-Artuby 105
Comtat Venaissin 43, 44, 49
Conrad I, Count of Ventimiglia 98
Constantine I, Emperor 144, 146
Consulates 231
Conversion chart 237
Le Corbusier 23, 98
  Cité Radieuse (Marseille) 54, 152
Cordes 38, 39
Corpus Christi 14
Corso de la Lavande (Digne-les-
  Bains) 31, 35
Côte d'Azur 10
  beaches 28, 31
  festivals 31
Côte d'Azur Airport (Nice) 238
Côte Bleue
  beaches 28
  wildlife 16
Côte Varoise, beaches 29
Côteau Fleuri (Grimaud) 198
Côtes du Luberon wine 207
Côtes de Provence wine 207
Côtes-du-Rhône wine 206
Cotignac 101, 105
  hotels 198
Council Travel (Aix-en-Provence) 239
Courbet, Gustave 152
Cousteau, Jacques 94, 101, 112
Coward, Noël 52
Crafts 219
Credit cards
  lost 232
  in restaurants 202
Cresta Holidays 239
Crime 230
CRIR 243

CROUS (Centre Régional de Oeuvres
  Universitaires et Scolaires) 192
Crucifixion (Bréa) 25
Cruises 245
Crusades 42–3
Cunningham, Merce 76
Currency 233
Customs and immigration **236**, 237
Cycling 244
Le Cygne (Beaucaire) 245

D
Dance 222
Dante 89, 142
Daudet, Alphonse 15, 26, 127, 140
  Moulin de Daudet 143
Daumier, Honoré 152
David, Jacques Louis, *Napoleon
  Crossing the Alps* 179
David-Néel, Alexandra 180
Davis, Miles 222
Deauville, le Champ de Courses
  (Dufy) 121
Delon, Alain 15
Delta 239
Les Demoiselles d'Avignon
  (Picasso) 73
Deneuve, Catherine 75
Dentelles de Montmirail,
  Tour of 159
Depardieu, Gérard 15
Département postcodes 235
Derain, André 153
Les Deux Frères (Roquebrune-Cap-
  Martin) 211
Les Deux Garçons (Aix-en-
  Provence) 202, **217**
Diaghilev, Sergei 93
Dialling codes 235
Digne-les-Bains 21, 175, 179, **180**
  festivals 31, 35
  restaurants 215
Disabled travellers 192, **193**, 229
  in restaurants 203
Disco 7 (Cannes) 225
Discotheques 223
Discounts
  student 229, **237**
  train tickets 241
  travel agencies 239
Diving 29
Doisneau, Robert 66
Domaine de Cabasse (Séguret)
  201
Domaine de Valmouriane (St-Rémy-
  de-Provence) 200
Donat, Saint 181
Dongen, Kees van 85
Draguignan 106–7
  tourist office 229
Dufy, Raoul 24, 78, 99
  Deauville, le Champ de Courses 121
  La Jetée Promenade à Nice 25

Dumas, Alexandre 26, 150, 152, 168
Duncan, Isadora 85
Durance river 54, 176
Durand, Maire 135
Dürer, Albrecht 142
  Rhinoceros woodcut **47**, 152
Durrell, Lawrence 27
Düsseldorf School 151
Duty-free limits 236
Duty-paid limits 236

E
Easter 14, 30
Easyjet 239
L'Echalote (St-Tropez) 212
Ecole de Nice 85
Eden Roc (Cap d'Antibes) 191, 196
Edward VII, King 93
Electrical adaptors 237
Ellington, Duke 76
Ellis, William Webb 99
Emergencies 231
Enclos de la Fontaine (Nîmes) 214
Entertainment 222–5
  bullfighting 223, 225
  buying tickets **222**, 224
  cinema 223, 225
  dance 222, 224
  discotheques and nightclubs **223**,
    224–5
  gambling **223**, 225
  information 229
  opera and classical music 222, 224
  participant sports **224**, 225
  practical information 222
  rock and jazz **222–3**, 224
  spectator sports **223**, 225
  theatre **222**, 224
Entrecasteau, Marquis of 148
Entrecasteaux 104, 105
  Côtes de Provence tour 108
Entremont 40
Entrevaux 175, 181, **187**
  festivals 31
Ephrussi de Rothschild, Béatrice 86–7
Epiphany 33
Ernst, Max 72, 106
L'Escale (Carry-le-Rouet) 213
Escoffier, Auguste 75
  Musée Escoffier (Villeneuve-
    Loubet) 74
Espace IGN 243
Espace Julien (Marseille) 224
Espuno (Nice) 217
Esterel, beaches 29
Estienne, André 173
L'Etang d'Estagel, entertainment 225
Etiquette 236
L'Etrier (L'Etang d'Estagel) 225
Eugène of Savoy 48
Eugénie, Empress 50, 98
Eurocamp 192
Eurocheques 232
Eurolines 243

Europa and the Bull (mosaic) 146
Europcar 243
L'Europe (Avignon) 194, **201**
European Union 14
Exposition Internationale de la Fleur
    (Cagnes-sur-Mer) 30
Eze 18, **88**
    cafés and bars 217
    hotels 196
    restaurants 210

F

Fabre, General Alexandre 106
Fabre, Jean-Henri, Maison J-H Fabre
    (Orange) 161
Fabrique de Pipes Courrieu (Cogolin)
    219
Faïence 49, 186
"Fairy Stone" 39, 107
Fayence 106
    hotels 198
    restaurants 212
Fédération d'Etudes et de Sports
    Sous-Marins 225
Fédération Française de Camping-
    Caravaning 192
Fédération Française de
    Canoë-kayak 225
Fédération Française de Voile 245
Fédération Française de
    Vol Libre 225
Félibrige 26, 50
Feria (Nîmes) 30
Féria Pascale (Arles) 30
Féria des Vendanges (Nîmes) 32
Ferme auberge 202
La Ferme Jamet (Avignon) 200
Ferries 245
Festin es Courgourdons (Nice) 30
Le Festival (Juan-les-Pins) 217
Festival d'Avignon 31, 35, **224**, 229
Festival du Cirque (Monaco) 33
Festival International d'Aix 31
Festival International de la Danse
    (Cannes) 32
Festival International du Film
    (Cannes) 30, 53, 55, 68
Festival International de la Musique
    (Toulon) 224
Festival International de Musique
    Classique (Cannes) 224
Festival du Jazz (Juan-les-Pins) 224
Festival du Jazz (Nice) 224
Festival du Jazz (Toulon) 31
Festival de Musique (Menton) 31
Festival de la Navigation de
    Plaisance (Cannes) 32
Festivals 30–33, 34–5
Fête des Bergers (Les-Baux-de-
    Provence) 33
Fête du Citron (Menton) 33
Fête des Gardians (Arles) 30
Fête du Jasmin (Grasse) 31

Fête de Mimosa (Bormes-les-
    Mimosas) 33
Fête des Prémices du Riz (Arles) 32
Fête de St-Jean 31
Fête de Sainte Marie Salome (Saintes-
    Maries-de-la-Mer) 32
Fête de la Tarasque (Tarascon) 31
Fête des Vignerons (Châteauneuf-
    du-Pape) 30
Fête du Vin (Bandol) 33
Films *see* Cinema
Fire services 230, 231
Fires, forest 54, 231
Fish, Iles d'Hyères 114–15
Fishing 29
Fitzgerald, F Scott 27, 52, 61, 72, 75
Fitzgerald, Zelda 27, 52
The Flagellation of Christ (15th-
    century German School) 151
Flamingoes 137
Flashman's (Monaco) 217
Flayosc
    Côtes de Provence tour 109
Les Florets (Gigondas) 215
Flowers 16–17, **160**
    lavender **182**, 183
FNAC 224
Foire Internationale de Marseille 32
Foire aux Santons (Marseille) 33
Fondation Vasarely (Aix-en-Provence)
    149
Fontaine-de-Vaucluse 165
    festivals 31
Fontvieille 143
    hotels 198
    restaurants 213
Food and Drink
    cafés, bars and casual eating 216–17
    What to Buy in Provence 221
    What to Drink in Provence 206–7
    What to Eat in Provence 204–5
    see also Restaurants
Forcalquier 182
    festivals 32
    hotels 201
Foreign Legion 153
Forest fires 54, 231
Forêt de Turini 97
Fortified wines 207
Formule One 192
Forum Nice Nord (Nice) 224
Fossatti, Dominique 106
Foster, Norman 132
Fountains 19
Le Four des Navettes (Marseille) 217
Fourchette II (Avignon) 214
Fox-Amphoux, hotels 198
Fragonard, Jean-Honoré 25
    If he were as faithful to me 86
    Villa-Musée Fragonard (Grasse) 66
Le France (Fayence) 212
France-Lodge 192-3
France-Station-Voile (Cannes) 225
Francis di Paola, St 117

François I, King
    Château d'If (Marseille) 152
    St-Paul-de-Vence 18, 19, 75
    Vence 74
Franks 42
Fréjus 125
    history 54
    railway station 241
Fréjus-Plage 29
"French Connection" drug ring
    55
French Government Tourist
    Office 192
French Railways 241
La Fresnaye, Roger de, *Le Rameur* 120
Froment, Nicolas, *Burning Bush
    Triptych* 46–7, 148
FUAJ (Fédération Unie des Auberges
    de Jeunesse) 192

G

Galerie des Arcades (Biot) 196
Galleries *see* Museums and galleries
Gallo-Roman Provence 40–41
Gambling 94, **223**, 225
Garbo, Greta 61, 75
La Garde-Freinet
    Massif des Maures tour 117
    restaurants 212
Gardens *see* Parks and gardens
Gardians, Camargue 20, 136, 138
La Gardiole (Cap d'Antibes) 196
Garnier, Charles
    Casino (Monaco) 92, 94
    Monte-Carlo Opéra 51, 92
    Musée des Automates et Poupées
        d'Autrefois (Monaco) 94
    Salle Garnier (Monte-Carlo) 93
Gassendi, Pierre 180
Gates, village 19
Giacometti, Alberto, *L'Homme
    Qui Marche I* 76
Gigondas
    restaurant 215
    Tour of the Dentelles 159
Gilles, St 139
Gilot, Françoise 73
Ginoux, Charles 116
Giono, Jean 26, 182
Giovanetti, Matteo 168
    Prophets Fresco 44
Giovanetti da Viterbo 130
Gîtes de France 192, 193
Glanum 22, **40–41**, 141
Glassware 74, 220
Gleize, Jany 209
The Goat (Picasso) 73
Godeau, Bishop 75
Golf 225
Golf de Cannes 225
Golf Grand Avignon 225
Golf de la Salette (Marseille) 225
Gorbio 98

Gordes 38, 156, **169**
Gorges du Cians 64
Gorges du Loup 65
Gorges du Verdon 59, 175, 186
   Tour of 184–5
   wildlife 17
Gorges de la Vésubie 17, 95
Gould, Frank Jay 72
Gourdon 65
Goya, Francisco de 142
Grace, Princess 54, 55, 91, 94
Grammont, Georges 120
Le Grand (Bormes-les-Mimosas) 198
Le Grand Arbre à Ste-Maxime
   (Dufy) 80
Le Grand Café de Turin (Nice) 217
Grand Hôtel du Cap-Ferrat (St-Jean-
   Cap-Ferrat) 191, 197
Grand Luberon 172
Grand Opéra-Théâtre (Toulon) 224
Le Grand Paris (Digne-les-Bains) 215
Le Grand Pavois (Nice) 211
Grand Prix Automobile de Formula 1
   (Monaco) 13, 30, 52, 94, 223
Grand Siècle (Avignon) 217
Granet, François 149
Grasse 66–7, 179
   festivals 31
   perfume 50
   shops 219
Grasse, Admiral Count de 66
Great Plague 48–9
Greeks 38
Greene, Graham 15, 27, 55, 84
Gregory XI, Pope 45
Gréoux-les-Bains 182–3
Le Griffu (Richier) 144
Grimaldi, François 90
Grimaldi, Gibelin de 123
Grimaldi, Hannibal 64
Grimaldi family
   Château de Roquebrune 98
   Château Grimaldi (Cagnes) 78–9
   counts of Beuil 64
   Grimaud 123
   Monaco 45, 90, 94
Grimaud 123
   hotels 198
   Massif des Maures tour 116–7
Guarinone, Guarino 81
Guiberto, J-A 80
Guiramand, Jean 148
Gyptis 38

H
L'Hacienda (Aix-en-Provence) 213
Hackman, Gene 15
Le Hameau (St-Paul-de-Vence) 197
Hannibal 39, 164
Haussmann, Baron 106
Haut Var 104–5
Haute Provence Geological
   Reserve 17

Health 231
Hemingway, Ernest 27, 72
L'Herbier de Provence (St-Rémy-de-
   Provence) 219
Hermentaire, St 107
L'Hermitage (Monaco) 195, **197**
Hertz 243
Hiély-Lucullus (Avignon) 208, **214**
History 37–55
Hitch-hiking 244
Hole in the Wall (Nice) 217
Holidays, public 33
Holy Roman Empire 42, 43
L'Homme au Mouton (Picasso)
   72, 73
L'Homme Qui Marche I
   (Giacometti) 76
Honorat, St 70, 89
Horse riding 225
Horses, Camargue 136
Hospitals 231
Hostellerie Bérard (La Cadière
   d'Azur) 198, 212
Hostellerie des Deux Lions
   (Forcalquier) 201
Hostellerie de la Fuste
   (Manosque) 215
Hostellerie le Paradou
   (Lourmarin) 201
Hostels 192, **193**, 237
Hot Brass (Aix-en-Provence) 224
Hôtel d'Arlatan (Arles) 199
Hôtel de l'Atelier
   (Villeneuve-lès-Avignon) 200
Hôtel des Augustins (Aix-en-
   Provence) 194, **199**
Hôtel de Cacharel (Saintes-
   Maries-de-la-Mer) 200
Hôtel Calendal (Arles) 199
Hôtel des Deux Rocs (Seillans) 199
Hôtel les Géraniums (Le Barroux) 201
Hôtel Mercure Beauvau (Marseille)
   199
Hôtel Métropole (Beaulieu) 196
Hôtel des Mimosas (Juan-les-Pins) 196
Hôtel le Minaret (Cagnes-sur-Mer)
   196
Hôtel Molière (Cannes) 196
Hôtel de Paris (Monaco) 191, 197
Hôtel Welcome (Villefranche) 197
Hôtel Windsor (Nice) 197
Hotels 190–201
   Aix-en-Provence 199
   Antibes 196
   Les Arcs 198
   Arles 199
   Avignon 200–201
   Le Barroux 201
   Les-Baux-de-Provence 199
   Beaulieu 196
   Biot 196
   Bonnieux 201
   booking 191
   Bormes-les-Mimoas 198

Hotels (cont.)
   La Cadière d'Azur 198
   Cagnes-sur-Mer 196
   Cannes 196
   Cap d'Antibes 196
   Cassis 199
   Château-Arnoux 201
   children in 191
   Cogolin 198
   Cotignac 198
   disabled travellers 193
   Eze 196
   Fayence 198
   Fontvieille 198
   Forcalquier 201
   Fox-Amphoux 198
   Grimaud 198
   Iles d'Hyères 198
   Juan-les-Pins 196
   Lourmarin 201
   Marseille 199
   Maussane-les-Alpilles 200
   Menton 196
   Monaco 197
   Nice 197
   Nîmes 200
   Pernes-la-Fontaine 201
   prices 190–91
   Provence's Best 194–5
   Reillane 201
   Roussillon 201
   St-Jean-Cap-Ferrat 197
   Saintes-Maries-de-la-Mer 200
   St-Paul-de-Vence 197
   St-Pierre-de-Tortour 198–9
   St-Rémy-de-Provence 200
   St-Tropez 199
   Salon-de-Provence 200
   Séguret 201
   Seillans 199
   Vaison-la-Romaine 201
   Vence 197
   Villefranche 197
   Villeneuve-lès-Avignon 200
   where to look and stay 190
Hugo, Victor 26
Hunting 231
Huxley, Aldous 27, 112
Hyères 115
   entertainment 225
Hypermarkets 218

I
Ibis/Arcade 192
If he were as faithful to me
   (Fragonard) 86
Ile du Levant 52
Ile St-Honorat 70
Ile Ste-Marguerite 70–71
Iles d'Hyères 17, 58, **114–15**
   festivals 34
   hotels 198
   restaurants 212

Iles de Lérins 70–71
Imports 236
Ingram, Sir William 98
Ingres, Jean Auguste Dominique 149, 152
Innocent VI, Pope 44, 45, 130
Insurance 230
   cars 242
Intercars 243
Intérieur au Phonographe (Matisse) 25
Interpreters 230, 231
Ironwork bell towers 21
Islam 14, 237
L'Isle-sur-la-Sorgue 165
Isnard, Jean-Esprit 110
Isola 2000 55, 96, 225
Les Issambres 103

J

Le Jardin de Fréderic (St-Rémy-de-Provence) 214
Les Jardins de Cassis (Cassis) 199
Jazz 222–3
Jazz à Juan 31
Jean de Florette 15, 153
Jeanne, Queen 47
La Jetée Promenade à Nice (Dufy) 25
Jews
   Carpentras 164
   history 44, 47, 48
   Musée Juif Comtadin (Cavaillon) 170
   synagogues 237
   in Vaucluse 155
Jimmy'Z (Cannes) 225
Jimmy'Z (Monaco) 225
John XXII, Pope 44, 45, 164
La Joie de Vivre (Picasso) 73
Joinville-le-Pont, entertainment 225
Josephine, Empress 85, 94
Jou, Louis 142
Jour de Nationale (Monaco) 32
Les Journées Médiévales (Entrevaux) 31
Juan-les-Pins 72
   beaches 29
   cafés and bars 217
   entertainment 224, 225
   festivals 31
   hotels 196
   restaurants 210
Julius II, Pope 168

K

Karr, Jean-Baptiste 124
Kayaking 225
Kisling, Moise 78
Klein, Yves, *Anthropométrie* 85
De Klomp (Nice) 217
Knights Templar 64, 74, 123, 183
Kuoni Travel (Nice) 245

L

Labadié, Alexandre 151
Lac de Ste-Croix 184
Lacoste
   Tour of the Petit Luberon 170–71
Lambot, J 109
Lartigue, Florette 66
Lartigue, Jacques-Henri 66
Lascaris-Ventimiglia family 85
Le Lavandou 116
   beaches 29
Lavender 35, **182**, 183, 220
Lawrence, DH 52, 74
Lectrice à la Table Jaune (Matisse) 83
Legal assistance 230
Léger, Fernand 25, 72
   Musée Fernand Léger (Biot) 74
     La Partie de Campagne 77
Lent 34
Léopold II, King of the Belgians 50, 85, 86
   Côtes de Provence tour 109
   hotels 198
Letters 234
Le Levant 114
Lhote, André 169
Lichtenstein, Roy 85
Liégeard, Stéphen 26
Ligurians 38
Liszt, Franz 171
Livingstone, David 88
Lloyds Bank 232
Logis du Guetteur (Les Arcs) 198
Lombard, Louis de 65
Loren, Sophia 75
Lorgues 108
   Côtes de Provence tour 109
Lou Calen (Cotignac) 198
Lou Marques (Arles) 213
Louis, St, Bishop of Toulouse 109
Louis II, Prince of Monaco 52
Louis II of Anjou 47, 140, 148
Louis IX (St Louis), King
   Aigues-Mortes 23, 127, 134–5
   Crusades 42, 43
Louis XI, King, 46
Louis XIII, King 48
Le Louis XIII (Hyères) 225
Louis XIV, King 48, 71
   La Turbie 89
   Monaco 94
   Orange 161
Le Louis XV (Monaco) 209, **210**
Louis-Philippe, King 68
Lourmarin
   hotels 201
   restaurants 215
   Tour of the Petit Luberon 170–71
Luberon 172
   prehistoric monuments 39
   Tour of 170–71
   wildlife 16

Lucéram 95
Lumière, Louis 223
Lurs 181

M

McDowell, Malcolm 27
McGarvie-Munn, Ian 105
Maeght, Aimé 75, 76
Maeght, Marguerite 75, 76
Le Magali (Menton) 196
Magazines, entertainments listings 222, 229
Maginot Line 98
La Magnaneraie (Villeneuve-lès-Avignon) 200
Mail services 234–5
Maillol, Aristide
   L'Action Enchaînée 64
   La Nymphe 121
Maison des Gîtes de France 192
Malaucène
   Tour of the Dentelles 159
Mallet-Stevens, Robert 115
Malraux, André 76
Man in the Iron Mask 70–71
Manchello 99
Manet, Edouard 168
Mann, Heinrich 27
Mann, Thomas 27, 112
Le Manoir (Les Iles d'Hyères) 198
Manon des Sources 15, 153
Manosque 175, **182**
   restaurants 215
Mansfield, Katherine 27, 99
Manufacture de Tapis (Cogolin) 219
Maps
   Aigues-Mortes 134–5
   Aix-en-Provence 149
   Alpes d'Azur 96
   Alpes-de-Haute-Provence 176–7
   Arles 144–5
   Avignon 166–7
   The Best of Provence 58–9
   Bouches-du-Rhône and Nîmes 128–9
   Camargue 136–7
   Cannes 69
   Côtes de Provence tour 108–9
   Dentelles tour 159
   for drivers 243
   France 10–11
   Gorges du Verdon tour 184–5
   Iles d'Hyères 114
   Iles de Lérins 70–71
   Marseille 152
   Massif des Maures tour 116–17
   Nice 80–81, 84
   Nîmes 133
   Petit Luberon tour 170–71

Maps (cont.)
  Pont du Gard 131
  Riviera and the Alpes Maritimes 62–3
  St-Tropez 118–19
  Toulon 113
  Var and the Iles d'Hyères 102–3
  Vaucluse 156–7
Maquis resistance 52–3
Marcel, St 104
Mardi Gras 34
Marie-Antoinette, Queen 65, 86
Marine life, Port-Cros 114–15
Marius, Consul 40
Markets 218
Marseille 37, 129, **150–52**
  airport 238, 239
  banks and *bureaux de change* 232
  bookshops 235
  cafés and bars 217
  customs information 237
  entertainment 224, 225
  festivals 31, 32, 33
  Great Plague 48–9
  history 38, 50, 51, 53
  hospitals 231
  hotels 199
  map 152
  railway station 241
  restaurants 213–14
  Roman remains 41
  shops 219
  student information 237
  tourist office 229
  travel agencies 239
  youth hostels 237
Marseille Exhibition (1922) 53
Martha, St 31, 43, 138, 140
Martigues 147
Martini, Simone 168
Mary Jacobea, St 35, 41, **138**
Mary Magdalene, St
  relics 43, 58, 110
  Saintes-Maries-de-la-Mer 35, 41, 138
  St-Maximin-la-Ste-Baume 58, 110
Mary Salome, St 35, 41, 138
Mas 20–21
Mas de la Bonoty (Pernes-la-Fontaine) 201
Mas de la Fouque (Saintes-Maries-de-la-Mer) 200
Le Mas de Garrigon (Roussillon) 201
Mas du Langoustier 212
Masséna, Marshal 85, 97
Massif de l'Esterel 17, **124**
Massif des Maures 17
  Tour of 116–17
Massif de la Ste-Baume 17
Master of Aix,
  The Annunciation 47

Matisse, Henri 24, 54, 153
  Chapelle de Rosaire (Vence) 75, 82
  Intérieur au Phonographe 25
  Lectrice à la Table Jaune 83
  Musée Matisse (Nice) 59, **82–3**
  Nature Morte aux Grenades 83
  Nu Bleu IV 82
  Torse Debout 83
Maugham, W Somerset 27, 85
Maurice of Nassau 161
Maussane-les-Alpilles
  hotels 200
  restaurants 214
Maximin, St 110
Mayle, Peter 27, 155, 171
Mazarin, Archbishop Michel 148
Le Mazagran (St-Tropez) 209, 212
Le Mazarin (Aix-en-Provence) 225
Mazoyer, Georges 173
Médecin, Jacques 55, 84
Medical treatment 231
Medieval architecture 23
Medieval Provence 42–3
Mediterranean ports 245
Ménerbes
  Tour of the Petit Luberon 170–71
Menton 98–9
  beaches 28, 29
  festivals 31, 33
  history 50
  hotels 196
  restaurants 210
Menus 203
Mercure/Altéa 192
Mercury Cinéma (Nice) 225
La Mère Besson (Cannes) 210
La Mère Germaine (Châteauneuf-du-Pape) 215
Mérimée, Prosper 26, 108
Minitel 235
Mirabeau, Comte de 148, 152, 173
Mirailhet, Jean 81
Le Miramar (Marseille) 208, **214**
Mireio (Avignon) 245
Miró, Joan 72, 75
  L'Oiseau Lunaire 77
Mistral, Frédéric 26, 127
  Félibrige 50
  Mirèio 26, 51, 139
  Museon Arlaten (Arles) 146
Mistral (Nîmes) 219
Mistral wind 21, 30, 31, 33
Mithraism 14
Modigliani, Amedeo 61, 75
Moissac-Bellevue 104
La Môle, restaurants 212
Monaco 90–95
  banks and *bureaux de change* 232
  bookshops 235
  cafés and bars 217
  entertainment 225
  festivals 32, 33
  Grand Prix 13, 30, 52, 94, 223

Monaco (cont.)
  history 50
  hotels 197
  restaurants 210
Monet, Claude 24
Money 233
  banks 232
  bureaux de change 232
  credit cards 232
  Eurocheques 232
  travellers' cheques 230, 232
Mons 105
Mont Bégo 39, 97
Mont Pelat 179
Mont Ste-Victoire 104
Mont Ventoux 16, **160**
Mont Vinaigre 124
Montand, Yves 15, 75
Montauroux 106
  restaurants 212
Monte-Carlo 51, **92–3**
  beaches 28
  festivals 33
  Monte-Carlo Casino Interior (Bokelman) 50–51
Montfort, Simon de 43
Montpellier, airport 238
Montpensier, Duchess of 148
Mossa, Alexis 34
  Musée-Mossa (Nice) 81
Motorail 241
Motorways 242, 243
Mougins 66
  restaurants 210–11
Moulin de la Camandoule (Fayence) 198
Moulin de Daudet 143
Moulin à l'huile (Grasse) 219
Moulin de Lourmarin (Lourmarin) 194, **201**, **215**
Le Moulin de Mougins (Mougins) 209, **210–11**
Moulins de Paillas 117
Mountains, walking in 231
Moustiers-Ste-Marie 43, **186**
  faïence 49
  Gorges du Verdon tour 184
Moyenne Corniche 90
Muret, Battle of (1213) 43
Muscat de Beaumes-de-Venise 207
Museums and galleries
  opening hours 229
  Arènes de Fréjus 125
  Carré d'Art (Nîmes) 132
  Cathédrale d'Images (Les-Baux-de-Provence) 142–3
  Le Centre d'Art Presence Van Gogh (St-Rémy-de-Provence) 140, 141
  Le Centre de Ginès (Camargue) 138
  Fondation Alexandra David-Néel (Digne-les-Bains) 180
  Fondation Emile Hughes (Vence) 74, 75

Museums and galleries (cont.)
Fondation Louis Jou (Les-Baux-de-Provence) 142
Fondation Maeght (St-Paul-de-Vence) 55, 59, 75, **76–7**
Hôtel de Sade (St-Rémy-de-Provence) 140, 141
Maison de Tartarin (Tarascon) 140
Le Monde Souterrain de Norbert Casteret (Fontaine-de-Vaucluse) 165
Musée des Alpilles (St-Rémy-de-Provence) 140, 141
Musée Angladon (Avignon) 168
Musée de l'Annonciade (St-Tropez) 59, **120–21**
Musée d'Anthropologie Préhistorique (Monaco) 94
Musée Archéologique (Apt) 172
Musée Archéologique (Cavaillon) 170
Musée Archéologique (Nîmes) 132–3
Musée Archéologique (St-Raphaël) 124
Musée de l'Arles Antique (Arles) 146
Musée des Arômes de Provence (St-Rémy-de-Provence) 140, 141
Musée d'Art Contemporain (Nice) 23, 85
Musée d'Art et d'Histoire de Provence (Grasse) 66
Musée d'Art Naïf (Gourdon) 65
Musée d'Art de Toulon 113
Musée Arts et Histoire (Bormes-les-Mimosas) 117
Musée des Arts Asiatiques (Nice) 85
Musée des Arts et Traditions Populaires de Moyenne Provence (Draguignan) 107
Musée Théodore Aubanel (Avignon) 167, 168
Musée de l'Automobiliste (Mougins) 66
Musée des Beaux-Arts (Marseille) 152
Musée des Beaux-Arts (Menton) 99
Musée des Beaux-Arts (Nice) 85
Musée des Beaux-Arts (Nîmes) 133
Musée Baroncelli (Camargue) 138
Musée de la Boulangerie (Bonnieux) 171
Musée Calvet (Avignon) 168
Musée Camarguais (Camargue) 139
Musée Cantini (Marseille) 151
Musée de la Castre (Cannes) 69
Musée Chagall (Nice) 85
Musée Henry Clews (La Napoule) 124
Musée Comtadin (Carpentras) 164
Musée des Docks Romains (Marseille) 150
Musée de l'Empéri (Salon-de-Provence) 147
Musée Ephrussi de Rothschild (Cap Ferrat) 59, **86–7**

Museums and galleries (cont.)
Musée Escoffier (Villeneuve-Loubet) 74
Musée Extraordinaire de Georges Mazoyer (Ansouis) 173
Musée de la Faïence (Marseille) **151**, 152
Musée de la Faïence (Moustiers-Ste-Marie) 186
Musée Granet (Aix-en-Provence) 149
Musée Grobet-Labadié (Marseille) 151
Musée d'Histoire et d'Archéologie (Antibes) 72
Musée d'Histoire de Marseille (Marseille) 151
Musée de l'Histoire du Pays d'Aigues et Musée des Faïences (La Tour d'Aigues) 173
Musée d'Histoire de St-Paul (St-Paul-de-Vence) 75
Musée Historique (Gourdon) 65
Musée International de la Parfumerie (Grasse) 66
Musée Juif Comtadin (Cavaillon) 170
Musée Lapidaire (Avignon) 168
Musée Fernand Léger (Biot) 74
Musée de la Légion Etrangère (Aubagne) 153
Musée de la Ligne Maginot des Alpes (Sospel) 98
Musée Magnelli (Vallauris) 72
Musée de la Marine (Grasse) 66
Musée de la Marine (Toulon) 112, 113
Musée Masséna (Nice) 85
Musée Matisse (Nice) 59, **82–3**
Musée Mossa (Nice) 81
Musée Municipal (Cassis) 153
Musée Municipal (Digne-les-Bains) 180
Musée Municipal (Draguignan) 107
Musée Municipal (Orange) 161
Musée National (Poupées et Automates d'Autrefois (Monaco) 94
Musée National (Poupées et Automates d'Autrefois (Monaco) 94
Musée Nature en Provence (Riez) 183
Musée Naval de St-Tropez 122
Musée Océanographique (Monaco) 91, **94**
Musée de l'Olivier (Château Grimaldi) 78
Musée de Paléontologie (Apt) 172
Musée du Pays Brignolais (Brignoles) 109
Musée du Père Anselme de Vignerons (Châteauneuf-du-Pape) 164
Musée du Petit Palais (Avignon) 167, 168

Museums and galleries (cont.)
Musée Pétrarque (Fontaine-de-Vaucluse) 165
Musée de la Photographie (Mougins) 66
Musée Picasso (Antibes) 72
Musée Picasso (Vallauris) 72
Musée Pierre de Luxembourg (Villeneuve-lès-Avignon) 130
Musée de la Préhistoire Régionale (Menton) 99
Musée Provençal du Costume et du Bijou (Grasse) 66
Musée Réattu (Arles) 144, **146**
Musée Renoir (Cagnes-sur-Mer) 78
Musée de la Résistance (Fontaine-de-Vaucluse) 165
Musée des Santons (Les-Baux-de-Provence) 142
Musée Simon Segal (Aups) 104, 105
Musée Souléiado (Tarascon) 140
Musée des Souvenirs Napoléoniens (Monaco) 90, **94**
Musée des Tapisseries (Aix-en-Provence) 23, **148**
Musée de la Tour du Brau (Les-Baux-de-Provence) 168
Musée des Traditions Locales (Ste-Maxime) 123
Musée du Trophée des Alpes (La Turbie) 89
Musée de la Vallée de l'Ubaye (Barcelonnette) 179
Musée du Vieil Aix (Aix-en-Provence) 148
Musée du Vieux Marseille (Marseille) 151
Musée du Vieux Nîmes (Nîmes) 132
Musée du Vieux Toulon (Toulon) 113
Musée Vivant de l'Abeille (Valensole) 183
Musée Ziem (Martigues) 147
Muséon Arlaten (Arles) 144, **146**
Muséum d'Histoire Naturelle (Aix-en-Provence) 148
Pavillon de Vendôme (Aix-en-Provence) 149
St-Paul-de-Mausole (St-Rémy-de-Provence) 141
La Verrerie de Biot 74
Villa-Musée Fragonard (Grasse) 66
Music
dance 222
discotheques and nightclubs 223
opera and classical 222
rock and jazz 222–3

N

Napoleon I, Emperor **179**, 194
lands at Golfe-Juan 50, 72
Musée des Souvenirs Napoléoniens (Monaco) 94

Napoleon I (cont)
  Musée du Vieux Toulon 113
  St-Raphaël 124
  Toulon siege 49
Napoleon Crossing the Alps
  (David) 179
Napoleon III, Emperor 85
La Napoule 124
Natural history 16–17
Nature Morte aux Grenades
  (Matisse) 83
Nautique de Voile (Juan-les-Pins) 225
Navig France 245
Négresco, Henri 84
Le Négresco (Nice) 23, 190, 195, **197**
Nelson, Admiral 183
Nero, Emperor 34
Newspapers 229, **235**
Nice 61, 63, **80–85**
  airport 238
  area map 84
  banks and *bureaux de change* 232
  beaches 28, 29, 54
  bookshops 235
  cafés and bars 217
  customs information 237
  entertainment 224, 225
  festivals 30, 33, 34
  history 48, 49, 50, 51
  hospitals 231
  hotels 197
  Musée Matisse 82–3
  Old Town 13
  railway station 241
  restaurants 211
  shops 219
  Street-by-Street map 80–81
  student information 237
  tourist office 229
  travel agencies 239
  Visitors' checklist 81
  youth hostels 237
Nice Leader Apollo (Nice) 225
Nice School 25
Nicholas II, Tsar 84, 85
Nietzsche, Friedrich 26
Nightclubs 223
Nijinsky 93
Nîmes 54, **132–3**
  airport 238
  cafés and bars 217
  entertainment 225
  festivals 30, 32, 34–5
  hotels 200
  map 133
  railway station 241
  restaurants 214
  Roman remains 22, 40
  shops 219
Niven, David 85
Noailles, Vicomte de 115
Noce imaginaire (Cocteau) 24
Nonn, Alain 117
Nord Pinus (Arles) 199

Nostradamus 26, 46
  birthplace 140
  Salon-de-Provence 147
Le Nôtre, André 65, 105
Notre-Dame-des-Anges
  Massif des Maures tour 116
Notre-Dame de Secours (Ronzen) 64
Novak, Kim 55
Novotel 192
Nu Bleu IV (Matisse) 82
Nu Devant la Cheminée (Bonnard)
  120
Nudist beaches 29
La Nymphe (Maillol) 121

O

L'Obéissance Récompensée
  (Boucher) 133
Office Municipal pour Handicapés
  et Inadaptés (Marseille) 229
L'Oiseau Lunaire (Miró) 77
Les Oiseaux Noirs (Braque) 77
Olives
  Musée de l'Olivier (Château
    Grimaldi) 78
  olivier millénaire 98
*Open Window on the Harbour at
  St-Tropez* (Camoin) 119
Opening hours 228
  banks 232
  museums 229
  restaurants 228
  shops 218
Opera 222
Opéra de Nice 224
Opéra Municipal (Marseille) 224
Oppède, Baron of 155, 170
Oppède-le-Vieux
  restaurants 215
  Tour of the Petit Luberon 170–71
Oppidum (Oppède-le-Vieux) 215
L'Orage (Signac) 120
Orange 21, **161–3**
  festivals 31
  history 49
  restaurants 215
  Roman remains 40, 41, 58
  Théâtre Antique d'Orange 162–3
Orange, Counts of 159
Orange, princes of 161
Otéro, La Belle 89
L'Oustaloun (Maussane-les-Alpilles) 200
Oustaó de Baumanière (Les-Baux-de-
  Provence) 208, **213**

P

Package holidays 239
Pagnol, Marcel 26, 53, 127, **153**, 223
  birthplace 153
  death 27
  Jean de Florette 15, 153
  Manon des Sources 15, 153
  Marseille Trilogy 27, 52

Painters 24–5
Palais des Sports (Marseille) 225
Palais des Sports (Nice) 225
La Palme d'Or (Cannes) 209, **210**
La Palud-sur-Verdon
  Gorges du Verdon tour 185
Pam-Pam (Juan-les-Pins) 217
Papal Avignon 44–5, 58
Parascending 225
Parc National du Mercantour 17, 62,
  96, **97**
Parc Naturel Régional 170
Parc des Sports (Avignon) 225
Parking 230, 244
Parks and gardens
  Jardin Biovès (Menton) 99
  Jardin Botanique des Cordeliers
    (Digne-les-Bains) 180
  Jardin Botanique Exotique
    (Menton) 99
  Jardin des Colombières (Menton) 99
  Jardin Exotique (Eze) 88
  Jardin Exotique (Monaco) 94
  Jardin Exotique (Monte-Carlo) 92
  Jardin Exotique et Zoo de Sanary-
    Bandol 112
  Jardin de la Fontaine (Nîmes) 133
  Jardins Olbius Riquier (Hyères) 115
  Musée Ephrussi de Rothschild 87
La Partie de Campagne (Léger) 77
Passports, stolen 230
Pasteur, Louis 158
Paul III, Pope 74
Pavillon, Pierre 148
Paysage en Cannet (Bonnard) 76
Paysage Méditerranéen (Staël) 25
Peille 95
Peillon 18, 95
  restaurants 211
Le Pêle-Mêle (Marseille) 224
Pélerinage des Gitans (Stes-Maries-
  de-la-Mer) 30, 34–5
Pénétrable (Soto) 77
Les Penitents des Mées 15, 43, 181
Perched villages **18–19**, 42
Perfumes **67**, 220
  duty-free and duty-paid limits 236
  Grasse 50
  Musée International de la
    Parfumerie (Grasse) 66
Le Périgordin (Monaco) 210
Pernes-les-Fontaines 22, 43, 49, **164**
  hotels 201
La Pérouse (Nice) 197
Pertuis 173
La Pescalune (Aigues-Mortes) 245
La Pesquière (St-Tropez) 209, 212
Pétanque 224
Le Petit Bedon (Avignon) 214
Petit Luberon
  Tour of 170–71
La Petite Bourse (Nîmes) 217

Le Petit Nice (Marseille) 214
Le Petit Pascal (Manosque) 215
Le Petit Prince (Saint-Exupéry) 27
La Petite Fontaine
    (Collobrières) 212
La Petite France (Maussane-les-
    Alpilles) 214
Petrarch 26, 44, 45, 155, 160
    Musée Pétrarque (Fontaine-de-
    Vaucluse) 165
Petrol 244
Pharmacies 231
Philipe, Gérard 117
Phoenicians 38
Phonecards 234
Piaf, Edith 85
Piat, Yann 15
Picasso, Pablo 13, 24, **73**
    ceramics 24, 72
    death 55
    Les Demoiselles d'Avignon 73
    The Goat 73
    Grimaldi Castle paintings 54
    La Guerre et la Paix 72, 73
    L'Homme au Mouton 72, 73
    La Joie de Vivre 73
    at Mougins 66
    Musée Picasso (Antibes) 72
    Musée Picasso (Vallauris) 72
    Violin and Sheet of Music 73
Pickpockets 230
Picnics 216–17
Pierre de la Fée 39, 107
Plage de Piémanson 29
Plague 48–9
Plaine de la Crau 16
Plans-Guides Blay 243
Plants 16–17, **160**
Plazza (Nîmes) 200
Point Sublime
    Gorges du Verdon tour 185
Les Poissons (Braque) 76
Polanski, Roman 68
Police 230, 231
Pollution 231
Pompey 40
La Ponche (St-Tropez) 199
Pont de l'Artuby
    Gorges du Verdon tour 185
Pont du Bornègre 131
Pont du Gard 131
Pont Julien 40
Pont de la Lône 131
Pont Rou 131
Porquerolles 114
Port-Cros 114–15
Port-Grimaud 54, **123**
Postal services 234–5
Postcodes 235
Post-Impressionists 120
Pottery **106**, 220
    Moustiers faïence 186
    tiles 105
    Vallauris 72

Prassinos, Mario 141
Prehistoric man 38–9
Prévot (Cavaillon) 208, **214**
Le Prieuré (Aix-en-Provence) 199
Procession aux Limaces
    (Roquebrune-Cap-Martin) 30
Procession de la Mer de Sainte Sarah
    (Saintes-Maries-de-la-Mer) 30
Procession de la Passion
    (Roquebrune-Cap-Martin) 31
Protis 38
Provence, Counts of 95, 109
Provence, Marcel 186
Pub Z (Avignon) 217
Public holidays 33
Public toilets 231
Puget, Pierre 25, 108
    Hôtel Boyer d'Eguilles (Aix-en-
    Provence) 148
    Pavillon de Vendôme (Aix) 148
    figures 48
    Le Sacrifice de Noé 152
    St-Etienne (Bargemon) angels 106
    Toulon figures 112–13
    Vieille Charité (Marseille) 150
Puget-Théniers 64
Puy, Delphine de 173
Puyricard (Aix-en-Provence) 217

Q

Quenin, St 159

R

RADAR (Royal Association for
    Disability and Rehabilitation) 192
Radio 229, **235**
Rail Europe 240–1
Rail services *see* Trains
Raimbaud 159
Rainier III, Prince of Monaco 54, 91
Rallye de Monte-Carlo 33
Ramatuelle 117
Le Rameur (de la Fresnaye) 120
Ramparts 19
Rasputin 99
Rasteau wine 207
Raymond IV, Count of Toulouse 139
Raymond-Bérenger III 43
Raymond-Bérenger IV 173
Raymond-Bérenger V 178
Réattu, Jacques 146
Red wines 207
Le Régalido (Fontvieille) 198, **213**
Reillanne, hotels 201
Reinach, Théodore 88
Relais Ste-Victoire (Aix-en-
    Provence) 213
Religion 14
Religious services 237
Rembrandt 65, 107
Rencontres Internationales de la
    Photographie (Arles) 31

René, Good King 37, **46–7**, 127
    Aix-en-Provence 148
    Château de Tarascon 140
Les Renforts (Calder) 76
Renoir, Pierre-Auguste 24, 25, 168
    Les Collettes (Cagnes-sur-Mer) 78
    Musée Renoir
    (Cagnes-sur-Mer) 78
Rent A Car 243
La Résistance 52–3
Restaurants 202–16
    Aigues-Mortes 213
    Aix-en-Provence 213
    Arles 213
    Avignon 214
    Bar-sur-Loup 210
    Les-Baux-de-Provence 213
    Biot 210
    Bormes-les-Mimosas 212
    La Cadière d'Azur 212
    Cagnes-sur-Mer 210
    Cannes 210
    Carry-le-Rouet 213
    Cavaillon 214
    Château-Arnoux 215
    Châteauneuf-du-Pape 215
    children in 203
    choice of wine 203
    Collobrières 212
    Digne-les-Bains 215
    Eze 210
    Fayence 212
    Fontvieille 213
    La Garde-Freinet 212
    Gigondas 215
    in hotels 191
    how much to pay 202
    Juan-les-Pins 210
    Lourmarin 215
    Manosque 215
    Marseille 213–14
    Maussane-les-Alpilles 214
    Menton 210
    La Môle 212
    Monaco 210
    Montauroux 212
    Mougins 210–11
    Nice 211
    Nîmes 214
    opening hours 229
    Oppède-de-Vieux 215
    Orange 215
    Peillon 211
    Provence's Best 208–9
    reading the menu 203
    reservations 202–3
    Roquebrune-Cap-Martin 211
    Roussillon 215
    Ste-Agnès 211
    St-Jean-Cap-Ferrat 211
    St-Paul-de-Vence 211
    St-Rémy-de-Provence 214
    St-Tropez 212
    Séguret 215

Restaurants (cont.)
Touët-sur-Var 211
types 202
vegetarian food 203
Vence 211
Villefranche 211
What to eat in Provence 204–5
wheelchair access 203
Le Rêve (Hyères) 225
Reyer, Ernest 116
Rhinoceros woodcut (Dürer) **47**, 152
Rhône, river, 164
Rhône delta, beaches 28
Rhône villages wine 207
Le Riboto de Taven (Les-Baux-de-Provence) 213
Richelieu, Cardinal 70, 123, 139
Le Richèlm (Aix-en-Provence) 217
Richier, Germaine, *Le Griffu* 144
Rieu, Charloun 142
Riez 183
Riquier, Guiraut 43
River trips 245
Riviera 10, 61–99
beaches 29
Exploring 62–3
festivals 34
hotels 196–7
restaurants 210–11
Rocher de la Baume 177
Rock music 222–3
Rodin, Auguste 107, 133
Roger Collet (Vallauris) 219
Rognes 51
Le Roi du Couscous (Marseille) 213
Roman Catholic Church
Papal Avignon 44–5
services 237
Roman de la Rose 107
Roman Empire 40–41
Aix-en-Provence 148
architecture 22
Arles 146
Cavaillon 170
Fréjus 125
Glanum 141
Gréoux-les-Bains 182–3
Nîmes 132
Orange 161
Pont du Gard 131
Riez 183
roche taillée aqueduct (Mons) 105
Théâtre Antique d'Orange 162–3
Le Trophée des Alpes 89
Vaison-la-Romaine 158
Vaucluse 155
Romanesque architecture 22
Romany festivals 34–5
Ronzen, Antoine, *Notre-Dame de Secours* 64
Ronzen, François, Retable 110
Roquebrune-Cap-Martin 19, 61, 63, **98**
festivals 30, 31
history 50

Roquebrune-Cap-Martin (cont.)
restaurants 211
Rosé wines 206
La Roseraie (Vence) 197
Rostand, Edmond 26
Rouget de Lisle, Claude Joseph 49
Roumanille 26
Rousseau, Le Douanier 65
Roussillon 169
hotels 201
restaurants 215
Les Routiers 202
Roux brothers 159
Rubens, Peter Paul 66, 152
Ruhl, Henri 69
Le Ruhl (Marseille) 199
Ruhl-Plage (Nice) 29
Rural architecture 20–21

S

Sabran, Elzéar de 173
Sabran, Gersende de 173
Sabran family 173
Le Sacrifice de Noé (Puget) 152
Sade, Marquis de 26, 155, 170
Château de Lacoste 171
Safety 230–31
Sagan, Françoise 27
Sagy, Léon 172
Sailing 225, 245
Ste-Agnès 98
restaurants 211
St-André-les-Alpes 187
St-Blaise 38, 39
St Bonnet 131
St-Cézaire-sur-Siagne 64–5
Saint-Exupéry, Antoine de 27, 52, 124
St-Gilles-du-Gard 139
St-Honorat et les Saints de Lérins 70
Le Saint Jean (St-Jean-Cap-Ferrat) 211
St-Jean-Cap-Ferrat 85
cafés and bars 217
hotels 197
restaurants 211
St Laurent, Yves 66
Ste-Marie-Madeleine (St-Maximin-la-Ste-Baume) 110–11
Saintes-Maries-de-la-Mer 138
festivals 30, 32, 34–5
history 40, 41
hotels 200
St-Martin-Vésubie 23
Ste-Maxime 123
St-Maximin-la-Ste-Baume 43, 58, **110–11**
St-Paul-de-Vence 55, **75**
cafés and bars 217
hotels 197
ramparts 18, 19
restaurants 211
St-Pierre-de-Tortour, hotels 198–9

St-Raphaël 29, **124**
entertainment 225
St-Rémy-de-Provence **140–41**, 219
hotels 200
restaurants 214
shops 219
Saint-Roch (Avignon) 200
St-Tropez 55, 101, 103, **118–22**, 219
beaches 29
cafés and bars 217
entertainment 225
festivals 30, 34
hotels 199
restaurants 212
Street-by-Street map 118–19
tourist office 229
St-Tropez, la Place des Lices et le Café des Arts (Camoin) 120
Salernes 104–5
Salon-de-Provence 147
hotels 200
Salt lagoons 137
Sanary-sur-Mer 29, **112**
Santon cribs **48**, 142
Saorge 97
Saracens 42, 43, 75, 117
Sarah, Saint 35
Le Sarrasin (Ste-Agnès) 211
Sartre, Jean-Paul 75
Le Scat (Aix-en-Provence) 224
Scipio 140
Scuba-diving 225
Sea fishing 29
Security 230–31
Segal, Simon
Musée Simon Segal (Aups) 104, 105
Séguret
hotels 201
restaurants 215
Seillans 106
hotels 199
Le Select Hôtel (Beaulieu) 196
Self-catering accommodation 192, **193**
Le Sémaphore (Nîmes) 225
Sénanque *see* Abbaye de Sénanque
Senequier (St-Tropez) 217
Septentrion 72
Sernhac gallery 131
Serre, Michel 152
Vue du Cours pendant la Peste 48–9
Sert, Josep Lluis 75, 76
Seyne 22, **178**
Shops 218–21
arts and crafts 219
bookshops 235
larger shops 218
local wines 219
markets 218
opening hours 218
regional specialities 219
specialist shops 218
tax-free goods 236
What to Buy in Provence 220–21
Sightseeing 229

Signac, Paul 24
  L'Age de l'Harmonie 121
  L'Orage 120
  in St-Tropez 122
Signoret, Simone 75
Silvacane *see* Abbaye de Silvacane
Simpson, Tommy 160
Sisteron 14, 21, **178**, 179
  history 53
Skiing 225
  Alpes d'Azur 96
Smollett, Tobias 26
Snakes 231
SNCF 241
SNCM Ferryterranée 245
Société Française des Traducteurs
  Professionels 231
Sofitel 192
Solidor, Suzy 78
Son-et-Lumière (Fontaine-de-
  Vaucluse) 31
Sophia-Antipolis technology
  park 55
Sospel 98
Soto, Jésus Raphael, *Pénétrable* 77
Souleïado (Avignon) 219
Soutine, Chaim 168
Spas
  Digne-les-Bains 180
  Gréoux-les-Bains 182–3
Speed limits 243
Spoerry, François 54, 123
Sports **223–4**, 225
Stade Vélodrome (Marseille) 224
Staël, Nicolas de 72
  Paysage Méditerranéen 25
Stahly, François 121
Stamps 234
Stanfords (London) 243
Stanley, HM 88
Starck, Philippe, *Bus Stop* 54
Stendhal 168
Stephanie, Princess of
  Monaco 91
Student information 237
Süe, Louis 120
Suffren, Admiral
  Pierre André de 122
  statue of 119
Sunshine 31
Süskind, Patrick 67
Sutherland, Graham 99
Swimming 231
Synagogues 237
Syrah grapes 206

T

La Table du Comtat (Séguret) 215
Tahiti-Plage (St-Tropez) 29
Take-away food 216–17
Tarascon 140
  festivals 31
  history 46, 47

Tarasque monster 31, 42, 140
Tax-free goods 236
Taxis 238, 244
Telephones 234–5
Television 235
Temperature chart 33
Templars 64, 74, 123, 183
Tende 39, **97**
Tennis 225
Tennis Municipaux (Marseille) 225
La Terrasse (Juan-les-Pins) 210
TGV (Train à Grande Vitesse) **240**,
  241
Theatre 222
Théâtre de l'Alphabet (Nice) 224
Théâtre Antique d'Orange 162–3
Théâtre des Carmes (Avignon) 224
Théâtre du Cour (Nice) 224
Théâtre de la Criée (Marseille) 224
Théâtre du Merlan (Marseille) 224
Théâtre de la Sémeuse (Nice) 224
Thoronet *see* Abbaye du Thoronet
Le Thoronet
  Côtes de Provence tour 108
Tickets
  entertainment 222
  museums 229
  trains 240–41
Tiles, ceramic 105
Time zones 237
Tintoretto 75
Tipping, in restaurants 202
Titian, *Charles V* 47
Tobacconists 229
Toilets, public 231
Tolls, autoroutes 242
Torpès, St 34, 122
Torse Debout (Matisse) 83
"Tortoise Village" 116
Touët-sur-Var 64
  restaurants 211
Toulon 112–13
  airport 238
  boat-building 48
  entertainment 224
  festivals 31
  history 46, 48–9
  railway station 241
  restaurants 212
  World War II 53
La Tour d'Aigues 173
Tourrettes 106
Tourist information 228
Tourist offices 192, 229
Tours by car
  Côtes de Provence 108–9
  The Dentelles 159
  Gorges du Verdon 184–5
  Massif des Maures 116–17
  Petit Luberon 170–71
Tourtour 104
Traffic information 243
Traffic signs 242, 243
Trailfinders (London) 239

Trains 240–41
  fly-rail package holidays 239
  Le Train des Pignes 181
Translation services 230, 231
Travel 238–45
  air 238–9
  boats 245
  buses and coaches 238, 243,
    244
  cars 242–4
  cycling 244
  helicopters 238
  hitch-hiking 244
  taxis 238, 244
  Le Train des Pignes 181
  trains 240–41
Travel agencies 239
Travel Cuts (London) 241
Travellers' cheques 230, 232
Les Trois Diables (Nice) 217
Le Trophée des Alpes 89
Trophime, St 143, 146
Troubadours 26, 37, 43
Truffles 32, 105
TT leasing, cars 242, 243
Tuck, Edward 89
La Turbie 40, **89**

U

UCRIF (Union des Centres de
  Rencontres Internationales de
  France) 192
Universities 237
Urban V, Pope 45
Urban VI, Pope 44
Utrillo, Maurice 99

V

Le Vaccarès (Arles) 213
Vacqueyras
  Tour of the Dentelles 159
Vadim, Roger 54
Vaison-la-Romaine 158
  history 55
  hotels 201
  Roman remains 40, 41
  Tour of the Dentelles 159
Valard, Antoine 167
Valberg 96
Valensole 176, **183**
Vallauris **72**, 73
  shops 219
Vallée des Merveilles 39, 62, 97
Vallée de la Vésubie 95
Van Gogh, Vincent 51
  in Arles 145
  L'Arlésienne 145
  Le Centre d'Art Presence Van Gogh
    (St-Rémy-de-Provence) 140, 141
  Van Gogh's Chair 24
Van Loo, Carle 85
Van Loo, Jean-Baptiste 89, 113

Van Meegeren, Hans 24
Var 100–25
    beaches 28
    Exploring the Var and the Iles
    d'Hyères 102–3
    festivals 34
    hotels 198–9
    restaurants 212
Vasarély, Victor 24, 123, 149, 169
VAT 236
Vauban, Marshal Sébastien 19, 49
    Antibes 72
    Colmars 180
    Entrevaux 187
    Fort Ste-Marguerite 70
    Seyne 178
    Toulon 48
Vaucluse 154–73
    Exploring Vaucluse 156–7
    festivals 35
    hotels 200–1
    restaurants 214–15
Vegetarian food 203
Vence 19, **74–5**
    hotels 197
    restaurants 211
Vendôme, Cardinal de 149
Verdon Plus (Riez) 225
Vergé, Roger 66
Veronese 89
Victoria, Queen 50, 66, 84, 98
Vidauban
    Côtes de Provence tour 109
La Vie (Chagall) 76
Vierge de Pitié (Avignon School) 167
Vilar, Jean 35
Le Village (Juan-les-Pins) 225
Village des Tortues
    Massif des Maures tour 116
Villages perchés **18–19**, 42
Villecroze 104, 228
Villefranche 88
    cafés and bars 217
    hotels 197
    restaurants 211

Villeneuve, Admiral 183
Villeneuve, Arnaud de 107
Villeneuve, Roseline de 107
Villeneuve family 74
Villeneuve-lès-Avignon 130
    bookshops 235
    hotels 200
Villeneuve-Loubet 74
Vineyards 51
Viognier grape 206
Violin and Sheet of Music
    (Picasso) 73
Virgin Megastore 224
Visas 236
Visigoths 41
Vitamine (Arles) 213
La Voile d'Or (St-Jean-Cap-Ferrat)
    197
Voyages Wasteels (Marseille) 239
Vue du Cours pendant la Peste
    (Serre) 48–9
Vuillard, Edouard 85

W

Wagner, Richard 171
Walking, in mountains 231
Warhol, Andy 85
Wars of Religion 46–7
Watersports 29
Watteau, Antoine 133
Weather in Provence 30–33
Wells, Charles Deville 93
Wharton, Edith 26
Wheelchair access *see* Disabled
    travellers
Whisky à Gogo (Juan-les-Pins) 225
White wines 206
Wildlife 16–17
    Luberon 170–71
    Marineland (Villeneuve-Loubet) 74
    Le Parc National du
    Mercantour 96, **97**
    Parc Ornithologique du Pont-
    de-Gau 136, 138

Wildlife (cont.)
    Port-Cros 114–15
    Vallée des Merveilles 97
William the Good 123
Winds 30
    Mistral 21, 30, 31, 33
Windsor, Duchess of (Wallis
    Simpson) 52, 85
Windsor, Duke of 85
Windsurfing 225
Wine 219
    duty-free and duty-paid limits 236
    in restaurants 203
    What to Drink in Provence
    206–207
Winter in Provence 33
World War I 52
World War II 52–3
Writers 26–7
Wylie, Laurence 155, 169

Y

Le Yaca (Orange) 215
Yachts 245
Yeats, WB 98
YHA (Youth Hostel Association,
    UK) 192
Youssoupov, Prince 99
Youth hostels 237

Z

Zeiger, Augustin 108
Zenith-Oméga (Toulon) 224
Ziem, Félix 147, 153
    Camargue, Côté Soleil 24
Zola, Emile 26, 149
Zoos
    Jardin Exotique et Zoo de
    Sanary-Bandol 112
    Jardins Olbius Riquier (Hyères) 115
    Parc Zoologique (Cap Ferrat) 85
Le Zouk-Times (Marseille) 224

Acknowledgments

DORLING KINDERSLEY would like to thank the following people whose contributions and assistance have made the preparation of this book possible.

MAIN CONTRIBUTOR

Roger Williams is a writer and editor who was for many years associated with the *Sunday Times* magazine. He has written two novels and a number of guide books, on places ranging from Barcelona to the Baltic States, and was a contributor to *Over Europe*, the first aerial record of the united continent. He visits France regularly, and has been writing about Provence for more than 20 years.

CONTRIBUTORS

John Flower, Jim Keeble, Anthony Rose, Martin Walters.

ADDITIONAL PHOTOGRAPHY

Andy Crawford, Lisa Cupolo, Nick Goodall, Steve Gorton, John Heseltine, Richard McConnell, Neil Mersh, Clive Streeter.

ADDITIONAL ILLUSTRATORS

Simon Calder, Paul Guest, Aziz Khan, Tristan Spaargaren, Ann Winterbotham, John Woodcock.

CARTOGRAPHIC RESEARCH

Jane Hugill, Samantha James, Jennifer Skelley, Martin Smith (Lovell Johns).

DESIGN AND EDITORIAL

MANAGING EDITOR Georgina Matthews
DEPUTY EDITORIAL DIRECTOR Douglas Amrine
DEPUTY ART DIRECTOR Gaye Allen
PRODUCTION CONTROLLER Hilary Stephens
PICTURE RESEARCH Susan Mennell
DTP DESIGNER Salim Qurashi
MAP CO-ORDINATORS Simon Farbrother, David Pugh
MAPS Jennifer Skelley, Samantha James
(Lovell Johns Ltd, Oxford)
RESEARCHER Philippa Richmond
Vincent Allonier, Rosemary Bailey, Laetitia Benloulou, Josie Bernard, Hilary Bird, Kevin Brown, Margaret Chang, Cooling Brown Partnership, Guy Dimond, Joy Fitzsimmonds, Jackie Grosvenor, Annette Jacobs, Nancy Jones, Erika Lang, Francesca Machiavelli, James Marlow, Helen Partington, Katie Peacock, Alice Peebles, Carolyn Pyrah, Amanda Tomeh, Daphne Trotter, Janis Utton.

SPECIAL ASSISTANCE

Louise Abbott; Manade Gilbert Arnaud; Brigitte Charles, Monaco Tourist Board, London; Sabine Giraud, Terres du Sud, Venasque; Emma Heath; Nathalie Lavarenne, Musée Matisse, Nice; Ella Milroy; Marianne Petrou; Andrew Sanger; David Tse.

PHOTOGRAPHIC REFERENCE

Bernard Beaujard, Vézénobres.

PHOTOGRAPHY PERMISSIONS

Dorling Kindersley would like to thank the following for their assistance and kind permission to photograph at their establishments: Fondation Marguerite et Aimé Maeght, St-Paul-de-Vence; Hotel Négresco, Nice; Monsieur J-F Campana, Mairie de Nice; Monsieur Froumessol, Mairie de Cagnes-sur-Mer; Musée Ephrussi de Rothschild, St-Jean-Cap-Ferrat; Musée Jean Cocteau, Menton; Musée International de la Parfumerie, Grasse; Musée Matisse, Nice; Musée National Message Biblique Marc Chagall, Nice; Musée Océanographique, Monaco; Musée Picasso/Château Grimaldi, Antibes; Salle des Mariages, Hôtel de Ville, Menton, and all other churches, museums, hotels, restaurants, shops and sights too numerous to thank individually.

PICTURE CREDITS

t = top; tl = top left; tc = top centre; tr = top right; cla = centre left above; ca = centre above; cra = centre right above; cl = centre left; c = centre; cr = centre right; clb = centre left below; cb = centre below; crb = centre right below; bl = bottom left; b = bottom; bc = bottom centre; br = bottom right; bla = bottom left above; bca = bottom centre above; bra = bottom right above; blb = bottom left below; bcb = bottom centre below; brb = bottom right below.

Every effort has been made to trace the copyright holders and we apologize in advance for any unintentional omissions. We would be pleased to insert the appropriate acknowledgments in any subsequent edition of this publication.

Works of art have been reproduced with the permission of the following copyright holders:

© ADAGP, Paris and DACS, London 1995: 25b, 54br, 59tl, 76t, ca, cb, 77c and b, 78c, 85b, 106b, 119b, 120ca, 144t; © ADAGP/SPADEM, Paris and DACS, London 1995: 76(b), 120 (b); © DACS, London 1995: 24t and b, 25t, 28tr, 73tl, tr, cl, cr and b, 74t, 77t, 78b, 99t, 120cb; 121t; 121ca; 121cb; © Succession Henri Matisse/DACS 1995: 25c, 82t and b, 83t, c and br.

The publisher would like to thank the following individuals, companies and picture libraries for permission to reproduce their photographs:.

ANCIENT ART AND ARCHITECTURE COLLECTION: 39t and cb, 40bl, 43t; ARCHIVES DE L'AUTOMOBILE CLUB DE MONACO: 52ca; ARTEPHOT, PARIS: Plassart 25c; ASSOCIATED PRESS LTD: 27cb.

LA BELLE AURORE: 30b, 35t; BRIDGEMAN ART LIBRARY: Christie's, London 47crb, 50–51; Giraudon 47t, 48bl; Schloss Charlottenburg, Berlin 179t.

CAMPAGNE, CAMPAGNE!, PARIS: Jolyot 92br; JL Julien 29bl; Meissonnier 159b; Meschinet 138c; Moirenc 239; Pambour 171t, 172t; Picard 159t; Pyszel 90t; CEPHAS: Mick Rock 206br, 207ca and br; JEAN-LOUP CHARMET, PARIS: 26cl, 27tl; © Antoine de Saint-Exupéry/Gallimard 27ca; 37b, 42bl, 46ca and cb, 49t and cla, 50tl and tr, 52t, 53t, 132cl, 140t, 153t, 160cl; BRUCE COLEMAN: Adrian Davies 114bl; JLG Grande 136bca; George McCarthy 17tl; Andrew J Purcell 115cb and bl; Hans Reinhard 137t, 171bl, bc and br; Dr Frieder Sauer 114c; Robert Wanscheidt 160bl; K Wothe 160bc; Paul van Gaalen 136bra; JOE CORNISH: 21tr, 188, 226; JULIAN COTTON PICTURE LIBRARY: Jason Hawkes aerial collection 11, 56–7; CULTURE ESPACES, PARIS: 86t and ca; Véran 87t.

PHOTO DASPET, AVIGNON: Musée du Petit Palais, Avignon 44t, 45bc; Palais des Papes, Avignon 44crb and b; DIAF, PARIS: J-P Garcin 31cb; J-C Gérard 34t and b, 151b; Camille

Moirenc 162c; Bernard Régent 24t; Patrick Somelet 158b; DIRECTION DES AFFAIRES CULTURELLES, MONACO: 91c.

MARY EVANS: 9 inset, 26t, bl and br, 27bl, 45br and t, 46b, 57inset, 189inset, 227inset; JANE EWART: 20cb, 21c, 22tl, 23cb, 58tl, 76cb, 127b, 163ca and cb, 203b, 209bl, 229b, 236b; EXPLORER ARCHIVES, PARIS: L Bertrand 38cb; Jean-Loup Charmet 67t, 124c, 147b; Coll. ES 42t, 46cb and bl; Coll. Sauvel 13t; G Garde 31ca; J P Hervey 64t; J & C Lenars 39c; J-P Lescourret 165c; M C Noailles 65b; Peter Willi 40ca; A Wolf 43clb.

FONDATION AUGUSTE ESCOFFIER, VILLENEUVE-LOUBET: 74c; FONDATION MAEGHT, SAINT-PAUL-DE-VENCE, FRANCE: Claude Germain 77t and c; Coll. M et Mme Adrien Maeght 77b; FRANK LANE PICTURE AGENCY: N Clark 170b; Fritz Polking 16tr; M B Withers 136bla.

GALERIE INTEMPOREL, PARIS: Les Films Ariane, Paris 54–5; EDITIONS GAUD, MOISENAY: 70bl, 86b, 87bl and br, 142t, 181c; GIRAUDON, PARIS: 25t, bl and br, 26cr, 30t, 36, 40br, 48ca and br, 133b, 145b, 172c; Lauros-Giraudon 38ca, 45cb, 46tr (detail), 46–7, 49clb, 51clb, 53clb (all rights reserved), 73tl and tr, 110bl, 125b, 134t, 144t, 146t; Musée de la Vieille Charité, Marseille 38tr; Musée de la Ville de Paris, Musée du Petit Palais/Lauros-Giraudon 24bl; Musée des Beaux-Arts, Marseille 48–9, 49b, 152b; Musée du Louvre, Paris 8–9; Musée du Vieux Marseille, Marseille 48cb, 50ca; GRAND HOTEL DU CAP FERRAT: 191t; RONALD GRANT ARCHIVE: Warner Brothers 27br; GROTTES DE ST-CÉZAIRE: 65c.

ROBERT HARDING: 33b, 238t, 240b; HOTEL EDEN ROC, CAP D'ANTIBES: 191b; HULTON-DEUTSCH COLLECTION: 26c, 27cb, 52br; Keystone 94t.

ILLUSTRATED LONDON NEWS PICTURE LIBRARY: 50b.

CATHERINE KARNOW, SAN FRANCISCO: 110c; THE KOBAL COLLECTION: United Artists 71tl.

DANIEL MADELEINE: 183b; MAGNUM PHOTOS: Bruno Barbey 34c; René Burri 55clb; Robert Capa 82c; Elliott Erwitt 91br; Guy le Querrec 223b; MAIRIE DE NÎMES: Jean-Charles Blais 132t (all rights reserved); Francis Bacon 223b (all rights reserved); MANSELL COLLECTION: 39b, 42br, 43b, 51cla, 52bl; EDITIONS MOLIPOR, MONACO: 94b; courtesy of SBM 51crb, 94c; MUSÉE DE L'ANNONCIADE, ST-TROPEZ: E Vila Mateu 119b, 120–21; MUSÉE D'ANTHROPOLOGIE, MONACO: J-F Buissière 38tl; MUSÉE ARCHÉOLOGIQUE DE LA VAISON-LA-ROMAINE: Christine Bézin 41clb; MUSÉE D'ART MODERNE ET D'ART CONTEMPORAIN, NICE: 54br, 85b; MUSÉE FABRE,

MONTPELLIER: Leenhardt 135b; MUSÉE DE LA PHOTOGRAPHIE, MOUGINS: 66b; MUSÉE MATISSE, NICE: © Service photographique, Ville de Nice 82t and b, 83t, c and br.

REPRODUCED BY COURTESY OF THE TRUSTEES, THE NATIONAL GALLERY, LONDON: 24c; NATURE PHOTOGRAPHERS: Carlson 16ca; Michael Gore 16b; NETWORK PHOTOGRAPHERS/RAPHO: Mark Buscail 184t.

L'OEIL ET LA MÉMOIRE/BIBLIOTHÈQUE MUNICIPALE D'AVIGNON: Atlas 24, folio 147 42cb; OXFORD SCIENTIFIC FILMS: Mike Hill 136blb; Tom Leach 160br; Frank Schneidermeyer 136brb.

JOHN PARKER: 19bl, 22b, 58tr, 108t, 157; PICTURES COLOUR LIBRARY: 185b; PHOTO RESOURCES: CM Dixon 41cbr; PLANET EARTH PICTURES: Richard Coomber 136bcb; John Neuschwander 114br; Peter Scoones 17b; POPPERFOTO: 27tc, 72b.

RANGE: Bettmann 26crb, 27tr and crb; RETROGRAPH ARCHIVE, LONDON: © Martin Breese 28tr, 69b; ROGER-VIOLLET, PARIS: 47cla, 51t, 52cb, 163b.

SERVICE DE PRESSE DE LA VILLE DE CAGNES-SUR-MER: 78c and b, 79b; ROGER SMITH, EZE: 86cb, 87c; SNCF/FRENCH RAILWAYS LTD., LONDON: 55b, 241b; FRANK SPOONER PICTURES: Robin 67b; P Siccoli 54cb; Gamma/T Pelisier 38b; Gamma/Christian Vioujard 67cra and cb; SYGMA: 75t; James Andanson 122b; 68b; H Conant 54bl; J Donoso 67crb; Diego Goldberg 55crb; Keystone 52–3; 53cla and b; Leo Mirkine 55cl.

EDITIONS TALLENDIER, PARIS: Bibliothèque Nationale 42–3; TERRES DU SUD, VENASQUE: Philippe Giraud 2, 44clb, 45c and bl, 46tl and br, 64b, 70br, 81ca, 105b, 166t, 167cb, 168b; TONY STONE IMAGES: Joe Cornish 12; TRAVEL LIBRARY: Philip Enticknap 93t and br.

WALLIS PHOTOTHÈQUE, MARSEILLE: Clasen 55t, 67cla; Constant 182b; Di Meglio 115ca; Giani 96t, 223t; Huet 185t; LCI 29br, 176t; Leroux 14b; Poulet 96cl; Royer 96cr and b; Tarta 193b.

ROGER WILLIAMS: 101, 138b, 165t, 170c, 181b, 185ca.

Front endpaper: all commissioned photography.

Jacket: all commissioned photography with the exception of TERRES DU SUD, VENASQUE: Philippe Giraud br and IMAGES COLOUR LIBRARY: tr.

DORLING KINDERSLEY SPECIAL EDITIONS

Dorling Kindersley books can be purchased in bulk quantities at discounted prices for use in promotions or as premiums. We are also able to offer special editions and personalized jackets, corporate imprints, and excerpts from all of our books, tailored specifically to meet your own needs.

To find out more, please contact: (in the United Kingdom) – SPECIAL SALES, DORLING KINDERSLEY LIMITED, 9 HENRIETTA STREET, COVENT GARDEN, LONDON WC2E 8PS; TEL. 020 7753 3572;

(in the United States) – SPECIAL MARKETS DEPARTMENT, DORLING KINDERSLEY, INC., 95 MADISON AVENUE, NEW YORK, NY 10016.

Phrase Book

IN EMERGENCY

Help!	**Au secours!**	oh se**koor**
Stop!	**Arrêtez!**	aret-**ay**
Call a doctor!	**Appelez un médecin!**	apuh-**lay** uñ medsañ
Call an ambulance!	**Appelez une ambulance!**	apuh-**lay** oon oñboo-**loñs**
Call the police!	**Appelez la police!**	apuh-**lay** lah poh-**lees**
Call the fire brigade!	**Appelez les pompiers!**	apuh-lay leh poñ-**peeyay**
Where is the nearest telephone?	**Où est le téléphone le plus proche?**	oo ay luh tehleh**fon** luh ploo **prosh**
Where is the nearest hospital?	**Où est l'hôpital le plus proche?**	oo ay l'**opee**tal luh ploo **prosh**

COMMUNICATION ESSENTIALS

Yes	**Oui**	wee
No	**Non**	noñ
Please	**S'il vous plaît**	seel voo **play**
Thank you	**Merci**	mer-**see**
Excuse me	**Excusez-moi**	exkoo-**zay** mwah
Hello	**Bonjour**	boñ**zhoor**
Goodbye	**Au revoir**	oh ruh-**vwar**
Good night	**Bonsoir**	boñ-**swar**
Morning	**Le matin**	matañ
Afternoon	**L'après-midi**	l'apreh-**meedee**
Evening	**Le soir**	swar
Yesterday	**Hier**	eeyehr
Today	**Aujourd'hui**	oh-zhoor-**dwee**
Tomorrow	**Demain**	duh**mañ**
Here	**Ici**	ee-**see**
There	**Là**	lah
What?	**Quel, quelle?**	kel, kel
When?	**Quand?**	koñ
Why?	**Pourquoi?**	poor-**kwah**
Where?	**Où?**	oo

USEFUL PHRASES

How are you?	**Comment allez-vous?**	kom-moñ tal**ay voo**
Very well, thank you.	**Très bien, merci.**	treh byañ, mer-**see**
Pleased to meet you.	**Enchanté de faire votre connaissance.**	oñshoñ-**tay** duh fehr votr kon-ay-**sans**
See you soon.	**A bientôt.**	byañ-**toh**
That's fine.	**Voilà qui est parfait.**	vwalah kee ay parfay
Where is/are...?	**Où est/sont...?**	oo ay/soñ
How far is it to...?	**Combien de kilomètres d'ici à...?**	kom-**byañ** duh is keelo-**metr** d'ee-**see** ah
Which way to...?	**Quelle est la direction pour...?**	kel ay lah deer-ek-**syoñ** poor
Do you speak English?	**Parlez-vous anglais?**	par-**lay** voo oñg-**lay**
I don't understand.	**Je ne comprends pas.**	zhuh nuh kom-**proñ** pah

Could you speak slowly, please?	**Pouvez-vous parler moins vite, s'il vous plaît?**	poo-**vay** voo par-**lay** mwañ veet seel voo play
I'm sorry.	**Excusez-moi.**	exkoo-**zay** mwah

USEFUL WORDS

big	**grand**	groñ
small	**petit**	puh-**tee**
hot	**chaud**	show
cold	**froid**	frwah
good	**bon**	boñ
bad	**mauvais**	moh-**veh**
enough	**assez**	as**say**
well	**bien**	byañ
open	**ouvert**	oo-**ver**
closed	**fermé**	fer-**meh**
left	**gauche**	gohsh
right	**droit**	drwah
straight on	**tout droit**	too drwah
near	**près**	preh
far	**loin**	lwañ
up	**en haut**	oñ oh
down	**en bas**	oñ bah
early	**de bonne heure**	duh bon **urr**
late	**en retard**	oñ ruh-**tar**
entrance	**l'entrée**	l'on-**tray**
exit	**la sortie**	sor-**tee**
toilet	**les toilettes, les WC**	twah-let, vay-**see**
unoccupied	**libre**	leebr
no charge	**gratuit**	grah-**twee**

MAKING A TELEPHONE CALL

I'd like to place a long-distance call.	**Je voudrais faire un interurbain.**	zhuh voo-dreh fehr uñ añter-oorbañ
I'd like to make a reverse-charge call.	**Je voudrais faire une communication PCV.**	zhuh voo**dreh** fehr oon kom-oonikah-**syoñ** peh-seh-veh
I'll try again later.	**Je rappelerai plus tard.**	zhuh rapeler**ay** ploo tar
Can I leave a message?	**Est-ce que je peux laisser un message?**	es-**keh** zhuh puh leh-**say** uñ mehsazh
Hold on.	**Ne quittez pas, s'il vous plaît.**	nuh kee-**tay** pah seel voo play.
Could you speak up a little please?	**Pouvez-vous parler un peu plus fort?**	poo-**vay** voo par-**lay** uñ puh ploo for
local call	**la communication locale**	komoonikah-**syoñ** low-**kal**

SHOPPING

How much does this cost?	**C'est combien s'il vous plaît?**	say kom-**byañ** seel voo play
Do you take credit cards?	**Est-ce que vous acceptez les cartes de crédit?**	es-**kuh** voo zaksept-**ay** leh kart duh kreh-**dee**

Do you take travellers' cheques?	**Est-ce que vous acceptez les chèques de voyage?**	es-**kuh** voo zaksept-**ay** leh shek duh vwa**yazh**
I would like ...	**Je voudrais...**	zhuh voo-**dray**
Do you have?	**Est-ce que vous avez?**	es-**kuh** voo zav**ay**
I'm just looking.	**Je regarde seulement.**	zhuh ruh**gar** suhl**moñ**
What time do you open?	**A quelle heure vous êtes ouvert?**	ah kel urr voo zet oo-**ver**
What time do you close?	**A quelle heure vous êtes fermé?**	ah kel urr voo zet fer-**may**
This one	**Celui-ci**	suhl-wee-**see**
That one	**Celui-là**	suhl-wee-**lah**
expensive	**cher**	shehr
cheap	**pas cher, bon marché**	pah shehr, boñ mar-**shay**
size, clothes	**la taille**	tye
size, shoes	**la pointure**	pwañ-**tur**
white	**blanc**	bloñ
black	**noir**	nwahr
red	**rouge**	roozh
yellow	**jaune**	zhohwn
green	**vert**	vehr
blue	**bleu**	bluh

TYPES OF SHOP

antique shop	**le magasin d'antiquités**	maga-**zañ** d'oñteekee-**tay**
bakery	**la boulangerie**	booloñ-**zhuree**
bank	**la banque**	boñk
book shop	**la librairie**	lee-**brehree**
butcher	**la boucherie**	boo-**shehree**
cake shop	**la pâtisserie**	patee-**sree**
cheese shop	**la fromagerie**	fromazh-**ree**
chemist	**la pharmacie**	farmah-**see**
dairy	**la crémerie**	krem-**ree**
department store	**le grand magasin**	groñ maga-**zañ**
delicatessen	**la charcuterie**	sharkoot-**ree**
fishmonger	**la poissonnerie**	pwasson-**ree**
gift shop	**le magasin de cadeaux**	maga-**zañ** duh kadoh
greengrocer	**le marchand de légumes**	mar-**shoñ** duh lay-**goom**
grocery	**l'alimentation**	alee-moñta-**syoñ**
hairdresser	**le coiffeur**	kwa**fuhr**
market	**le marché**	marsh-**ay**
newsagent	**le magasin de journaux**	maga-**zañ** duh zhoor-**no**
post office	**la poste, le bureau de poste, le PTT**	pohst, booroh duh pohst, peh-tch-tch
shoe shop	**le magasin de chaussures**	maga-**zañ** duh show-**soor**
supermarket	**le super-marché**	soo pehr-**marshay**
tobacconist	**le tabac**	tabah
travel agent	**l'agence de voyages**	l'azhoñs duh vwayazh

MENU DECODER

l'agneau	l'an**yoh**	lamb
l'ail	l'eye	garlic
la banane	ba**nan**	banana
le beurre	burr	butter
la bière	bee-**yehr**	beer
le bifteck, le steak	beef-**tek**, stek	steak
le boeuf	buhf	beef
bouilli	boo-**yee**	boiled
le café	kah-**fay**	coffee
le canard	kan**ar**	duck
le citron pressé	see-**troñ** press-**eh**	fresh lemon juice
les crevettes	kruh-**vet**	prawns
les crustacés	**kroos**-ta-say	shellfish
cuit au four	kweet oh foor	baked
le dessert	deh-**ser**	dessert
l'eau minérale	l'oh **meeney**-ral	mineral water
les escargots	leh zes-kar-**goh**	snails
les frites	freet	chips
le fromage	from-**azh**	cheese
le fruit frais	frwee freh	fresh fruit
les fruits de mer	frwee duh mer	seafood
le gâteau	gah-**toh**	cake
la glace	glas	ice, ice cream
grillé	gree-**yay**	grilled
le homard	om**ahr**	lobster
l'huile	l'weel	oil
le jambon	zhoñ-**boñ**	ham
le lait	leh	milk
les légumes	lay-**goom**	vegetables
la moutarde	moo-**tard**	mustard
l'oeuf	l'uf	egg
les oignons	leh zon**yoñ**	onions
les olives	leh zol**eev**	olives
l'orange pressée	l'oroñzh press-**eh**	fresh orange juice
le pain	pan	bread
le petit pain	puh-**tee** pañ	roll
poché	posh-**ay**	poached
le poisson	pwah-**ssoñ**	fish
le poivre	pwavr	pepper
la pomme	pom	apple
les pommes de terre	pom-duh tehr	potatoes
le porc	por	pork
le potage	poh-**tazh**	soup
le poulet	poo-**lay**	chicken
le riz	ree	rice
rôti	row-**tee**	roast
la sauce	sohs	sauce
la saucisse	sohsees	sausage, fresh
sec	sek	dry
le sel	sel	salt
le sucre	sookr	sugar
le thé	tay	tea
le toast	toast	toast
la viande	vee-**yand**	meat
le vin blanc	vañ **bloñ**	white wine
le vin rouge	vañ **roozh**	red wine
le vinaigre	vee**naygr**	vinegar

EATING OUT

Have you got a table?	Avez-vous une table libre?	avay-**voo** oon tahbl leebr
I want to reserve a table.	Je voudrais réserver une table.	zhuh voo-**dray** rayzehr-**vay** oon tahbl
The bill, please.	L'addition, s'il vous plaît.	l'adee-**syoñ** seel voo play
I am a vegetarian.	Je suis végétarien.	zhuh swee vezhay-**tehryañ**
Waitress/ waiter	Madame, Mademoiselle/ Monsieur	mah-**dam**, mah-dem wah zel/muh-**syuh**
menu	le menu, la carte	men-**oo**, kart
fixed-price menu	le menu à prix fixe	men-**oo** ah pree feeks
cover charge	le couvert	koo-**vehr**
wine list	la carte des vins	**kart**-deh vañ
glass	le verre	vehr
bottle	la bouteille	boo-**tay**
knife	le couteau	koo-**toh**
fork	la fourchette	for-**shet**
spoon	la cuillère	kwee-**yehr**
breakfast	le petit déjeuner	puh-**tee** deh-**zhuh**-nay
lunch	le déjeuner	deh-**zhuh**-nay
dinner	le dîner	dee-**nay**
main course	le plat principal	plah prañsee-**pal**
starter, first course	l'entrée, le hors d'oeuvre	l'oñ-**tray**, or-duhvr
dish of the day	le plat du jour	plah doo zhoor
wine bar	le bar à vin	bar ah vañ
café	le café	ka-**fay**
rare	saignant	**say**-noñ
medium	à point	ah **pwañ**
well done	bien cuit	byañ **kwee**

STAYING IN A HOTEL

Do you have a vacant room?	Est-ce que vous avez une chambre?	es-kuh voo-**zavay** oon shambr
double room	la chambre à deux	shambr ah duh
with double bed	personnes, avec un grand lit	pehr-**son** avek un groñn lee
twin room	la chambre à deux lits	shambr ah duh lee
single room	la chambre à une personne	shambr ah oon pehr-**son**
room with a bath, shower	la chambre avec salle de bains, une douche	shambr avek sal duh bañ, oon doosh
porter	le garçon	gar-**soñ**
key	la clef	klay
I have a reservation.	J'ai fait une réservation.	zhay fay oon rayzehrva-**syoñ**

SIGHTSEEING

abbey	l'abbaye	l'abay-**ee**
art gallery	le galerie d'art	galer-**ree** dart
cathedral	la cathédrale	katay-**dral**
church	l'église	l'ay**gleez**

garden	le jardin	zhar-**dañ**
library	la bibliothèque	beebleeo-tek
museum	le musée	moo-**zay**
railway station	la gare (SNCF)	gahr (es-en-say-ef)
bus station	la gare routière	gahr roo-tee-**yehr**
tourist information office	les renseigne-- ments touristiques, le syndicat d'initiative	roñsayn-**moñ** too-rees-**teek**, sandee-ka d'eenee-sya**teev**
town hall	l'hôtel de ville	l'ohtel duh veel
private mansion	l'hôtel particulier	l'ohtel partikoo-**lyay**
closed for public holiday	fermeture jour férié	fehrmeh-**tur** zhoor fehree-**ay**

NUMBERS

0	zéro	zeh-**roh**
1	un, une	uñ, oon
2	deux	duh
3	trois	trwah
4	quatre	katr
5	cinq	sañk
6	six	sees
7	sept	set
8	huit	weet
9	neuf	nerf
10	dix	dees
11	onze	oñz
12	douze	dooz
13	treize	trehz
14	quatorze	ka**torz**
15	quinze	kañz
16	seize	sehz
17	dix-sept	dees-**set**
18	dix-huit	dees-**weet**
19	dix-neuf	dees-**nerf**
20	vingt	vañ
30	trente	tront
40	quarante	karoñt
50	cinquante	sañkoñt
60	soixante	swasoñt
70	soixante-dix	swasoñt-**dees**
80	quatre-vingts	katr-**vañ**
90	quatre-vingts- dix	katr-vañ- dees
100	cent	soñ
1,000	mille	meel

TIME

one minute	une minute	oon mee-**noot**
one hour	une heure	oon urr
half an hour	une demi-heure	oon **duh-mee** urr
Monday	lundi	luñ-**dee**
Tuesday	mardi	mar-**dee**
Wednesday	mercredi	mehrkruh-**dee**
Thursday	jeudi	zhuh-**dee**
Friday	vendredi	voñdruh-**dee**
Saturday	samedi	sam-**dee**
Sunday	dimanche	dee-**moñsh**

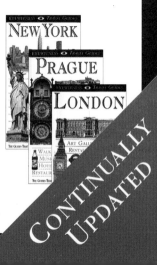

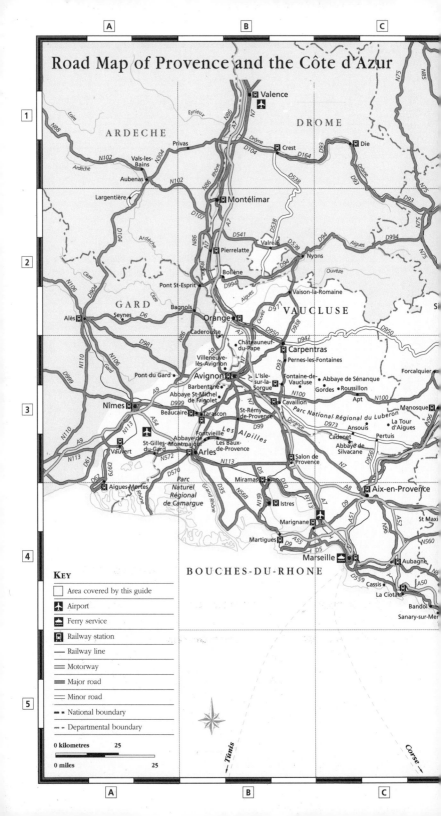